C-UNIT

SEARCH FOR COMMUNITY IN PRISON

ELLIOT STUDT

SHELDON L. MESSINGER

THOMAS P. WILSON

RUSSELL SAGE FOUNDATION, NEW YORK, 1968

PUBLICATIONS OF RUSSELL SAGE FOUNDATION

Russell Sage Foundation was established in 1907 by Mrs. Russell Sage for the improvement of social and living conditions in the United States. In carrying out its purpose the Foundation conducts research under the direction of members of the staff or in close collaboration with other institutions, and supports programs designed to improve the utilization of social science knowledge. As an integral part of its operations, the Foundation from time to time publishes books or pamphlets resulting from these activities. Publication under the imprint of the Foundation does not necessarily imply agreement by the Foundation, its Trustees, or its staff with the interpretations or conclusions of the authors.

FOREWORD

C-UNIT is an account of one small effort to refresh and affirm the human spirit. In the unquiet recesses of a California prison, there was enacted a drama of faith and frustration that is only partly obscured by the apparatus of social research and by the painstaking quest for theoretical understanding.

Dr. Elliot Studt brought to the C-Unit Project a long experience in dealing with offenders. She and her collaborators tried to put into practice, and to study at the same time, a distinctive philosophy of corrections. It is no derogation of their achievement to say that what was done in C-Unit amounted to taking seriously an ancient belief in the dignity and worth of human beings. This is not the first piece of social research to be, in effect, a mission to administrators, a reminder that they may fail to grasp the human and practical significance of treating men as persons.

That the underlying truth is a familiar one does not detract from the need for inquiry. General principles are notoriously inadequate as guides to policy and administration. Ideals have a certain abstract innocence; action is concrete and messy. There is always a need to discover anew what maturity, fairness, responsibility, or love may mean in circumstances that set their own problems and make their own demands.

In C-Unit we see an effort to specify and make relevant a person-in-context approach to the administration of corrections. The persons who need "treatment," it turns out, are staff as well as inmates. And this insight leads, in turn, to an interactional, problem-solving model of community.

The inmate-staff community is the indispensable context for authentic, self-affirming action.

The report unfolds a number of themes that seem to me especially noteworthy:

(1) *The postulate of normality, competence, and worth.* If offenders are to be dealt with as human beings, it must be assumed that they are basically like everyone else; only their circumstances are special. Every administrative device that negates this principle, and any therapy that ignores it, must be questioned and, if possible, set aside.

(2) *Salience of the micro-world.* Men live out their lives in specific settings, and it is there, in the crucible of interaction, that potentialities are sealed off or released. The micro-world is the world of here-and-now; if an inmate's future is to be affected, that future should have a dynamic, existential connection with the experienced present.

(3) *The poverty of power.* An administration that relies solely on its own coercive resources can make little contribution to the reconstruction of prison life or to the creation of environments that encourage autonomy and self-respect.

(4) *Order as tension and achievement.* Quiescent conformity imposed from above is a parody of social order, not its fulfillment. A system that validates the humanity of its participants, and engages their full resources, accepts the risk of disorder and even, from time to time, of searing confrontations.

(5) *Justice as therapy.* A concern for fairness and civic validation should permeate the entire administration of criminal law, including the daily life of the prisoner. That treatment will be most effective which does the most for the inmate's sense of self-worth and responsibility. Nothing contributes more to these feelings than a social environment whose constitutive principle is justice, with its corollaries of participation, giving reasons, and protecting personal dignity.

These themes suggest the complex argument of the book and its relevance for the sociology of organizations, deviance, and social control. Although the work deals with a quite specialized context, I believe that students of human organization can gain a fresh perspective from it.

The explicit purpose of the C-Unit Project was to develop new modes of rehabilitation, in the hope that many inmates might be returned to a constructive community life and the state rewarded with a reduction of recidivism. Without questioning the worth of these objectives, it may be asked: Is it the public policy to punish offenders, especially young offenders, beyond the fact of imprisonment itself? If not, does humane and respectful treatment, not as therapy but as civilized conduct, require a special justification?

In seeking to make criminal justice more redemptive and less punitive, we may have asked too much of institutions that can barely hold their own, let alone develop the competence to be curers of souls. A retreat from rosy hopes may well be inevitable, if only because rehabilitation entails supervision, and ineffective rehabilitation coupled with open-ended control has little to commend it. As the dialogue proceeds and experience is assessed, we may well conclude that the real worth of the "treatment perspective," in its various forms, has been to serve as a civilizing influence on correctional systems. If that should be so, then a theory of corrections that envisions the creation of viable, working communities, based on a postulate of normality, will have most to offer.

PHILIP SELZNICK
Chairman, Center for the
Study of Law and Society

University of California
Berkeley
September 15, 1967

PREFACE

SOME of the diverse factors that combine to shape or influence the program of a public correctional institution may be deeply rooted in the culture and tradition of the citizens in our communities, of the correctional workers, and of the inmates. Ambivalent attitudes over punishment and rehabilitation of offenders are but one example.

Some other conditions that contribute to the degree of success and what success means in correctional programs are of more immediate consequence. These may range from an unquestioned need to prevent violence and maintain security to a practical realization of the limits of tax-dollar financing.

Of major significance is a lack of knowledge and understanding of just what practices and efforts have a positive effect in changing human behavior.

We still do a great many things in prison as a matter of tradition or in the untested belief that they are necessary and beneficial. This is true with respect both to rigid security measures and to the most liberal and expensive training and treatment efforts.

In the corrections field, as in other areas of endeavor concerned with human behavior, there is a general and longstanding need to test and evaluate the old ways of doing things. We also need quite urgently to discover and develop new and more effective methods, and perhaps even some new basic philosophies.

The C-Unit Project described and evaluated in this report is an example of the creative and searching experimentation so urgently required. It is this very type of pioneering which we have attempted to encourage in the California Department of Corrections since our formal research program was initiated a few years ago.

One noteworthy aspect of the Project, I believe, was the multi-agency interest and financial support that cut across the sometimes insurmountable barriers of organizational and governmental jurisdiction. This same type of cooperative endeavor will become increasingly important with the growth of knowledge and experience through correctional research.

When the Project was first proposed, some difficult operational problems were logically anticipated. An experimental project of this type in the midst of a large operating institution was bound to generate conflicts and differences of opinion.

Some inevitable differences did arise. The sincere efforts that were made to resolve or compromise these conflicts are a credit both to the Project workers and to the administration and staff of Deuel Vocational Institution.

There is a good deal to be gained in the reading of this report. One value to correctional administrators is insight into the difficulties and frustrations of experimental programming within the framework and controls of day-to-day prison operation.

For the California Department of Corrections, I extend appreciation and compliments to the persevering and creative individuals who inspired the C-Unit Project and carried it to conclusion.

WALTER DUNBAR
Director of Corrections

Sacramento, California
May 26, 1967

ACKNOWLEDGMENTS

EVEN a cursory glance at the C-Unit story reveals that the Project was the work of many persons. That C-Unit happened at all is a tribute to the creativity, patience, investment of effort beyond the call of duty, and tolerance of ambiguity of many whose contributions cannot be adequately recognized here.

Among those to whom we wish to express special appreciation are Allen Cook, Superintendent, and Keith Edwards, Associate Superintendent, Custody, Deuel Vocational Institution, for their gracious and unstinting hospitality to the Project's action and research programs. Although C-Unit's activities constituted a heavy burden on administration, Mr. Cook and Mr. Edwards were always ready to consult on Project proposals and to facilitate activities that did not run counter to the integrity of their own perspectives. The Project staff, all of whom were raw recruits to prison management, learned much from the opportunity to work with these veterans of practice.

During the early stages of the C-Unit experience Richard A. McGee was Director of the California Department of Corrections. His statesmanlike approach to the difficult work of corrections made possible the experimental activities of C-Unit. Mr. McGee was followed as Department Director by Walter Dunbar, who continued to give active support to the Project and to the subsequent use of certain of its proposals in correctional institutions for adult offenders throughout California. Many members of the staff of the Department of Corrections and the Department of the

Youth Authority helped to implement the procedural changes authorized by Mr. McGee and Mr. Dunbar. Among these, Milton Burdman and John Conrad are especially remembered for their continuity of interest and consultative help. Although differences of opinion between the researchers and Department representatives occurred, Mr. Burdman and Mr. Conrad consistently supported the right and duty of the researchers to present for public examination the findings that in their judgment most accurately described the C-Unit experience. In reading the report, it should be remembered that its formulations and recommendations are the responsibility of the authors and do not necessarily reflect the official position of the California Department of Corrections.

Philip Selznick's wise counsel and guidance has been invaluable in the translation of the complexities of our experience in the Project into communicable ideas. He and Martin Trow, Sheldon L. Messinger, Albert K. Cohen, and Donald Garrity acted as consultants to the Project's research program. Their contributions were many. All participated in stimulating seminar discussions of conceptual problems. Messinger studied Deuel Vocational Institution as the organizational environment in which C-Unit developed. Trow supervised the Inmate System Study, which is reported in Chapter VIII. Garrity assisted in the initial formulation of the research studies. Leonard S. Cottrell, Jr., of Russell Sage Foundation and Lloyd E. Ohlin, Associate Director of the President's Commission on Law Enforcement and Administration of Justice, gave valuable support and guidance to Studt in developing the ideas that ultimately took shape in the C-Unit action program. Stanton Wheeler of Russell Sage Foundation acted as a perceptive editorial guide during the work of revision.

Six persons besides the senior author assumed responsibility for portions of the research program. Messinger's contribution has already been noted; he was assisted by Herbert Mills. Thomas P. Wilson, Alvin Rudoff, and Jorgen Jepson were full-time research associates in the Inmate-Staff Community Project. They were assisted by Michael Otten.

In the story to follow it will become evident that the "men of C-Unit" contributed at least as much as, and perhaps more than, official staff members to the substance of this report. We cannot list here the names of all those who helped us understand the nature of "life inside" and whose efforts made possible the emergence of the C-Unit community. A number of C-Unit men became deeply involved in the production of "our book"; among them were the research clerks who not only performed the drudgery of statistical routines, but also spent many hours with us discussing events and issues in a spirit of disciplined honesty characteristic of shared scientific endeavor.

Susan Reid's contribution as secretary during the preparation of the first draft of *C-Unit* was that of an active partner in intellectual endeavor. Thanks are also due to Mary Alden, Gloria Neal, and Paula Marshall who shared the work of preparing the manuscript in final form.

Many agencies have contributed to the financial support of the Inmate-Staff Community Project. A grant from Russell Sage Foundation to the School of Social Work of Rutgers—the State University made possible for the senior author two years of intellectual exploration preceding the C-Unit plan. The C-Unit action program and the first seven months of the research program were supported by the California State Department of Corrections. The National Institute of Mental Health provided a small proposal-writing grant in 1960, and continued its financial support of research activities from May, 1961, through August, 1963. The Ford Foundation made two small grants available to support Wilson's participation in the Project from June, 1960, through May, 1961. The National Institute of Mental Health and The Ford Foundation grants were made to the Institute for the Study of Crime and Delinquency, Sacramento, California, and were administered by that body. The Center for the Study of Law and Society has provided many services in the final preparation of the Project report. These services, including a portion of Messinger's time, were supported by a grant to the Center from the Office of Juvenile Delinquency and Youth Development, Department of Health, Education, and Welfare.

These acknowledgments would not be complete without recognition that C-Unit was based in its essentials on the work of Ray Nash Studt, who, as Superintendent of the Denver Detention Home from April, 1942, through June, 1944, shared with Elliot Studt in developing an institutional program as a "transitional community." Although he was not present in the C-Unit experience, his profound sense of social process and his faith in the potentialities of socially discarded persons infused the Project's endeavor in ways that those who knew him will recognize.

This report of the C-Unit experience has been revised twice since the first manuscript was completed in August, 1963. The primary message of the story has not been changed by reexamination. The model for using a prison community to develop the social competence of its members has been more fully developed. All three authors have been engaged in the revision process. Most of the report as submitted for publication was written by Studt. Messinger prepared an extensive document on DVI's history and operation in the Department of Corrections, and portions of this have been used in Chapters II and IV, although perspectives from his study are interwoven throughout the book. Wilson's study of the C-Unit Inmate System is presented in Chapter VIII. He is co-author of that chapter, and he wrote the explanatory appendices. In a major sense, however, the clarification of concepts resulting from the revisions is the product of continued collaboration among the three authors.

The authors gratefully acknowledge their great indebtedness to the many persons and agencies that have contributed to the successful completion of the Project and the preparation of this report. However, it is only fair to relieve them of any responsibility for the findings and conclusions here reported. For these, the authors must be held solely responsible.

E S
S L M
T P W

March 10, 1967

CONTENTS

TABLES, CHARTS, EXHIBITS

TABLES

CHARTS

EXHIBITS

C-UNIT

NOTE TO READER. Throughout the volume we have used staff and inmate "lingo" where it helped to communicate a special sense of places, events, and persons. We have "translated" such lingo, usually in a footnote, unless the context makes the meaning apparent. Two terms call for particular note: "A#s" and "YAs." Inmates under the jurisdiction of the California Department of Corrections are frequently referred to as "A#s"; inmates under the jurisdiction of the California Department of the Youth Authority—a separate correctional department —are called "YAs." This usage, which begins in Chapter II, derives from the correctional system practice of assigning to inmates identification numbers that begin with "A" and "YA," depending on the department having jurisdiction over them. The C-Unit Project was conducted in a correctional institution housing both A#s and YAs. Throughout the volume the names used in case stories are fictitious.

I - PERSPECTIVES

THE MODERN PRISON is asked to perform three tasks: (1) to make explicit in action that the community will not tolerate certain destructive behaviors; (2) to protect the community, for at least temporary periods of time, through the segregation of those persons whose acts have shown that they can be socially dangerous; and (3) to prepare such persons to be responsible members of the community when they are released from prison. The C-Unit Project selected the third task for special attention. It sought to discover how the current resources of the prison might be used to better advantage in preparing inmates for their probable futures in the free community.[1]

---

[1] The functions of the prison in the administration of criminal justice are undergoing major changes because of the increased use of probation, on the one hand, and parole and other community-based services on the other. In the foreseeable future "preparation for futures in the free community" may have quite different connotations, owing to the specially selected nature of the imprisoned population and the related changes in the length of time usually spent in prison. Nevertheless, we consider it important to think seriously about what happens to prison inmates in preparation for release at this time in correctional history. What we learn as we attempt to improve our present correctional tools will profoundly influence the direction of change. Major changes in policy for the use of prison are often discussed long before they become actual in practice, and not all jurisdictions are equally ready to make such changes. Meanwhile we have generations of committed offenders who can expect to spend considerable time in prison and who will be ultimately released to do what they can with their lives in the community. It is of major importance both to those persons and to the community that will receive them back that we do what is possible now to avoid the customary deterioration of human capacity in prison. See Morris, Norval, "Prison in Evolution," in Grygier,

The Project attempted first of all to establish in prison the conditions under which the offenders could begin while imprisoned to act as responsible members of a community. This choice of direction reflects four basic assumptions about offenders:

1. Imprisoned offenders are like other people in desiring to walk with dignity among their fellows, to give as well as to receive, and to behave as responsible members of a community. Under conditions that support the expression of these desires in behavior, most offenders reveal some capacity to act accordingly.

2. Men who have had the opportunity to act as responsible community members during their stay in prison should be better able on release to meet the expectations of the free community. At the least, a life in prison that encourages an inmate to exercise the social competence of which he is capable will do minimal harm to his readiness to behave responsibly; at best, such an experience will increase the inmate's ability to perform consistently within the community's basic moral code.

3. Most offenders experience the sequence of offense, arrest, interrogation, detention, adjudication, and imprisonment as a major life crisis that disrupts accustomed adaptations and requires some sort of reorganization of the self in relation to society. Like other persons in crisis, most offenders can use assistance in making constructive adaptations, the kind of help needed depending on their problems, resources, and goals. The help indicated may range from fairly simple human supports through various kinds of skill training to complicated therapies. What help is appropriate for which inmates can be most economically determined under conditions that encourage each person to act in the present at the top of his social capacity.

4. Prison inmates, like other people, make effective use of proffered help only as they act on their immediate reality. The inmates do the work of preparing themselves for membership in the free community or it does not get done; official helpers can only encourage and influence the direction of learning, growth, and change. Conditions that support any person in efforts to improve his social performance include: recognition of his essential contribution to the task, encouragement to work with others in the achievement of common goals, opportunities to come to grips with problems like those he will be expected to meet in the future, and training in problem-solving skills.

The C-Unit Project attempted to establish such conditions in prison to

Tadeusz, Howard Jones, and John C. Spencer, editors, *Criminology in Transition,* Tavistock Publications, Ltd., London, 1965, pp. 267–292, for an analysis of current trends in the organization and use of prisons.

support inmates in living decently today so that those who chose could prepare themselves for release.

CENTRAL CONCEPTS

Four concepts informed the Project's attempt to create conditions in prison under which inmates could live from day to day as responsible community members. The terms "moral," "community," "problem-solving," and "resocialization" will appear throughout the report; and the use made by the Project of these terms should be explicit.

THE MORAL ISSUE

In the Project's perspective the issue around which the community and the offender confront each other is fundamentally moral. The offender has violated the basic moral code of our society as it is formulated in the penal code. The community has reacted by labeling him "bad" and by segregating him for a time from those who are presumed to be law-abiding. An important mandate from the community to the prison is to do something during the holding period that will make it more probable that the offender will be "good" when he is released. The community's question on the offender's return is essentially, "Can we trust him not to disrupt the social patterns essential to the maintenance of group processes among free persons? Is he *safe* to have among us?"

We use the word "moral" here to denote the character of social relationships essential for the existence of group life.[2] Specifically we consider that a moral relationship is characterized by ascription of dignity to individuals, respect and concern for the rights and welfare of others in pursuing individual interests, and reliance on positive social controls rather than on force or manipulation to regulate interaction. Relationships that are moral in this sense can and do vary in behaviors according to cultural prescriptions, but they lose the basic characteristics of morality if they represent the superimposition of class or ethnic mores by more powerful on less powerful subgroups. Our use of the term "moral" also rejects the narrow meaning of the word as puritanical concern with the suppression of "vice." Under our definition, an act is not immoral simply because its behaviors offend the cultural preferences of a dominant class or because it is deemed evil by some, even though no clear harm is intended or perpetuated.

---

[2] Miller, Daniel R., and Guy E. Swanson, *The Changing American Parent.* John Wiley and Sons, New York, 1958, p. 166.

When we say that the central issue in the community's dealing with crime is moral, we recognize the inherent necessity for any community to be concerned about acts that violate the conditions without which the reciprocities of group life cannot be preserved. We also assert the obligation of the community to observe rigorously its own standards in identifying and dealing with those of its members who commit such acts. No person should be subjected to the major penalty of loss of liberty unless he has threatened the fundamental conditions for trust and security among men. At the same time, it is dangerous to the moral welfare of the community if it uses such instances as occasions to abrogate dignity, mutuality, and good faith in its operation toward individuals. Morality is a reciprocal relationship and cannot be reinstated in the relationship between a person and his community after an offense unless both parties—the community as well as the offender—participate actively in healing the breach of confidence they have suffered.

In our society the fundamental moral concern of the community is implemented through a complicated institutional framework in which prisons perform a central function. Because our society is human and subject to error, many acts that are clearly immoral under this definition are not treated as such; and some persons whose acts are offensive rather than immoral are sent to prison. Under these circumstances the prison's task is particularly critical. It accepts responsibility for persons at the crucial juncture when a legally instituted impasse has been established in the relationship between the individual and his community. An important function of the modern prison is to initiate the process by which this breach can be healed and the conditions for safe interaction reinstated. It can perform this function only by engaging the individual once again in acceptable social relations with his fellows and by representing to the offender the values of the community that seeks his ultimate return.

Accordingly, in attempting to create conditions under which imprisoned offenders can prepare themselves for membership in the free community, the Project was specifically concerned to encourage the maximum development of moral relationships among inmates and prison staff.

COMMUNITY AS CONTEXT

Moral values are evoked, become explicit for groups, and gain power to influence behavior only within some institutional context.[3] The values of individuals also are strengthened or changed, not by direct attack, but by

---

[3] We use "institutional" here in the broad sociological sense.

changing the context of opportunities, expectations, rewards, and penalties within which persons act.[4] The Project was concerned, therefore, to establish within the prison an institutional context for inmate and staff associations that would effectively evoke moral issues and encourage responsible behavior in resolving such issues.

Correctional programs tend to use some normal community institution or process as the model for their efforts to prepare offenders for the responsibilities of life in the free community. Bentham first envisaged prisons as factories to train a work force for the new industries. Correctional institutions for children and youth have called themselves "homes," using the family as a model; or even more frequently have thought of their function as primarily educational and have called themselves "schools." Certain recent programs for youthful offenders, such as Highfields and Provo, have used the youth peer group as the type of association whose dynamics they utilize in shaping their programs. And "community" has recently become a popular term for characterizing institutional programs that involve inmates as well as staff in the consideration of common problems. The model chosen by any program has important consequences for the issues to which the program will attend and the processes that will appear appropriate for dealing with those issues.

The C-Unit Project chose *community* as the model for the institutional context in which to develop moral associations among staff and inmates.

Fundamentally, the Project conceived of the community in the real world as the social institution within which the basic moral code must develop in order to regularize the complex interactions among the many disparate and potentially conflicting interests that occupy an identifiable area.[5] Community is the one form of human association that is both sufficiently comprehensive to include the range of roles, activities, and processes through which moral orientations are pervasively expressed and intimately enough related to individuals to impinge directly on patterns of behavior. Because the community is comprehensive in this sense, it is the social unit that can develop and enforce social norms sufficiently general

---

[4] Holmberg, Allan R., "The Changing Values and Institutions of Vicos in the Context of National Development," *American Behavioral Scientist*, vol. 3, March, 1965, p. 5.

[5] Kai T. Erikson speaks of communities as those social units that establish the "boundaries in social space" which are necessary for coherent relationships among persons. A primary boundary-maintaining process used by such social units is the definition of deviance for that community's culture and the formal expression of the community's reactions against behavior that violates its values. See Erikson's *Wayward Puritans: A Study in the Sociology of Deviance*, John Wiley and Sons, New York, 1966, pp. 5ff.

to permit the emergence of subcultural patterns for the expression of moral orientations in a heterogeneous population. And the community is the natural system that generates and shapes the array of socializing processes on which all of us depend for support in finding moral solutions to changing life problems. Thus in the Project's framework, "member of a community" was conceived of as the basic role in our society, ascribing to each person within the community's boundaries the rights and obligations out of which morality-relevant issues arise. And it was this role of *member* that the Project assigned to inmates and staff members alike to signify the common task for which they were associated and the common privileges and responsibilities they shared in their work.

In modeling its institutional context after a community, the Project recognized that a prison community can never become exactly like the free community; and that, in fact, it may be more effective in influencing the moral context of social relationships because it can be designed to accomplish that specific task.

The community established in prison differs from the more loosely organized and complex free community since it is focused on a primary task. Because of the nature of this task, the prison community should delevop a code of behavior that is highly visible and more cohesive than is possible in the free community where value systems often compete in a way that may obscure the moral core in each. Since the task must typically be accomplished in a brief span of time, the link between individual and community should be close rather than extensively mediated, entailing a limit on the number of persons who can be included in a single prison community. Community processes should be immediately available instruments for dealing with problems important to individual members in order to reward acceptable performance as a community member with positive satisfactions in goal achievement. Thus the prison community can be expected to differ from the normal community in its task focus, cohesion, limited size, direct involvement of all members in community activities, and explicit relationship between community and individual welfare.

However, the prison community should also be transitional if it is to prepare its members for release, and so must be part of a continuum with the normal community. The task, so conceived, is not to maintain offenders as inmates but to prepare them for futures in the free community. Accordingly, the prison community should be "like" the normal community in selecting from the range of possible activities those with most relevance for the problems which offenders can expect to meet after release. The roles it develops and the problems to which it gives attention should be treated as sample experiences, archetypal in the sense that the principles of action developed in the prison community can be easily transferred to the less simply defined roles and problems that will be confronted in the normal community. And the boundaries of the artificial community should be highly "permeable," permitting easy participation by persons from the free community who can act as resources, role models, and visible testimony that the free community desires the return of imprisoned offenders to full membership on the outside.

It is evident that the C-Unit Project's conception of the prison community differed in important respects from some versions of the "therapeutic community."[6] In common with other community approaches, the Project saw the prison community as a primary tool for influencing offenders, but it did not define the community as an extension of group therapy designed primarily to remake personalities. Rather, it conceived of the prison community as a political association within which an emergent rule of law would become an instrument for achieving individual and group welfare. In the Project's framework, community was to be used as the context for problem-solving action in the present, thereby developing the social competence of its members, rather than as an instrument for the direct analysis and reduction of intrapsychic difficulties. Because the Project sought to maximize the continuity between the prison and the free community, it emphasized the importance of role design and learning.[7] All staff members and inmates were expected to share the common role of member of the community, and to increase the flexibility with which they assumed new roles, but functional distinctions among staff members and between inmates and staff members were not to be blurred. In fact, diversity and uniqueness in roles was valued as enhancing both the contribution of individuals to the resources of the group and the development of individual potentialities. The goal was to provide social conditions that would permit and encourage inmates to become trustworthy persons capable of operating acceptably in a variety of roles, rather than therapists.[8] Accordingly, no single mechanism for association, such as the "community meeting," was stipulated for evoking the community in action. All normal proc-

---

[6] See Jones, Maxwell, *The Therapeutic Community: A New Treatment Method in Psychiatry*, Basic Books, New York, 1953.

[7] Shortly after C-Unit's first year of operation the director visited Austen Riggs Center in Stockbridge, Massachusetts, whose community program for mental patients proved to be similar in this respect to that in C-Unit. See Talbot, Eugene, Stuart C. Miller, and Robert B. White, "Some Aspects of Self-Conception and Role-Demands in a Therapeutic Community," *Journal of Abnormal and Social Psychology*, vol. 63, no. 2, 1961, pp. 338–345.

[8] For an explicit formulation of the spreading of therapist roles through the therapeutic community, according to one model, see Rapoport, Robert N., *Community as Doctor: New Perspectives on a Therapeutic Community*, Tavistock Publications, Ltd., London, 1960, pp. 100–103.

esses through which any community becomes self-governing were seen as potentially useful, depending on the task at hand and covering the range from one-to-one relationships to convocations of the whole to public opinion polls. The community was expected to emerge as a recognizable entity as all processes of decision-making were infused with a common orientation and made subservient to a primary task of importance to all its members.

PROBLEM-SOLVING AS PROCESS

The Project conceived of problem-solving as the process through which the prison community would be created.

Problem-solving is used here to mean a specific and desirable mode for dealing with problems[9] as they concern individuals, groups, or larger, more complex social units. The dynamics of problem-solving as defined in the Project's framework included:

—Attention to problems of immediate concern to community members as defined by inmates as well as by staff.

—Collaboration of all persons relevant to the problem under consideration in the analysis of problems and in action to resolve problems.

—Task-focused action involving commitment on the part of all relevant persons, staff as well as inmates, to make the changes indicated by problem analysis.

—Evaluation of problem-solving success against standards combining concern for the development of moral relationships with concern for the efficient manipulation of reality.

The Project anticipated that both organizational forms and people would change in the problem-solving search for what disrupts social functioning and for what is available to correct what is wrong. Efficient communication systems would have to be created to aid in securing and channeling relevant information. Roles would be modified as persons became more flexible in the identification and use of latent resources. Increased organizational complexity could be expected as one consequence of the identification of subgroup needs and action to meet those needs. And

---

[9] A more elaborate definition of the problem-solving process as envisioned by the Project is found in Kenneth D. Benne's "Deliberate Changing as the Facilitation of Growth," in Bennis, Warren G., Kenneth D. Benne, and Robert Chin editors, *The Planning of Change*, Holt, Rinehart and Winston, New York, 1961, pp. 230–234.

community goals would emerge to influence action and to enrich the culture with symbols concerned with "we" as well as with "I."

In the Project's strategy, the community could not be established by fiat from above. Community would emerge from the process of involving inmates with staff in action to deal with problems experienced in the present. Structure would follow the necessities of agreed action and would be tested by usefulness in accomplishing tasks; it would accordingly be subject to change as the definition of problems and the tasks needed to resolve problems changed. The community would be made by its participants as they worked to serve the needs and goals of all.

Because such pooling of human interests would necessitate the establishment of certain regularities, an effective set of generally accepted rules could be expected to emerge to govern participation in that community. In this process it was hoped that imprisoned offenders would learn directly how responsible relationships both enhance human satisfaction in the attainment of goals and increase the probability that the needs of each individual will be met; and that both staff and inmates would grow in the social skills needed by all persons if they are to attain their own ends through participation with others. For all, the image of community should begin to be transformed from that of a superimposed organization used by some to punish others to that of a responsive social instrument for achieving group and individual welfare.

Creating such an image of individual-community relationships in the minds of imprisoned offenders was considered by the Project to be a first step in enabling inmates to be responsible men and in preparing those who could make the grade for return to the free community.

A RESOCIALIZING MODEL FOR TREATMENT

When one examines current prison operation one can discern four distinct models for doing something about what is wrong with imprisoned offenders. Most prison treatments fall within the scope of one of the following models: *custodial, educational, psychotherapeutic,* and *group treatment.* Each of these models selects one normal socializing process and elaborates it into a method for dealing with what is presumed to be wrong with offenders. Therefore each can be characterized as method focused. Each model is buttressed by a recognizable ideology and espoused by articulate adherents who often compete within the prison organization for recognition, resources, and control over inmates. And as now applied, the various treatments act on the individual offender as fragmentary and often conflicting pressures to change, offering no consistent goal for successful striving.

We shall briefly summarize the treatment ideologies current in most modern prisons in order to clarify the special characteristics of the C-Unit approach.

The Custodial Treatment: Obedience Training.[10] The first and controlling treatment ideology provides the rationale for incarceration as an instrument of reform.[11] It is professed by the largest body of personnel in the prison, the custody force. Because these officials are responsible for security twenty-four hours a day throughout the prison, their treatment approach is both pervasive and dominant in its impact on the individual offender.

In the custodial ideology the offender is perceived much as he is by the criminal law, as a social unit subject to definitions applying to all inmates rather than as a unique individual responding to particular problematic situations. Because he has violated one social norm, the offender is assumed to be a person of bad intent and potentially capable of violating all accepted norms. The process of changing such persons is conceived of as largely a matter of conditioning, with punishment as the chief means available for habituating offenders to conformity.

The technique associated with this ideology or treatment formulation relies on consistency rather than individuation. Its tools are detailed rules governing every aspect of daily life, gradations of punishment that can be invoked for each single violation, and minimal rewards attainable only by total conformity. Its goal is the well-behaved inmate, not the active problem-solver. In this perspective the task of the prison is to return the offender by force to a childlike dependence on external controls. The expectation is that, given sufficient exposure to institutional rules, the offender will learn to obey the law.

Educational Treatment: Training in Specific Role Skills. The first treatment programs designed to supplement the reform efforts of custody were

---

[10] See Gilbert, Doris C., and Daniel J. Levinson, "Role Performance, Ideology and Personality in Mental Hospital Aides," in Greenblatt, Milton, Daniel J. Levinson, and Richard H. Williams, editors, *The Patient and the Mental Hospital,* The Free Press, Glencoe, Ill., 1957, pp. 197–208, for a discussion of custodialism as it appears in the mental hospital.

[11] Although many custodial procedures are responsive primarily to the necessities of managing populations of offenders rather than to a preconceived treatment rationale, the design of custodial activities reflects a set of assumptions about what is wrong with offenders and what must be done to change them. The treatment rationale for custodial activity has become more explicit as the custodial role has been professionalized, but, explicit or not, this ideology is consonant both with the common-sense perspectives of our culture and with the deeper unconscious response of the law-abiding toward violators of the basic moral code. (See Mead, George H., "The Psychology of Punitive Justice," *American Journal of Sociology,* vol. 23, March, 1918, pp. 577–602.)

devised in the late nineteenth century. They brought into the prison representative units of the socializing agencies found in the free community, such as the church and the school. Today many modern prisons have educational, vocational, religious, and recreational programs manned by small groups of employees having the appropriate skills. Each such program, in its own way, attempts to make up the deficiencies in an offender's character and social skills in preparation for the roles that he will be expected to perform on release to the community.

The educational treatment ideology conceives of offenders as inadequate rather than as necessarily bad. In general, the approach classifies offenders, using their capacities, backgrounds, and anticipated opportunities as the determining variables in the planning of training programs. Educational processes emphasizing moral values and social skills are the characteristic tools of these socializing programs. The goal of treatment is to provide the offender with a repertory of roles that will allow him to participate in a legitimate social environment on his release. With this training, he is expected to be able to make a choice between crime and conformity. The task of the prison, in this perspective, is to keep the offender accessible to a variety of resocializing processes.

The presence of various educational treatments in prisons was responsible in the second decade of the twentieth century for an important change in prison organization, the introduction of *classification*. Up to this point educational treatment personnel had had little influence in prison decision-making because, although they were superior to custody personnel in education and community prestige, they were outnumbered and inferior in authority. Over the years many prisons have established classification committees, composed of representatives of the various prison treatments and responsible for scheduling specific programs for each inmate.

These committees act as high-level forums where adjustments are reached between those who operate on the principle of uniformity and those who seek to vary programs in response to different types of problems. Although security and institutional necessity continue to take priority in most classification decisions, such a committee has raised treatment personnel to a position of formal equality with those responsible for security. This somewhat unwieldy collection of "representatives," the Classification Committee, is today the primary means for adapting the prison program to the needs of the individual offender.

Individual Psychotherapy: Personality Change Through Remedial Relationships. During the first quarter of the twentieth century the newly emerging psychoanalytic treatment was proposed as a specific corrective for criminality. By 1932–1934 there were enough psychiatric programs in prisons, staffed by psychiatrists, psychologists, and social workers, to involve the American Prison Association in an intensive three-year debate concerning the function of this kind of treatment in the prison.[12]

According to the psychotherapeutic treatment formulation, offenders are psychologically disturbed persons who have been driven to illegal behavior by unconscious forces over which they have no control. The source of the disturbance is to be found in the offender's emotional relationships with parents and siblings experienced in his early life. The hostilities, sexual conflicts, and guilts, generated but unresolved in these relations with significant others, are acted out later in offenses toward persons who symbolize in the offender's internal drama the original objects of his love and hate. According to this formulation of the problem, the only effective treatment is a therapeutic relationship within which the offender, as patient, reexperiences early emotional difficulties, learns to distinguish between feelings aroused by his first family and feelings appropriate in current social relations, and ultimately understands himself in a way that enables him to control his behavior. In this perspective the problem is unique to the individual and the treatment must be specific to him.

This complex and highly individualized therapeutic process is posited on assumptions about the way the environmental conditions provided by prison management should support the treatment endeavor. The offender, perceived as patient, should be understood rather than judged. He should learn under guidance to make his own decisions by experimenting with behavior over a range not usually tolerated in individuals who are psychologically well. He should be dealt with on each occasion in terms of his needs and capacities as an individual rather than under rules governing everyone in his class. And the general principles of the psychotherapeutic approach should, so far as possible, be expressed in the behavior of all

---

[12] See Brenham, V. C., "Report of Committee on Casework and Treatment for Prisoners," *Proceedings of the American Prison Association,* 1932, pp. 147–179; and Spradley, J. B., "Psychiatric Case Work in the New Jersey Penal and Correctional System," *Proceedings of the American Prison Association,* 1934, pp. 186–198. It is significant that this debate focused on whether professional personnel were to be used as aides to administration in improving the management of all prison activities for all inmates, or as diagnostic and treatment specialists for those inmates who were perceived as psychologically ill. The decision favored the sequestration of professional treatment persons in separate divisions and made them responsible for specialized functions remote from influence on general prison management.

It is likely that in the early stages of the introduction of a new perspective, like that associated with psychotherapy, into an ongoing organization, some degree of insulation will prove necessary; otherwise the chances of corruption of the perspective would be vastly increased. The danger, of course, is that the insulation will not be overcome, and that in time it will become isolation.

officials who deal with him. To implement such a treatment program, highly specialized practitioners are needed; conditions favorable to their work must be provided; and the psychotherapeutic process should be given priority over all other prison activities.[13]

The parallels between this set of treatment formulations and the assumptions of the custodial treatment ideology are as striking as the points of divergence. Both treatment ideologies locate the source of the difficulty to be treated in the offender's personality; both assume that their formulations are appropriate for all offenders; both propose a corrective child-like experience as the cure; and both claim control over the conditions of institutional living as essential to effective treatment. But here the similarity between them ends. For the proponents of one treatment method the offender is ill; for the other he is bad.[14] The conditions perceived as necessary for treating the psychologically ill conflict in many ways with those necessary for training bad persons in obedience, especially in the contrast between individual and mass approaches. The knowledge and skills required to practice each of the two treatment methods are located at opposite ends of the theoretical and vocational spectrum. When psychotherapeutic personnel are added to the institutional staff, two relatively powerful types of personnel claim the right to make the crucial decisions in the prison organization.

The resultant organizational dissonance is obvious in many modern prisons. In most institutions some version of the custodial treatment ideology controls the decisions that affect the inmate's daily life. Personnel in the psychotherapeutic treatment program have access to the inmate only during specified hours, and their recommendations are seldom permitted to supervene custodial concerns at critical decision points. The offender therefore learns to be a patient in one facet of his prison experience and an inmate during the remaining portion of his time.[15] Organizational resources tend to be dissipated in conflict between staff groups with com-

---

[13] Robert B. White and Joan Erikson criticize this "sanctuary" formulation of the inmate role in the mental institution in "Some Relationships Between Individual Psychotherapy and the Social Dynamics of the Psychiatric Sanitarium," an unpublished paper presented to the Massachusetts Psychological Association, May 17, 1953, which suggests that certain patient roles should represent the "demands of an honest, not artificial or contrived social reality" (p. 2).

[14] See Aubert, Vilhelm, and Sheldon L. Messinger, "The Criminal and the Sick," *Inquiry*, vol. 1, no. 3, 1958, pp. 137–160.

[15] See Ohlin, Lloyd E., and William C. Lawrence, "Social Interaction Among Clients as a Treatment Problem," *Social Work*, vol. 4, April 1959, pp. 1–13; and Polsky, Howard W., *Cottage Six: The Social System of Delinquent Boys in Residential Treatment*, Russell Sage Foundation, New York, 1962.

peting ideologies. And each treatment group blames the other for inability
to achieve treatment goals. Today, although some prominent correctional
theorists assert that no institution with the task of implementing a sentence
of punishment can effectively integrate treatment (defined according to
the psychotherapeutic model) within its organization,[16] many persons in
the participating professions assume that the ideal prison should be organized much like a mental hospital and administered primarily to facilitate psychotherapeutic treatment.[17]

Group Treatment: Value Change Through Peer Influence. During the past
thirty years the human being has been increasingly perceived as simultaneously an individual psyche and a social unit. In this perspective, criminal deviance appears as a problem of the individual's relations with
groups. Whether the offender is seen as a disintegrated personality unable
to respond to group norms, or as a member of delinquent groups in an
anomic society, treatment by the group method is proposed as a specific
for the problem.

The group method consists primarily in bringing offenders together to
influence each other toward reform.[18] The individual offender is exposed
to a significant group of peers who can talk his language, establish acceptable norms, correct his behavior, and support him in legitimate striving.
The goal of treatment is to develop the capacity to maintain effective membership in the normal groups that are essential to an acceptable mode of

---

[16] Cressey, Donald R., "Limitations on Organization of Treatment in the Modern
Prison," in *Theoretical Studies in Social Organization of the Prison,* Social Science
Research Council, Pamphlet 15, New York, 1960, pp. 78–110; Powelson, Harvey,
and Reinhard Bendix, "Psychiatry in Prison," in Rose, Arnold M., editor, *Mental
Health and Mental Disorder,* W. W. Norton and Co., New York, 1955, pp. 459–481.

[17] This orientation does not sufficiently take into account the fact that the mental
hospital also suffers organizationally from potentially conflicting goals and treatment ideologies. See Cumming, John and Elaine, *Ego and Milieu,* Atherton Press,
New York, 1962, p. 108. See also Strauss, Anselm, and others, *Psychiatric Ideologies
and Institutions,* The Free Press of Glencoe, New York, 1964.

[18] For various formulations of this treatment method, see Cressey, Donald R., "Changing Criminals: The Application of the Theory of Differential Association," *American Journal of Sociology,* vol. 61, September, 1955, pp. 116–120; Empey, LeMar
T., and Jerome Rabow, "The Provo Experiment in Delinquency Rehabilitation,"
American Sociological Review, vol. 26, October, 1961, pp. 679–695; Fenton, Nor-
man, *An Introduction to Group Counseling in State Correctional Service,* American
Correctional Association, New York, 1958; Jones, Maxwell, *The Therapeutic Community, op. cit.;* Wilmer, Harry A., *Social Psychiatry in Action: A Therapeutic
Community,* Charles C Thomas, Springfield, Ill., 1958; Kassebaum, Gene, David
Ward, and Daniel Wilner, *Group Treatment by Correctional Personnel: A Survey of
the California Department of Corrections,* California Board of Corrections Mono-
graph 3, January, 1963; and McCorkle, Lloyd W., Albert Elias, and F. Lovell
Bixby, *The Highfield Story,* Henry Holt and Co., New York, 1958.

life in the free community—family, work, school, or recreation. The collection of offenders in prison is conceived of as a natural opportunity to use groups of offenders to help each other in becoming resocialized.

At present, the group treatment ideology lacks a consistent theory, and no single professional discipline is offering leadership in the use of the method. Some proponents adhere to strict psychoanalytical formulations and use the group primarily as a setting for individual therapy. Others follow sociological or group dynamics assumptions and focus on the group itself, adopt an eclectic position, or operate in terms of the wisdom gained by experience. Therefore group programs in prisons vary widely in goals, techniques, and the kinds of personnel involved in leadership. Each such program tends to evolve its own definitions of the group as a treatment tool, of the role of inmates in the treatment group, and of the subjects appropriate for group consideration. The one thread that links most group programs seems to be the proposition that *relations among inmates are potentially useful for treatment rather than an unavoidable evil to be discouraged.*

For our analysis the importance of this currently popular prison treatment method lies in its potential for instigating conflict and change in the prison as it is typically organized. Acknowledging the inmate as a significant participant in the treatment of his fellows raises his status vis-à-vis the staff. When the implications of this change of role are carried to the logical conclusion in action, major consequences for all other prison roles can be expected. In addition, inmate groups that achieve treatment significance gain organizational power, in contrast to the passive role required of inmates by the custodial ideology. Inherent in the group treatment method, regardless of the behavioral theory to which its practitioners subscribe, is the perception of the offender as a powerful force in his own resocialization and that of others. Inevitably, any attempt to apply this method will be the least potentially disruptive of many of the traditional patterns by which the prison organization has accommodated the other three treatment ideologies.[19]

The C-Unit Treatment Model: Resocialization. In the C-Unit perspective none of the prison treatments currently in use adequately addresses the task of the prison community when it is conceived of as the preparation of

---

[19] No brief and schematic summary of this nature can do justice to the variations in conceptual and technical approaches that exist within the broad practices of any one of the prison treatments. The obvious differences in assumptions of these four approaches do, however, point to the issues that tend to introduce distance or conflict among various kinds of practitioners when they are combined in current prison programs.

imprisoned offenders to act as morally responsible members of the free community. Each offers one method by which orientations and behavior may be changed but also elevates the method to an ideology. The disparate assumptions used by the various treatment proponents encourage conflicting approaches among the different sets of practitioners, thereby losing the value of mutual reinforcement possible when each treatment is seen simply as one of the potential socializing processes within the prison community to be used flexibly as needed.

For the C-Unit Project the treatment task called for influencing the expression of values in social relations; and for this comprehensive task treatment becomes not the application of a single method, but the management of all the socializing processes available in prison life to achieve a cohesive moral influence. Thus the Project did not consider itself to be competing with any one of the treatments currently established in the prison program, but rather to be undertaking to relate these methods together with other socializing processes in a comprehensive effort to enable prison inmates to live as moral men in present reality.

To distinguish "the management of socializing processes" from other treatment approaches, the Project chose the label "resocializing." This term is not completely satisfactory because it seems to imply that all prison inmates need to have their moral orientations overhauled and fundamentally changed. Such an assumption does not square with the reality one discovers in learning to know a population of imprisoned offenders. Only a very few give explicit allegiance to antisocial values; most offenders are in agreement with the general moral orientations of law-abiding persons. Many have lived so long under conditions that did not support moral behavior that they may need help in responding to more favorable conditions. Many need training in one or more of the social and technical skills essential for acceptable role performance; and some are handicapped by personality distortions that seriously limit their ability to perceive or act according to acceptable social norms. In addition, all prison inmates need protection against the value-debilitating effects of routine imprisonment. But the nature of the prison's task is fundamentally distorted if imprisoned offenders are conceived of as primarily persons of evil intent and tastes.

The term "resocialization" also suffers from the possible connotation of "clock fixing" or "brain washing," as though moral persons could be created by superior others doing something to them to correct faults in the inner mechanisms. The essence of moral behavior is responsibility for self in dealing with others, and acceptance of responsibility cannot be imposed. To avoid the implication of imposition from without, potential in the term "resocialization," the Project emphasized its own responsibility for creating conditions in which moral behavior is possible and rewarded, while insisting that the individual inmate must take action on his own behalf in order to use the conditions so provided.

Resocializing as a label for the Project's action model does draw attention to the fact that a particularly stringent form of adult socialization is initiated when a person's social status is drastically revised by imprisonment for a penal offense.[20] In this action the individual's old roles are suspended and many normal supports are withdrawn. The stress of crisis is deliberately applied by the community and the individual is given the task of earning his way out of the social degradation to which he has been subjected.[21] Under such conditions some changes in adaptive patterns can be expected to occur within each inmate; and the socializing conditions provided in prison life will influence the kind of reintegration that can occur.

Thus the Project used the term "resocialization" to direct attention to the fact that each prison inmate is, by the nature of his situation, forced to create for himself an identity that incorporates his new role in the community. He may or may not choose to use this opportunity for positive change; indeed, he may accept as appropriate for himself the degraded status assigned to him. But regardless of the inmate's choice, the dynamics of change will have been initiated in his life by the fact of imprisonment; and the kind of socializing processes to which he is exposed in prison will influence in some way the direction of change.

In the Project's lexicon, the resocializing model for treatment meant managing all the socializing processes available in prison life to encourage inmates to use the socially induced crisis of imprisonment for change toward moral maturity and increased social competence.

THE CHAPTERS TO COME

The pages that follow describe the Project's experience in attempting to build a resocializing community in a modern, humane, but traditionally organized, reformatory for young adult male offenders. The report takes on the form of a case history, although throughout we shall analyze the data for their contribution to emergent theoretical perspectives. In a deeper sense this document reports a voyage of intellectual discovery,

---

[20] See Broom, Leonard, and Philip Selznick, Sociology, 3d ed., Harper and Row, New York, 1963, pp. 114–123, for a summary of current tentative propositions about resocialization as a form of adult socialization.

[21] Garfinkel, Harold, "Conditions of Successful Degradation Ceremonies," American Journal of Sociology, vol. 61, March, 1956, pp. 420–424.

seeking the significant variables to be understood and managed if this kind of prison program is to be effective in the lives of human beings.

Chapter II sets the stage for the report of two years' activity involving 291 inmates and the appropriate staff based in one housing unit, known as C-Unit.[22] Here we introduce the reader to the conditions within which this particular inmate-staff community developed: the institution providing the Project's immediate organizational environment; the basic design for community created by a series of decisions made during the planning period; the human resources, both inmate and staff; and the physical plant. These were relatively constant factors in the life of the Project, establishing the direction of its development, setting limits, and providing certain potentialities for change and growth. Understanding the specific conditions that determined the nature of this community should help to differentiate between those features of the Project that were idiosyncratic to a particular place and time, and others with more general implications for the study of organizational change.

Chapters III through IX tell the story of community action during the two-year period. The sequence of chapters is organized around three primary foci.

The patterns for social relationships as they developed over time and became institutionalized in the C-Unit community are described in Chapters III, IV, and V. This history of the emerging community prepares the reader for the later analysis of interaction among staff and inmates by outlining the issues that engaged them and the means available for dealing with those issues. Three chapters are required for this topic because two central themes focused the attention of staff and inmates as they struggled to establish the relationship patterns appropriate for resocializing work. Chapter III describes what happened during the first year in the attempt to organize community relationships for welfare. Chapter IV traces the parallel attempt in the same twelve-month period to establish similar relationships for social control. Because the outcomes of these two organizational efforts were quite divergent, the community, as it was stabilized during the second year, was bifurcated rather than coherent. Chapter V sketches the quite divergent kinds of action of which such a community proved to be capable. This community, with its potentialities and flaws, constituted the dynamic social setting within which the staff and the inmates can be observed interacting. The remaining chapters analyze the participation of each in the community they helped to create.

---

[22] Between the initiation of the Project and the withdrawal of the research staff two years later, 291 inmates were selected for C-Unit. The first 266 of these were included in the study population.

Chapters VI and VII examine the critical role of the Project staff in discharging its responsibility for creating community. Again, more than one chapter is needed for this subject matter because both the composition of the staff and the conditions for its work were different for the two years. Although in the original plan, the second year's activity was expected to be continuous with the first and devoted to further refinement of the resocialization model, the changes introduced at the end of the first year so drastically modified the style and content of staff activity that we have, as it were, a "natural experiment." Comparing the style of management used by the first staff with that characterizing the work of the second staff allows us to examine those conditions favorable to community relationships against other less favorable conditions. The analysis of staff work in both years reveals the processes through which the organization of official relationships influences the nature of the inmate-staff community and leads to useful propositions about the role of official personnel in work toward the resocializing goal.

In Chapters VIII and IX we turn to the experiences of inmates in the C-Unit community. Chapter VIII describes the patterns for informal relations that developed among the C-Unit inmates as those patterns could be observed at one point in time through the lens of a survey that compared the C-Unit inmate system with the inmate systems existing in two other housing units in the same institution. This chapter differs from others in that it is a "still photograph" rather than a report of action in process. It does, however, allow us to identify the mechanisms through which officials in the prison organization gained access to influence within the inmate system. It also provides a check on the indications from observational data that changes in the desired direction were occurring in the relationships established by C-Unit inmates among themselves; and permits us to compare an important aspect of their social experience with that to which other inmates living in the same institution were exposed. In Chapter IX we examine the way the C-Unit community affected the institutional careers of individual inmate members, seeking to identify the processes through which organizational change accomplishes its purpose in the lives of the persons whom it engages in action.

The final chapter focuses attention on the tentative principles for organizing human resources to influence offenders that emerged in the C-Unit experience. We shall be concerned in this chapter with the original Project expectations that were supported or disproved; and with the issues for which no resolution was discovered in this particular endeavor. We use this concluding chapter to share with the reader our thoughts on the conditions that affect the success or failure of such an attempt to create a resocializing community in prison; and on the implications of such attempts for correctional programs of the future as well as for the many other community institutions that also face the critical issue of how to organize human relations to secure the welfare of individuals and groups.

In presenting this report it is important to alert the reader to a major limitation in its discussion of the variables affecting organizational change. It is already evident that the Project's strategy for organizational change was to begin at the bottom of the organizational ladder in order to evoke and study in action the elements of community processes in prison. This focus was deliberately chosen. For many years innovations in prison programming have been initiated at upper administrative levels on the basis of limited descriptive data about what occurs in the action arena where the program affects the inmates. In consequence, unidentified variables often obscure the findings and limit their use for future planning. The Project hoped to use the C-Unit community as a laboratory in which to observe in microcosm the action consequences of proposed organizational changes; and later to use the findings of this experience in refining the model and proposing policies to guide administration in planning more extensive programs of this nature.

Because of this focus on the elements of action within the developing prison community, the Project has limited data about the decisions made in its organizational environment—the institution and the Department of Corrections—that seriously affected the course of the Project's career. The Project planners had originally expected that information about the rationale for upper administrative decisions would become available in the course of action; and that such information could be recorded and analyzed along with other data about responsive action within the C-Unit community. Perhaps one of the Project's more important findings concerns the serious lacunae existing in the communication lines between a single unit such as the Project and upper administration in the institution, as well as between the institution and the central office of the Department of Corrections; and the recognition that these gaps could not be successfully bridged by efforts from within the Project alone even though they constituted a serious handicap to the continuity of experimental action. As a consequence, Project personnel were often not adequately informed about the constraints under which upper administration made their decisions; and so cannot report the rationale for such decisions with the understanding that informs that part of the story in whose action the writers were intimately involved.

Therefore we shall have to report certain critical decisions made about the Project without the explanatory analysis that would help the reader understand an important arena of action affecting the Project's successes and failures. During the two years of the Project's life, and later in retrospective analysis, we formulated a number of "educated guesses" about the dynamic variables in the Project's organizational environment. They appear in this report primarily as background for events that blocked program development in certain directions while supporting it in others. Subsequent study is now under way that should give a fuller understanding of the problems that such an experiment in using a small unit for organizational change poses for the larger systems in which it operates.

Meanwhile *C-Unit* should be read in the light of its modest objectives. We seek to identify and describe the elements of action among prison inmates and the personnel directly related to them that must be taken into account when the prison task is conceived of as establishing the conditions for moral behavior in the present. The story that follows identifies some of the problems to be expected in such an undertaking, the phases through which the emerging community may have to pass, the processes by which staff and inmates influence each other, and the conditions that facilitate problem-solving work toward resocialization.

II - LAUNCHING THE PROGRAM

DEUEL VOCATIONAL INSTITUTION, the site of the C-Unit Project, stands on a 760-acre plot of flat land at the northern end of the fertile San Joaquin Valley, near the town of Tracy, California, about 60 miles east of San Francisco. Surrounded by fruit orchards, truck and dairy farms, and grazing lands, "DVI" is bounded in the distance on the west by the low rim of the Coast Range and on the east by the foothills of the Sierra Nevada. In the summer, the land of the broad flat valley to the south disappears into the blaze and glare of hot, cloudless days; and in the winter, into the thick grayness of fog and low clouds coming in from the Pacific Ocean.

An access road from the highway leads to the institution. Driving in, to the left, two cyclone fences, separated by a fifteen-foot gravel strip and topped with barbed accordion wire, enclose an oblong "security area" approximately 1,600 feet wide by 1,000 feet deep. Along the fences, custodial officers in tan uniforms look down from eight gun towers. On foggy days, additional officers armed with shotguns patrol the fences on foot.

To the right across neat lawns, in front of the institution but outside the fences, are several buildings for staff use. Further away, nine ranch-style, state-owned houses, rented by DVI officials, stand amidst colorful gardens. Straight ahead are a number of facilities for maintaining and operating the institution's physical plant. At a greater distance are farm buildings used for dairy and hog-raising activities.

Inside the security area, reached through the steel door of the small entrance building and the sliding gate of the second fence, one sees spread out with geometric regularity, the square-cut, yellow-tinted concrete buildings of the institution: in the center, the administration building; to the left, the protruding wings of the housing units and the hospital, and in the distance, the reception center for new arrivals; to the right, the wings housing the library, academic classrooms, and the trade training shops; straight ahead, not visible to the eye from the main entrance, the kitchen and dining halls, industrial shops, chapels, and the recreational facilities, including the field house and yard.[1]

In 1960, when the C-Unit Project began, DVI was one of seven correctional institutions for males under the jurisdiction of the California Department of Corrections. On any given day during the Project, about 1,400 inmates occupied its main buildings.[2] Over three-quarters of them were from eighteen to twenty-four years of age. Like many correctional institutions serving this age group, DVI's program stressed educational activities. The trade training program was especially well developed, with some 20 instructors teaching courses in well-appointed shops, including aircraft,[3] mill cabinetwork, landscaping, refrigeration, dry cleaning, shoe repairing, sheet metalwork, machine shop, welding, drafting and mechanical drawing, electricity, painting, and plastering. About 550 inmates at any given time were enrolled in trade training work, usually on a half-day basis. Roughly the same number was enrolled in academic classes offered by a dozen certified teachers.[4] In addition, the institution operated a metal products factory, bedding factory, and farm. Some 250 inmates participated in one of these operations, usually on a full-day basis. Further, approximately 80 groups of 5 to 15 inmates met weekly for one hour, with a

---

[1] Chart 1 suggests the layout of Deuel Vocational Institution during 1960–1962. From 1946, when DVI received its first inmates, until 1953, the institution was located in temporary quarters near the town of Lancaster in southern California. These temporary quarters were smaller, housing about 500 inmates; the staff was proportionately smaller at Lancaster as well.

[2] Another 300 inmates were housed in the reception center; they were served by about 50 staff members. We shall not be concerned with the operation of the reception center, except incidentally. Although under the supervision of the Superintendent of DVI, it was operated as a separate institution. Only a portion of the inmates processed in the reception center were assigned to DVI.

[3] The airframe and airplane engine mechanics shops were the most prestigious of DVI's trade training operations. The institution had been granted an Air Agency Certificate by the U.S. Civil Aeronautics Administration in 1958, empowering it to operate an approved school in airframe and powerplant.

[4] Most academic pupils also attended on a half-day basis. Taking into account those inmates assigned to both academic and trade training classes, about half of the inmate population were participating in the educational program at any given time during 1960–1962.

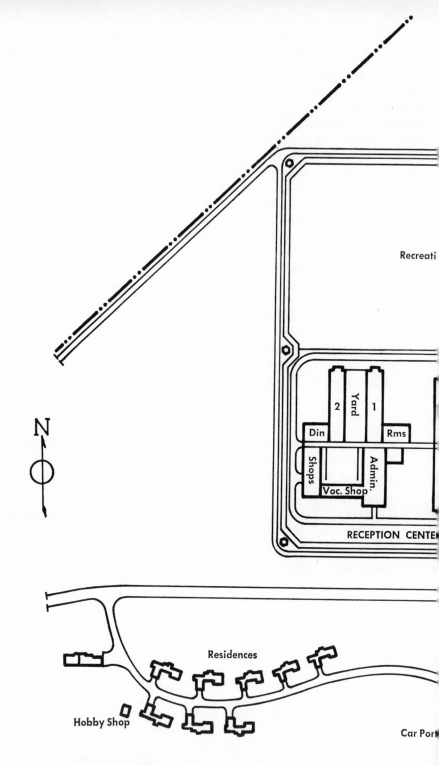

N

Recreati

2 | Yard | 1

Din | Rms

Shops

Voc. Shop

Admin.

RECEPTION CENTE

Residences

Hobby Shop

Car Por

CHART 1. PLOT PLAN
DEUEL VOCATIONAL INSTITUTION
Tracy, California

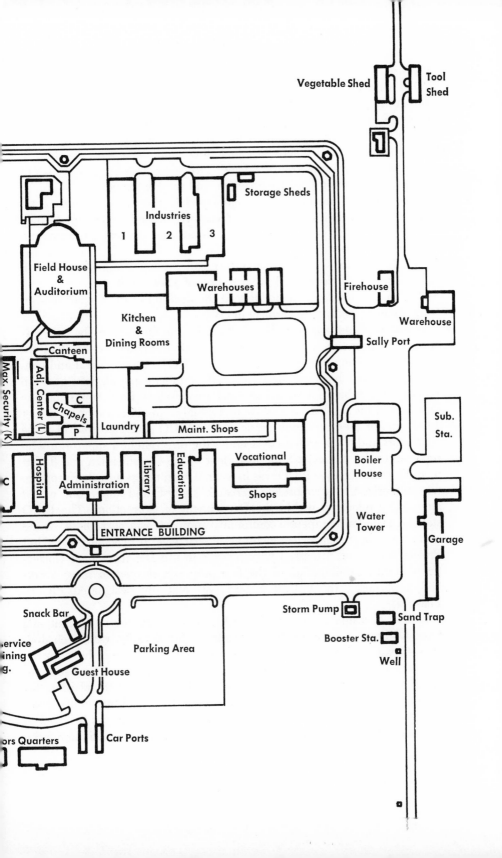

variety of staff members for counseling classes (as such groups were called at DVI). At any given time, about half of the inmates were members of some group counseling class, partly because the paroling authorities often suggested to inmates that participation in this voluntary activity was the better part of wisdom. Finally, DVI provided a number of other recreational and rehabilitative activities, including handicrafts, a drama club, an Alcoholics Anonymous group, a Dale Carnegie course, regular religious services, a swimming pool, gymnasium, and weekly movies.

Some 400 staff members were employed in the main institution, organized into six divisions: Custody, Classification and Treatment (which was responsible for group counseling), Education, Medical, Business, and Correctional Industries (which was responsible for the factories and the farm). In addition, the Superintendent had a small administrative staff. Chart 2 indicates the formal organization of DVI's staff.

Two main considerations influenced the decision of the Department of Corrections to conduct the Project in DVI:

1. The decision was heavily weighted by the fact that a five-year experimental program was already based in DVI. Known as the Pilot Intensive Counseling Organization (called "PICO"), experimental and control groups had been selected from DVI's inmate population, and the experimental subjects assigned to special counselors. Each counselor saw members of his caseload in weekly individual counseling sessions and met with some of them in group sessions. The PICO staff consisted of three counselors and a research analyst under the direction of a supervisor who reported to the Associate Superintendent of the Classification and Treatment Division. In 1960 PICO was in its final year; unless a further program was authorized, the counselors, research analyst, and supervisor would have to be relocated within the Department of Corrections. The PICO staff suggested a therapeutic community approach as a next phase. At the same time the action research program that was to become the C-Unit Project was being discussed with officials in the Department of Corrections. Since a combination of the two proposals seemed to serve everybody's purposes, the C-Unit Project was officially designated PICO–Phase II.

2. DVI also met a number of the Project's criteria for an institutional base. DVI was a large institution organized functionally, with each division—Custody, Treatment, Training—managing its own procedures for the institution as a whole. From the perspective of the Project, any such institution could be improved by using smaller multifunctional units for relating staff with inmates. DVI's plant provided housing units small enough to restrict the living group to 130 inmates, which was believed to be about the maximum number of inmates for the kind of community the

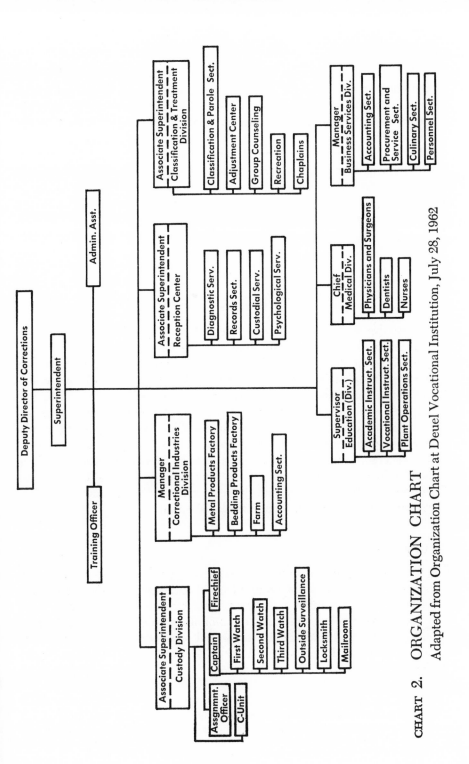

CHART 2. ORGANIZATION CHART

Adapted from Organization Chart at Deuel Vocational Institution, July 28, 1962

Project sought to develop. The inmate population at DVI consisted of younger men who had relatively short sentences, few of whom had settled down to prison as a way of life. Of primary importance, DVI's administrators had a tradition of pioneering and had expressed interest in the Project. They had an impressive trade training program developed in consultation with representatives of labor, management, and government employment agencies, who were organized into a Trade Advisory Council that met quarterly. Further, under their leadership DVI had been one of the first of California's correctional institutions to employ group counseling on a wide scale.[5] Moreover, DVI's administrators indicated a willingness to accept the necessary conditions, to be discussed below, for the beginning of community action.

PROJECT PLANNING

Once the institution had been selected, the Project director, together with personnel from the institution and the Department of Corrections, spent three months planning the program, a shorter period than had been expected. Original arrangements between the Department of Corrections and the director had provided that the director should have at least one year's experience in the regular prison operation before writing a proposal for action research. When it proved impossible to pay the director to obtain such experience in the Department, a small proposal-writing grant was secured from the National Institute of Mental Health and three months for planning had to suffice. Accordingly, the Project itself was designed to be exploratory, and the research was directed toward the discovery of variables rather than toward evaluation.

OLD PATTERNS

Consideration of the Project's operational goal—to engage staff and inmates in responsible action on problems of real concern in the present and relevant for the futures of inmates—suggested that arrangements were needed that would counteract, or minimize the development of, three characteristics of traditionally organized correctional institutions. Observation during the planning period made it clear that DVI shared these characteristics.

---

[5] The group counseling program was initiated in DVI during 1955. Prior to that time DVI had an individual counseling program in which inmates consulted individually staff members. Staff members from all divisions were involved, but existing records did not permit us to estimate the extensiveness of the program.

1. The first may be called "segmentation." This term is intended to refer, on the one hand, to the barriers that develop between staff groups organized into functional divisions, for example, Custody and Treatment. The members of the different divisions seldom talk to each other about their work. They tend to define problems in terms of the specific functions of their divisions, and they lack information about how other parts of the organization affect and are affected by their activities. Without occasion or means to formulate and work toward a common goal, the staff tend to be integrated if at all by the pervasive interest of custody in institutional security, and to compete in other areas for resources and influence over inmates.

The term "segmentation" is also intended to refer to the barrier that develops between staff and inmates. Behind this barrier, across which inmates and staff do not "talk serious,"[6] individual inmates pursue private goals so far as limited resources permit, supported by the explicit norm of "do your own time."

The Project accordingly had to find means to relate staff members from different functional groups to each other and to inmates within a single organization where common problems would become salient and communication about how to solve the problems necessary.

2. A second characteristic common to traditional correctional institutions is a hierarchical pattern for decision-making that reserves initiative and discretion for upper-level staff members, limiting the involvement of lower-level staff members and inmates.

When initiative and decision-making authority are reserved for upper-level administrative personnel, the lower-level staff members who implement the decisions act without adequate information, substitute conformity for problem-solving, lack means to contribute their specialized information to program-planning, and seldom experience the discretion necessary to adapt work to the requirements of particular situations. A prescribed role, rather than his actual capacity to contribute, determines what the individual staff member puts into the enterprise; and the exchange between the individual staff member and his organization is limited to utilitarian matters that cannot motivate him either to strive for excellence or to examine value-laden issues.

Inmates are even more limited by their organizational role in prison. Remote decision-makers move them about within a mass program with what is often only token concern for their individual interests, differentiating among them primarily as they fall into gross categories, for example, "conforming" or "bad actor," bright or dull, skilled or unskilled. The ex-

---

[6] *Talk serious:* inmate term for open communication about issues of real concern to those communicating.

change between the individual inmate and the organization occurs at a primitive level, with the inmate offering conformity in exchange for minimal harassment. In consequence, inmates learn to present themselves to officials according to the accepted stereotypes, manipulating specific parts of the organization behind the scenes for private goals. They are seldom engaged with staff at those deeper motivational levels where influence becomes effective and reciprocity develops.

The Project was thus necessarily concerned to establish patterns for decision-making that would engage staff and inmates in conversation and action over real issues, evoke individual initiative and investment in outcomes, and permit flexibility of organizational response to individuals.

3. Finally, traditionally organized correctional institutions share the characteristic of "discontinuity"; they develop limited means for relating the programs of individual inmates to parole-planning, thus diminishing the effectiveness of efforts to make the prison experience a transitional preparation for future responsibilities.

Institutional staff members, lacking significant information about the social realities to which inmates are to be released, frequently design programs that accommodate individuals to institutional necessities or direct them toward unrealistic goals. Prison activities are accordingly often more effective in training offenders to be successful inmates than in preparing men for their future roles outside the prison.

In response, prison inmates often become incapable of conceiving of the future except as a desired state of freedom seen through rose-colored glasses. The free role is pictured primarily as it contrasts with the deprivations and irritations of the inmate role, as if the inmate will become a totally new self upon release. And so the newly released parolee is likely to find himself ill-prepared for the increased stimuli, the complex responsibilities, and the specific problems demanding immediate solution that bombard him when the dependency-inducing supports of the prison are withdrawn. This abrupt change from a severely restricted life to the uncharted complexity of "the streets" frequently precipitates for the new parolee a profound experience of discontinuity in himself as a person.

The parole agent, who is expected to aid the individual in this transitional crisis, also lacks information. The new parolee's problems, capacities, and recent experiences in prison are largely unknown to the agent and he must thus focus on the specific demands of the parolee's new roles without being able to evoke what has been useful in the individual's recent past for use in present exigencies.

Thus in the parolee's perspective, the move from inmate role to parolee role tends to become a break in continuity rather than a transition, and the patterns learned in prison a crippling handicap to be overcome rather than preparation for greater responsibilities. Accordingly, the Project wanted to establish organizational bridges from the prison experience to the parole experience that would substitute transition for discontinuity in the individual offender's move from prison to parole.

NEW PATTERNS

The Project saw itself as a laboratory within which Project personnel could experiment, together with DVI's administrators, in an attempt to discover a more satisfactory model for institutional management, beginning at the housing-unit level. The housing unit was conceived, to use an analogy, as the neighborhood within which the desired relations among inmates, among staff members, and between inmates and staff members could develop.

Although it was known that the individual inmate at DVI mingled with other segments of the inmate population during work and educational assignments, at mess and recreation, it was believed that his housing unit was the location where he experienced some stability of relationships with other inmates as he showered, lined up for clothing change, watched TV, played cards, or chatted while waiting for the bellowing institutional horn to announce the next movement. With some procedural changes, it was reasoned, these relations might be made even more stable and meaningful. It was also believed that the housing unit could provide a focus for relatively stable relationships among staff members, relationships that would cut across traditional divisional lines. Since the housing unit appeared to provide the best potential center in DVI for developing relatively meaningful and stable relationships between staff and inmates, it was decided to use a housing unit to determine the boundaries of the Project.

The program was to be limited, moreover, to one housing unit. In part, this limitation was in line with the departmental practice of using small, especially designed units to test new treatment ideas. In part, it served to place personnel relatively inexperienced in institutional management at an appropriate administrative level. It also fit within the Project's strategy for discovering what specific organizational changes were needed by working up and out from the level of direct action among inmates and between inmates and staff members. One housing unit, finally, would provide a relatively limited situation to facilitate early identification of problems and precise analysis of action consequences.

Project personnel expected that the two-year period of action would be a time of tension between the single unit and its quite different organizational environment.[7] But if Project ideals were achieved, much of this tension would be used for learning in the long, slow process of testing experiments through public examination of their consequences. In line with this strategy of change, it was important that C-Unit not be so different from the rest of the institution that its problems would be perceived as completely dissimilar. Accordingly, the request for initial changes was limited to those held to be essential. They were the following:

1. As noted, a single housing unit was to be selected as the locale of the project. The inmate population of the Unit was to be limited to 130 men at any given time by assigning one man to a room. Inmates would be selected randomly from an eligible pool representing a cross section of the institutional population.[8] Once selected for the Unit, inmates would remain until released from the institution, approximately six to eighteen months. If the behavior of C-Unit inmates warranted temporary segregation, they were to be housed elsewhere but returned to the Unit upon release from such segregation.

2. The immediate Project staff was to be composed of persons representing five functions: administration, counseling, custody, research, and secretarial, all of whom would be members of the C-Unit community. Staff members would not be routinely rotated to other posts in the institution; they were to remain with the Project as long as possible. Their major responsibility would be the C-Unit population, which was to be treated as a distinct caseload. Both custody officers and counselors were to have offices in the Unit. Counselors were to have caseloads of 40 to 45 inmates and were to be responsible throughout each inmate's career in DVI for both the necessary procedural tasks and the therapeutic functions previously performed by the PICO staff. As case managers for individual inmates, further, counselors were to confer with institutional personnel in other parts of DVI's program, for example, work and educational assignments. Finally, C-Unit staff members, along with other relevant institutional personnel and the concerned inmate, would in time form subcommittees to make decisions about each inmate's institutional program ("classification") and discipline.

Through the use of these measures, the Project hoped to establish identity-forming boundaries for the new community; to provide opportunities for the frequent face-to-face encounters out of which enduring relation-

---

[7] In the original plan the two-year developmental period was to have been followed by three additional years devoted to consolidating C-Unit's program and introducing its organization of staff functions into other living units. This integrating process did, in fact, occur but without an accompanying research program.

[8] See Appendix A for selection procedures.

ships might develop; and to ensure the confrontation of diverse staff and inmate interests that would bring problems of importance to more than one grouping into focus for common attention and action. Although C-Unit inmates would be scheduled for much of their time outside the Unit's boundaries, participating in work, school, feeding, and recreation with the rest of DVI's inmates, the decisions about each inmate's classification and discipline, and about communications to parole authorities were ultimately to be located at the level of persons who had first-hand information about problems, who could act together to resolve conflicts, and who were responsible for implementing decisions once they were made. Making members of the community responsible for outcomes in matters of importance to them was expected to create conditions in which individuals could be involved in work on community tasks.

3. Finally, provisions for "bridges to the community" constituted the Project's scheme for emphasizing the transitional character of the prison experience.

C-Unit inmates were to be selected from those in DVI who had been committed from three major metropolitan areas in California and who therefore might be expected to return to these areas on parole. At least one parole agent from each of the state's two correctional agencies[9] in each of these areas was to be assigned to duty in the C-Unit program and to be present in the institution one day a month. The individual parole agent was to become acquainted with inmates to be released to his area soon after each one's admission to the Unit. In the ensuing months the agent would participate in decisions about the inmate's institutional program, would secure pertinent information about "back home" conditions as needed by the inmate and his counselor, and would begin planning for the parole program. Parole agents would assume membership in the C-Unit community during attendance at the institution, and at those times Project activities would be designed to focus the attention of C-Unit inmates and staff on preparation for specific futures.

By establishing bridges to the community, the Project hoped to make problem-solving in the institution more than a simple disposition of problems in the present. With the perspective of relevance for the future built firmly into the Project organization, it was hoped that it would become possible to introduce continuity and significance into the institutional lives of those who would otherwise be mainly "doing time."

---

[9] California has two correctional agencies: the Department of Corrections and the Department of the Youth Authority. As noted earlier, DVI was operated by the Department of Corrections. It housed inmates under the jurisdiction of both departments. This matter will be discussed further below.

It is also important to note the conditions which the Project did not require in order to begin its work.

1. The Project did not exclude any inmates from the Unit population on the basis of behavioral, personal, or social characteristics. So far as possible, the Unit population was expected to be similar to that of DVI. Although the goal of population selection was not representativeness, the Project did seek exposure to the range of problems that DVI staff members and inmates might expect to encounter.

2. The Project did not ask for control over the selection of personnel. Given the goal of organizational change, it was deemed essential to work with the personnel normally available to the institution. Thus selection of personnel followed the usual civil service procedures.

3. The Project did not require revisions in the mechanisms for classification and control of inmate behavior as a condition for starting the Project. It did secure administrative agreement that experimentation with these procedures would be permitted as experience was gained and specific plans for change were formulated.

Thus the Project began with a set of conditions that might reasonably be duplicated in housing units throughout the institution, provided it demonstrated sufficient improvement in management and services to warrant the wider adoption of the plan. Its stipulations were modest and within the range of practical next steps for the institution as a whole.

DIFFERENCES FROM DVI

Withal, the organizational arrangements proposed by C-Unit were considerably different from those to be found in most traditional correctional institutions, including DVI. The nature and import of these differences will be treated more fully in subsequent chapters; however, they are briefly outlined here.

DVI's administration did not consider or treat individual housing units as equivalent entities, each managing its own problems. Instead, all were thought of as forming a "system" in which particular units or groups of units had special functions; and all were governed by centralized authority. The main division of units was between "nonhonor"[10] and "honor" units. Newly arrived inmates entered nonhonor units, where relatively strict surveillance was exercised and regimentation prevailed. After accu-

---

[10] These were called "mainline" or "skid row" units at DVI. We have chosen the more cumbersome term—"nonhonor" unit—to avoid confusion with another common use of the term "mainline" to refer to any unit housing those not under special disciplinary restrictions.

mulating a sufficient period of time without a serious disciplinary infraction ("clean time"), inmates were moved to honor units, where less strict surveillance and regimentation were enforced. Prior to the establishment of the Project in C-Unit, there were four nonhonor units: C, D, H, and J. Wings E, F, and G were used as honor units, as well as parts of units K and L.

It was not institutional practice to assign inmates to live in a particular housing unit throughout their careers in DVI; instead, men were moved for control purposes not only from nonhonor to honor units, but between the various nonhonor and honor units as well. In addition, serious disciplinary infractions typically led to removal to the "isolation" cells in K-Unit, and inmates from honor units who met this fate were inevitably sent to a nonhonor unit upon release to begin the trek, through clean time, back to an honor unit. In general, too, inmates removed to isolation from a nonhonor unit returned to a different nonhonor unit. Those inmates who caused persistent trouble were typically assigned to L-Unit, the adjustment center. Here they would remain for three months or more—the center provided a program which included some education and counseling within its confines—eventually to be returned to a nonhonor unit. If the institution decided that nothing could be done with a recalcitrant inmate, he might be confined in the "administrative segregation section," located in K-Unit. There he would spend twenty-two hours a day in his cell, with two hours to walk the adjacent corridor, until transferred to another institution or released by discharge or parole.

In brief, inmates typically moved from unit to unit; they did not stay long in any one location.[11] As is also apparent from this brief description, and as will become quite evident in Chapter IV, housing assignments were intimately connected with the institution's arrangements for motivating inmates to conform to institutional rules and for dealing with deviant conduct.

Limiting the unit population to 130 men and providing each with his own room was also different from the general practice at DVI. Although the institution had been built to house approximately 130 men in each housing unit, within a few years of its activation in 1953, a number of rooms had been "double bunked." As a consequence, units housed up to

---

[11] Of course, some inmates managed to stay in one room for fairly long periods; this was hardly the institutional norm, however. During one 13-week period in 1962, there were 1,520 moves between housing units and 1,153 moves between rooms and tiers within housing units. (Moves between rooms and tiers also had control significance since inmates preferred some locations on units to others.) These moves, it should be noted, do not include movement to or from the reception center, the hospital, court, nor to parole, discharge, or other institutions (transfer).

185 men. Indeed, "single rooms" were viewed by inmates as something of value; some requested not to be transferred to honor units in order to retain single rooms. From the administration's point of view, single rooms were a semi-precious resource to be used as rewards and as a safeguard when inmates were felt to be untrustworthy. All segregation units—isolation, segregation, the adjustment center—were single bunked; but even in these units, in times of crisis, inmates were sometimes placed two in a room, one sleeping on the floor.

It is also to be noted that personnel, like inmates, had no particular connections with individual housing units.[12] Responsibility for all the housing units was assigned to the Custody Division. Institutional practice was to rotate custodial officers (including middle management, that is, sergeants and lieutenants) from assignment to assignment, the avowed object being to provide them with wide experience in the various tasks to be performed. Counselors were assigned counselees in a fashion that meant each counselor would have under his supervision inmates widely scattered among the housing units: each counselor was assigned those incoming inmates whose identification numbers ended with particular digits. This practice was, in part, a means of ensuring that particular inmates were served by the same counselor throughout their careers in DVI. It is evident that, given the institutional practice of moving inmates from unit to unit, this was the only means of providing continuity of relations between inmate and counselor. Secretaries were assigned to institutional divisions; and researchers, of course, were a rarity. Administrators other than custodial were responsible for specific functions and across-the-board programs not related to housing units.

Nor were DVI's regular counselors in any real sense "case managers," as those in C-Unit were expected to be. Although each inmate was assigned to a counselor, each of the six "regular" counselors at DVI had a caseload of about 250 inmates. Counselors had their offices in the administration building and rarely saw an inmate where he lived or worked. Each inmate was typically interviewed by his counselor shortly after arriving at DVI. On the basis of this interview (and recommendations made by reception center personnel), the counselor prepared a report used by the institution's Classification Committee to assign inmates a custodial rating and a training program. The Classification Committee was typically composed of a supervising counselor, the institution's assignment lieutenant—a custodial officer who kept track of the jobs that needed to be filled and the places open in the education program—and a representative of the Education Division; the inmate's counselor seldom had

---

[12] The adjustment center was a partial exception.

time to attend. Further, although the Classification Committee periodically reviewed the program of individual inmates to consider changes, the counselor was not consulted about these decisions. Inmates might see their counselors by requesting an interview through the office of the custodial captain; these requests were ordinarily honored within a few days. It was clear, however, that many inmates seldom requested such interviews, and some did not see their counselors a second time until they were being considered for parole. At that time, the counselor interviewed each inmate again to prepare a report on his progress for the paroling authorities.

Other personnel, for example, schoolteachers, trade training instructors, or work supervisors, had no routine way of affecting the overall programs arranged by the Classification Committee. They periodically checked forms assessing the progress of individual inmates in their specific programs and sent them to the Classification Committee, but they were seldom consulted directly about individual inmates.

The discipline process was also centralized; like housing, with which it was intimately connected, it was primarily the responsibility of the Custody Division.[13] Inmates accused of rule infractions appeared before the Disciplinary Court, conducted by the Associate Superintendent, Custody, or a substitute custodial officer, which was held each morning. Cases calling for something less than confinement in an isolation cell were disposed of by the Court. More serious cases were referred to the Disciplinary Committee, composed of the Associate Superintendent, Custody, the head of the adjustment center, and a supervising correctional counselor. This Committee met once a week. Its sanctions ranged from withdrawal of the privilege card for a specified period of time to confinement in an isolation cell for up to twenty-nine days, through more or less permanent segregation in the adjustment center, to a recommendation that an inmate's date for parole consideration be delayed or his actual date of parole be set back. Observation of this Committee in action showed considerable effort on the part of its members to be fair, for instance, to listen to inmate explanations and to mete out roughly equal punishment for offenses deemed equally serious. Observation also suggested that rule violations did not provide an occasion for examination of the rules themselves—the rules were taken as given; it was the "bad actors" who provided trouble. And no staff person who knew the inmate well was involved in making the discipline decision.

---

[13] This is not to say, however, that members of other divisions were expected to disregard rule violations. On the contrary, they were constantly exhorted by custodial administrators to attend to "the security of the institution." They were expected to write CDC 115's (disciplinary reports) on observing rule infractions, as were the custody officers.

The Project's proposal to integrate parole agents into the C-Unit community was quite different from current practice at DVI. For the most part, DVI's lack of participating parole agents had nothing to do with the intentions of DVI's administrators. DVI housed inmates from all sections of California, and the parole divisions of the Department of Corrections and the Department of the Youth Authority had no provisions for agents to visit institutions on a regular basis. Instead, a more formal kind of contact prevailed. When an inmate's parole date had been determined,[14] his records were forwarded to the parole office to which the inmate would be reporting. These were used by parole officers to help them develop parole plans, such as those for living accommodations, a job. At some time during the period between the parole hearing and the actual date of release, most Department of Corrections inmates attended a group lecture on parole conditions (called a "pre-parole class") offered by a visiting parole official; such a meeting took place about once every two months. Youth Authority inmates attended a similar lecture offered about every two weeks. In addition, Youth Authority inmates, as indicated above, saw the parole board again, briefly, to discuss the plans that had been made. On balance, however, it seemed clear that parole planning for inmates under the jurisdiction of either department remained rather sketchy and that parole was anticipated by most inmates with anxiety as well as with elation.

Finally, in C-Unit, staff and inmates were to share a common role, that of member of the community. No such provision for including inmates with staff in the distribution of responsibility existed elsewhere in DVI.

RELATING THE PROJECT TO DVI AND TO THE DEPARTMENT

In view of these differences, it was not immediately evident how the Project should be located within already existing patterns of authority and activities. Accordingly, it was necessary to specify how the Project was to be related to other parts of DVI and to authorities in the central office of the Department of Corrections.

Because of the pervasive responsibilities of the Custody Division, it was

---

[14] The parole board serving inmates under the jurisdiction of the Department of Corrections (the Adult Authority) set a definite parole date for each inmate at the same time that it set his sentence; for example, an inmate sentenced to one to fifteen years might, near the end of the second year, receive a definite sentence of two and a half years in the institution and two and a half years on parole. After taking this action, the board would not ordinarly see the inmate again in the institution. The parole board serving inmates under the jurisdiction of the Department of the Youth Authority (the Youth Authority Board) did not ordinarily specify a definite period of parole, but set a date for release. About sixty days later, this board would again see the inmate in the institution to review such parole plans as had been made in the interim.

decided that the Project would be located within it. The Project's supervisor would occupy a rank at the level of a custody captain and report directly to the Associate Superintendent, Custody. Both the Project director and supervisor would be members of the Division's weekly conference, composed of the Associate Superintendent, Custody, the captain, and the 12 lieutenants, although they were not similarly included in the activities of other divisions to which they were also functionally related. It was expected that locating the Project in the Custody Division would greatly facilitate the Project's acceptance throughout the institution. It would establish C-Unit's image in DVI as not "just another tacked-on treatment program"; and enable the Project to rely on custody's recognized authority in DVI for sponsorship and for support in making the procedural changes needed in the initial stages of the program.

The relationships between the Project and the central office of the Department of Corrections were less clearly outlined during the planning period. For most purposes Project administrators were expected to rely on DVI's Superintendent for authority to proceed with its activities; and to seek appropriate functional assistance from the central office as needed for specific tasks. In addition, the Research Division of the Department of Corrections was to supervise the Project's research activities as well as those aspects of the program closely related to the research perspective; and the director was to be responsible to the Central Office for the administration of National Institute of Mental Health grants to the Project. When part of the action program, such as that involving parole participation in C-Unit, required action at the state level, the Project administrators were expected to deal directly with the appropriate authorities in the Department of Corrections and the Department of the Youth Authority.

In the story to follow it will become evident that this general plan for locating the C-Unit Project in its organizational environment was less well thought out than were the provisions for relating staff and inmates within C-Unit itself. At that early period no one fully appreciated the communication problems that can arise when a small multifunctional unit is established within a highly departmentalized larger organization.

PROJECT ORGANIZATION

Although the National Institute of Mental Health grant was not received until May, 1961, the action program began during September, 1960.[15] In

---

[15] One housing unit in the institution had been emptied by the removal of its inmates to the newly opened reception center. In addition, both the director and PICO personnel would need to find other employment unless the Project was launched.

consequence, the Project operated for seven months without the security of a definite future; and the research program was not fully staffed until August of 1961, after nearly a year of operation. Nevertheless, the Project was committed to studying change in a prison under realistic conditions. It soon found that meeting exigencies that did not fit into a preplanned schedule was one of the requirements of that task.

From the beginning the Project's task was considered the responsibility of the staff as a group. The staff work group was to define the task in operational terms, develop the plan for accomplishing the task, and allocate subtasks to its members. Individual staff members would perform specialized functions but each would carry additional responsibilities as a member of the staff work group and would be held accountable by that group for his contribution to the total enterprise.

In attempting to create a unified staff work group, various differentiations among subgroups in the staff had to be taken into account. It was expected that the way these subgroups were related to each other and to the staff as a whole would strongly influence the kind of community that might develop in C-Unit.

One kind of differentiation within the staff occurred because some were civil service employees and others were paid by funds from outside sources. The civil service paid personnel in the Project staff constituted a core group of persons who could perform all major functions of the C-Unit community after the demonstration period had been completed: a supervisor, three counselors, three custody officers, two secretaries, and a research associate.[16] The Foundation paid group was smaller, including only the Project director, two research associates, and various secretarial and technical personnel as they were needed for research activities.

In order to minimize the possibility that these two segments of staff would develop separate interests and identities, all Foundation-paid personnel accepted from the beginning the basic obligations expected of their civil service colleagues. Unless they had duties elsewhere, for example, at the University 60 miles distant from DVI or at the state central office 75 miles in another direction, they were on duty at DVI during regular working hours five days a week. Foundation-paid personnel in the Project carried DVI identification cards, ate in the staff dining room, slept on occasion in the staff quarters provided at the institution, obeyed the same rules in dealing with inmates that were mandatory for civil service employees, and expected to perform any duties that might have been asked of them

---

[16] A lieutenant was added to the Project staff at a later date.

if they had been employed in similar capacities by DVI.[17] Homogeneity of staff performance was also encouraged because the research associates acted as a unified subgroup in the Project, including as one of the three the PICO research analyst who was a civil service employee; and Foundation-employed secretaries assumed general duties in the clerical pool which handled the work of both the action and the research programs. Accordingly, there was little observable difference among staff members in day-to-day activities that could be attributed to the way they were paid. Nevertheless, the basic fact remained that the civil service employees in the Project were pursuing careers within the Department of Corrections and were subject to sanctions of a different order from those applicable to Foundation-paid personnel. It was understandable that for DVI's administration a distinction remained between those Project staff members who were "ours" and who would be continuing in the institution after the demonstration period, and other staff members who were "with us" for a temporary period.

The functional subgroups in the Project staff were much more pertinent for understanding the kind of community that developed in C-Unit.

ADMINISTRATION

The Project's first administrative team consisted of the civil service-paid supervisor and the Foundation-paid director, both professional social workers with experience in institutional administration.[18] Because of his place in the bureaucratic line, the supervisor was made officially responsible for all the usual activities necessary to manage the C-Unit inmates and their cases. He was the supervisor of the custody officers, the counselors, and the secretaries, reporting directly to the Associate Superintendent, Custody, on the activities of his combined staff. He presided at all Unit staff meetings and those meetings between staff and inmates that dealt with basic policy issues. For all concerned with the Project—DVI administration and line personnel, the Project staff including the Foundation-paid personnel, and inmates—he was the responsible executive of the Project.

The director's role was less easy to define, although the term "leader" might best describe the implied content of the job. In general, the direc-

---

[17] The Foundation-paid personnel put in a great deal of overtime as well. For long periods the director and two research associates stayed overnight once or twice a week to conduct meetings with inmates and to observe evening activities.

[18] In the second year the lieutenant was appointed to act as assistant supervisor, adding a third member to the group of administrative personnel within the Project.

tor's role was originally conceived of as a combination of "idea man," staff trainer, question asker, experimenter, and link between research and action. For example, during the first several months of the Project when most of the action staff were unfamiliar with the ideas embodied in the Project's proposals, and were frequently confused about what to do in interaction with inmates, the director sought by asking questions and noting the significance of events to direct their attention to the factors that needed to be considered for effective action. In addition, the director offered suggestions, but refrained from imposing them as orders, since the leadership task was to get the action staff to the point at which it could see what needed to be done and design the appropriate action. She was also expected on occasion to substitute for the supervisor in presiding at meetings and to participate with him in policy discussions with DVI's administration. In line with her interest in discovering the elements of problem-solving action in this kind of organizational setting, the director also acted as a counselor for a small caseload of inmates and assumed responsibility for certain inmate task groups. In addition, she had primary responsibility for administering the research program and its supporting grants.

The exigencies of the Project's first year greatly widened the scope of the director's responsibilities, and by the end of the first twelve months she had performed in almost every staff role in the Project. Two months after the start of the C-Unit program the Project supervisor became seriously ill, and within five months he was replaced by a custody lieutenant. By special authorization from DVI's Superintendent, the director was made officially responsible, first, for the total project in the absences of the original supervisor, later, for the Project's treatment functions in cooperation with the second supervisor, as well as for most communication with the state central office. It was not until the third supervisor was appointed, a full year after the beginning of the Project, that the director returned to a role more nearly like that originally conceived.

The most consistent role for the director was that of administrative supervisor of the research program. The same conceptual framework governed both the action program and the research program; and the chief task of research was to describe and analyze the process of planned change as it emerged in the action program. To maintain conceptual congruence between the two programs, the director was expected to assume responsibilities in both the service and the research programs. For the first four months of the Project a part-time co-director in charge of research had assumed primary responsibility for the research design. However, he unexpectedly left for a year's study abroad early in 1961. Consultants from the University of California at Berkeley were then secured to supervise various segments of the research program and their work was coordinated by the director.

COUNSELORS

Three correctional counselors, all professional social workers, began work with the Project on its first day. Within fourteen months all three had been replaced by counselors who had experience but no specific professional education. Because the first three counselors had formed the nucleus of the original PICO-I staff and had a more flexible schedule than the custody officers, they assumed primary responsibility in the first few months for program-planning, and continued to lead in performing this function. In addition, each counselor was responsible for individual planning and treatment as needed by one-third of C-Unit's population. In order to facilitate work between the counselor and the parole agents assigned to C-Unit from that area, each counselor's caseload roughly corresponded with the group of inmates who would be returning to one of the three major metropolitan areas used in the selection process. In addition, counselors led most of the cross-caseload inmate groups that proliferated as the program developed.

CUSTODY OFFICERS

Three correctional officers were responsible for supervision of the Unit during most of the waking hours of each week: a morning officer, who awakened the inmates and remained on duty with a break for lunch until 3:30 or four in the afternoon; an evening shift officer, who came on duty about three in the afternoon and remained until after inmates were locked in their rooms for the night at 10:00 P.M.; and a relief officer, who substituted for the other two on their days off. These officers were not used elsewhere in the institution except in emergencies. Because of the overlap in shifts, the officers were able to keep each other informed about daily developments in the Unit and to confer about custodial practices. The overlap also made it possible to schedule daytime staff meetings when at least two of the three officers could attend. Although responsibility for supervision on the floor of the Unit kept the officers continuously occupied while on duty, it was possible to arrange schedules so that each could assume on occasion responsibilities for inmate counseling or group leadership.

SECRETARIES

The Project clerical pool varied in number between two and four, depending in part on the volume of research materials to be processed. The bulk of clerical work was initially devoted to maintaining the departmentally required inmate case records. As the program developed, weekly schedules, notices of meetings, memoranda, and working papers were added to the clerical load. When an inmate newspaper was established, C-Unit inmates helped with preparing "dittoes" and running the duplicating machine. By the middle of the first year secretaries were participating in staff meetings whenever the agenda related to their concerns, leading inmate Interest Groups, and attending Unit functions such as the Christmas Party. Although inmate-secretary interaction was somewhat limited because most secretaries were women and the clerical pool was located inside an area where women were closely supervised, the Project found ways to involve several secretaries as active participants in the C-Unit community activities.

PAROLE AGENTS

After August, 1961, one Youth Authority and one Department of Corrections parole agent from each of the appropriate district offices in the state were assigned to the C-Unit Project. Those who traveled from the south were present in the institution two days every two months; those located in the north came for one day each month. Because of the size of the geographical areas from which C-Unit inmates were selected, not every inmate was able to talk with the agent who would supervise him on parole. However, some parole services were provided for all C-Unit inmates during the second year of operation. In the Unit each parole agent learned to know all the inmates who would be released to his area, beginning soon after each individual was admitted to C-Unit. He conferred with the inmate and his counselor about the institutional program as it related to the individual's goals for the future. Between visits he communicated with family and possible employers and gathered the information needed to relate outside concerns with institutional plans in those cases for which he was responsible. When he was present in C-Unit, he conducted pre-parole discussions, attended Project staff meetings, talked with work instructors and academic teachers, and participated in community activities such as the monthly C-Unit dinners.

RESEARCHERS

The research group consisted of the Project director and the three research associates who had backgrounds in psychology, sociology, and law. During the first program year there were only two associates, the third coming to the Project in August, 1961. They were assisted by two research assistants employed part-time at different periods during the Project, and by a group of inmate clerks from C-Unit, varying in number from one to four, depending on the volume of work and the availability of inmates with suitable backgrounds. The action staff, particularly the counselors, also helped the research effort by writing reports of their experiences with inmates as individuals and in groups.

Although the researchers did not assume responsibility for inmate management or service functions, they were so continuously present in C-Unit activities that they were seen by staff and inmates primarily as informed members of the community who acted as question askers and helpful listeners. However, because they did not implement the community program, they will be much less visible in the story to follow than are the members of the other staff role groups. Therefore we shall pause briefly here to describe their activities in more detail than has been necessary in introducing the functions of the other groups of project personnel.

The researchers had two primary functions in the Project. First, because the same conceptual framework governed both the action program and the research study, the researchers were expected to participate in action-planning by contributing to conceptual clarification and by feeding information from data analysis into the considerations of the action staff. A second major research function was to study the action program and to record its experiences in a form that made action available for analysis.

The research design provided for a number of closely related small studies, each seeking to tap one aspect of C-Unit community life. These studies utilized a variety of methods depending in part, on the nature of the phenomenon to be studied, for example, an action process as it occurred over time, the state of a subsystem within the Project at a given point in its history, or the characteristics of a relevant population. Thus the research activities ranged from systematic surveys to all kinds of observational procedures, and from the search of documents to informal interviews exploring critical events. In the course of the two years, all the research staff participated in some way in each kind of research activity, although each associate was expected to use the help of others as appropriate in his assigned study area.

We shall not attempt here to list all the studies that contributed to the mass of data ultimately accumulated about C-Unit inmates, the development of the C-Unit community, and the institution within which it operated. Some studies were quite small and will be mentioned either in the text or in footnotes when data derived from such sources are used. However, the major studies, the findings from which are interwoven throughout the story to follow, will be briefly outlined here.

During the three months prior to the launching of the C-Unit program, a baseline study of DVI's staff and inmates was conducted. A single questionnaire was used with a staff sample, stratified for functional positions, and with a sample of all inmates housed at that time in DVI. The questions focused on the respondent's value orientations and perception of the roles of self and others in the institutional complex. This same questionnaire was used during the first nine months with new selectees for C-Unit and was readministered as C-Unit inmates left for parole. The findings of this study are extensively reported in an unpublished doctoral dissertation by Alvin Rudoff, "Prison Inmates—An Involuntary Association" (University of California, Berkeley, 1964).

Throughout the entire two years, research associates attended and recorded all staff meetings and all "community meetings" involving staff and inmates. Other group meetings, such as those of committees or of Interest Groups, were selectively observed and recorded, sometimes by the research associate who was following a particular action process or critical event, sometimes by the staff member responsible for the group.

Throughout the first eighteen months demographic data were collected on all C-Unit selectees and on a comparison sample of inmates drawn from the same eligible pool. Similar data were assembled for those inmates living in two other housing units who were interviewed in the inmate system study. An analysis of these background variables describing the C-Unit population as it existed at one point in time and comparing it with inmates in other housing units will be found in Appendix D.

During the latter part of the first year, three general areas of inquiry were identified as critical for understanding the action trends revealed in the observational data: the role of the staff organization in the C-Unit community; the effect of the honor system's control patterns on relationships among inmates and staff in C-Unit; and the nature of the inmate system in C-Unit. Accordingly, three surveys were conducted during the second year. One used focused interviews with members of both the first and the second staffs to identify staff members' perceptions of the organizational relationships among themselves and of the changes in these relationships that appeared under the different conditions provided at different times in the Project's history. Another study collected information about the honor system controversy between the Project and DVI's administration, using interviews with both staff members and inmates to discover how various events connected with this issue had been perceived by the respondents.[19] A third survey used a pretested schedule in interviews with 120 inmates then resident in C-Unit and with a sample of inmates in

---

[19] Jorgen Jepson was the research associate responsible for surveying the honor system and staff experiences. Many of the summarized critical events to be found in subsequent pages are based on his work.

each of two other housing units to discover the nature of the C-Unit Inmate System and to compare it with inmate systems existing elsewhere in the institution. The findings from this third survey are used extensively in Chapter VIII and have been more elaborately analyzed by Thomas P. Wilson in his doctoral dissertation, "Some Effects of Different Patterns of Management on Inmate Behavior in a Correctional Institution" (Columbia University, 1965).

Beginning in August, 1961, and continuing throughout the rest of the Project, the director maintained a daily log to which all three of the research associates contributed. Since the director was in contact with action processes at all levels of project activities, the log provided important clues to understanding how various subsystems affected each other within the community complex and enabled the researchers to identify the major action themes as they appeared over time in the histories of the various groups and individuals in C-Unit.

Finally, during the first year of the Project it became increasingly evident that DVI, as the institutional environment of the C-Unit community, was a primary factor in determining what happened within C-Unit; and that DVI could not be understood in full from within the Project itself. Accordingly, a sociologist from the Center for the Study of Law and Society at the University of California was secured to study DVI as an entity in its own right. He began his work in early 1962 near the conclusion of the action program and was aided in data collection by a graduate student in political science, also employed by the Center. Neither participated in the C-Unit action program. The findings of this study are reported more fully in an unpublished report by Sheldon L. Messinger, "The Setting of C-Unit" (Center for the Study of Law and Society, University of California, Berkeley, 1963). These findings provided background for the analysis presented in this volume and some portions of the study report are integrated at appropriate points in the text.

OTHERS

As the C-Unit program developed, this pool of staff members was augmented by other persons who carried semi-official responsibilities of many kinds. Volunteers and students from nearby colleges contributed much to the group program and were involved with staff in many ways. From the inmate population in the Unit a set of leaders were recruited to fill inmate clerk positions and their duties included program leadership tasks. Gradually, as the Project became known throughout the institution, staff members from other departments participated in one way or another in Project activities. And more than one Department of Corrections official was active in program with inmates as well as with staff.

THE HUMAN RESOURCES

THE INMATES

The first 125 young men brought into C-Unit were admitted in groups of approximately ten a week between September, 1960, and January, 1961. Ultimately, 291 men participated in C-Unit during the 22-month demonstration project. For 266 of these, comprehensive background data are available.[20]

Although there are many ways to describe the C-Unit population, our major interest at this point is in those characteristics that affected the program and services. As we shall see later, whether an inmate was under the jurisdiction of the Department of Corrections or the Department of the Youth Authority made a great deal of difference both to the inmates and to the program. Because this is not an ordinary "demographic characteristic," it is germane to begin with a brief discussion of this distinction.

As noted earlier, California has two correctional systems. Inmates under the jurisdiction of the Department of Corrections were usually called "A#s" (A-numbers) and sometimes "adult commitments" at DVI; those under the jurisdiction of the Department of the Youth Authority were usually called "YAs" (Y-As).[21]

The distinction between A#s and YAs was, first of all, a legal one. Persons eighteen years of age or over accused of public offenses in California are ordinarily tried by the criminal court. A#s had been tried by the criminal court, convicted of crime, and committed to the Department of Corrections. By law, A#s are typically required to serve minimum terms in correctional institutions before they can be paroled by the state parole board for adult males, the Adult Authority. Legal limits on maximum sentences for A#s often run to many years or are indefinite, and these limits vary by offense and the proven past record of the offender.[22] About half of the inmates at DVI were A#s during 1960–1962.

---

[20] See Appendix A for a description of selection procedures; and Appendix D for an analysis of background variables.

[21] The terms derive from the correctional system practice of assigning identification numbers to inmates beginning with "A" and "YA."

[22] The Adult Authority, besides paroling inmates, was empowered to set and reset sentences for A#s within statutory limits. Some minimum and maximum limits:

Inmates under the jurisdiction of the Department of the Youth Authority, YAs, fell into two broad subgroupings. First, and most numerous at DVI (about 40 per cent of DVI's inmate population during 1960–1962), were "youth offenders." Youth offenders were ordinarily persons eighteen years old or over who had been accused of a public offense, tried by the criminal court, convicted of crime, and committed to the Youth Authority instead of to the Department of Corrections, an option open to the court for most offenders under twenty-one years of age at the time of apprehension.[23] Such a commitment carried significant limitations on the penalties that could be administered. No minimum terms were required of youth offenders; they could be discharged or paroled at the discretion of the Youth Authority Board, the sentence-setting and parole board for youths (and, as we shall note, for "juvenile offenders"). Further, state jurisdiction over youths ordinarily lapsed when the offender was twenty-three or twenty-five years old, depending on his crime, and maximum limits were not extended by a youth's proven past record of offenses.

"Juvenile offenders" made up a second grouping of YAs, comprising about 10 per cent of DVI's inmate population during 1960–1962. Persons under eighteen years of age in California accused of a public offense are ordinarily heard by a juvenile court. Juveniles had been made wards of the court and committed to the Youth Authority. Like youths, they could be discharged or paroled at the discretion of the Youth Authority Board. State jurisdiction over this group of YAs ordinarily lapsed when they were twenty-one years of age.[24]

Perhaps the major difference between A#s and YAs at DVI (others are described below) was to be found in the different amounts of time they typically served at DVI for similar offenses. (See Table 1.)[25] On the average, YAs served about one year at DVI; A#s, on the other hand, closer to two years. In part, this simply reflected the letter of the laws governing

---

Manslaughter, 6 mo.–10 years; Robbery 1st, 5 years–life; Robbery 2nd, 1 year–life; Burglary 1st, 5 years–life; Burglary 2nd, 1–15 years; Grand Theft, 6 mo.–10 years; Forgery or Fictitious Checks, 6 mo.–14 years; Rape, 50 years. (Cal. Pen. Codes 193, 213, 461, 489, 470, 476, 264.)

[23] Offenders convicted of crimes with mandatory sentences of life imprisonment or death could not be committed to the Youth Authority. Data supplied by the Research Division of the Department of the Youth Authority indicate that during 1960–1962 between 70 and 80 per cent of those criminal offenders under twenty-one at the time of apprehension were committed to the Youth Authority rather than to Corrections.

[24] Juvenile commitments were not included in the eligible population for C-Unit.

[25] Because of the Project's requirements for eligibility, A#s coming to C-Unit had already spent some time in DVI, while YAs were admitted directly from the reception center. See Appendix A for elaboration.

A#s and YAs: many adults could not be released as quickly as youths or juveniles because of the minimum terms of imprisonment imposed by statute for A#s. But DVI staff members and inmates alike believed that the temper of the two parole boards differed as well; it was said that the Youth Authority Board "thinks in months" but the Adult Authority "thinks in years." The term-setting practices of the two boards tended to confirm this belief.

TABLE 1. *Months Served in Institution by Inmates First Paroled From DVI for Selected Offenses During 1960*[a]

Youth Authority Parolees			Adult Authority Parolees		
Median	Range	Middle 80%	Median	Range	Middle 80%
Robbery (N = 63)			Robbery (N = 39)		
14	3–28	10–17	30	15–72	18–49
Burglary (N = 98)			Burglary (N = 38)		
11	1–20	6–16	18	11–60	12–37
Theft except auto (N = 26)			Theft except auto (N = 11)		
10.5	4–25	7–14	18	7–48	15–34
Auto theft (N = 36)			Auto theft (N = 12)		
10	1–19	4–16	13.5	10–24	11–20
Forgery and fictitious checks (N = 24)			Forgery and fictitious checks (N = 30)		
10	4–15	8–13	18	12–30	13–26
Narcotics (N = 37)			Narcotics (N = 17)		
10	2–22	3–15	18	12–45	15–30

[a] Data supplied by Department of the Youth Authority, Research Division, and Department of Corrections, Research Division. These categories represent 78.7 per cent of all YAs and 86 per cent of all A#s first paroled from DVI during 1960.

For reasons explained in Appendix A, the C-Unit inmate population excluded certain groups of A#s and YAs. A#s who were members of DVI's Adult Work Crew, assigned to key maintenance jobs, were largely excluded. There were about 200 such A#s at DVI at any given time during 1960–1962. Further, YAs committed by the juvenile court were excluded by Youth Authority request. And for a time, youth offender YAs who had been transferred to DVI from other institutions were excluded. This provision was changed during the fourteenth month of the action program, when its effect on selection was discovered. With these major exceptions,

A#s appearing to have six to eighteen months remaining before release and all YAs newly committed to DVI, so long as they came from the selected geographical areas, were eligible for inclusion in C-Unit; by and large, the C-Unit inmate population was representative of the majority of DVI's inmates.[26]

Although at any one time there might have been a disproportion between the A#s and YAs actually housed in C-Unit, the record shows that an equal number of each group was included in the study population. Since age was one factor determining whether an offender would be handled by the Youth Authority or be committed to the Department of Corrections, we could expect to find two modal age groups in any unit that housed both types of commitments in equal numbers. In the C-Unit study population, the ages ranged from 17 to 40, with only 11 per cent under 19 and only 1 per cent over 30. About 57 per cent of the YAs were in the age bracket of 20 to 21; while 57 per cent of the A#s were 24 to 27 years of age. These age differences produced clusters of inmates within the population, differing in self-images, social orientations, and tastes. The meaning of institutionalization and of membership in C-Unit was different for inmates in each of these age groups, and each group made different demands on program.

In characteristics that indicate personal equipment for learning and doing, the C-Unit population was especially diverse. Twenty-eight per cent of the 266 men for whom comprehensive background data were available had tested above normal in intelligence when studied in the reception center before commitment to DVI, while 24 per cent registered as below normal. In educational background, 19 per cent were recorded as having achieved the fifth grade or less; 45 per cent had reached an educational level between the sixth and eighth grades; 27 per cent were in the high school grade range; and 2 per cent had twelfth-grade education or more. These young men had also been reared in families with diverse backgrounds. Nine per cent came from families with white-collar or professional histories; while the fathers of 30 per cent were skilled workmen, and 33 per cent had fathers who were semi-skilled or without any employment skill.[27] C-Unit would, as would any community, depend for many of its activities on the verbal skills and organizational know-how of a leadership group. At the same time, a program that could challenge the group

---

[26] Appendix D compares the characteristics of C-Unit inmates with inmates housed in a nonhonor unit and an honor unit.

[27] Information on the father's occupation was not available for 27 per cent of the inmates.

with better than normal personal competencies would not reach or serve the inmates at the lower range of adequacy. Thus the very composition of the population demanded that the program be directed to building a community with a wide range of resources for meeting diverse needs and with mechanisms for the flexible use of many levels of ability.

The C-Unit population was also an interethnic group, and each different ethnic group brought its own culture into the C-Unit community. Eighteen per cent of the C-Unit men were of Mexican descent, and 21 per cent were Negroes. The rest (except for an occasional Japanese or American Indian) were part of the vague American composite designated "white." As might be expected, the minority groups were more homogeneous than the white group. The Mexicans and the Negroes tended to form their own friendship groups, each with significantly different social characteristics. Although these differentiating tendencies were brought into the C-Unit community by inmates who had learned them in the outside community, in the institution the differences tended to appear in exaggerated form as each minority inmate sought out "his people" in an unfriendly world created and governed largely by "whites."

C-Unit men also had been exposed to a wide range of criminal activities and correctional processes. Of the 266, 2 per cent were committed for sex offenses; 18 per cent for offenses connected with narcotics; 40 per cent for property offenses; and 35 per cent for some sort of violence against persons. Only 21 per cent had experienced fewer than three arrests prior to this commitment; and 49 per cent came from families with histories of arrests. Forty-seven per cent of the 266 had at some earlier time been committed to jail; 8 per cent had served time in prison for a previous offense; and 42 per cent had previously been committed to one or more institutions for delinquent youths. Although there was an occasional first offender among the group, most of the young men in C-Unit had had considerable experience as delinquents and were sophisticated about "doing time." Also, there were social differences among the subgroups determined by criminal history and these affected programming. Inmates with drug histories tended to find each other companionable; while the "hypes" were often disliked and distrusted by the proper criminals who had attacked property or persons. Even program details such as the kind of music to be played on the record player reflected the diverse tastes of different kinds of persons.

Among the 266 C-Unit men in the study group, a few had identifiable psychiatric disorders. Nine per cent had shown sufficient personality disturbance to have been diagnosed at some time as psychologically ill, including an occasional overt schizophrenic. A still larger proportion suffered from medically recognized behavior disorders, including 9 per cent with a known history of homosexuality; 31 per cent with an alcoholic problem; 18 per cent with a history of opiate use; and 31 per cent reporting use of pills or marijuana, or both.

Thus the C-Unit population was a conglomerate group of individuals who had participated in various forms of deviance and had been exposed to a variety of processes for correcting deviance. Although they were all identified offenders and inmates, they tended to reject each other for disparate kinds of deviance even more intensely than does the society that had rejected them all. The C-Unit community, compared with communities outside the institution, at first evidenced more than its share of prejudice against subgroup members such as "hypes," "dings," "smokes," and "punks." At the same time, this very diversity, described here largely in terms of problems for building the program, could also be perceived as providing a wide range of potential capacities. It sharply defined the task for the problem-solving community. Inmates would need to accept and understand both themselves and very different others if they were to become part of a C-Unit community or to qualify for membership in the free community to which they would be released.

THE STAFF

In the pool of official persons associated with C-Unit during the two-year developmental period, we can find almost as much diversity as that evidenced by the inmate population. Although most staff members were men, women were represented by the Project director and by several of the secretaries, as well as by volunteers and guests at the various Unit get-togethers. Educational backgrounds ranged from high school education to a doctoral degree. Three counselors were social workers with a master's degree, while others had majored in college in criminology and political science. Several members of the staff had extensive military backgrounds, including a custody officer who was a retired marine sergeant; a counselor who had been a member of the Air Force Police; and a secretary who had eight years' experience as a supervising secretary in the Navy. One researcher, two counselors, and the director had experience in parole work before entering the institution. One secretary had been a newspaper reporter. One research associate was a visitor from Denmark. Two of the staff were Negroes and one was Japanese. Volunteers included a chaplain intern at DVI, a high school art teacher, a jazz critic, and a housewife who was also an artist. Every participant brought with him a fund of human experience and some contributing skill. Program changed shape throughout the two years, depending on the needs presented and the human resources available.

PHYSICAL RESOURCES: THE PLANT

One approaches C-Unit through a long corridor, after having been admitted to the security area through four electrically controlled locked doors. From windows that permit observation from the corridor, one sees first the Unit TV room with its fixed benches and then the long gray nave of the Unit, around which the 133 rooms are ranged in three tiers. The visitor rings the bell at C-Unit's door and awaits the busy custody officer's key; then steps into the cement-floored, echoing hallway with its distant end windows overlooking "the free world" from which one has just come.

One notes, first, that the wall consists largely of doors. One-third of the inmate rooms open directly onto the main floor of the Unit; the others are ranged along two upper, horseshoe-shaped galleries that jut out from the interior wall. On further exploration, one finds that each room has a window to the outside, its own toilet and washing facilities, and a single bunk. An open shower room is located on the main floor and two others on the upper tiers. Bulletin boards on each side of the Unit are placed so that inmates can read notices before taking the stairways to upper tiers. On the main floor, a small office with its adjacent linen room is the center of much activity as inmates check with the supervising officer about details. Later one learns that scattered around the Unit are four additional "offices"—actually converted inmate rooms—used for counseling. In the center of the open floor are square tables, with an odd assortment of chairs, used for dominoes, checkers, and card games during free hours. The inmates wear denim trousers and blue shirts or white T-shirts; the officer wears a tan uniform.

During the first weeks, all program activities were housed in C-Unit. For small group meetings, chairs were arranged in a circle at one end of the Unit or in front of the benches in the TV room, and individual conferences were conducted in the offices. As the program expanded, space was provided for Project activities in the Annex,[28] another wing some distance down the corridor with one floor partitioned into offices and meeting rooms, each open to observation through windows along the corridor wall. The research and secretarial offices were located in the Annex where staff meetings were held, and much administrative work conducted. Gradually the C-Unit program filled both the Unit and the Annex, and both staff and inmate activities occurred in either location as suitable for the job to be

---

[28] "Annex" was the name used at DVI for the second floor of the wing housing the library. (See Chart 1.)

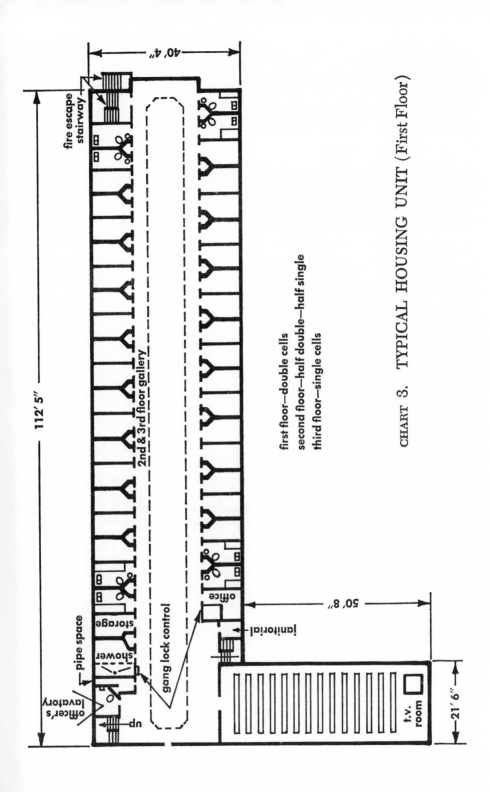

2nd & 3rd floor gallery

storage

pipe space

shower

officer's lavatory

gang lock control

up

office

janitorial

50' 8"

t.v. room

21' 6"

first floor—double cells
second floor—half double—half single
third floor—single cells

CHART 3.   TYPICAL HOUSING UNIT (First Floor)

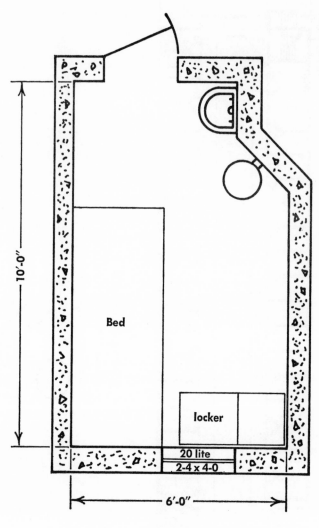

CHART 4.   TYPICAL CELL

done.[29] Later C-Unit activities were occasionally scheduled for one of the
mess halls or for the Field House.

---

[29] Since the Project director was a woman, certain adjustments in procedures were
made to allow for her appearance in either location; for example, the open shower
room on the lower floor of the Unit was not used when she was on duty.

THE FIRST DAY

The Project program began on September 19, 1960, with its first 20 inmates: 10 adult commitments, who had already spent considerable time in the institution; and 10 youth commitments fresh from the reception center. The time for initiating the program had been chosen because a transfer of inmates to the new reception center had freed one housing unit for Project intake, not because the staff were prepared for their new tasks.

There had been little staff planning for the program about to be launched. The core staff of supervisor and three counselors, inherited from the PICO project, had helped to prepare the proposal to the National Institute of Mental Health some months before, but the details of program were still largely a matter of speculation. PICO had operated in the institution for five years as an intensive counseling venture, providing individual and group therapy for inmates drawn randomly from the total institutional population. PICO counselors, each of whom had been in the institution from two to five years, had by design carried no responsibilities for the procedural work concerning the inmates on their caseloads and knew little of the daily routines of institutional life as lived by inmates and officers. Two weeks before the Project program was to begin, they had been freed of PICO duties and had set about planning their new activities. Since the officers for the Unit were selected only a day or two before the opening of program, they had not been part of planning. Two researchers had been in the institution for three months but they had been busy with a baseline study of the institution's staff and inmate population. This staff, whose members were so diverse and in some cases not acquainted with each other, was now to meet the first inmates.

The first 20 men had been transferred into the Unit on the evening before the first day of the program, during the time in the institution's schedule when all room transfers are implemented. During that first evening, the 20 inmates had rattled around in the large emptiness, observing the broken windows, the lack of tables and chairs, and the rundown condition of the Unit;[30] while the officer, accustomed to handling 165 men to a unit, wondered what he was going to do with his time. The inmates had all received a short explanatory note along with their notification of transfer to C-Unit. It had informed them of an orientation meeting scheduled for eight o'clock the next morning. Until the meeting, however, there were only rumors to answer the angry questions of the A#s who had been so

---

[30] C-Unit had been handled as a nonhonor unit for its previous population.

unceremoniously jerked out of their accustomed pathways, or to guide the bewildered YAs who were newly admitted to the institution.

When the counselors and researchers assembled on the Unit the following morning, there were no inmates. The ducats[31] for the meeting had not been distributed the previous evening, and the morning officer had had no choice but to release his charges to their regular work and educational assignments. The Project staff were, first, startled, then, anxious and tense. The supervisor's questions put the officer on the defensive. There was talk about the inefficiency of the central control office. One counselor strode back and forth between the supervisor and the telephone, trying to discover how the 20 inmates might be recalled. Chairs had not been secured for the Unit, so other counselors were sent to scrounge for seats for the meeting to be held once the inmates were rounded up. The locksmith and his crew were working on doors that had not yet been keyed, and voices rose as individuals attempted to be heard above the screech of tools on metal.

Inmates gradually drifted into the Unit, returning from their regular program assignments. They stood aloof, suspicious and sullen, far from the small staff huddles of two or three persons. The director walked across the empty floor to a tall Negro inmate who was standing alone, hunched in his navy blue work jacket, and asked him to join her in the circle of chairs now assembled at the end of the Unit. Together they walked the length of the Unit, watched but not joined by the others.[32] An hour later the meeting was convened and an inmate-staff community was in the process of birth.

---

[31] *Ducat:* written pass to meeting or interview.

[32] For two years this inmate, known as Big Mac, was an important leader in the program. His contribution to staff understanding will become evident in the story to follow.

III - PROGRAM FOR PROBLEM-SOLVING

THE PROJECT'S FIRST TASK was to get prison inmates to experience legitimate problem-solving as rewarding in and of itself. This could not be accomplished by telling them about the satisfactions they were missing, by instructing them in the process, or by providing material rewards for behaving in the desired fashion.[1] Only a problem felt strongly enough to motivate action; a process for successful problem resolution; and the actually experienced rewards of pride in self, safety with others, accomplishment and fellowship, would be sufficient to establish effective community values to govern action in prison.

STARTING THE PROBLEM-SOLVING PROCESS

The Project's beginning program consisted of arrangements for getting problem-solving started. These arrangements were expected to change over time with the nature of the problems to be tackled and the resources available for solving them. The initial program was accordingly tentative,

---

[1] In this connection it is useful to note that the C-Unit Project lacked special funds or equipment. The Robinson Crusoe environment of the institution, with its limited resources and cumbersome means for securing resources, constituted the arena in which problems arose and the setting within which resolution must be sought. The limit on external resources forced staff and inmates to identify and use previously unvalued resources—themselves and what they did have—thus hopefully linking rewards more closely with what persons did for themselves than with what others could give.

little more than a schedule for meetings between staff and inmates designed to start communication about felt problems.

Departmental administration found this conception of the program as scaffolding *ad hoc* and difficult to supervise. They asked for a "blueprint" of action—"what exactly are you going to do?"—and expected a manual to standardize the program within the first six months. With some hesitation they permitted the program to start with little on the drawing boards except orientation meetings, a weekly Staff-Inmate Group meeting to consider the "health of the Unit," and the promise that further groups would be established as problems were identified.

Before the opening of the action program, staff had been uneasy lest the inmates remain passive when given the opportunity to discuss problems. They were not prepared for the fact that the assignment to C-Unit would itself be a major problem for most inmates, one about which they would express themselves vociferously. "My only problem is how I can get out." "I didn't have any problems until you jerked me in here." "All you've done is to create problems I didn't have before." Attacking, suspicious, and manipulative, the newly admitted inmates demanded to be returned to the prison routine they knew. By establishing C-Unit a felt problem had been created.

CREATIVE DISORGANIZATION

The rage and anxiety expressed week after week in orientation and other meetings was clearly a reaction to widespread disruption of accustomed adaptations. As staff probed, "Just why is assignment to C-Unit so disturbing?" the answers revealed many levels of concern. A#s had lost access to the magazine routes established in former living units. One man had just moved into and cleaned up a room for which he had been angling for many months; now he had to settle into another room in a less favorable unit location. A YA had looked forward to the double rooming of the nonhonor unit where he could be with his buddy. A#s who had already learned how to "do time" in DVI were forced into close association with newly admitted YAs who had not yet proved themselves in the institution and who were accordingly considered to be unidentified sources of "trouble." The settled relations through which information could be secured, goods shared, debts collected, and game contests completed had been wiped out by the random selection for C-Unit and each man had to rebuild his social relations with new partners who were as uneasy as himself.[2]

---

[2] The A#s were more disturbed about these matters than the YAs because they had already spent time in the institution while the YAs were newly admitted from the

Fundamental to the inmates' sense of disorientation were the new expectations about relations between staff and inmates. The first orientation group stared at staff in disbelief when invited to discuss problems. At the end of the hour a quiet, intellectual inmate spoke for all: "It won't work. There's the inmate code." What about the inmate code? "You don't talk to the man." Repeatedly the theme that communication between staff and inmates is dangerous was elaborated. "They're using the fink system." "They're out to keep us here longer in order to *help* us." "They're using us as guinea pigs so they can find out something." "They don't know what they are doing. It's *my* time they're messing with." Much later a member of the first group of selectees who was then on parole remembered:

I was terribly frightened. Everything in me was focused on that Board hearing just ahead. I had it all set up to make it out this time, and I couldn't stand to have anything interfere. The Project was a completely new thing. None of us could tell what the staff could do to our time if they got to know us better. I thought I might have to stay longer just because staff thought I "needed" to, or because they caught me up on some little thing. I was just plain scared.

But the Project had provided that this was one problem that could not be solved by getting out. The Project could not make inmates participate usefully, but it could offer them means for determining the kind of environment in which they would live while they remained in the institution. Thus began the period of creative disorganization with problem-creating disruption of accustomed patterns, a refusal to permit problems to be solved by running away, and opportunities to make and to do in a relatively unstructured environment.

Since everyone was concerned with the problem created by C-Unit's expectations, and since additional men were brought in weekly to face it anew, there were many restatements about the primary difficulty. In essence, the Project expected inmates and staff to discuss mutual problems; while the inmate "code" proscribed discussion about real issues. Staff began to learn that according to the "code" there were only two categories of discussible problems; and for each the inmates' expectations restricted inmates and staff to stereotyped operation.

One kind of safe problem was "personal," such as an inmate's concern about his family, the anxiety caused by the diagnostic label he had acquired during the reception center study, or "why did I get into trouble?" The inmate was allowed to take this kind of problem confidentially to a

---

reception center. See rationales for selection of A#s and YAs in Appendix A. However, both suffered from the fact that in C-Unit they entered an informal system without stable patterns for inmate interaction.

counselor, expecting to receive sympathetic listening, advice, or some therapeutic magic. He did not expect to be asked about what he was doing in his own version of the institution's "underlife" nor to reveal anything about his relations with other inmates. Personnel other than counselors, who might observe the inmate during program activities, were not considered by inmates qualified to deal with "personal problems." Their job was to see that rules were obeyed, not to "mess with me."

The other kind of problem permitted in inmate and staff interchange concerned the handling of procedures. An inmate would be supported by his fellows in protesting against inequitable or harsh administration of institutional rules or in appealing for change toward leniency. In C-Unit's first meetings almost every discussion degenerated into what was later to be called the "gimmes." "If we are different why can't we have the lights on an hour later?" "Where are the butt cans and the shower benches?" "Why don't you stop all these room searches? Last week the A#s were all cleaned out of things we've had for months in the other units." In this kind of interchange the inmate role was to demand, test limits, and wrest minor concessions from the staff member. The staff role was to ignore or reprimand the obvious hostility, point to the rules, argue down rumored claims, deny the request, or give when accustomed inmate rights were invoked.

This limited definition of problems acceptable for discussion between staff and inmates was made explicit in many meetings. For instance, the inmates proposed at an early stage that they get together in meetings without staff present and prepare proposals to present to staff. The director suggested that this would be just a miniature Inmate Advisory Council[3] and might lead to nothing but manipulative bargaining. In response the following interchange occurred.

INMATE: "Doesn't it come down in the end to staff and inmates bargaining, no matter how you set it up?"
DIRECTOR: "This is your version of how staff-inmate relationships have to be?"
INMATE: "Is there another version? If so, I'd like to hear it."
DIRECTOR: "Is the only staff-inmate relationship a bargaining one?"
INMATE: "No. If I have a personal problem, I can go to my counselor."

And again in reply to a staff member's attempt to focus on "day-to-day problems of living in the institution":

---

[3] *Inmate Advisory Council:* an inmate body composed of elected representatives from each living unit. The Council formulated requests for privileges or rule changes; the Executive Committee presented these requests to DVI administration and attempted to secure the most favorable outcome from the inmate point of view.

FIRST INMATE: "What problems?"

SECOND INMATE: "Most guys I know can hold their own mud in the institution."

It was obvious that most staff members accepted both this definition of the problems appropriate for discussion with inmates and the definition of their proper roles as implicitly as did the inmates. In meetings they often responded only to that part of what was said that could be classified as either a personal problem or a procedural complaint. It was clear that the new C-Unit community would quickly establish old patterns for relating staff and inmates unless a wider range of problems appropriate for mutual consideration could be identified.

The first period of program, roughly the four months of weekly intake while the full Unit population was assembled, was chiefly concerned with getting inmate problems defined in open assembly where both inmates and staff could hear what was said. The activities of this period might be called "giving the inmates back their voices." As Big Mac said after two years in C-Unit: "When I was on the mainline before I was in C-Unit, it was as though I had no voice. Life was like a movie. I watched it but I didn't take part. Other people told me what to do but I was never asked what I thought. It was as though C-Unit gave me back my voice. I had something to say about my own life."

PROBLEM DEFINITION

During the first two months there was more noise about problems than definition and analysis.

From the first days three highly complex problems were so grossly evident that no one questioned the necessity of tackling them. Foremost in everyone's mind was the problem generated by the fact that two separate populations—A#s and YAs, respectively, honor and nonhonor in status— were living under different sets of rules in the same Unit.[4] This situation was as confusing to custody officers as to inmates, but no one could document the critical points where change might relieve tension. Related to this problem, but with its own special difficulties, was the mounting disorder in the TV room. By the end of the first month one custody officer was predicting a riot, although, again, it was not clear why the whole situation continued to be unmanageable. Complicating every other problem was the fact that staff efforts to communicate with inmates did not result in a steady flow of consistent information. In an attempt to analyze these

---

[4] See Chapter IV for a detailed discussion of this issue.

problems and to develop corrective measures three committees were added to the already scheduled weekly program of orientation and Staff-Inmate Group meetings: the Rules Committee, the TV Committee, and the Communications Committee.

It was immediately evident that neither the staff members who had already been working in DVI nor the inmates knew what to do in a problem-solving group.

The counselors were trained to use groups for therapy. In any stated problem they saw the underlying feelings of the individual speaker as the issue to be addressed. Accordingly, their participation in meetings tended to take the form of reflecting feelings, interpreting motivations, or, failing all else, repeating the now hackneyed formulations of the Project proposal: "We're here to solve problems together." The inmates rejected this kind of staff behavior with understandable frustration. They called staff "evasive"; responded to every staff comment with "You never give a straight answer. Just say yes or no"; and challenged, "Just tell me in one sentence what this is all about. I don't want to be taken on another trip."[5] Neither side was talking about the same kind of problem; and counselor attention seldom focused on what the inmate was loudly reporting to be a problem for him.[6]

Equally important, many staff members were unclear about the nature of problem-solving action. They tended to see inmates as unable to take action unless the individual changed his attitudes and behavior. Along with inmates, both the counselors and the custody officers defined action in administrative terms—getting the rules changed or securing resources; and in this area the Project staff was as dependent on upper-level administration as were the inmates. The same kind of confusion existed about "decisions." Almost everyone took it for granted that decisions were the prerogative of top administrative personnel and were recorded in memoranda. Few perceived that both staff and inmates made many decisions as they operated daily under these rules and policy statements, or that such lower-level decisions could be made explicit and modified.

Accordingly, problem analysis was frequently terminated prematurely by an inmate "vote" to request some procedural change, and the supervisor went off to confer with upper-level authorities only to find that what had been proposed could not be approved.

---

[5] *Trip:* a fanciful story believed by neither teller nor his audience; a way of using empty time.

[6] See Stanton, Alfred H., and Morris S. Schwartz, *The Mental Hospital*, Basic Books, New York, 1954, pp. 200–208, for a discussion of failures to hear patient reports of "real" problems on the part of the psychiatric staff.

Thus at the beginning few staff activities demonstrated to inmates how a problem could be defined, analyzed, and separated into its component parts in order to initiate appropriate action at various levels of responsibility.

There were other difficulties contributing to the delay in problem definition. The use of overlapping small groups in a period of rapid intake interfered with focus and the orderly flow of information.[7] In each small group there would be some inmate members who had already considered the questions raised by others. Because the most important problems of this early period were interconnected and affected everybody, each meeting tended to become a forum for the restatement of common irritations regardless of the purpose for which the meeting had been called. The most loudly verbal inmates dominated discussions, while more passive individuals lost the connection between the subject and their own experiences, picking up chiefly the anxiety and anger. In a system without known roles whose incumbents could not yet be held responsible for what they said, the "grapevine" carried rumors to greet each new set of men as they entered the Unit and to fill endless hours of gossip. "The director said she wanted us all to fink." "C-Unit men do longer time." "They have A#s here simply to control the YAs, exploiting us in order to keep the gunseling[8] down." "They're using C-Unit for training new custody officers because we're smaller. The officer said we'd have room searches every day." "The corridor officers are down on C-Unit. They give write-ups[9] just because you are a C-Unit inmate." "They're trying to make us talk about race. There *will* be trouble." The inmates repeatedly demanded a meeting of everybody to "get things settled" but in the echoing Unit hallway it was difficult to hear in groups larger than 12 or 15. In the current confusion it seemed that any statements made in a meeting of the whole had little chance of being commonly understood.

The inmates contributed to the delay in problem definition by their impatience with analysis and their grandiose plans for immediate action. The Communications Committee attracted the ablest men in the Unit and in a great burst of enthusiasm they set out to establish order on their own. They wrote a brochure (never completed) to be distributed to all entering inmates so that the new men would "get the lowdown from the inmates.

---

[7] The use of small groups was not necessarily contraindicated. This kind of confusion can characterize any new situation in which stable communication lines have not yet been established.

[8] *Gunsel:* term for young, irresponsible inmate whose disturbing behavior could range from noisy horseplay to criminal attacks on other inmates.

[9] *Write-up:* disciplinary report.

They'll believe another inmate." They sent inmate representatives to orientation meetings. When a second bulletin board was provided, they arranged for meeting announcements, sign-up sheets, and posters. Reporters were appointed to attend every group meeting and to write articles for a bi-monthly newspaper. But the leaders of this Committee were studying nights for their air mechanics certificate examination and did not have time to edit copy and prepare it for dittoing. Reporters forgot to act as observers in the meetings they attended and introduced their own urgent concerns into the discussions regardless of the agenda. Instead of writing reports about what happened, they turned in long, garbled statements in which fact and editorial comment were indistinguishable. When the staff sponsor suggested that certain articles be rewritten as either news or editorials, the editor protected himself from the anger of his reporters by publicly charging unwarranted staff censorship, although he had himself excluded certain items as unpublishable.

Thus the means for problem-solving devised by the inmates added to the confusion the staff were attempting to diminish. Unrealistic goals, inability to analyze a task and assess the costs involved in implementing decisions, impatience with and distrust of official processes for facilitating action, scapegoating of officials in order to protect self and other inmates from facing the consequences of bungling performance; these patterns were repeated in one form or another in all the early groups. In using their newly returned "voices," inmates revealed how they contributed to the problems to be dealt with.

One day toward the end of the first two months the unwieldy program disintegrated. Two meetings, one for the Rules Committee and the other for the Communications Committee, had been scheduled an hour apart on the Unit floor. A group of visiting officials from the Department appeared and joined the Rules Committee, whose members were at the peak of their exasperation about the confusion caused by different rules for A#s and YAs.[10] With such an audience the inmates stated everything in extremes. As the visitors left, the Rules Committee broke up and half its members joined the just assembling Communications Committee, noisily repeating the arguments from the previous meeting. The Communications Committee had been called to consider a reduction in its overextended responsibilities. Instead, all the problems in the Unit were redescribed in heated terms. The editor resigned, saying, "The staff talk a lot but they

---

[10] The YAs were new arrivals in the institution and were classified as nonhonor, a status involving more strict supervision than that required for the honor status A#s. See Chapter IV for an explanation of the honor-nonhonor conflict and what it meant for the C-Unit community.

aren't going to let us do anything. They can't even do their own jobs."[11] Five other members resigned, stating they would have nothing further to do with any part of the C-Unit program. Although four men remained behind to say they would like to go on with the Communications Committee —"I think it is important; and things aren't as bad as they were saying."— staff gave up for the moment. There would be no more committees until after the staff could devise a better plan and achieve some clarity in their own goals.

Meanwhile groups with a more flexible structure, and whose memberships cut across those of the more formally organized groups, were being used for less complex tasks.

Two counselors, who were concerned that C-Unit YAs as new inmates in DVI were not members of any of the institutional group counseling classes, made themselves available to all YAs who wanted to attend during the regular group counseling hour.[12] To their surprise the YAs, who had often remained silent in orientation meetings, began to use this opportunity to talk, not about "personal" problems, but about the issues concerning inmates in C-Unit. Monday evening Bull Sessions were already an accustomed event. Each week the director, a counselor, and a researcher appeared at the end of the Unit floor, where inmates could attend or not as they pleased, and remained for a two-hour session. The only ground rules were that staff as well as inmates could ask questions and that all participants would be as honest in answering as they could. No questions were barred.

The Bull Sessions continued as an important part of program throughout the four and a half months of intake, varying in size from 14 to 40. Often the two-hour session provided for two separate discussions as some inmates left for the field house and others moved in after a TV program. At first, inmate motivation for attending seemed little more than the attraction of one more opportunity to discharge anger at staff. Early meetings were endurance tests for the staff members who tried to make sense out of the highly emotional challenges hurled at them. Soon, however, it was possible to focus at least part of each meeting on a topic. "Why does it bother you to have counselors based on the Unit?" "Why is there such conflict between A#s and YAs?" "Why is it so disturbing to have counselors and custody work as a team?" "Why can't a program in prison help to prepare a man for parole?" "Why does having research as part of the

---

[11] Eight months later when on parole he revisited DVI and spent two hours with the C-Unit staff.

[12] The institution set aside one hour a week during which most other activities ceased and group counseling classes met.

C-Unit program make you angry?" As important topics were identified and worked over, appropriate visitors were asked to lead discussions. A Project research consultant spent an evening answering questions; members of the Adult Authority[13] told one session about their perspectives on prison treatment; and a visitor from a foundation led an absorbing discussion on maturity and the courtesies necessary for viable social life.

For the staff the Bull Sessions were a valuable educational experience about the nature of the inmate's social world. The image that emerged over the weeks was that of a society in which every man's hand is against another's. Among the inmates, A#s and YAs hated and distrusted each other. Although it was clear that incipient ethnic groups were forming in the Unit, each antagonistic to the other, the inmates were unwilling at this stage to talk about these conflicts. "If you talk about race, there *will* be trouble." In the official world the inmates saw counselors, custody officers, and parole agents as antagonistic to one another, with inmate safety depending on lack of communication among them. The Project staff was perceived as engaged in a mutually hostile battle with the DVI administration. In addition, the Project was exploiting the inmates: "You're just using us as guinea pigs so you can find out something to benefit other guys five years later"; and Project staff members were seen as persons who "are messing with us" for irresponsible personal motives like morbid curiosity and desire for prestige. "You get paid for it, don't you?" It was clear that offenders had brought into the institution a readiness to perceive social relationships as predatory and exploitative, and that the institution had fed into such perceptions by establishing hard and fast categories within which both staff and inmates were segregated.

In the informal atmosphere of the Bull Sessions, the staff began to hear about the practical concerns of inmates. There were frequent comments about the boredom of dead time, especially in the evenings when "there's nothing to do but trip with your friends"; and occasional suggestions about what inmates might like to do. "How about speakers from the outside every week?" "Could we have a practice room for musicians?" "How about a study hall for tutoring?" It was in the Bull Sessions that the staff first heard of the inmates' intense fear that C-Unit would "blow up" over the coming holidays. "Thanksgiving will start it; there will be more trouble on Christmas; but wait until New Year's. Then it will really come down."[14] "Holidays are hard on a man. There isn't enough to do. He remembers things. He thinks he might as well make a little hell, too."

Accordingly, a Holiday Committee with the modest task of planning

---

[13] Parole Board for A#s.

[14] *It will come down:* a major disturbance.

for C-Unit's Thanksgiving was convened, manned by some of the less belligerent inmates and including the two Mexican YAs who were known as "the children" because of their nuisance behavior. The Committee members asked for a party and added they would like to invite all personnel in the institution: "Like an open house so they can see we aren't all crazy in here." Most of all, they wanted a record player on the Unit, "so we can listen to the sides we want, not just sit glued to earphones in a room by yourself."[15] The party plan was turned down by upper-level administration, but the record player was approved. Staff assembled equipment and records from their own possessions; a team of mechanically sophisticated inmates assumed responsibility for managing the player in shifts; memoranda outlined procedures for storing the equipment and fixed the hours of play; and the inmates drew up rules for honoring requests. On Thanksgiving Day there were ten hours of music in C-Unit; and more than one custody lieutenant dropped in to have a cup of coffee with the listening inmates. On the next Monday a tense older man told his counselor: "This was the first time I've felt safe in C-Unit. I've been so tied up inside I was afraid I would blow so I have stayed away as much as I can. You don't know how good it was to lie back on my bunk and listen with everybody else relaxed around me. No yelling, just everybody listening." For once, something practical had been done by staff and inmates together to change the nature of a problematic situation.

With somewhat renewed confidence in their ability to assess a disturbing situation and to take appropriate action, the Project staff experimented with *ad hoc* groups from whom they sought advice in difficult situations. A naïve and puny YA had been threatened with sexual attack and was sent to the adjustment center for protection. After considerable exploration, it was decided to bring the man back to the Unit and deal with the problem there. Twelve of the Unit's inmate leaders were asked to discuss this decision with staff. It was a sober meeting in which the inmates talked guardedly about the problem. "Nobody will want to associate with him. It could mean trouble with whoever is after him." "An inmate can't interfere even if he sees what is going on. It might mean a fight and that would be a writeup on his record." But also, "We could see to it that he is included with some of the older men." In the end the inmates agreed. "Bring him back and we'll do what we can."

Partly as a result of this quiet but, as it turned out, effective handling of an incident, a Mexican gang leader told his counselor there were knives

---

[15] Each DVI inmate was issued earphones to keep in his room. With these he could listen to a full daily schedule of music and taped radio programs from the institution's radio room.

on the Unit. "We nearly had a rat pack[16] last weekend: Mexican and Negroes. The smokes are getting too salty[17] in TV." Again there were conferences: director, supervisor, counselor, and custody officer with the man
himself; and later with him and the leader of the Negro group. Knives
were turned in, some directly, while others were slipped under the counselor's door. Within a week the Mexican leader reported, "The Unit is
clean." And the Mexicans asked for a group where they could do something better with their time than "teach the youngest how to do an armed
robbery."

On Christmas Eve afternoon there was the first C-Unit Open House,
with record player, refreshments, and Christmas tree, attended by 50
institutional staff with their wives and friends. For two weeks before
Christmas, C-Unit, like the community outside the walls, was absorbed in
activity focused on a holiday. Every procedure had to be approved in
writing from permitting a "female plug for use with the record player to
be stored in the custody office" to changing work schedules so that the
showers could be cleaned, to permission for nonhonor men to be on the
floor to take part in the cleaning activities. Hobby craft articles were returned to inmates for display in their rooms. The Christmas tree was
nearly a fiasco because, after a scrawny leftover was secured from another
spot in the institution, it was stored in a hot cubby hole and dried up. In
desperation the supervisor was about to purchase a new tree with funds
from the staff when he found inmates and custody officers in the process
of remaking the C-Unit tree by inserting branches from the barren side
among those on the good side. Set against the window and trimmed, it
was a beautiful tree, more so because it was "ours." When there was talk
about the danger of fire, the custody officer said, "I would just like to see
what would happen to any gunsel who dared touch that tree with Big
Mac around."

When the Open House started, the inmates were withdrawn and moody;
and a few talked about "invasion of privacy by free people." But the host
committee was busy with introductions; the silent lineup for coffee and
cakes broke up into small groups; the inmates momentarily forgot they
had not talked to women for months; and those who did not want to cir-
culate could listen to the records. As the last guests were hurried out and
down the corridor before count,[18] a Mexican gang leader who had main-

---

[16] *Rat pack:* organized gang attack.   [17] *Salty:* provocative.

[18] *Count:* All inmates locked in their rooms and standing at their doors while an
officer counts men each tier. No inmate leaves his room until the central control
office has a count from all posts in the institution that checks with the figure for the
total inmate population at that time.

tained an inscrutable face toward every staff communication for three months, ran along the length of the TV room windows separating C-Unit from the corridor waving goodbye and smiling broadly as he called, "Merry Christmas."

The record player stayed on the Unit during Christmas Day, and was brought back for New Year's Day. When the expected howling of New Year's Eve beset the whole institution, C-Unit was quiet, much to the disgust of the next door unit whose inmates kept hollering, "Where are you, C-Unit? Come on, C-Unit."

C-Unit was beginning to find out where it was. But an illness of the supervisor necessitated his leaving, and it was over a month before a new supervisor could begin work. Nevertheless, on the Project drawing boards was a plan for C-Unit group activity, announced but not yet implemented. The staff responsible for implementing the program had found out what they wanted to use groups for and with the director's help had formulated a plan for problem-solving activities.

GROUPS FOR PROBLEM-SOLVING

A bulletin distributed to all C-Unit inmates on December 13, 1960, announced:

THERE WILL BE FOUR KINDS OF GROUPS ON C-UNIT:
Community groups for staff and inmate communication about mutual concerns;
Task groups to do specific jobs for the Unit;
Counseling groups for discussion of personal problems of inmates;
Interest groups for inmates with common leisure-time interests.

There followed an outline of the kinds of groups available in each category and the means by which inmates could become involved in them.

Aspects of this program that were important for later developments were as follows:

The primary community group, the Staff-Inmate Group, formerly a different set of staff selected inmates each week, would now meet for four weeks in succession in order to provide continuity of membership for the development of projects. In addition, elected representatives from the Unit to the institution's Inmate Advisory Council would become regular members of the Staff-Inmate Group during their term of office.

Task groups included the Research Seminar, the Holiday Committee, the Newspaper Group (newly reconstituted), and the TV Orderly Committee. Membership in these groups was often initiated by staff invitation, but openings were available for any inmate who expressed an interest.

Counseling groups included the Pre-Parole Group for A#s and groups established by the counselors and officers. The Pre-Parole group was composed of A#s who were within two months of release, although any A# with a parole date was welcome and several attended. Membership in other counseling groups was arranged by discussion with the individual inmate's counselor.

Interest groups were organized on inmate initiative with staff sponsors and met in the evening hours. Usually membership started with a small group of friends who either recruited among inmates known to them or used a sign-up sheet on the bulletin board. The first interests to become organized included art, music, chess, and "English-Speaking and Writing."

With the initiation of the revised program after the holiday season, group participation in C-Unit jumped from 26 per cent of the population in December, 1960, to 67 per cent in January, 1961. During the rest of the first program year, the percentage of inmates in C-Unit who were actively participating in groups ranged from 60 per cent (a low period during the summer heat when the yard with its swimming pool was open until late each evening) to a high of 78 per cent. It is important to note that many staff members took responsibility for more than one group, in addition to participating in the Staff-Inmate Group.[19]

Several facts about this group structure should be noted in order to understand the almost immediate development of new kinds of social relationships among staff and inmates on C-Unit.

Most groups were established to deal with problems that were both actually experienced by the inmates in their daily lives and had already been defined by them. Inmates were concerned about TV behavior. They had expressed uneasiness about "being researched." They did not like the tension on the Unit that inevitably developed during holiday season. They wanted to know more about parole rules. They had complained about empty evenings when there was nothing to do. Group activity thus became in large part voluntary, with staff facilitating work on problems that mattered to inmates. Since staff members were perceived as assisting inmates to work toward their own goals, they could begin to teach how goals are specified realistically, how means are selected, and how previously unrecognized resources might be identified and used.

This group structure also widened the range of inmate relationships contributing to the official program. The Interest Groups legitimated and

---

[19] At first no secretaries led groups and the regular relief officer did not accept responsibility for a group, although he attended community groups when his schedule permitted. Later, two secretaries assumed responsibility for Interest Groups, and students and volunteers were also used in this way.

made visible the small inmate friendship groups formed through informal association, permitting inmates to work together in formal program with other persons whom they already liked and believed they could trust. Thus inmate relationships that were already somewhat relaxed and friendly contributed energy to the accomplishment of official program.

At the same time, the staff made sure that inmates were exposed to new relationships across the barriers of their initial stereotypes. By plan, community and task groups always included A#s and YAs, members of the three ethnic groups, oldtimers and newcomers, inmate leaders and less mature individuals. Inmates met other inmates to whom they would not otherwise have spoken in groups focused on common concerns and in roles that permitted expression of different perspectives. In the same structure most inmates were related with several different staff members in complementary rather than competitive roles.

It was also important that in these groups the actual inmate leaders were given responsibility by staff in a way that supported their leadership with peers. An inmate did not have to be known as favorable to staff to secure staff help in setting up an Interest Group for his friends. The invitations to the Research Seminar were issued to inmates who had the capacity to think in a disciplined fashion and who could express general inmate concerns. Consequently, although this was a high prestige activity, the Seminar membership included as many inmates who were actively hostile to the Project as those who were beginning to be known as "with program." Legitimating inmate interests regardless of who represented them made it possible for any inmate leader to get payoff from peers by dealing openly with staff and encouraged an atmosphere in which it was permissible for any individual who desired to associate with officials.

Finally, this group structure permitted work on a variety of tasks that were appropriate for inmates of different maturity levels. Thus the Newspaper Group, the Research Seminar, and the first Music Group challenged the best minds in the Unit. In contrast, the English-Speaking Group was tailored to meet the needs of relatively unacculturated Mexicans and the Painting Class was a valuable resource for inadequate individuals who lacked ability to express themselves except in action, as well as for those with already recognized talent. The Holiday Committee welcomed both those inmates who could organize and those who were best used by assignment to the cleanup squad. As individual inmates achieved success at one task level, they often moved into more demanding group experiences. The research staff began to observe a phenomenon they called "careers in C-Unit" as individuals moved from one group assignment to another, evidencing previously unidentified abilities.

With the initiation of the new group program, the staff found themselves under pressure to facilitate more creative proposals than the available man hours permitted. But this was a very different kind of pressure from that which they had experienced when most meetings with inmates required absorption of an almost radioactive hostility. Now the surprise of the new idea and the pleasure of working with rather than against compensated for the extensive work necessary to invent means for responding positively to proposals. Most staff members put in many hours of overtime in order to manage both the daytime routines and the evening group responsibilities. Later, when the program had been stabilized, it was possible to organize a less demanding worklife. At this stage of spontaneous innovation, requiring as it did much learning by both staff and inmates, there was never enough time to keep up with the emerging possibilities.

A PROBLEM-SOLVING COMMUNITY

In April, 1961, C-Unit had its first experience as a community. An institutionwide disturbance, triggered by Mexican-Negro antagonism, occurred in the yard. The next morning Project staff were met by C-Unit men with glowing faces reporting how good it had been in C-Unit; and for a week little else was discussed. The inmates said, "It felt safe in C-Unit. All I could think about was getting back to the Unit where I knew everybody." "We felt separate from the hassel, hardly interested. We looked out of the Unit windows at the fighting in the corridor and it was like looking at TV." "It was nice to see a colored fellow and know his face and name. You knew he wasn't an enemy." "We knew C-Unit fellows were regular. If you didn't know them any other way, you had met them in groups." "We were worried about the guys who hadn't got back to the Unit yet." "Everyone was kind of helpful. That was the kind of contagion that swept our Unit." "I was standing at the Unit window with a Negro fellow and we were watching a white guy get stomped in the corridor by a colored gang. We looked at each other and shook our heads. We didn't think 'look what your race is doing to my race.' We just both felt bad it was happening." No C-Unit inmate had been involved in the fighting that occurred in the yard and the corridors. For the first time, C-Unit men went around the institution proud that they were "different."

During the following four months, the theme of program activity was the identification of subgroups with different needs and interests and the mobilization of community resources to respond to them. This theme had already been established by staff in their response to interest groups. Now the inmates took the initiative.

THE SEMINAR WORKING GROUP

Three quite different subgroups with special needs were identified by the Seminar Working Group that met during April and May to formulate inmate views on program policy. On the basis of the group's discussion, the inmate chairman wrote a paper (see Exhibit 1) for presentation at one of the monthly Project policy sessions when institutional administration, departmental representatives, and Project staff met together to evaluate program and formulate directions. In preparation for the presentation, the members of the Seminar Working Group interviewed many C-Unit inmates and circulated the paper on the Unit in rough draft before its final writing. The inmate members of the group were in charge of the half-day policy session at which they presented the paper, each member speaking to one point and leading the active discussion with DVI and departmental administrators that followed. According to the Seminar Working Group, more attention should be given to the needs and participation of *newcomers to the Unit, custody officers,* and the *undereducated.* The Seminar Working Group members themselves took action to do something about one of the subgroups it had identified by constituting themselves as an Orientation Committee. By the middle of April, they were handling the first orientation session of each new group of C-Unit selectees, turning the new men over to staff when the inmate discussion had ended.

THE WELFARE FUND

Other subgroups received consideration in Staff-Inmate Group meetings. One Staff-Inmate Group spent its month in office considering the needs of "gunsels" at the request of two self-identified gunsel YAs who felt they were changing and would like to involve others previously unreached by the Project program. What they proposed was a version of a counseling group, a kind of Gunseling Anonymous self-help movement. The next month's Staff-Inmate Group began by suggesting that money be collected to adopt a Korean child by C-Unit, and went on to propose, "If we are going to give money out of our draw,[20] why don't we give it to people at home instead of to somebody across the ocean we don't even know. There are men right in our Unit who don't get any draw from home and have to smoke this dust the State calls tobacco."

The identification of the economically underprivileged within C-Unit as a subgroup needing community resources opened a wide range of issues

---

[20] *Draw:* up to $20 made available once a month to the inmate with money from home for purchases from the canteen.

EXHIBIT 1 **Inmate Analysis and Proposals for C-Unit Community Living**

June 9, 1961

(Document written by inmates and not edited by staff)

This paper was developed over a period of seven weeks—by a Seminar Working Group meeting once a week—maintaining a group of ten to twelve men. The membership changed as men expended their ideas to be replaced by other C-Unit inmates. We feel a good representation of C-Unit thinking was ensured in this manner. The tone of each meeting was of sincerity and thoughtfulness, with a sense of responsibility.

It was decided in the first meeting to follow an outline of discussion that would be chronologically similar to the inmates progressive absorption into C-Unit; beginning with selection and ending with parole. In ths paper we will summarize the results of the discussion and follow the same sequence of development.

I. Selection

The Problem

At the present time a small percentage of C-Unit inmates are unable to read. This skill deficiency results in a communications breakdown which leaves the vis-à-vis counseling situation as the only possible way to reveal to the inmate community-living concepts. This has the effect of draining off an inordinate amount of staff time, with the result that large areas of program that require an optimum of staff time are slighted.

Proposals

1. We reviewed the existing criteria. We decided on one more: A literary efficiency level of sixth-grade reading ability would help to eliminate this drain on staff time. Youth Authority inmates assigned to this institution will be the only ones affected. Adult Authority inmates when assigned to this institution for program training usually have a reading skill.

2. It was thought that a pre-C-Unit diagnostic workup, handled by C-Unit staff to determine motivation, interests, would facilitate engaging the inmate's individual needs by the community. This essentially would be a refinement of the classification effort done on the broader institutional level.

II. How to Build C-Unit into a Whole

The Problem

When inmates first enter the Unit certain needs have to be met. The first thing is to negate, by the positive, the misinformation from the patois of the rest of the institution, the current one being that they were selected because "they are crazy," "they will do more time," "twice the time on parole," "lose certain privileges," "they are going to Disneyland," etc. This reinforces the natural resistance to being manipulated, sustains the protective subcultures that form along ethnic lines, and, in general, creates negative attitudes that take months to overcome.

Proposals

1. To help eliminate this condition it was suggested to catch the inmates immediately upon entering the Unit with a combination orientation. The combination would consist of an inmate group developed along a service line, working in conjunction with the regular staff group orientation.

2. Have them given ducats to all C-Unit activities to familiarize them with all C-Unit phases.

3. To eliminate the present status distinction between custody and counselors inherent in inmate attitudes, have officers wear civilian clothes.

III. Program

The Problem

As every program issue was discussed it became evident that every problem hinges on three needs: the limitations of staff time, spatial limitation, and lack of having autonomy for policy-making.

The Problem Analyzed

At present there is no general unit sense of purpose. The feeling of continuity, plus awareness of ongoing interaction is lacking. Staff time is spread so thin that a large area of diverse interests and needs are neglected.

The rest of the institution program is either vague or ill-equipped to support and supplement in a dynamic C-Unit program that has, theoretically, a time limitation of six to eighteen months to prepare a man for the street.

Proposals

1. Increase the staff in some manner, perhaps by allowing university students studying in this field to participate.

2. Opportunity to acquire transferable skills, direct and indirect, could be made available if interest groups were increased and the existing ones improved.

3. Set up procedure for every inmate to be seen at least once a month by his counselor.

4. Increase the interest in community living by making it visible to all; one example would be to plan occasional community meetings when appropriate.

5. Emphasize the concept that staff is inseparable from community living by having staff—on an informal basis—in more frequent evidence on the unit.

6. Try to interest outside service groups—speakers and people with skills—that C-Unit could identify with and profit from.

7. Acquire one-half of the adjacent hospital yard, which is in disuse, to build—utilizing the TV room wall—a three-sided room for community activities, such as talks by visiting speakers.

8. Set up supplementary educational programs to provide individual inmates with a more adequate and direct means of acquiring skills pertinent to their individual needs. Suggested ways for doing this were: (a) correspondence courses; (b) investigating the feasibility of educational machines (Grolier; $20) that have been used in similar situations (prisons). They offer the advantage of cutting instructor time to the minimum of proctoring the final testing; also the advantage that course learning time is cut in half; (c) the use of the State Library in Sacramento.

9. Initiate C-Unit tradition of pride, etc., by creating unit service groups who would perform maintenance services such as: room painting, helping with clerical work, etc.

10. Screen prospective C-Unit officers for the ability to handle caseloads and group counseling, and to learn therapeutic philosophy.

11. Establish a viable communication program to effect a sense of pace and momentum in the Unit and to point out the varied facets of community living.

IV. Bridges to the Community

The Problem

Based on the past experience of some, and drawing upon the thinking of those presently involved, pre-parole is the most crucial time an inmate faces.

At present, when an inmate reaches this juncture everything suddenly goes beyond him or his experience. Sometimes there is very little sense of relationship between the institution's program and the inmate's situation on the outside.

Proposals

1. Continue the compulsory pre-parole group.

2. Create volunteer parole-oriented group sessions to point out how the present learning is applicable to life on parole.

3. Permit the earliest relationship to develop between Outside Parole officer and inmate; possibly beginning at the initial classification of the inmate to help ensure a realistic program for eventual parole.

4. Recognize the different parole needs of YAs and A#s and design program and pre-parole activities accordingly.

5. Establish a stronger triad relationship, consisting of family, parole officer, and inmate.

6. Establish policy of allowing furloughs for job interviews.

7. Have inmates who have proved, and are proving, themselves on parole visit the Unit accompanied by outside parole officers.

8. Make coherent use—from beginning to end—of all employment resources, consisting of the Department of Employment, counselor, the parole officer, and the inmate.

9. Bring inmates back for a ninety-day suspension period of parole who are beginning to show regressive patterns.

10. Provide counseling on the psychiatric level if and when a parolee's situation appears to need it.

THE SEMINAR WORKING GROUP

for consideration. The inmates immediately pointed out that providing even limited funds for those who were without canteen money could cut down on the cell robbing that was currently plaguing the Unit. They then considered what it might mean to a man to be known as a recipient of "relief" and discussed how the needy could be identified without exposing them to their fellows.

Because such a plan depended on the willingness of inmates with funds to give their own money, the group members decided it was necessary to assess opinion on the Unit more thoroughly than ever before. A systematic poll was proposed, and with the help of a researcher, a committee of six men drew up a short survey form. Each of the six inmates interviewed the men on one-half tier in the Unit, using a checklist provided by the officers. When over 80 per cent of the Unit were reported as favorable to a welfare fund for C-Unit, the supervisor undertook the long process of working out procedures with the business office and upper administration, ultimately securing the necessary approval from the Department of Corrections' central office.[21] (See Exhibit 2.)

Meanwhile C-Unit groups went on to discuss many of the critical issues facing any community that undertakes to help its needy. How to define eligibility? What about the inmate who applied for relief and is known to other inmates as "running a business?" How to ensure confidentiality for the individual applicant while maintaining control over possible abuses? Would it be better to buy and distribute goods such as shaving soap and tooth powder, or should a recipient be allowed to "blow" his pittance on

---

[21] The permissions needed included the Attorney-General's agreement that it was not illegal for inmates in a correctional institution to give from their own funds to other inmates.

candy, ice cream, and cigarettes if he so desired? What limits should be
set on monthly grants and over what period might they continue? Could
part of the collected funds be set aside for equipment that would benefit
the Unit as a whole? And how could the Unit population determine what
purchases would be most useful for the largest number of inmates?

In this new approach to subgroups and the relation between their welfare of the whole, C-Unit inmates went on to reexamine the cartoon versus
sports interests in the TV programming controversy.[22] For the first time
inmates talked good naturedly about "minority" interests, noting that a
majority could and perhaps should voluntarily provide opportunities for
those in the minority to satisfy their less popular tastes. Later this perspective bore fruit in an agreement that certain program periods would be set
aside for the sports fans, and that during those periods the TV program
would not be interrupted by calling for a vote.

THE RACE RELATIONS GROUP

Partly as a result of the success of the Welfare Fund poll, real conflicts
of interest among ethnic groups appeared openly in C-Unit discussions for
the first time. Essentially what happened was that a minority group used
the new social mechanism of the poll to push its own interests at the expense of other subgroups.

The record player had become a regular part of C-Unit programming
for holidays, but as early as Easter, 1961, it was apparent that Mexicans,
Negroes, and whites liked different kinds of music and had different patterns for getting their desires expressed. The Negroes liked blues played
very loudly. They tended to gang around the record player and to dominate the request list. The Mexicans wanted guitar music but refused to ask
the inmate in charge of the record player for the records they liked. "I
can't go up in front of a bunch of guys and say I want that side. They
might not like it and be mad. All I can do is go off in a corner and mumble-
jumble about how they don't play my music." The whites had formed
several different factions. The quiet, more studious men wanted the music
period to be limited to two hours at a time and resented the loud playing
enjoyed by the Negroes. The sophisticated "hypes" asked for more modern
jazz. A few inmates requested a larger selection of classical records.

Just as these differences were being formulated, a group of Negroes
who had been active in promoting the Welfare Fund plan decided to poll

---

[22] Cartoons and sports typified the two levels of program tastes among C-Unit inmates.
Since there was only one TV on the Unit, program interests often clashed, with
considerable ill feeling on both sides. See "The TV Story," Chapter IV.

EXHIBIT 2 **Proposal for C-Unit Welfare Fund**

July 19, 1961

(Memorandum prepared by staff for administrative use)

C-Unit inmates have proposed that a Unit Welfare Fund be established. The fund would be accumulated through donations from inmates in C-Unit. The fund would be administered by a Committee of C-Unit inmates and staff which would establish policies for the collection of the fund and its use. The moneys so collected would be used for:

1. Canteen slips for C-Unit inmates who are without any source of outside income.

2. To provide the Unit with recreational and educational items not provided in the regular institutional budget, such as: a supply of swimsuits for loan to men without funds to purchase them, a large dictionary for use of men studying on the Unit, or supplies needed for a Unit event such as an Interest Group festival.

The ISCP* Project director and the Project supervisor will be responsible for the collection of contributions and the selection of inmates to whom funds would be distributed.

This Project is seen as particularly valuable for the development of a community spirit on C-Unit. It is significant that this suggestion came from the men themselves and that the proposal was developed by the men in a series of discussions accompanied by a poll of the complete Unit in which about 80 per cent indicated a willingness to contribute. The proposal evidences a readiness in C-Unit inmates to use their own resources, to be concerned about other human beings, and to think as a community about the welfare of its members. This readiness suggests that a different kind of culture is being substituted for the "do your own time" culture more common in the institution. Considerable social training will be possible in working on this kind of project with the men as they consider the problems and responsibilities of such welfare efforts.

This proposal has been staffed with the DVI Business Manager who agrees that such a project could be managed without too much additional strain on the business office. He suggests that inmates wishing to contribute to the fund could do so by signing a "Trust Withdrawal Slip" indicating the amount of contribution. To facilitate bookkeeping, contributions would be made as follows:

1. Inmates with odd change of less than one dollar could donate that amount.

2. Inmates wishing to contribute more would make their contributions in an even amount of one or two dollars. All contributions would be limited to not more than two dollars per inmate per month. Where an inmate wishes to contribute one or two dollars in a lump sum to cover contributions at the rate of some speci-

fied amount per month (such as $.25 a month), the ISCP office will keep track of the pledge and notify the inmate at the end of his period of contribution so he can renew his pledge.

All contributions would be pooled in one fund and withdrawals would be arranged either through $1.00 canteen slips, to be distributed to needy inmates, or by checks to the Project supervisor for agreed-upon purchases.

The Project has been discussed in detail with [institutional and state officials], all of whom have agreed that the project has considerable merit and would be a useful small experiment in facilitating the concern of inmates for the welfare of all. Permission to proceed with the C-Unit Inmate Welfare Fund is hereby requested.

---

* The Project was called the Inmate-Staff Community Project for NIMH purposes; and PICO, Phase II, for many DVI and departmental uses.

---

the Unit with the request that the record player be made available on the Unit every weekend. The polling was done under pressure—"An inmate can't say no openly when other inmates are trying to get a special privilege"—and a group of white inmates asked the staff to block what had appeared to be an overwhelming inmate request for weekend record playing. The supervisor refused to approve a plan that forced a minority to suffer under conditions they could not get away from, that is, continuous loud music in the living quarters.[23] Although several different subgroups had been identified in this process, for the inmates the matter had become a racial issue and feelings ran high.

For the first time C-Unit inmates were willing to talk about race relations in a group with staff. During a two-month period a Race Relations Working Group, composed of two Negroes, two Mexicans, and two whites, interviewed C-Unit inmates and analyzed the C-Unit experience. At first, they found it very difficult to discover the facts that lay behind the myths of this long verboten subject. A Mexican member of the group said:

Guys won't tell another inmate what they really believe. In fact, they hardly know what they do believe. I know how it is myself. Maybe I work next to a

---

[23] It should be noted that this administrative decision prevented the use of the C-Unit pattern for problem-solving among potentially conflicting subgroups. Discussion of the general problem was permitted in the Race Relations Group but the specific issue was disposed of by fiat without requiring the immediately involved individuals and groups to work out their differences together.

Negro and while we are in the shop, he and I are buddies. I walk down the corridor alongside a Mexican, and he says to me, "I sure hate those smokes; they're all dirty and loud." I say, "Sure, man. I feel the same way." In the Unit a white man says, "The way to get along is for the races to leave each other alone" and I go along with him too. Now we have a group where we are supposed to say what we really think, and although I guess it is safe, I'm not sure. Even if I was sure, I wouldn't really know what to say.

In spite of difficulty in securing wide participation from other inmates in their study, the Race Relations Working Group offered the following report:

Although there is currently more talk about racial antagonism on the Unit, there is no increased tension. C-Unit men are simply more free than before to express their antagonisms verbally.

Racial tension is always present and tends to be the lightning rod that attracts and focuses tension arising in other problem areas such as conflicts over TV programming.

Resolution of such problems through interracial groups reduces the tendency to turn arguments about special interests into racial conflicts.

Inmates who would formerly express their racial antagonisms in fights are now talking to staff about them, although there still remains much fear that discussing racial problems in any way will lead to trouble.[24]

THE EMERGENCY PLAN

In August a second period of institutional racial tension blossomed into a full-fledged disturbance and once again C-Unit men were not involved. Inmate leaders of all three ethnic groups came to the staff asking: "Why did we have to be locked up in our rooms after we were all in the Unit? Nobody in C-Unit was making trouble."

DVI's policy in times of unrest was to lock all men in their cells, sometimes for periods of several days until "the air cleared." This simple procedure facilitated management in several ways: it inactivated hostile racial gangs; it freed custody officers from close unit supervision so that they could be concentrated in areas presenting serious problems; it allowed the orderly removal of an inmate from a unit for questioning by custody; and it protected official personnel from possible spontaneous group attacks. After the second disturbance in the summer of 1961, all DVI inmates were confined in their rooms for three days.

As soon as the regular schedule was reinstated an interracial group of

---

[24] Adapted from the director's Quarterly Report, August 1, 1961 (edited for clarity in this context).

inmate leaders from C-Unit asked the Project staff if C-Unit inmates could
be given the chance to look out for themselves during such periods without having to be locked up like the rest of the institution. They said that
there was little or no racial grouping in the Unit, even during periods of
disturbance, and reported that C-Unit inmates had developed their own
group code: "You don't shoot at a C-Unit man." "You don't take out your
racial dislike on C-Unit inmates." "In C-Unit you are safe."

The C-Unit custody officers agreed that racial grouping was not a problem on the Unit and thought a special C-Unit plan for these periods would
be highly desirable. Staff immediately began working with various groups
of inmates to devise a plan allowing C-Unit to carry on "business as usual"
—with access to TV, card games, and showers, while other living units
were locked up. The plan was prepared as a proposal and sent to higher
institutional officials. Less than two weeks later, the Associate Superintendent of Custody gave official approval to the C-Unit Emergency Plan.

Even though there was no further cause to put the plan into effect that
summer, both staff and inmates felt a great sense of accomplishment. Inmates saw the Emergency Plan as a symbol of the C-Unit staff's willingness to listen to them, to take their views into account, to plan with them,
and to take the necessary action for approval. Big Mac later reported that
the Emergency Plan gave C-Unit inmates something very important to
say in response to gibes from other units about C-Unit being a "nut ward."
Most important, this was one action in which custody, counselors, and inmates acted together as a unified group working for a common goal. (See
Exhibit 3.)

In the first twelve months of operation the staff and inmates of C-Unit
had learned that to be one community it was necessary not to eliminate
subgroups, but to provide for differences in needs and interests. Being
different had been legitimated by belonging to a larger whole; and belonging involved both obligations to contribute out of difference and
claims to special response from the total community.

NEW CHANNELS FOR STAFF AND INMATE COMMUNICATION

No longer concerned that community would be lost in diversity, staff
and inmates went on to solve the communication problem that had been
troubling everyone since the beginning of the Unit program. There had
been repeated discussions of the fact that not all inmates had equal access
to information and problem-solving activities. Meetings of the whole were
not feasible. Small groups did not reach everybody. The Staff-Inmate
Group had been redesigned once in an effort to gain greater respresenta-
tiveness plus continuity of effort. But no way had been found to make sure

EXHIBIT 3 **The Emergency Plan Proposal**

August 25, 1961

(Memorandum prepared by staff for administrative use)

The following plan was proposed by the C-Unit Project staff following two periods when the Unit was observed to be quiet, well behaved, and relatively undisturbed, although the institution was experiencing interracial difficulties. The plan has been thoroughly staffed with C-Unit custodial officers who not only approve but believe such a plan would be highly desirable. The plan is proposed because all staff believe C-Unit population is ready for additional responsibility and would benefit from some recognition, through differentiating procedures, of their ability to handle themselves as a group during periods of institutional tension.

The plan involves continuing an organization of all noncustody male personnel attached to the Project, including both counselors and researchers, to provide at least two additional free persons for C-Unit supervision immediately following any upsetting institutional episode. The C-Unit officer would call the Project Supervisor, who in turn would get in touch with the assigned O.D. (officer of the day) from the Project. If the Project supervisor is not available, the officer would call the O.D., who would then get in touch with at least one more staff person to complete the emergency team. Whenever possible at least both the Project supervisor and the assigned O.D. will report to C-Unit.

Emergency procedures following a recall, including lockup, would be the same for C-Unit as for other units until the additional staff team could arrive on the Unit. However, when the additional staff had arrived, C-Unit would be released to carry on business as usual, with availability to TV, card games, showers, etc. Inmates would agree not to gang up at TV windows or around the Unit door, and the additional staff would be posted in such a way as to assist the officer in maintaining order away from the windows.

If the institutional authorities need a C-Unit inmate for investigation in connection with the institutional difficulty, three alternative plans are available in order of preference:

1. C-Unit would be notified that the inmate is needed and the personnel in C-Unit would deliver him to the designated place.

2. The inmate would be picked up after the ten o'clock count.

3. A temporary lockup would be called, during which the man would be removed from the Unit.

Because C-Unit personnel know the Unit population in more detail than is possible in the usual unit, it is suggested that personnel on the Unit be given the option of plan (1) above and allowed to indicate whether or not in their judgment such a plan is feasible. A decision between plan (2) and plan (3) can then be made.

It is conceivable that this plan for emergency staffing could not be put into effect on the first day of trouble because of absences among the Project staff. The C-Unit population would be made aware ahead of time of the possibility that on the first evening of a period of institutional unrest, the Unit would be handled in the same manner as all other units. However, during the days immediately following an institutional episode, teams of Project staff would be selected to be available on call; and enriched staffing would be provided until institutional tension was reduced, even if no further emergency occurred.

It is understood that if the situation does not warrant the execution of this plan, C-Unit will be dealt with as would any other unit.

---

that every C-Unit man had an opportunity to hear about and participate in the issues that concerned him. Suddenly a quite simple plan appeared possible; it was quickly formulated by staff and approved in discussion with inmates.

The plan called for a meeting of each counselor with half of his caseload during the weekly hour provided by the institutional program for group counseling. Within each two-week period there could be six Half-Caseload Group meetings, involving all the inmates in the Unit. Representatives from these groups would meet weekly with staff as a Unit Council (in place of the old Staff-Inmate Group) to coordinate opinions and to identify issues that should be discussed in the Half-Caseload Groups. Other task and interest groups would continue as usual, but now there would be a communications system through which they could send information and secure response.

Because of the turnover in Project personnel at the end of August, 1961, the Half-Caseload Program could not be implemented until the following January, after new staff had been secured. However, the C-Unit community had experienced the need for total Unit involvement around some issues as well as for subgroup participation in others, and had invented the necessary devices for maintaining community through the activities of small groups within itself. It was now ready to become the responsible political entity serving the welfare of individuals and groups envisioned in the Project's model for the resocializing prison community.

However, the problem-solving process developed in C-Unit for dealing with welfare issues did not result in congruent institutions for controlling the behavior of its members because, throughout the developmental first year, another critical issue was never successfully resolved. To understand why C-Unit was able to invent means for the constructive use of leisure time, for maintaining economic welfare, and for democratic policy-making but was not able to establish the appropriate sanctioning machinery to control deviant behavior, we must review those events in the first year that concerned the Project's efforts to modify DVI's patterns for control over inmate behavior.

IV - CONTROL BY COMMUNITY

LIKE ALL OTHER ORGANIZATIONS, every prison develops means for creating and maintaining order among its participants. Such means include incentives intended to promote conformance to normative regulations, devices for detecting and coping with incipient disorder, and sanctions to deal with deviance. Together, these incentives, devices, and sanctions, and the social arrangements that embody them, may be called a "system of social control." Such a system serves to elucidate, communicate, and enforce institutional norms of order to those who are to be guided by them, including both staff and inmates.

Prison administrators necessarily give special attention to those aspects of the system of social control that govern inmates. Inmates are, first of all, persons removed from their ordinary situations, including the informal and formal patterns for order on which they formerly relied in the free community. In addition, inmates are identified as socially dangerous, as persons who cannot be trusted to create a benign social order for themselves. And prison administrators desire, above all, to create a benign social order; their jobs and sometimes their personal safety depend on it, as well as the personal safety of inmates. Further, a benign social order is in modern prisons, including DVI, conceived as an important prerequisite for carrying on the work of rehabilitation. For all these reasons, the creation and maintenance of a strong official system of social control is deemed of critical importance.

Given the importance of the control system, it is not difficult to understand that it is more likely than any other part of the prison's structure to embody directly the basic conception of order held by the prison's administrators. Their notion of what order among persons *is*, and ought to be, is contained in prescriptions for proper relations among inmates and between staff and inmates. Such prescriptions, too, communicate directly the official conception of the natural proclivities of inmates, ideas about how inmates will behave given that they are law violators held in prison against their will.

Thus it was no accident that the critical issue between the Project and DVI's administration concerned the character of the system of social control that would be institutionalized within C-Unit. For the Project and for DVI, this issue was central to its integrity as an organization.

DVI's control system embodied a set of conceptions about inmates, often explicitly stated, that ran somewhat as follows: Inmates are chiefly motivated by egoistic concerns both because convicted offenders are that kind of person and because any person in prison will be principally interested in his own "time" or "getting out." Some inmates are just "bad" and nothing much can be done about them except to see that they do not have the chance to infect others. And, if not closely watched, inmates will form groups to exploit each other, threatening official attempts to maintain order. Accordingly, DVI's control system made it advantageous for individual inmates to limit their involvements with other inmates; it also institutionalized means for segregating "bad actors" from conforming inmates and for avoiding the formation of inmate "cliques."

In contrast, the Project saw inmates as similar to other people in being capable of both good and bad behavior, depending in large part on the kind of controls to which they were exposed. It was assumed that most inmates would be responsive to goals that looked beyond immediate self-interest; that much disruptive behavior could be avoided by providing more opportunities to cope with tension and to gain satisfaction through legitimate means; and that given such goals and opportunities, with rewards for using opportunities and achieving larger goals, inmate peer groups would emerge to structure and control the behavior of potential "bad actors." Project strategy accordingly emphasized the discovery and legitimation of inmate concerns, the encouragement of inmate groups to deal with these interests, and the institutionalization of means through which the staff and inmates could deal with problem behavior in line with values established by the community as a whole.

Most important, DVI and the Project had different conceptions of the overall goal of the control system. DVI sought inmate conformity to norms handed down from the top, maintaining that "learning to obey orders" was essential for their future success on parole. DVI's guiding norm for inmates was unquestioning subordination, as individuals, to officials. In contrast, the Project hoped to encourage the inmates in the exercise of initiative and responsibility as individuals and as groups. The Project conceived of the inmate who was ready for parole as a man who was aware of value alternatives, who could make choices, and who could seek out and use peer relationships to support acceptable behavior. Accordingly, the Project attempted to develop in the C-Unit community those processes for promoting conformance and controlling deviance that would encourage such behavior while its inmate members were still in the institution.

In DVI, the "honor system" in conjunction with the disciplinary process was the pervasive internal, administratively controlled mechanism for inducing inmate conformity[1] and for segregating "bad actors" for special supervision. This system became throughout C-Unit's first year the subject of much disagreement both within the community and between its members and DVI's administration. Disagreement was typically over procedural matters that often seemed superficial; actually, it reflected the much more basic differences in goals and values outlined above. Accordingly, we must reexamine C-Unit's first year in order to trace the sequence of events that made up the controversy about the honor system. Only then can we understand why, in the long run, the C-Unit community was never able to institutionalize a control system congruent with the moral customs emerging elsewhere in its activities.

---

[1] For most inmates, it seems clear that "time," i.e., length of sentence, was the primary incentive for conformance, and not the rewards and punishments produced by the honor system and disciplinary process. DVI's administration did not control sentences, however, which were set by the two parole boards. Indeed, in the case of A#s, institutional personnel were not permitted to make direct recommendations for release.

On the other hand, the honor system and disciplinary process were linked to sentences, since both parole boards (but particularly the adult board) took movement to honor status as well as misconduct into account when making release decisions. And the institution could and sometimes did recommend delay of both parole consideration and parole dates to the boards as a means of dealing with misconduct, recommendations which inmates believed were of import to the board in making release decisions.

Further, as many of our data illustrate, it is well not to underestimate the motivational value of situational differences that seem small from an outsider's perspective. Not only may such differences loom large in themselves, but they may achieve a symbolic significance difficult to appreciate unless seen in context. (See, for example, "The Screen Story," pp. 121–124.)

Finally, we suggest that all these points be kept in mind when considering the evident commitment of top DVI staff to the honor system.

THE HONOR SYSTEM IN DVI

In the opinion of DVI's top administrators, its "honor system" was essential for safeguarding order within the institution. The honor system arrangements provided incentives for inmate conformance. At the same time it was a device for deploying relatively scanty custodial resources to manage the identification, close supervision, and relative segregation of "bad actors."

The concern of DVI's administration with "bad actors" was based on the fact that any population of older youthful offenders who have already been through many less stringent correctional processes is always a difficult and volatile group to manage in a closed institution; and DVI had been originally established in the Department of Corrections to house those older YAs who seemed to require more supervision than Youth Authority institutions ordinarily provided. In addition, by 1960 when the C-Unit Project began, DVI's administrators had reason to believe that the institution was receiving the "bottom of the barrel," the worst individuals that the Youth Authority had to offer. Memoranda prepared by DVI administrators during 1960 and 1961 put the matter this way:

The present criteria for transfer of YA wards [from the reception centers to DVI] leaves us largely with the hoodlum type of inmate with whom to try to carry on a program. Figuratively speaking, only Eagle Scouts are to go to Ontario; 1st, 2nd, and 3rd class Scouts to Soledad and Camps [all of which housed older YAs]; and we keep what is left. This policy is resulting in the concentration at DVI of a highly explosive and dangerous type of inmate. . . . We recognize that we must keep more than our share of this type, but concentrating the cast-offs of more than 2,500 [older] YA wards in this one institution is likely to cause a bad explosion. . . .

Because of the continued "skimming off" of all potential management problems for retention at DVI, the quality of our YA population has become increasingly lower. [Further] under present criteria, aggressive or acting out behavior or other management problems not screened out [for retention at DVI in the first place] are returned to DVI as soon as they give any trouble [at Ontario, Soledad, or Camps]. Because of this consistent lowering of quality, YA wards who would ordinarily conform in a better, more acceptable manner are now conforming to the more delinquent, unacceptable patterns.

The honor system and other parts of the social control system were seen by DVI as largely a response to and safeguard against the kinds of disorder produced by the "hoodlum type of inmate" DVI was expected to manage.[2]

---

[2] A#s were generally regarded as presenting fewer problems. Among the many reasons offered by the administration for this difference between the A# and YA

Although the procedures making up the honor system were never formulated in a manual, they may be readily described.[3]

The honor system created two kinds of "regular housing" in DVI by establishing different degrees of surveillance and regimentation in different housing units.[4] With few exceptions, newly admitted inmates were housed under conditions of relatively strict surveillance and regimentation in "nonhonor" units.[5] Eligibility for transfer to an "honor" unit was earned by achieving seniority in accumulated "clean time"[6] on the list of nonhonor inmates maintained by the Custody Division. Transfer to an honor unit occurred when there was a vacant bed. Retransfer to a nonhonor unit could follow any disciplinary infraction.

The period during which an inmate had to maintain "clean time" before transfer to an honor unit had varied in DVI's history from as little as six weeks to as much as five months, depending on the proportion of inmate rooms in the whole institution classified as "honor" by the Custody Division. Just prior to the beginning of the Project, there were four nonhonor units; three housing units plus portions of two others provided honor rooms; thus about 40 per cent of available beds were classified as "honor." This proportion produced a three to six months' waiting period for in-

---

populations in DVI were two, based on policy: (1) selection and transfer policy directed that A#s defined as "trainable" were to be selected for housing at CVI, while A#s defined as potential "troublemakers" were to be housed at other prisons; (2) parole board policy suggested that the adult parole board evaluated disciplinary reports in the institution more seriously than did the Youth Authority Board in setting sentences and releasing to parole. In addition, A#s selected for DVI were generally older than many in the YA population and A#s were accordingly expected to be more settled and experienced in "getting along" than were the YAs. Finally, DVI's experience was that YAs were more extensively involved in behavior requiring disciplinary action than were A#s. See Chart 5.

[3] These procedures were essentially created and implemented by the Custody Division. As we noted in Chapter II, the management of housing in DVI was generally regarded as the special prerogative and responsibility of the Custody Division; and, except for the adjustment center which was not a "regular" housing unit in any case, personnel from other divisions rarely entered a housing unit or expressed concern about the procedures governing the basic living arrangements for inmates.

[4] We refer to "regular" housing to differentiate it from "special" disciplinary housing, i.e., isolation, administrative segregation, and the adjustment center. As we shall note, inmates could also be placed on "room confinement" while remaining in the "regular" housing unit when a penalty was needed for a relatively minor disciplinary infraction.

[5] As noted in Chapter II, these were called "mainline" or "skid row" units in DVI. We have chosen the more cumbersome term "nonhonor unit" to avoid confusion with another use of the term "mainline," i.e., to refer to any unit housing those not under special disciplinary restrictions.

[6] *Clean time:* a period free of disciplinary reports.

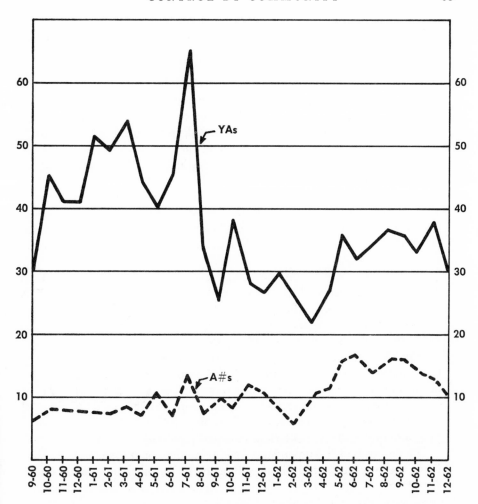

CHART 5. OFFICIAL DISCIPLINARY ACTIONS PER 100 YAs AND A#s AT DVI, September, 1960, through December, 1962

Source: Institutional records. "Official disciplinary actions" includes actions by Disciplinary Court and Disciplinary Committee. Actions against inmates housed in C-Unit or the reception and guidance centers not included. Population base composed of month-end totals plus departures during month.

mates at the bottom of the seniority list. An individual's waiting period might be much longer, of course, if clean time was not consistently maintained.

Procedures for managing the two types of units were quite different. In the nonhonor units, inmates were tightly scheduled and closely supervised. They had no room keys; they entered and left their rooms at half-hour intervals—"room calls"—when the lock bar on each half-tier was thrown by the officer. Nonhonor men were allowed nowhere on the Unit except in their own rooms or the TV room, and they had to pass directly from the Unit entrance to their approved destinations. They showered on schedule and had to leave the Unit for the yard at a certain time before lunch call. They were permitted to use the TV room only at scheduled periods, were searched before they entered, and were supervised in the TV room by a correctional officer. They viewed only those programs scheduled by a weekly inmate vote conducted by the institution's Inmate Advisory Council.

In the honor units, on the other hand, each inmate had a key to his own room, which permitted him to enter or leave it during free periods. This key served as a pass in the corridors at times when nonhonor men were not permitted to move about the buildings. Honor men could move freely about the unit, visiting at each other's doors, showering, entering or leaving the TV room at will, or using the game tables on the main floor of the unit (such tables were not provided in the nonhonor units). All facilities of the honor unit were open to inmates during periods when they were not on work assignments or locked in their rooms for the night. No special supervision was provided for the TV room, and the inmates determined programming by the vote of viewers actually present.

The purposes of the procedures making up the honor system were clear. First, the waiting period for new inmates in the nonhonor units, under conditions of regimentation and close supervision, was held to provide a "test" permitting identification of "bad actors"[7] as well as a goad to "good" ones. Although no definite policy governed the number of honor rooms, the custody personnel were quite definite that a restricted number was necessary, for some period of waiting was "needed" before moving an inmate to honor status. Because nonhonor units were used for this testing purpose, correctional officers showed greater readiness to write discipli-

---

[7] Inmates who arrived at the institution predefined as "bad actors," that is, inmates transferred from other institutions as "agitators," were usually sent by the custodial officer in charge directly to special housing set aside for troublemakers before release to even a nonhonor unit. In reference to this practice, a custodial official said: "It's just as well to let them get a look at it" (the special housing).

nary reports for minor rule infractions by nonhonor inmates than was the case in the honor units.

Second, the provision of two kinds of units was believed to permit the separation of "good" and "bad" inmates, limiting the corrupting influence of the latter on the former. A high custodial official suggested the importance of this purpose.

The big thing about the honor system is that it provides a means for segregating troublemakers. More specifically, it provides a means through which agitators are segregated from, and thereby kept from infecting, those who would otherwise be manageable. There are some people on the staff, of course, who believe that the more manageable elements can control the troublemakers, but it has never worked out that way.

Finally, the separation of these two types of inmates into two kinds of housing units permitted concentration of the always scanty supervisory forces: the "bad actors" could receive the extra supervision felt needed to prevent disorder.

A major consequence of the honor system was the support, if not the creation, of something approaching two inmate cultures at DVI. On the one hand, the honor-unit culture tended to be characterized by compliant orientations toward staff coupled with "making out" in ways informally countenanced or not easily detected. Inmates in the honor units appeared to concentrate on "doing their own time." On the other hand, the nonhonor unit culture was characterized by the dominance of gunsels; showing that one could "take it" from staff and would not "take it" from other inmates, and "the hell with the consequences," was the pervading orientation. Because inmates with current disciplinary records were not transferred to honor units, and inmates who committed infractions were returned, the nonhonor units tended to collect together a "hard core" of delinquently oriented inmates.[8] Banded together in small groups for self-protection and exploitation of others, the hard core dominated the culture of the nonhonor units as well as the thinking of custody personnel about problems of control. YAs tended to be concentrated in the nonhonor units; for many,

---

[8] Thus a survey of a random sample of the disciplinary records of one-third of the inmates in one honor and one nonhonor unit during 1962 showed the following: Honor-unit inmates (N=59) had been in the institution longer; about half had been in DVI 13 months or more, compared to 14 per cent of the nonhonor-inmates (N=57). Notwithstanding their longer "exposure time," honor inmates had notably fewer recorded disciplinary infractions. Over half (57.6 per cent) had no recorded infractions, compared to just over a third (38.6 per cent) of the nonhonor inmates. Almost no honor inmates (3.4 per cent) showed a rate of infractions as high as four per year, compared to over one quarter (28.1 per cent) of the nonhonor inmates.

given their short sentences, the nonhonor units (interspersed with stays in disciplinary units) provided the only housing—and subcultural milieu— experienced during their tenure at DVI.[9]

From the point of view of DVI's administrators, particularly those in the Custody Division, the gunsel culture was *contained* by the honor system, rather than created or supported by it. As we have noted, "bad actors," particularly among YAs, were seen as the particular burden assigned to DVI by the Department of Corrections. And the honor system and other elements of the social control system were conceived of as mechanisms for lightening the load as much as possible, given the resources at hand. The Project's view, on the other hand, came to be that the honor system, as it operated in DVI, might be making a difficult task even more difficult, and that alternative arrangements and uses of available resources could not only be imagined but should be tried.

We have described the honor system at some length because it was the particular part of DVI's social control system that became the center of the extended controversy between DVI's administration and the Project to be described and analyzed in the remainder of this chapter. Further, the honor system was a prototype of the broader system of control in DVI, a system that included other means for identifying potential antagonists and separating them, for short-circuiting the development of close, informal relations among inmates, for increasing surveillance of and restrictions on inmates who violated institutional regulations, and, finally, for more or less permanently separating "bad actors" from other inmates.[10]

It is worth noting that this strategy of control, differentiating levels of deprivations, restrictions and supervision, was applied within housing units as well as between them, with different parts of a single floor or different floors in a single unit housing inmates believed to be more or less willing to conform. This in combination with techniques for moving inmates from room to room within units and from unit to unit, produced a kind of complicated Chinese box effect, with inmates in the innermost box required to traverse each enclosing one on the way to relative freedom. These elaborate segregation and mobility procedures strongly influenced the kinds as well as degrees of solidarity that could develop among inmates. And this is precisely what they were intended to accomplish.

---

[9] At the time of the survey of disciplinary records mentioned above, 23 per cent of the inmates in honor units were YAs (as estimated from the survey sample); 60 per cent of the inmates in nonhonor units were YAs. The proportion of YAs in the institutional population as a whole was about 40 per cent.

[10] We have briefly described these other parts of DVI's system of social control in Chapter II.

During the planning period, Project personnel had taken note of the disparity between its own approach to social control and that of DVI's administration. Partly because of administrative insistence, but also because change should grow naturally out of the necessities of experience, the Project began its action program with the honor system built into its operation. However, the Project proposal stipulated that there would be experimentation and change in the control operations of C-Unit. The section of the proposal dealing with "Organizational Arrangements" included these paragraphs:

It is anticipated that by the end of the first year C-Unit will have its own classification subcommittee and its own discipline subcommittee. . . . All discipline incidents involving C-Unit inmates regardless of where they occur in the institution will become the responsibility of the C-Unit subcommittee.

There will be experimentation with the process by which inmates are promoted to honor status.

In spite of this agreement, DVI's arrangements for control by segregation remained essentially intact in the Project's program throughout its history.

TWO CLASSES IN C-UNIT

One day during the third week of proposal planning, the Project director and supervisor were for the first time admitted to C-Unit to observe procedures during count.[11] After the inmates had filed out to mess, the Project administrators remained in the empty Unit hall, noting its more obvious features: the custody office, the TV room, the stairways and their adjacent shower rooms, and the walls of doorways to the rooms in which C-Unit inmates would live. One of their tasks was to select the rooms to be converted into offices for counselors. They agreed that the staff offices should be located about the Unit, one to a half-tier, in order to avoid creating a solid bank of official doors as a physical division between inmate land and staff land. Suddenly they turned to each other with a common thought: honor and nonhonor statuses; rooms keyed and not keyed; two classes of inmates located in different sections of the Unit. This must not happen. Their first request to administration was that rooms without keys remain scattered among the rooms to be occupied by key-carrying honor men in order to avoid a skid row on C-Unit.[12]

---

[11] At that time C-Unit was filled with reception center inmates.

[12] See p. 94, note 5.

In spite of this forethought, C-Unit started community life with its own built-in skid row. Nonhonor rooms on each half-tier were opened at stated times for groups of inmates by throwing a lock bar at one end of the tier. When the bar was thrown, all the rooms on that half-tier were also unlocked whether they had been keyed for honor men or were occupied by nonhonor men. Because the opening doors blocked the officer's view of what was happening on the walkway, he could not observe that the nonhonor men who had assembled for room-call were not entering rooms other than their own, and so could not protect honor rooms located on the same tier (whose occupants probably would not be present at room call) from cell robbing. In order to solve this supervision problem, honor rooms in C-Unit were keyed in a solid block beginning on one side of the ground-floor tier, and nonhonor inmates occupied rooms not yet provided with keys. As additional rooms were keyed during the first months of intake to accommodate the weekly intake of new honor selectees, skid row was pushed upward to the unkeyed rooms on the tiers above. By the time the Unit was fully occupied, the ground-floor tier and one-half of the second floor housed honor men. The third tier and one-half of the second constituted skid row.

The honor-nonhonor division within the C-Unit population, made visible by the allocation of inmates to either an advantaged or disadvantaged site within the Unit, was intensified because in C-Unit's first population all but one of the A#s were honor men. Administration had not anticipated that almost every A# who became eligible for C-Unit selection by being within six to eighteen months of release would have already achieved honor status in DVI. Nevertheless, it turned out that most A#s came to C-Unit requiring keys; while all YAs for C-Unit were automatically nonhonor because they had just been admitted to DVI from the reception center and still had to earn the period of clean time required for advancement to honor status. Consequently, in C-Unit, honor status was from the beginning equated with being an A# and nonhonor status with being a YA.

The social characteristics of the YAs and A#s selected for DVI could have tended, under the most favorable circumstances, to differentiate the two groups as they were brought together, each comprising half of C-Unit's population. Many of the YAs were younger, in their late teens. In general, they seemed less well-educated, were often assigned to less demanding training programs in the institution, and tended at any one time to have a higher proportion of ethnic minority members. YAs anticipated short terms in DVI, roughly nine to fourteen months; they would be paroled under a relatively lenient set of requirements about institutional behavior; and were accordingly more prone to minor types of forbidden behavior such as "horseplay." In contrast, the A#s were older. They had been selected for DVI as "trainable," and a much larger proportion of them than of the YAs took their vocational training seriously. They had already been in DVI for months or even years and had settled patterns for doing time, often involving study or the pursuit of hobbies. A#s were handled by a paroling authority that took seriously any discipline infraction; an A#'s next parole hearing could be delayed as much as a year by a single writeup, and most A#s were noticeably careful to avoid the appearance of misbehavior. As a consequence of the different characteristics and orientations of the two populations from which C-Unit inmates were selected, C-Unit might have been expected to divide along A#–YA lines as the "men" distinguished themselves in tastes, habits, and goals from the "youths."

The different styles of life provided under the honor system for honor A#s and nonhonor YAs greatly intensified the apparent differences in their modes of life. Honor men were frequently on the floor of the Unit when most nonhonor men were locked in their rooms. They moved about the Unit freely, swinging their keys as evidence that they enjoyed a status as much like that of an adult in the free community as was permitted to any inmate in DVI. In contrast, nonhonor men in C-Unit moved along strictly limited pathways in response to room calls. The regimented schedule imposed on the inmates assigned to this more childlike status was visible to all as nonhonor men responded in groups to the frequent shouted orders from custody officers.

Thus the probability that a two-class system would develop in the C-Unit community was overdetermined by the differences between A#s and YAs in legal status, social characteristics, location in the Unit, and styles of life permitted by honor and nonhonor statuses.

When the two statuses were located together in a single unit, it was almost inevitable that the two classes so formed would be in conflict from the start, because the procedures for handling the two sorts of inmates collided at many points, primarily to the disadvantage of the honor men. A#s, transferred from regular honor units, were resubjected to the noise of half-hour room calls even though they did not have to depend on the calls for access to their rooms. The TV officer, later brought into C-Unit to supervise the nonhonor inmates in the TV room, also supervised honor men. The half of the Unit allocated to nonhonor inmates was out of bounds for honor inmates, blocking access to the upper-tier windows from which the outside world could be watched. Because amenities such as shower benches, trash cans, game tables, and ash trays were not provided in DVI nonhonor units, C-Unit was not originally provided with such equipment and there were delays in securing it because of the presence of nonhonor inmates. Room-search teams did not discriminate between honor and nonhonor rooms located in a single unit when removing unauthorized articles. Most irritating to the honor men was the fact that any adjustment designed to remedy these disadvantages involved giving greater privileges to the nonhonor inmates as well as to the honor men. Nonhonor YAs in C-Unit had not had to earn these privileges "the hard way" as had the honor A#s, who had spent weeks or months in a skid-row unit before achieving honor status. Most frightening to the honor A#s was the fact that once again they were forced to associate with nonhonor men who were seen as potential sources of trouble for those around them. From the first day A#s responded to this situation with anger and alarm.

The impact on YAs of combining the two statuses in a single unit was quite different. The YAs came to C-Unit directly from the reception center where rumor had it that selection for C-Unit meant your lucky number had turned up. Although most of them did not know what a nonhonor unit would have been like, they were aware that, by the chance of random selection for C-Unit, they had moved at once into the high-status position of having a single-bunked room, a privilege usually associated in DVI with seniority. In addition, the YAs in C-Unit had relatively easy access to counselors who spent considerable time arranging desirable work and academic assignments for them. As might be expected, the YAs tended to believe that allocation to C-Unit meant "doing easy time" and reduced responsibility. A few of them tested this presumption by misbehaving and telling custody officers outside C-Unit, "You can't write me up. I belong to C-Unit," thus, according to the A#s, attracting unfavorable attention to all C-Unit inmates. The YAs' problem was that they had to watch the honor men—"other cons like me"—enjoying the use of game tables, visiting with each other throughout the Unit, and using room keys, while they suffered the hostile superiority expressed by A#s toward YAs. Without understanding that A#s found C-Unit a situation in which they did "harder time," the YAs turned sullen and passive in meetings; made full use of their voting privileges in the TV room, where they usually outnumbered the A#s, who had other alternatives for filling time; and at moments of intense annoyance harassed the honor men by yelling when locked in their rooms and by sweeping dust from the upper skid-row walkways onto the heads of the honor men at the game tables.

In consequence, the honor system became the first major problem of equal concern to staff and inmates in C-Unit. The hostile stereotyping of class by class proved to be a major barrier to efforts to develop community. Because the honor system procedures had to be taken into account in every part of the program, many discussions focused on irritations occasioned by the honor system regardless of the planned agenda. And because honor status had become equated with A# and nonhonor status with YA, each issue tended to be discussed as a conflict between A#s and YAs.

By the end of the first six weeks when approximately half the Unit population had been assembled, it was clear to both staff and inmates that something should be done about honor system procedures to avoid a permanent two-class system in the C-Unit community. The director wrote a working paper analyzing the issues as they had been experienced up to October 31, 1960. (See Exhibit 4 for that part of the paper documenting the issues.) This paper was distributed to the staff with the expectation that resolving the honor system difficulty through problem-solving would in itself constitute a major step in establishing the organization necessary to support the new social relations expected of the C-Unit community.

When DVI's administration proved unwilling to permit any general change in honor system procedures in C-Unit at this early stage, staff and inmates tried to deal piecemeal with the honor system as it affected particular segments of the program. The TV story illustrates the way the honor system defeated the use of practical measures to relieve tension in specific issues, producing blame of one class by the other and demands from inmates that all problems be resolved by resegregating A#s and YAs into separate units.

THE TV STORY

For the first two days of the action program, C-Unit officers sent the nonhonor YAs to a skid-row unit during the evening TV period because as nonhonor men they were not permitted to vote on programs to be viewed. This procedure confused both inmates and officers and worked a hardship on the other unit. The problem was discussed in the second orientation meeting with the first group of 20 inmates. The A#s proposed that YAs be permitted to remain in C-Unit during TV hours and that the honor system of voting on programs be instituted for all C-Unit men. The A#s, having come out of honor units where newcomers (particularly the YAs) accepted the informal agreements about programs to be viewed that had been already established by men with seniority, made it explicit that this move on their part was an effort to establish their preferences in procedures to govern both the YAs and the new selectees for C-Unit to be admitted in the coming weeks. "We will set it up before new men come in. Then we can control it and the new men will just have to fall in line." This suggestion was quickly approved by the Associate Superintendent, Custody, in order to avoid the evening transfer of C-Unit YAs from one unit to another.

EXHIBIT 4   **Structure of Inmate Population in C-Unit**

October 31, 1960

(A document written for staff use by the director)

Because of the nature of the selection process a marked and rigid "class" system (the inmates call it "class") has emerged on C-Unit which has crystallized
around the A#—YA separation. This was not so evident when the population was
small, and there are a few YAs who have "passed" into the A# group simply because of their more mature interests, intellectual ability, and desire to participate
in the community. But in large measure, problems such as the TV hassel of last
week tend to become dramatized beyond their real significance because they are
used as symptoms of the A#—YA split. The facts of the split are as follows.

Almost all A#s are already on honor status. They worked hard and waited
long to achieve this status. At the same time, as they see YAs receiving certain
privileges (which they had to work for) simply by admission to C-Unit, they find
that they have lost certain privileges and advantages which they enjoyed in their
former units. The C-Unit move has meant for them:

Lack of freedom to move about the entire Unit.

Separation from friends and accommodation patterns long established.

Less control over TV programming.

Rooms that are run down and in need of renovating.

Irritation from the few "gunsels" who make noise and get involved in horseplay.

A feeling of vulnerability to custody; C-Unit gets attention from custody, some
of it unfavorable, because individual C-Unit members have flaunted their
supposed "specialness" outside the Unit.

Increased severity in the application of rules about contraband and locking
the outside door of the Unit.

A feeling of increased vulnerability in relation to time, because the tension on
C-Unit between A#s and YAs means potential trouble in which they may get
involved unwittingly unless they withdraw from everything.

The YAs break down into three groups: a small number who are with the program and whose interests tend to go along with those of the A#s; a middle
group who are passive, nonverbal, not troublemakers, but not involved in program developed so far; and a small group of troublemakers.

The A#s and YAs differ significantly in:

Age: There is a four-year mean difference in ages of the two populations, and
there are evident major taste differences between the two groups.

Stage of institutionalization: YAs are straight from reception center; most of them are new to the institution and are as ready to settle for C-Unit as for any other Unit (although a few have friends on other Units from whom they feel separated). A#s have already settled into the institution, have spent months or years building comfortable patterns of accommodation, and are in many cases in the last stages of training programs which are important to them.

Vulnerability: An A# may lose a year if he is involved in trouble. The YA risks only a month or two at most.

Possible racial composition: The YAs seem to contain more minority group members than do the A#s, and these comprise largely the members of the community who are as yet unreached.

Involvement in leadership and voluntary activities in the Unit: The natural leadership roles have in general fallen to the A#s except for the small minority of YAs who have joined them. There are four YAs out of ten on the voluntary communications committee. At the last Bull Session only three YAs attended and one of them left when the going got tough.

Available resources, both personal and institutional: For much of the free time the YAs are faced with a choice of being locked in their rooms or sitting in TV. Except in the TV room they have little opportunity to sit and talk together and they seem to use the TV offices* for this kind of activity. In general, they are a group who have not yet developed the program and individual interests which characterize the A#s—studying, hobbycraft, membership in clubs, etc.

The A#s have taken three kinds of action about the problems arising from this two-class system:

At first they asked that YAs be admitted to floor privileges from six to seven in the evening and to weekend TV. This was supposed to make it possible for A#s and YAs to get acquainted and to avoid the hostility of YAs against A#s expressed by yelling when locked in rooms, jamming the TV vote, sweeping room dust down onto the heads of A#s on the main floor.

When it became obvious that YAs were always the majority in the TV room because of limited access to other activities, and that certain individuals were causing trouble on the floor from six to seven, the A#s became very angry and drew up a petition asking to have all the extra privileges of the YAs withdrawn. It was noticeable during this weekend that although the YAs also had a meeting they were much less capable of forming and acting as a group. They do not tend to take a stand that holds for all of them.

In the discussions about TV privileges which followed during the week after the petition, both A#s and YAs agreed that the only solution was to give all members of C-Unit honor status at once, and then withdraw this privilege from individuals who could not live up to the responsibilities of this status. It was believed that such a move would break down the artificiality of the A# versus YA split and make it possible to identify individuals who cannot live up to their responsibilities and to form groups of common interests regardless of A#—YA differences. The YA resentment against the special privileges of the A#s would be lessened and because YAs would have wider access to activities, there would be less jamming of the TV room and fewer annoyances from yelling and other expressions of hostility.

---

* Temporary offices had been constructed at the end of the TV room. These were later removed because of Fire Marshal regulations.

C-Unit inmates soon began to complain that the vote in TV usually split along A#—YA lines. The split reflected a consistent difference in tastes between the younger YAs and the somewhat older A#s, resulting in repeated showdowns over the choice between cartoons and sports programs scheduled for the same periods over different channels. For the YAs, as nonhonor men, sitting in the TV room was the only alternative to being locked in their rooms during the free evening period, while the A#s could use the game tables, shower, or visit at their friends' doors. In addition, many more A#s than YAs studied or worked at hobbies during the evening. Consequently, YAs tended to be in the majority in the C-Unit TV room and the A#s were often voted down.

The first inmate effort to resolve this conflict of interests was constructive. A#s pointed out that YAs had no place to go but the TV room during the evening hours and therefore could neither talk with their friends nor get acquainted with the A#s. In part, to "take the pressure off TV" and, in part, to enable honor and nonhonor inmates to get acquainted with each other, it was proposed and officially approved that the floor of the Unit be open to nonhonor men during the period after dinner and before the 7:00 P.M. count. However, it was soon evident that this adjustment was not enough to solve the TV problem. The conflict continued during the 7 to 10 P.M. viewing period and throughout the weekends.

The A#s reacted by invoking the expectations of the DVI honor system. They claimed the "right" as honor men to determine TV programming and insisted that in the honor units there was a rule—at least informally accepted—that sports had preference over all other programs. When this question was put to the Associate Superintendent, Custody, he denied that such a rule existed. Consequently, the hassels continued. The A#s indiscriminately blamed the YAs for the difficulties, claiming that the YAs were intruders and "gunsels" and should voluntarily respect the "earned rights" of the honor A#s. The YAs, on the other hand, insisted that the A#s had no such "rights," and accused all A#s of being "snooty" and "clannish." As the conflict sharpened, the YAs began packing the vote in the TV room and yelling or talking in the background when they were occasionally voted down. The problem of noise was further aggravated by the honor system rule that nonhonor men who were outvoted were not allowed to leave the TV room until the next room call, which might be as much as half an hour later. As could be expected, the nonhonor men tended to use the TV room as a dayroom for conversations with their friends.

The A#s next drew up an angry petition requesting staff to withdraw all the privileges that had been granted to the nonhonor men in C-Unit. Project administration responded by calling a meeting of inmate leaders with the Unit officers and counselors. Exchanges like the following occurred:

A YA: One of the troubles is skid row and honor in the same unit.

AN A#: That's getting at a lot of it. YAs don't understand what a skid row or honor unit is like—they're fresh from the reception center. Another thing is YAs sweep stuff on the A#s down below.

ANOTHER YA: It's because YAs are hot about the TV and are getting back at A#s.

AN A#: It's not A# versus YA.

A COUNSELOR: Well, what is it?

A#: It's honor versus nonhonor.

THE OFFICER: The split makes a big difference in running the Unit. Why don't we send YAs who voted against a TV program back to their rooms after the vote without waiting for the room call?

A#: That would be good as I see it, since I'm honor. But how would the YAs feel? They would just have to be locked up.

This discussion about TV, like many others, ended in extensive proposals to modify the honor system by opening the floor to nonhonor men during evenings and weekends or by giving each man a key as he entered C-Unit. Because this approach was blocked by administrative refusal to change additional rules related to the honor system, inmates began to say in meetings, "Shit, lock us all up. It doesn't make any difference." Also, "What's all this talk about? It doesn't get us anywhere."

A TV committee was established composed of inmate orderlies, A# and YA, to manage the vote during regular periods of TV use. The staff purchased a weekly *TV Guide* to help inmates anticipate the programs in which they might be interested until the subscription, usually provided by the institution for each honor unit, could be secured for C-Unit. Rules were posted, including the stipulation that no one except the orderly was to switch channels and the arrangement that votes should be scheduled for each half-hour even if an hour program was in progress. But YA orderlies tended to side with other YAs; they were accused of miscounting votes in favor of YA preferences; reputedly they rounded up other YAs ahead of time in order to make sure that on any given vote the nonhonor men would be in the majority. Meanwhile the A#s were increasingly boycotting the TV room in order to avoid the possibility of trouble; and it proved difficult to get any responsible A# to accept assignment as a TV orderly, because few A#s wished to commit themselves to an entire evening of TV. After a Mexican ratpack against Negroes was narrowly averted one weekend over the TV issue, a regular TV officer was assigned to C-Unit during evening viewing hours. Except for the fact that all viewers voted on programming, C-Unit's TV room was handled for the next three months as it would have been in a nonhonor unit.

The presence of the TV officer was an added grievance to the honor inmates who now demanded that staff, (1) "Let us take care of the TV problem; there'll be a few heads broken but we'll clean it up"; or (2) give every YA who talks in the TV room a discipline writeup, followed by room confinement or a sentence to isolation; or (3) eliminate the YAs from the Unit and run it as an honor unit. "Shut up the loudmouths." "Pick out the troublemakers and get rid of them." Violence or resegregation was the only alternative according to the inmates by which control could be reestablished.

TV problems ceased to be the major issue after the YAs were advanced to honor status in sufficient numbers to have alternative ways of spending free time out of their rooms. TV orderlies were made responsible to the C-Unit evening officer; and by March, 1961, it was possible to remove the special TV officer from C-Unit because of relaxation over the TV programming issue.

But the TV room continued to be a sensitive barometer of Unit morale. Much later when a new wave of intake brought many new men into the Unit on nonhonor status, TV became a critical issue once more, was defined as a conflict between A#s and YAs, and again resulted in strong inmate demands that staff control the "gunsels" by segregating them in some fashion. (See Exhibit 5.)

RESTRICTION ON COMMUNICATION

The interclass conflict was sharper because honor system segregation in the Unit population limited communication between honor and nonhonor men to formal meetings where they often dealt with each other as representatives of hostile groups each causing trouble for the other.

EXHIBIT 5 **Editorial from The Spectrum, February, 1961: Committee Shows How Not to Solve Problems**

Well, we had another one of those wonderful Staff-Inmate meetings. We didn't get much done, but the atmosphere was just wonderful.

Really.

I mean where else can an inmate get together with staff and other inmates and with complete impunity, try to foist off outlandish, ridiculous, and completely absurd solutions(?) to pressing problems?

Take, for instance, the solution offered by (Inmate A—) to the problem of noise and gunseling in the unit. While it is, at the very least, unrealistic, it is, nevertheless, the opinion of more than a few A-number inmates, including Mr. A—, that we "just get rid of the noise-making YAs."

Exactly how we should get rid of them he didn't say, but I feel safe in saying that he meant nothing more drastic than moving them to another unit.

Obviously we can't get rid of anyone by moving him to another unit. Even if we could, it wouldn't be solving the problem, but merely ignoring it. If ignoring a problem would solve it there would be no United Nations, no aid to foreign countries, and we'd all still be paying a tax on tea.

The point is, it's not only the YAs. Age doesn't carry with it the guarantee of maturity (whatever that is). If we're going to ask for consideration from other inmates, we're going to have to give it to others; and this includes not supposing that our young friends are gunsels simply because they are fortunate enough to have a Y in front of their number.

Although nonhonor men could be "ducated" to group meetings as were honor men, and, in fact, staff made a special effort to ensure that nonhonor YAs were equally represented with A#s on community and task groups, the participation of many YAs in discussion was seriously limited by their nonhonor status. Because of restrictions on the mobility of nonhonor inmates in the Unit, the YAs were neither known nor trusted by the A#s whom they met only in the official groups, and were much less aware of the issues discussed or the positions taken by the freer portion of the community. In addition, each nonhonor man had to speak for himself because his legitimate association with fellow YAs was so limited. Therefore, no clear YA position emerged. Nonhonor men suffered from the stereotype "gunsel" applied by A#s to all nonhonor YAs and were hesitant to express their opinions in the hostile atmosphere created in group meetings by the

A#s. This feeling of incapacity to enter freely into group discussion with A#s was expressed by one YA, who wistfully suggested that it would be nice to have a YA committee. Staff found it necessary to provide a period during orientation sessions when the YAs sat alone with staff in order to get from them a statement of their real concerns.

Even later, after stereotyping had almost disappeared, a YA said in the Staff-Inmate Group that now that he had earned his honor status after three months on the Unit, he was just beginning to get acquainted with inmates other than those who lived on each side of his room. Throughout the life of the Project, men who were nonhonor when selected for C-Unit were always delayed by their segregated status in becoming active members of the community; and the new values of C-Unit depending, as they did, on the communication and enforcement of norms through peer relationships had limited influence over newcomers until after they had achieved honor status.

THE SKID-ROW SUBCULTURE

Partly because the problems between honor and nonhonor men could not be solved by practical changes in procedures, by the middle of December, 1961, an organized skid-row group had appeared among C-Unit's nonhonor men, similar to that expected in DVI's nonhonor units.

The skid-row subculture, so generated, differed from the earlier sporadic annoying behavior of the C-Unit nonhonor men in that it was spread by a self-styled gang led by a "duke"[13] and two lieutenants who professed, even to staff, their loyalty to a romanticized criminal code of behavior. This group specialized in serious aggression against fellow inmates, including cell-robbing, sex pressure, beatings administered in the third-tier shower, and fire setting. Many of these acts were not performed by the leaders themselves, but by weaker YAs who were controlled by fear and obligations and who were ordered to beat up "that fink," to throw lighted papers down a stairwell from which smoke billowed forth to fill the rooms of noninvolved inmates after night lockup, or to begin howling as soon as lights were out. These events were salient enough to evoke both editorial comment and cartoons in the inmate newspaper, *The Spectrum,* relating to immature inmates with the disease "howlitis" and those who were childish enough to set fires. Accordingly, it was difficult to identify and

---

[13] *Duke:* inmates' term meaning an inmate who had established domination over others through fear and manipulation of resources.

deal with those individuals who were primarily responsible. The leaders recruited among the new YAs recently admitted to the Unit, oriented them to assume a cynical antistaff attitude, and spread mutual distrust and anger among all the inmates in the Unit.

Although there were other factors favoring the development of an openly criminal culture in the skid-row segment of the Unit, the implementation of the honor system in the Unit contributed to its flowering and diminished the ability of the staff to handle it through problem-solving with inmates.

The decision of DVI's administration to have only three half-tiers in C-Unit keyed for honor rooms was partly responsible. The administrative position was that since the total institution operated with approximately half its units on honor status and the other half nonhonor, the same proportion should obtain in C-Unit. It was anticipated that C-Unit honor rooms would become available to YAs as A#s left on parole and that eligibility for advancement to honor status would be based on seniority in clean time earned over an indefinite waiting period.

However, there were several unique factors operating in the C-Unit situation. Because of conditions established legislatively and by the research plan, a rough approximation to a 50–50 balance between A#s and YAs on the Unit was required. In order to maintain this balance, when an A# left on parole another A# was selected to replace him. Such selectees were almost sure to have already attained honor status and were therefore moved into the empty honor rooms. YAs had observed that honor rooms could be created on C-Unit by the simple process of keying more rooms. Those who believed they had earned honor status became disgruntled as new A#s were moved into the empty honor rooms and YAs remained on nonhonor status. Because DVI's administration had stated that there would be no additional honor rooms, the Project temporarily suspended selection of A#s in favor of YAs during the final period of first population intake in order to make it possible to advance eligible YAs to honor status. Consequently, nonhonor YAs soon outnumbered the A# honor men in the C-Unit population.[14] At this point, the ability of the more mature inmates to influence the Unit's code of behavior was seriously diminished and C-Unit became even more stereotyped by both inmates and staff in DVI as another skid row.

In addition, C-Unit rooms had been keyed from the bottom tiers upward,

---

[14] The actual numbers of A#s and YAs in the Unit during these months were: September—15 A#s/15YAs; October—35/36; November—58/57; December—54/64; January—55/72; February—53/73; March—60/70; April—61/68; May—67/69; June —69/66. (These figures include intake during the month, so occasionally they exceed the capacity of the Unit.)

with the result that nonhonor rooms were located on the second and third-floor tiers. Consequently, nonhonor men were associating during periods of inmate movement in a segregated section of the Unit that was also remote from supervision. A less expensive key had been used in C-Unit, and inmates soon learned that many of these keys fit more than one door or could be easily filed for use in cell robbing. Project administration proved increasingly unable to cope with these difficulties after the Project supervisor became ill in December, 1960 (the third month of its operation), and left the institution in early January. In response, the inmates were much less willing than before to help staff identify the groups causing the problems about which they complained. Instead, they resorted to hostile demands that Project staff clean up the mess.

Dealing with the skid-row subculture was the first task of the new supervisor, a custody lieutenant appointed late in January, 1961. Together with his officers on the Unit, he identified the chief troublemakers by the use of traditional custody measures, such as the interrogation of informers, and in February the duke and his two lieutenants were removed from C-Unit to the adjustment center. These men were the only inmates formally extruded from the C-Unit population by Project initiative during the first year of operation.[15] Although other equally difficult persons had already been handled by staff and inmate problem-solving action, the group processes used earlier (see Chapter III) were too new (as well as unfamiliar to the new supervisor) to be invoked for dealing with an organized attack on staff and inmates alike. In order to protect the weaker inmates who were already under the control of the duke and his lieutenants, it was necessary to use the strategy of segregation and to eliminate the leaders of the gang permanently from the Unit.

INTERFERENCE WITH THE DEVELOPMENT
OF NEW PATTERNS

Of particular importance for Project goals was the honor system's interference with inmate and staff efforts to institutionalize the new kinds of social relations proposed as necessary for a resocializing community.

When discussions about problems such as the handling of TV or the contraband rules bogged down because honor system procedures interfered with solutions, the inmates quite realistically addressed themselves

---

[15] At the end of the first three months of operation, an additional C-Unit A# had been transferred to another institution when the DVI administration discovered that he had a history of aggressive homosexuality.

to discussion of the kind of social arrangements that would work better in a unit where the two groups had to live together. This was exactly the kind of problem-solving effort the Project wanted to encourage because the issues raised were fundamental for the emergence of community. The inmates were concerned with such matters as: Should all inmates start equal and have keys withdrawn only on evidence that they could not respect the rights of others? What kind of behavior should be so penalized? (There was considerable insistence that making noise after lights were out should be a more serious cause for removing honor freedom than some violation of the rules that did not disturb one's peers.) Should new inmates be granted this improved status when others had had to earn their keys the "hard way?" ("I worked eight months for my key.") Could additional rewards be devised, such as permitting personal possessions and conveniences in their rooms, for men who made real contributions to the Unit? Should taking part in community activities have anything to do with earning a key? Should inmates help staff decide who should have a key? Throughout the discussions ran the insistence that somehow C-Unit had to become "one unit" instead of two warring camps if staff and inmates were to get on with the other matters that were supposed to help inmates "make it" on parole.

In response to this inmate readiness to deal with the basic issues of organization for community, Project staff (relying on the original agreement with administration that honor system procedures were subject to experiment in C-Unit) encouraged these discussions in Bull Sessions, probed for specific first steps concerning which there could be general agreement, and even scheduled special meetings for the discussion of criteria to govern advancement to honor status in C-Unit.

In these discussions inmates came to moments of general consensus about proposed arrangements.

YA: Could we have a YA committee? I want to help the Unit, too.
A#: That would split us even more. Why can't we be one Unit?
ANOTHER A#: Why not every one honor?
ANOTHER A#: Why not key all the rooms and then when a guy messes up, a staff committee take his key? (Group approval).
COUNSELOR: How about the argument that A#s worked for their keys?
A#: You weren't at the last Bull Session. Every A# said he'd gladly accept it.
ANOTHER A# (to Project supervisor): What are the possibilities?
SUPERVISOR: I'm not sure about getting additional rooms keyed.
A#: There could be a C-Unit way of doing things until we get the rooms keyed.

RESEARCHER: What will be the reaction of other units?

ANOTHER A#: Other units see this is a special project. They don't know what is going on here.

DIRECTOR: Suggests agenda for next meeting concerning "our way of admitting inmates to honor status in C-Unit."

Serious plans to implement such proposals could have led to the invention of patterns in C-Unit for the assignment of rights and the distribution of rewards and penalties appropriate for the new social relationships expected to develop among inmates as members of a community. However, administrative refusal to permit action on the first proposals to overhaul the honor system resulted in frustration among the inmates and a serious loss in the problem-solving momentum that was evidently developing. The moments of consensus no longer occurred and again there were many warring voices. Because inmates and staff were not allowed to try out their initial proposals, they could not learn from experience what might or might not have worked; and the slowly emerging values of community in C-Unit became associated with what persons did when they were not dealing with the critical issues of conformity and deviance.

INCONGRUENT PENALTIES AND REWARDS

Meanwhile DVI's strategy of control became further institutionalized in C-Unit processes.

DISCIPLINE COURT

Soon after the lieutenant supervisor was appointed, C-Unit was permitted to establish its own discipline court. The supervisor and the counselors of any inmates charged with infractions met together in the first half hour of each day's schedule, interviewed the inmates so charged, and determined what penalties should be applied except in those cases of violations so serious that they had to be delayed for review by the institutional Discipline Committee.

In the Project's plan the establishment of C-Unit's discipline court was to have been accompanied by a careful study of rules, penalties, and rewards, and was expected to lead to changes both in the processes by which discipline incidents would be dealt with and in the rules themselves. However, the lieutenant supervisor was completely new to C-Unit's history and expectations; and the entire Unit was so weary of the uncertainties experienced during the weeks between the departure, because of illness, of one supervisor and the appointment of another, that no one was capable at that moment of the work that would have been necessary to examine the entire discipline process and to justify both procedural and substantive changes to DVI's administration. In consequence, the C-Unit Discipline Court quietly established in its own operations DVI's pattern for handling discipline incidents. Penalties all involved some sort of segregation from the community; the hearing was kept confidential, with staff responsible for all decisions; the isolated inmate who was to be disciplined confronted officials outside the purview of community concern; and no group of staff and inmates was assigned responsibility to consider what policies and procedures might be appropriate for dealing with instances of disapproved individual behavior in a community such as C-Unit was expected to become.[16]

REWARDS

Equally important was the way the honor system established a reward system in C-Unit that had nothing to do with the new norms emerging among C-Unit inmates. The story of the first advancement of C-Unit YAs to honor status illustrates how the honor system in C-Unit provided rewards that could be attained by simple conformance to institutional rules, leaving C-Unit without official sanctions to support positive involvement in the community.

The First Advancement of YAs to Honor Status. At the beginning of the Project, the honor system in DVI was managed according to an extensive body of unwritten rules within which discretion could be exercised in a way not visible to the majority of staff and inmates. Choosing the most consistent among the many myths and rumors associated with the honor system in DVI, the C-Unit staff had operated from the beginning on the understanding that eligibility for honor status was automatically earned by three months' "clean time" after the inmate reached DVI proper; and that clean time in the reception center did not count in the period that determined eligibility for honor status.

Staff had anticipated that nonhonor YAs from the first orientation group would be advanced to honor status as soon as its members had earned three months' clean time; and Project records of seniority were kept according to this rule. The Project supervisor, who was officially in a posi-

---

[16] It is notable, for instance, that after the first four months the staff never again used inmate groups to help them deal with such problems as the return to C-Unit of the inmate who had been subjected to sexual pressure or the presence of knives on the Unit. See Chapter III.

tion equal to that of Captain, in that he reported directly to the Associate Superintendent, Custody, had responsibility for room moves within the Unit and assumed that he, with the advice of the appropriate staff members, would also make the decisions about advancement to honor status, since such advancement required moves from unkeyed rooms to those provided with keys.

Furthermore, the counselors in working with nonhonor YAs who were initially misbehaving had used the fact that one might achieve honor status to motivate a number of potential "bad actors" to mend their ways and had been able to involve several of them in active use of counseling and other parts of the program. Accordingly, there was considerable interest among the YAs with seniority in C-Unit about which of them would rate the first moves to honor status. An unofficial list of those eligible for such moves (based on Project records) was used by the counselors in encouraging YAs who had made obvious improvement in behavior. The serious discussions about special criteria for earning honor status in C-Unit had encouraged both staff and inmates to assume that advancement to honor status would be based in part on the inmate's participation in the C-Unit community program.

The first sign that there was inconsistency between Project plans and the expectations of the DVI lieutenant responsible for room assignments came on Monday of Thanksgiving week in November, 1960, when a sophisticated manipulating YA was moved to a C-Unit honor room by an order communicated through the daily transfer sheet prepared by the room assignment officer. This inmate was low on the C-Unit list of eligibles and was perceived by staff and inmates as "putting on a shuck."[17] Both the counselors and the nonhonor YAs who had been told they had priority were upset and there were vociferous demands from inmates for explanations and from counselors for administrative clarification. At this point, C-Unit staff suddenly found that the Project office records were not accurate or up to date. After a good deal of confusion, a C-Unit list of six eligibles, still based on the rule of three months' clean time after admittance to DVI, was prepared on Wednesday and was posted on the Unit bulletin board. These transfers to honor status were expected to take place on the Friday after Thanksgiving and were ordered by the Project supervisor.

On Friday afternoon DVI's transfer list named ten C-Unit YAs for moves to honor rooms, only two of whom were on the C-Unit list. The Project supervisor talked with the DVI room assignment officer who stated

---

[17] *Putting on a shuck:* insincere presentation of self to staff as a "good" inmate interested in reform.

that the three months' clean time rule held[18] but that clean time earned by the YAs in the reception center also counted in the three months. Project staff frantically worked to reorganize their list, although they still found discrepancies between the Project records and the list posted by the assignment lieutenant. (It was later discovered that there were also inaccuracies in DVI's recording of disciplinary actions.) In the absence of both the Superintendent and the Associate Superintendent, Custody, the Project supervisor went to the Captain, requesting that all room moves be postponed until the return of upper officials when policy for advancement to honor status in C-Unit could be established. The Captain refused to delay the moves. The ten inmates on the DVI list were moved Friday evening, although in a meeting with them that evening several requested permission not to move until everything was settled, saying they did not want to take rooms rightfully belonging to other men and that they preferred not to clean up new rooms until they were sure they could remain in them.

When the Associate Superintendent, Custody, returned after the Thanksgiving holiday, he supported the Captain's decision. He confirmed the rule that clean time in the reception center before admittance to DVI would be counted in determining eligibility for honor status; and he placed control over advancement to honor status in C-Unit in the central custody office. From this time on, transfer to honor rooms in C-Unit was made by the institutional room assignment officer, and the Project supervisor had control only over which of the available rooms in C-Unit should be occupied by whom.

It is important to note that in this episode, staff had been trying—somewhat naïvely perhaps—to link institutionally provided rewards to behavior evidencing good citizenship rather than passive conformity. Since the Unit obviously had to live with the honor system for some time, it was important that advancement to honor status become visibly attached to efforts to participate constructively in the community, or at the very least to behavior in the Unit that respected the rights of other inmates. On the C-Unit list of six nonhonor YAs for advancement were several inmates who were visibly improving as community citizens. The institution's list of ten included certain inmates who were known to their fellows as "putting on a shuck" and others who passively conformed. One was also known as an uncaught troublemaker.

---

[18] It was learned only much later that the three-month rule was established simply to accommodate the new situation in C-Unit. Before then the length of time depended on the availability of honor rooms for those with some period of clean time in order of seniority.

Furthermore, since all YAs had spent six weeks or more of their first three months in the reception center, the rewards of advancement to honor status became openly attached to behavioral adaptations established before exposure to C-Unit. When DVI's administration decided, without consultation with Project staff, to count reception center time in advancing inmates to honor status in C-Unit, they diminished the possibility that the honor system could be integrated with the incentive system the Project was attempting to establish. From then on, C-Unit nonhonor inmates had to desire other kinds of rewards than those provided by the honor system in order to become involved in the resocializing program. C-Unit inmates *could* choose to do their own time without involvement in the community and still gain all institutionally permitted privileges. This fact served to establish a core of individuals in the Unit who continued to operate as they would have done in any other unit. The gunseling subculture could be controlled by custodial investigation and segregation. There were no available means except appeal to individuals that could break up the "honor system subculture" so institutionalized in C-Unit.

Up to this period, staff had been engaging inmates in considerable discussion about the honor system problem and its possible resolution. The inability of the Project staff to act in the episode of advancing YAs to honor status firmly established among the C-Unit inmates the staff's current lack of authority to implement their own proposals; and for some time honor system issues were dropped as questions to be considered seriously.

The inmate image of staff as unable to deal effectively with significant problems and therefore as resorting to much talk about minor issues from which no action was expected is illustrated by an article about the "Snark Threat" drawn from the first issue of the *Spectrum* published in February, 1961. (See Exhibit 6.)

CHANGED PATTERNS OF SOCIAL CONTROL IN C-UNIT

There was considerable modification in this unfavorable image of staff after the second Project supervisor was appointed in late January, 1961. This improvement began with a single action connected with the honor system that relieved much of the tension on the Unit and opened the way for the development of program in other directions. Because the new supervisor was a custody lieutenant who had been trained by the Associate Superintendent, Custody, and was trusted by him, he was able to secure permission for keying rooms as rapidly as needed to accommodate C-Unit YAs who had earned honor status under the three months' clean time rule. Partly because the next few months constituted a period of low intake, it was soon evident that the only nonhonor men in C-Unit were

EXHIBIT 6 **Article from The Spectrum, February, 1961: Problem-Solving by Staff as Seen by an Inmate**

Snark* Threat on Upsurge

In the weekly meeting of the C-Unit Staff-Inmate group, held last week, Inmate Clepe Gleet complained of the increase in the Snark problem in C-Unit.

"There have been numerous importunate requests from the inmates to 'get something done' about this problem," stated Gleet.

The problem (snark) was thrown open for discussion, whereupon, a staff member stated that "in a new project such as we have here, until things get squared away, this problem is to be expected."

"Yes," came the swift rejoinder from Gleet, "but as of late, the situation has gotten completely out of hand, and if something isn't done about it immediately, why, there's no telling what could happen. What I mean, it's swollen to gigantic proportions, the snark (problem)."

There followed a heated discussion as to whose responsibility it was to deal with the snark problem. The inmates maintained that it was the responsibility of the staff.

"It should have been anticipated and dealt with accordingly before the project even was started," complained Febul Grout, "we never had this problem (snark) in the other units before."

The staff then made the suggestion that the inmates form a committee to investigate ways and means of coping with the problem.

A nominating committee was formed to select a chairman of the Ways and Means Committee. Clepe Gleet was elected chairman of the nominating committee.

Orvile Heville, who was selected as chairman of the Ways and Means Committee, had this to say: "As far as I can see, there isn't no problem at all. Why let a few snarks bother you?"

---

* *Snark:* invented word, implying "big deal about nothing."

---

the few inmates who were chronic disciplinary problems. Stereotyping of YAs as gunsels practically disappeared, and the fact that the honor system no longer dominated every discussion freed staff and inmates to consider a number of proposed innovations.

During this period of stabilization, three additional modifications in the rules governing the honor system were achieved, each making C-Unit inmates more responsible for their own behavior. Two of these changes were made with the formal approval of upper administration: (1) The extra officer assigned for supervision of the TV room was withdrawn; (2) and the freedom of the floor was granted to nonhonor inmates on weekend evenings, a time when most honor inmates went to the movies.[19] Along with these changes, apparently through the informal process by which many relaxations of a rule led to its disappearance in practice, officers also became accustomed to allowing nonhonor men on the Unit floor during weekend days as well as on holidays when the record player was available.[20] By August, 1961, C-Unit was operating like an honor unit except for minimal restrictions on the few men in nonhonor rooms.[21]

At the same time, as we saw in Chapter III, C-Unit experimented with many other kinds of social control, not dependent on the formal sanctioning institutions, most of them suggested and implemented by the inmates themselves. The Interest Group, the Welfare Fund, and the Emergency Plan all had important implications for developing and supporting community norms for acceptable behavior. The effectiveness of these informal social controls in C-Unit was evidenced by the fact that during a period of general institutional tension, C-Unit YAs more often qualified for honor status according to DVI criteria than did youths in a comparison sample who lived during the same period under the the control system governing other units in the institution. (See Table 2.)

By the end of August, 1961, there was no longer any disagreement among C-Unit staff or inmates about the need to bring C-Unit's sanctioning institutions, such as the honor system, into line with the community's newly developed social values. At a staff meeting toward the end of the second supervisor's period of responsibility, in August, 1961, he and the officers directed much of the discussion to what they would do if "C-Unit was its own little institution and didn't have to worry about consistency with the rest of DVI." They said that the first thing they would do would be to give all inmates a key on entrance to the Unit and withdraw the key

---

[19] Nonhonor inmates in DVI attended movies during weekend day-time hours. Evening hours were preferred by almost all inmates.

[20] No official memorandum approving this practice can be found. When the officers were interviewed a year later, they insisted that the practice had been formally approved early in the spring of 1961 by the lieutenant supervisor.

[21] The evident institutional relaxation about honor system modifications during this period can be explained by several facts that should be kept in mind in evaluating it. With the additional keying of rooms, the large majority of C-Unit inmates had become honor men. This was a period of low intake. And C-Unit discipline rates had dropped dramatically since the elimination of the gunsel subculture leaders, stabilizing at an unexpectedly low point (about one-half the institutional rate).

TABLE 2. *Inmates in DVI for More Than Three Months Having Honor Status*

August 1961 Status	C-Unit		Comparison Sample[a]	
	Youths	*Adults*	*Youths*	*Adults*
	Per Cent			
Honor	76	97	48	87
Nonhonor because not eligible[b]	24	3	42	11
Eligible but nonhonor	0	0	10	2
Total	100	100	100	100
Base	(63)	(58)	(65)	(46)

[a] Comparison sample was drawn from the same universe as C-Unit inmates but was not representative of DVI as a whole.

[b] "Eligibility" defined as three months without disciplinary infractions.

primarily as a penalty for unacceptable behavior in the Unit. In staff meetings from August 11, 1961, to December 1, 1961, one or another officer would volunteer his version of the necessary next step: "Why not make the whole Unit an honor unit and give the new man a key when he comes in?" or "Why not make the Unit an honor unit and let the officer handle minor violations on the Unit by putting the man in temporary room arrest until he can report to the supervisor?"

In the same period, the inmates made it repeatedly clear that they had reached the same conclusion. An A# who had initially been very antagonistic to letting new C-Unit inmates receive keys until they had earned them the hard way came to the Project director with the comment: "I'm going to surprise you in the meeting today. I'm going to suggest that all men get a key when they are admitted to the Unit."

THE SCREEN STORY

During this period of developing program and increasing assumption by inmates of responsibility for social control, another honor-system linked issue was identified and discussed by inmates and staff. This time the inmates' concern was supported by greatly increased trust of each other. After their successful experiences in weathering the two summer riots as a community with solidarity, they asked to have the screens removed from the windows in room doors.

The screens on room door windows in C-Unit had been a sore issue for the inmates since the beginning of the Project. These wire-mesh screens were installed on the inside of the windows in the room doors. They protected the windows from breakage from the inside and also prevented stealing from locked rooms from the walkways, even when the glass had been broken. The inmates reported that the screens made the windows difficult to clean. Some of them complained that they were given "U's"[22] for dirty windows even though the screens prevented them from cleaning the windows properly without the investment of much effort and ingenuity.

The screens had an important symbolic meaning beyond their inconvenience. In DVI all the nonhonor rooms had screens on their door windows, placed there originally to protect officers from articles thrown out of rooms through broken windows. None of the honor units had window screens. For inmates who came into C-Unit from an honor unit, the presence of screens symbolized demotion to nonhonor status.

When the first supervisor raised this issue with the Associate Superintendent, Custody, he learned that the C-Unit screens would not be removed because DVI planned to install screens in all units throughout the institution. This report settled the matter for a long time, although new selectees kept asking about the screens. At the same time, the Maintenance Division postponed putting glass in C-Unit's broken windows, giving as one reason that no work could be started because the screens might have to come out first.

When the second Project supervisor was appointed, the inmates brought up the screen question once more. After observing that C-Unit inmates assumed increasing responsibility for their own behavior, the lieutenant supervisor became convinced that removal of the screens was a reasonable request. He took the C-Unit proposal to the Associate Superintendent, Custody, who indicated that he might consider removing the screens if the C-Unit inmates agreed among themselves that they wanted them out.

When the issue was returned to the inmates, their response was unequivocal:[23] they trusted the community code of "safety in C-Unit" enough to agree on wanting the screens removed. Unfortunately, the process for securing both staff and inmate agreement took two months, and by the

---

[22] *U's:* unit officer grade for unsatisfactory conduct, such as dirt in the inmate's room, not at the time warranting a writeup. Three U's in a month automatically constituted grounds for disciplinary action.

[23] Ascertained by a public opinion poll conducted by the inmate representatives in the Staff-Inmate Group.

time consensus was reached within C-Unit, the lieutenant supervisor who had been instrumental in interpreting the request to the Associate Superintendent, Custody, had left the Project.

The third Project supervisor appointed in September, 1961, was uneasy about proposing this change to the Associate Superintendent, Custody, so early in his administration. In a meeting shortly after his appointment, inmates reported that a recent poll on the Unit had shown an overwhelming majority for removing the screens. The supervisor commented that "There are certain things about this institution we just have to accept." However, when the officers supported the inmates and the background of the issue had been explained, the supervisor somewhat reluctantly agreed to take C-Unit's request to the Associate Superintendent, Custody. Nevertheless, the matter remained unsettled for several weeks, and he and the rest of the staff were unable to give definite answers to repeated inmate questions about action on the screen issue.

The question of screen removal was finally settled in late November, 1961, by a vote in the weekly meeting of the top DVI custody staff. The C-Unit supervisor made a vain attempt to interpret the Project's request. The proposal was voted down by a majority of the DVI lieutenants, who said that granting such a privilege to C-Unit inmates would cause jealousy in the nonhonor units.

In a staff meeting a week later in which the Associate Superintendent, Custody, was present, the Unit officers, who had not yet heard about the decision, brought up the matter anew. "The talk on the Unit is now: 'Why can't they give us a Christmas present and take those damn screens out?'" The supervisor reported that the request had been voted down by the lieutenants. One officer continued: "They say it is an honor unit, so the screens should not be there in the first place." The Associate Superintendent, Custody, firmly refused to reopen the issue, justifying his decision by fear of cell robbing, the expense, and institutional concern over the jealous reaction expected from the nonhonor units. This meeting settled the screen issue for good.

Research interviews with members of the Staff-Inmate Group during the following week[24] clearly reflected the inmate reaction to the decision:

"I think the Staff-Inmate Group is important if you can get things accomplished, but if you can't, people lose interest. For instance, the screens—people talked for six months, and we got some hope. But then it got turned down—so why bother in the future?"

---

[24] Part of a study of inmate attitudes toward work with staff in community groups during December, 1961.

"What is talked about (in Staff-Inmate Group meetings) is ridiculous. There are a lot of ridiculous motions, but nothing is accomplished—you don't get the screens off, and you can't get new mirrors."

"We don't bring up a lot on these meetings—you people can't do anything about them. . . . I think the staff-inmate meetings are a waste of time—you can't do anything."

"The staff is pretty powerless—they have somebody else they have to answer to, too."

"You have your own staff."

DVI's administration had once again refused to accept a C-Unit proposal to reduce the handicaps introduced by honor system provisions into the C-Unit community. This time the consequences for the C-Unit effort to develop its own institutions for control were especially serious. The inmate request to remove the screens was no longer a class or privilege issue. Instead, the men in C-Unit were asking to have their increased ability to maintain order recognized by granting them rights to legislate policy appropriate for a community that could generate mutuality and trust. The denial of this request by upper levels of administration meant to the C-Unit inmates that Project staff were powerless to act in terms of the philosophy they taught; and finally eliminated staff and inmate expectations that the official sanctioning system in C-Unit could be overhauled to support the new social values emerging informally in welfare aspects of program.

At no later time did the honor system, and the associated discipline process, become a subject for discussion among inmates and staff in C-Unit. A conference of the Project staff with upper DVI and Central Office administrators in December, 1961, resulted in the decision that no additional changes in the honor system would be permitted in C-Unit. And plans developed during the second year for reorganizing a second housing unit along C-Unit lines adopted the hybrid honor system as an integral part of the new unit's design.

Thus at the end of the first program year C-Unit had been explicitly defined as a colony. It was permitted some leeway in developing its own cultural activities, such as use of leisure time, communication media and welfare associations, along the lines indicated by its new social relationships. But its formal system of social control embodied the different values and goals of the governing institution. The next chapter summarizes the outcomes for the community of this conflict in community institutions between control by community and control by segregation.

V - THE SPLIT COMMUNITY

DURING C-Unit's second year the organizational themes elaborated in the two preceding chapters continued to develop side by side, although the dissonance between C-Unit's system of social control and its institutions for welfare and communication became increasingly apparent. The consequences for community were unfortunate.

Once the honor system and its related control mechanisms ceased to be a subject for staff and inmate discussion, the program in C-Unit focused on exploiting the potentialities for social activity made possible by the devices created during the first twelve months of the Project's experience rather than on continued reform of community institutions.

Two avenues for development remained available. New areas of group life could be investigated and utilized for program; and the community patterns for social intercourse already invented could be refined and used for increasingly complex activities. The first alternative proved to be almost exhausted by the extensive developments of the first year.

The areas of group life that remained to be incorporated into the C-Unit community program were restricted during the second year partly because DVI administration had reached the limits of its flexibility by the end of the first twelve months of operation. Many significant proposals discussed during the first year ultimately had to be dropped because of procedural barriers. From the beginning C-Unit inmates had wanted to organize for the maintenance and beautification of their quarters. After many conferences, the lack of money for paint, the rules forbidding decoration of walls, and the control over maintenance procedures by a separate division in the institution indicated that C-Unit inmates would not be allowed to muster their own manpower for civic improvement. Plans for special study halls were dropped for lack of rooms that could be supervised during the evening hours. A series of discussions about the availability of musical instruments for individual and group practice was ended by a veto from the education department whose personnel controlled the instruments and the practice room. A request for a C-Unit Christmas service in the chapel with family members attending was denied because of concern over contraband.[1]

DVI had been generous in making possible many innovations; but in the long run it seemed easier to manage such social occasions as the annual Christmas Open House and the monthly C-Unit dinners of the second year than to put inmates to work at tasks with deeper meaning for citizenship.

CONTINUITIES

In spite of these limitations on expansion, certain patterns of program development that had appeared in the first year continued into the second.

1. *Each invention of the first year opened up a series of unanticipated problems requiring revision of goals and adaptation to complexities unforeseen in the original plans.*

THE MUSIC INTEREST GROUP

The original Music Group studied different kinds of music and taped some of their presentations. These were so satisfying to the group that the members proposed to record a series of music appreciation programs to be played over the institution's radio. Suddenly they found themselves in a major controversy with the institutionwide Inmate Advisory Council whose Executive Committee had responsibility with DVI Classification and Treatment officials for radio programming. Acknowledging that they had been precipitate, the members of the Music Group spent two meetings with representatives from the Inmate Advisory Council discussing the many overlapping areas of interest, including the problem caused by

---

[1] *Contraband:* forbidden articles. Of particular concern was the possibility that inmate family members allowed inside the locked portions of the institution would smuggle in drugs, knives, and money.

withdrawing popular records from the central radio room for use in a single unit. As a consequence, the C-Unit music appreciation programs were scheduled as weekly events on the inmate radio system and were played throughout the institution. From then on C-Unit committees found ways of coordinating the Unit's musical activities with the procedures of the larger institution, ultimately sharing its sessions with a popular jazz critic with inmate guests from outside the Unit.

THE NEWSPAPER GROUP

The second inmate group to undertake a Unit newspaper in January, 1961, called itself the Magazine Interest Group and had big ideas about producing a "little magazine." The Magazine Group did not gauge their audience well; they published too little news and set impossible schedules for themselves without adequately assessing the time it took to write, edit, and make duplicate copies. When they ran into administrative censorship of suggestive words at the end of March, the key men resigned. However, in May those inmates who had survived both the ill-fated Communications Committee and the Magazine Group, together with some new members, formed a Newspaper Interest Group that realistically set out to meet the communication needs of the Unit. They used a newspaper format, reported Unit activities, and came to terms with both official censorship and the interests of their inmate audience. In the second year they added to their developing self-discipline by writing their own style book and devoting a number of sessions to group criticism of submitted articles, thus making the editorial process visible to all.

THE WELFARE FUND

The Welfare Fund Board, finally activated in January, 1962, spent three months planning what could be done for "The Unit as a whole" with the 30 per cent of the funds withheld from relief to individuals. First, proposals included a coffee urn for the Unit, cushions for the TV benches, and special equipment to improve reception on the TV. When none of these plans proved feasible, the Board settled for a supply of swimming trunks to be lent to men who could not provide their own; and a library of paperback books for C-Unit, including many reference volumes. The management of the library, in turn, developed into a project of considerable complexity, involving volunteer librarians, rules and fines, and procedures for increasing the book collection as more money was received.

Every group went through the process of revising unrealistic goals, discovering other interests that had to be taken into account, inventing in the face of limitations, and accepting the discipline of the work required for accomplishment of goals.

2. *Gradually an expertise in group process was acquired in the Unit population, and, in consequence, during the sceond year certain quite complex program activities could be managed by the inmates with relatively little facilitation from staff.*

THE C-UNIT FOOTBALL TEAM

For instance, the C-Unit Football Team was organized in January, 1962, as an expression of total Unit resources mobilized by the inmates themselves. In DVI, intramural football was traditionally conducted as a playoff among teams selected by inmate "managers" from among their friends, and no team had recognized identity beyond its place on the sports calendar. Therefore, the suggestion that a housing unit form its own team and enter the institutional contest was revolutionary for DVI.

The idea was proposed one evening on the Unit and discussed with much enthusiasm in the next Council meeting. The inmates pointed out that this plan would be "good for the community" and would help to counteract the "ding-wing" stereotypes about C-Unit still current in the rest of the institution. They believed that a C-Unit team would open opportunities to men who might not otherwise get involved in football, and that because C-Unit men were housed in one living unit, they would have an easier time getting together for practice. In 29 research interviews conducted the day after the team was discussed in the Council, 21 C-Unit inmates had heard about the idea already; all but two of the 29 were in favor of the plan, while 20 thought the team was not only a good idea but would also be "good for the Unit."[2] The day after permission was received from the institutional coach, a sign-up sheet on the bulletin board showed 66 names, including that of a problem inmate who added "water-carrier" after his name.

During the following months of practice, there were many sessions on the Unit floor with the staff blackboard used for diagramming plays, and uncountable hours on the practice field. Although many of the original volunteers dropped out because of the work required and the fact that only 33 uniforms were available, the morale remained high and the team was highlighted in the Unit newspaper. In actual competition the Unit football team fared well enough to be second in the institution, although it included many men who had never played before. At each game

---

[2] Of those who had heard about the team, 85 per cent thought it would be "good for the Unit," while among those who had not heard, only 25 per cent thought so.

C-Unit's team had a large rooting section,[3] the only team so supported. At the end of the season, one of the C-Unit dinners was called a "football banquet" and the team members, together with other sportsmen on C-Unit, were honored.

Staff were minimally involved in managing this community action. The meaning for C-Unit inmates is best revealed by a quotation from a research interview with Big Mac, the team manager and a former college football star, conducted just before he was paroled.

Mac then told a number of anecdotes about his experiences as manager of the team and his pride in being part of a group that had done so well under the handicaps of inexperience, inability to practice, and being the target for other teams to "get." He was particularly proud of the team for a game that they won 6–0 in which his inexperienced players performed so well that, although he was quarterbacking at the time, he simply stood at certain points and watched them play ball. Just before game time, the team had been grouped in the field-house dressing room waiting for one inmate to return from his Parole Board hearing. They believed that if he had had a bad session with the Board, he would go straight to the Unit rather than join in the play. No one knew whether he would show up or not, and Mac needed to know in order to complete his roster for the first lineup. The waiting team was quite silent and said little or nothing. When the missing inmate came in, the group let out a tremendous roar, and Mac, feeling that the team was ready to go, did not give them the usual pre-game pep talk. He simply led them out on the field and they played ball. This is a game that Mac will always remember.

THE GOODBYE PARTY

The Goodbye Party for the researchers in August, 1962, illustrates what the more complex C-Unit inmate system was able to accomplish for itself by the end of its first two years.

During the second year of program, the monthly C-Unit dinners[4] had been used not only for making announcements, but also as occasions for introducing new personnel and saying goodbye to departing staff. Program was necessarily limited on these occasions, because of the poor acoustics in the mess hall and because the hall was needed by the cleanup crew immediately after all had finished eating. However, when it was announced in June, 1962, that the research staff would soon withdraw

---

[3] Including staff members.

[4] One mess hall was reserved for one evening meal a month for C-Unit inmates, staff, and guests. The menu was the same as that served elsewhere in the institution. Staff members and guests distributed themselves along the serving line so there would be one to each table seating four persons. Sound equipment was used for announcements and program.

from DVI after two years of participation and study, it was generally assumed that a C-Unit dinner in their honor would serve to recognize this event.

At this time the Special Projects Interest Group was established by six C-Unit inmates. Administration was told that the first project to be planned by this group would be the program for the researchers' Good-bye Party, and that plans would be brought to administration for approval as soon as they were formulated. The planning was conducted with great secrecy.[5] At first the group asked for a banquet with a special menu in the staff dining-room where speeches could be given in a setting less noisy than the mess hall. When this proposal was denied because of expense, the group proposed a get-together after the evening meal in the field house, which was usually empty during summer evenings because the yard was open until dark. This request was granted, and Project staff was told to be present at 7:30 P.M. on the selected date. The inmates then asked staff to arrange for the sound equipment and for refreshments. The Committee handled the rest of the planning itself.

From the minute the research staff walked into the field house it was evident that this party was the inmates' own. Many associated personnel in the institution had been invited by C-Unit inmates and had brought their wives or friends. Corsages for the ladies had been provided with the help of the Agricultural Laboratory instructor. Members of the Special Projects Interest Group waited at the door to select the proper color of flowers for each woman guest and to offer help in pinning. Refreshments included not only the coffee and cookies provided by the institution, but also iced Kool Aid purchased by the C-Unit inmates from their Welfare Fund. Through the short program the Special Projects Interest Group presided, with the chairman as master of ceremonies and some presentation made by each member of the group. Staff members, including the Superintendent, were invited to the microphone, but instead of being asked to speak, they were interviewed humorously and allowed five minutes apiece for their answers. With considerable flair and pace the program was pushed along, with C-Unit inmates gently kidding themselves and staff, while allowing a moment of genuine poignancy when they presented a beautifully lettered scroll to the director, "A Certificate of Appreciation from the Men of C-Unit." An inmate photographer from the DVI newspaper recorded the high points of the event in pictures.

For two hours inmates, officials, and guests mingled in relaxed conversation while the Kool Aid was finished. No uniform was in sight, and

---

[5] The program was to be a surprise for the guests of honor.

the C-Unit officers (present on their own time) together with upper custody personnel wore civilian clothes. In every outward appearance the inmates were in charge, acting as hosts to the officials, who were on this occasion their guests. C-Unit men had learned how to perceive and use themselves as resources not only for their own welfare and the welfare of subgroups within the Unit, but also in giving to a larger whole of which they were a part.

In such program continuities we see the outlines of a prison community potentially quite different from the set of social relationships described by the inmates in the early Bull Sessions. The C-Unit community had openly adopted the norm that it should be "safe in C-Unit" for each of its members, and had been capable on occasion of being a source of security for all. The resources of its members had been pooled in response to different kinds of needs, and organizational means for the appropriate distribution of such resources had been devised. At its best, the C-Unit community was the arena for the critical discussion of value issues and for developing the social skills required to act on identified problems. The community had devised means by which every individual could participate in the democratic determination of policies to govern all; and, in the Emergency Plan, had shown its competence to take responsibility for itself in the name of the whole population. In necessarily limited ways, C-Unit had become able to relate with its environment through giving as well as receiving. In many facets of its life C-Unit appeared to be the kind of responsible political entity serving the welfare of its members that had been envisioned in the Project's model for the resocializing prison community.

However, in spite of the potentialities inherent in these program continuities, the C-Unit community contained a critical structural flaw in that it was never permitted to design its institutions for the control of deviance according to the value system developed in its welfare institutions. Thus its values lacked power in the governing of men, and were effective only when individuals and subgroups could be motivated to give them voluntary allegiance. As might be expected, this divergence between power and publicly expressed values led to an increasingly evident segmentation in the community between those who exercised power, the staff, and those who were essentially powerless, the inmates.

THE SPLIT BETWEEN CONTROL AND WELFARE

During its first year of program, C-Unit had managed to avoid a split between two inmate classes in spite of the tendency of the honor system to reactivate class antagonisms during each new period of high intake. By the end of the second year, however, a more serious split between the staff who controlled and the inmates who were controlled had emerged because the system of social control within C-Unit operated on different principles from those of its institutions for welfare and communication. Perhaps no other aspect of the C-Unit experience so strongly illustrates the importance of control mechanisms for community treatment in a prison.

The destructive relationships that could develop between staff and inmates under the hybrid honor system with its satellite welfare institutions is illustrated in the moving skid row episode, an event of June, 1962.

MOVING SKID ROW

On a Friday afternoon in June, 1962, the Project staff worked out what appeared to be a useful solution to two problems that had long been plaguing the Unit. One was the problem of inmate requests for room changes that were not deemed necessary for custodial efficiency. The other was the problem of the location of skid row in C-Unit.

The Problems. The first concerned inmate requests for room changes. In order to control room changes within the Unit, requests by C-Unit inmates desiring room changes had always been channeled through the counselors, who were expected to explore such requests and, after consultation with the Unit officers, make recommendations either for or against. This procedure proved to be cumbersome, and from time to time had led to open disagreement among the staff. For instance, an inmate could go to the Project supervisor who might approve a room change without finding out that the counselor had already denied the request; or two or more counselors might approve requests for moves to the same room. Each staff member tended to have a different set of reasons for approving room change requests and the counselors frequently expressed irritation concerning the many reasons advanced against room changes based on custodial interests proposed by the officers. A series of inmate requests, each of which seemed reasonable at the time, could result in the gathering of individuals in one area who then became a clique with a "turf" to protect within the Unit. Room change requests were particularly frequent when there was high turnover in the Unit as resident inmates picked rooms soon to be emptied and timed their requests accordingly. Meeting such requests when new men were brought in could produce a "fruit basket" effect requiring massive readjustments of officer information about who lived where.

As a result of continuing staff disagreement, C-Unit policy on room changes, although always controlled by staff, was often vague, swinging from periods when no room changes were granted through a cycle of gradual relaxation of policy, to yet another period of tightening up and denial of all requests except those justified by custodial reasons. During the administration of the second supervisor, room change policy was fairly relaxed and consistent. However, the lieutenant who became the assistant supervisor in November, 1961, was opposed to any room changes made at the request of an inmate, particularly when the request stipulated a particular room.[6] His recommendations had been frequently disputed or ignored by counselors and officers and he felt keenly this denial of his custodial authority.

From the inmates' point of view, this kind of staff limitation on room changes challenged an important custom in the DVI honor system tradition. Those who had long been in the institution insisted that by careful planning an honor inmate with seniority and knowledge of procedures could gradually work his way from one room to another until he ended up with the room of his choice. Since the supply of desirable rooms was limited in C-Unit by the fact that the rooms in only one Unit were available, men who had been denied by the Parole Board for another year and who therefore had more seniority in the institution and in the Unit than the majority of C-Unit inmates were particularly unhappy when a request for assignment to a particular room was denied and the room was then occupied by a newcomer to the Unit. In addition, the fact that the un-keyed rooms for skid-row inmates were located on the east side, third-floor half tier meant that nonhonor men occupied as many as 14 of the most desirable rooms[7] in the Unit, thus further decreasing the availability of preferred rooms for inmates with seniority and good conduct records.

As a consequence, the second related problem concerned the location of skid row. When the Unit rooms were first keyed as honor rooms, the locks had been changed as each new intake group was admitted, with just enough honor rooms provided as were required by the new selectees already on honor status. The first intake group pointed out that the least desirable rooms in the Unit—those west of the ground-floor tier—had been keyed first. Although there is no record of who decided where the keying

---

[6] His concern stemmed from custodial uneasiness about "cliques."

[7] *Desirable rooms:* Because of summer heat, east side rooms were often preferred. Rooms on the upper tiers were removed from the noise of activities on the floor, and those located at the far end of the unit were both less exposed to traffic along the walkway and provided views of the outside world from their windows.

process should begin, it was generally assumed that the locksmith, unaware that rooms on the third tier were preferred by honor men, had started with the most accessible rooms and had proceeded around the bottom tier and then up to the next as more and more honor rooms were added to accommodate C-Unit men on honor status. Probably the fact that the Unit began with a small group of inmates and was filled gradually had something to do with the fact that all inmates, honor and nonhonor, were first housed on the main floor where they were most accessible to supervision. As skid row was gradually reduced to a small number of rooms on the top tier, there were repeated complaints from inmates about harassment from the nonhonor men. From time to time certain inmates recommended that skid row be located on the first floor, although usually others objected on the grounds that shouting and noise from nonhonor men locked in ground-floor rooms would disturb the men using the game tables. Officers had also reported that illegal activities such as cell robbing and sex pressure were more difficult to control because nonhonor men were limited to the tier most remote from supervision.

Solution. The staff discussion began with the recurrent problem of room changes. The supervisor, two counselors, the two regular officers, and the director proposed, against the objections of the lieutenant and one counselor, that some room-change requests should be honored, although there was no agreement on criteria to govern approvals. For instance, one officer had wanted to move an A# when he was once again denied his parole date simply to ease his upset emotional state by some response from his environment. The director suggested that inmates who used their rooms for quiet work such as pursuing a hobby or reading could reasonably be given rooms away from stairways and shower rooms where the traffic was heavy, although the lieutenant believed that all such inmates wanted was a quiet place to sleep. The staff had already discussed this matter many times in preceding meetings and another impasse seemed inevitable.

The problem began to unravel when both the room-change requests and the location of skid row were examined as essentially two aspects of one problem concerning the supervision of the Unit by the custody officers. The solution called for:

Moving skid row to the main floor, west side, thus freeing 14 more desirable rooms on the upper tier to be occupied by honor men.

A rule for honoring one request for a room change from each man after he reached honor status in order of seniority.

Assigning responsibility for all room-change decisions to one custody officer who would consult with the appropriate counselor and with the other officers.

After reaching these agreements, the whole staff expressed a sense of accomplishment because they believed they had found a way to solve recurrent staff problems and at the same time respond to requests from inmates in a way that should please them.

However, the Project staff had long since ceased to discuss honor-system issues with inmates; and on this occasion they did not consider how to involve the inmates in planning for changes of such importance to them. Officers spoke to individual inmates with seniority, who understood that they could request specific rooms and immediately put in request slips. The impending change was announced during one week's meetings attended by approximately half of C-Unit's inmates, but there was no provision for discussion throughout the population prior to action. The list of moves was prepared by two members of the Unit staff who simply assigned men with seniority in the Unit to the new honor rooms now available on the top floor, starting at the least desirable end of the tier with the inmates who had top seniority.

Consequences. When the order directing the room moves was posted on the bulletin board, the inmates expressed anger instead of the appreciation expected by staff. Most inmates had believed that they would be allowed to designate the rooms they preferred, and some claimed that the officers had promised them either a certain room or priority in choosing. Others found that they were being moved to less desirable rooms. When they protested, they were informed that the one-room move allowed under the new procedures had already been granted and that they could not, therefore, request to be moved back into the rooms they originally occupied.

In an effort to postpone the moves until after reconsideration, the inmates drew up a petition signed by almost half of the men in the Unit, including many community leaders.[8] A committee delivered the petition to the Project supervisor in person, with a request for a meeting with staff. No meeting was called, and the moves were made as ordered.

The staff response was a feeling of real anger that "no matter what you do for inmates, they will always complain." Both counselors and custody officers blamed two inmates as "troublemakers" and agreed that if actual proof was available, the originators of the petition should go to isolation.

---

[8] Petitions from inmates were forbidden by Department of Corrections rules. However, in C-Unit, petitions had appeared at certain points of tension in the early period and had always resulted in opportunities for discussion between inmates and staff. (See TV Story, p. 103.) Since it was easier to request a meeting than to draw up petitions, such documents had not been used by inmates as a means for getting staff attention to a problem for some time.

Although the supervisor had promised that none of the petitioning inmate committee would be penalized because of the petition, the two who had been singled out by staff as responsible were subjected to unpleasant treatment by the Unit officers, who had themselves been reprimanded for not stopping the circulation of the petition.

A staff still sensitive to the issues raised during the honor system discussions would have been aware that arbitrary action affecting an inmate's living arrangements signifies to him the lack of respect for him as a person inherent in the inmate role under a system of control by segregation. It is the inmate's "house"[9] that is affected. In such actions, he is uprooted and replaced without an opportunity to influence decisions about matters of importance to him. Such a change forces him to give up accustomed patterns by which he manages the small area of self-determination permitted him in the institution and poses new problems for him. At the same time, the process communicates to him that in official eyes he is merely a pawn, to be manipulated in terms of some larger plan that does not recognize him as an individual.

Even more important for C-Unit as a community was the meaning for all inmates—whether or not they were moved during this episode—of staff's failure to discuss this issue with them. Throughout the Project's history C-Unit men had always had the right to discussion even when the final decisions were not in accord with their wishes. Now staff had made explicit in action that matters affecting controls and sanctions on the Unit were no longer considered appropriate for discussion with inmates. Not realizing what they had done, the staff had removed without notice the basis for inmate citizenship in the C-Unit community, and C-Unit inmates were left with no recourse other than individual manipulation of the rules, each in his own interest. With this massive reinstatement of the honor system ideology as the basis for staff action, C-Unit inmates could no longer say as one YA had said: "I know what C-Unit is about. It is to help us be men, not inmates."[10]

The Project had hoped to reintroduce prison inmates to membership in a community by requiring them to create their own community. In this process they were expected to learn in action the complexities inherent in political processes, the give and take required between the individual and the larger whole, the costs and rewards of responsible citizenship, and the necessity for rules and justice in a system that is also concerned with the welfare of the individual. As the C-Unit community ultimately developed,

---

[9] *House:* an inmate's room was spoken of as "my house."

[10] The failure of "control by community" in C-Unit was dramatically evidenced in August, 1962, when C-Unit's discipline rate doubled, reaching its highest point since January, 1961, when the gunsel subculture was at its peak.

it projected an image of government by a powerful ruling class that permitted a token democracy among its members only when the issue concerned the amenities of social life. The real lesson about the intimate relationship between control over deviant behavior and the welfare of individuals—the lesson most important for convicted offenders to experience in action—could not be taught in a system explicitly organized to deny its own central value of individual and group responsibility for moral behavior.

In an important sense, DVI's administration was more forthright with the inmates outside C-Unit than the Project in its later period was able to be with its inmate members. In DVI proper, where the system of social control was consistent with the official version of desirable social relations between staff and inmates, the inmate could easily discover the rules of the game and adapt himself accordingly. He knew he was an inmate subject to orders that did not take his wishes into account, but he was not expected at the same time to act in meetings as though he was a citizen with responsibilities. In the C-Unit community, as it operated at the end of the later period, the inmate role was blurred and oscillating. Inmates could ask for a "combo" to play at the annual Christmas Open House and could prepare elaborate decorations to make the third such event "the best yet." But they could not participate in decisions about how their community would be zoned. If the individual learned to manage the complexities of such divergent inmate roles, he could earn a good board report and petition for "goodies" of various kinds. But he did not experience what it meant to be a responsible man in a coherent set of roles governed by the values of the "good" community.

Nevertheless, it is important to keep in mind that throughout the two-year period reported here the C-Unit community of staff and inmates continued to have potentialities both for the high points of the Emergency Plan and the Goodbye Party and for the less desirable relationships evident in the gunsel subculture and the moving skid row episode. Although C-Unit did not become a cohesive and powerful moral community, because of the disparate patterns it used for dealing with value issues, it continued to provide certain resocializing opportunities for those individual inmates capable of utilizing them and motivated to do so.

With C-Unit's flaws and potentialities thus identified, it is useful now to examine the processes by which the Project staff and C-Unit inmates interacted in the community so produced. In the remaining chapters we shall seek to identify the elements of resocializing action and the conditions under which each part of the community made its own most effective contribution to the whole. We shall begin with an exploration of the role of staff in discharging its responsibility for creating the conditions necessary for a resocializing community.

VI - THE STAFF WORK GROUP

THE PROJECT charged the official segment of C-Unit's membership, the staff, with responsibility for building community. In this chapter and the next we shall follow the work of two staffs, each operating in one of the two program years, as they attempted to translate this charge into action under quite different conditions. Examination of their disparate experiences should help us understand the critical role of official personnel in the inmate-staff community, the problems they are likely to encounter, and the conditions that seem most favorable for effective work.

We should first make explicit the expectations built into the charge to the staff.

1. Every staff member was seen as a potential contributor to the socializing processes affecting the inmates in C-Unit. Some would interact more directly with inmates than others, but every staff activity would contribute to the total image of the official world projected to inmates.[1]

2. Since each staff member was seen as a culture carrier and socializing agent as he performed his individual assignment, each needed to be an

---

[1] See Studt, Elliot, "The Client's Image of the Juvenile Court," in Rosenheim, Margaret K., editor, *Justice for the Child*, The Free Press of Glencoe, New York, 1962, pp. 200–216, for the way administrative factors in another agency communicate values to the client.

active participant in the culture-creating body, the staff work group. Only such a group of colleagues could establish an official value system sufficiently broad and strong to supersede the idiosyncratic orientations of individuals and to be effective in guiding the behavior of staff members as they worked with inmates away from the direct influence of their colleagues.

3. From the perspective of the staff, the official program for work with inmates could be seen as the set of staff roles designed to initiate and sustain problem-solving throughout the C-Unit community. To create a coherent program from a set of discrete functional roles each staff member would need to contribute his specialized knowledge to the design that encompassed the work of all and to share in determining the part he would play in the total enterprise.

4. In assuming the program-planning and role-designing functions of administration, the staff work group would become a management body. Two consequences for the work of staff were expected: (1) The staff work group would be an important source of authority, to which each staff member would be responsible for the way he performed his share of the task. (2) Each staff member would share with his colleagues certain management functions in addition to the specialized functions of his primary job as he participated in planning how the joint task of building community was to be accomplished through the work of many individuals.

At the beginning of the action program only the director had a general image of how such a staff group should be organized. At first, the Project staff was simply a collection of individuals chosen from among certain functional groups in DVI: administration, counselors, custody officers, secretaries, and researchers. Except for the director none of the 12 individuals who comprised this pool of human resources had previously been part of an operation in which employees with different functions shared in the definition and implementation of a common task. On previous jobs they had been directly responsible to supervisors for specific jobs assigned to them as individuals. They had become accustomed to accept management as determined for them by relatively inaccessible administrators, to separate treatment functions from the management functions performed at all levels, and to practice specialized treatment methods uncoordinated with the methods used by others. Under the Project plan these individuals were expected to accept responsibility as a group for the institutional life of 130 inmates; and each was expected to assume a new function in helping to manage both the general design and the components of that life.

The Project plan did not stipulate how they were to organize themselves to accomplish this assignment. It did enjoin them to create their own organization by starting to solve the problems with which they were faced.

ROLE STRAINS IN ASSUMING MANAGEMENT
RESPONSIBILITIES

Any staff drawn from diverse assignments and committed to act as a group in managing a community could be expected to have initial difficulties in determining "who does what." Certain problems were particularly intense in the first period for the three basic groups—counselors, custody officers, and researchers—who started with the Project on its chaotic first day and organized their work in a way that made the next period possible.

ROLE REDEFINITION

Of all the staff groups, the first counselors were exposed to the most drastic changes in tasks and expectations. The problems they faced were intensified by their previous experiences in the institution. To understand the readjustments required of them we must remind the reader of their history in a previous project.

Five years before the Project was conceived, the Pilot Intensive Counseling Organization, known as PICO, had been established in DVI as a special demonstration project in institutional treatment. The PICO unit consisted of a supervisor and three counselors, all of whom were professionally educated social workers, plus a research analyst. With part-time consultation from a psychiatrist, each PICO counselor offered individual and group therapy to a small caseload of 20 to 30 YAs randomly selected from the inmate population.

The treatment model used by PICO followed the psychoanalytic tradition. Inmates were perceived as psychologically ill, and treatment was directed to encouraging the individual's development of insight. By design, PICO counselors assumed no responsibility for procedural decisions in their cases in order to avoid interference with the development of therapeutic relationships. Nor did the counselors attempt to direct what happened to their inmate clients in their institutional programs because it was considered important to keep attention focused on the individual's inner change. Inmates assigned to PICO caseloads did not live together in the institution. They were seen weekly or more often in individual interviews and, selectively, in therapeutic groups. PICO counselors did not share responsibilities for their cases with each other; and since communication from the inmate was considered confidential, the counselors did not discuss their cases with the other DVI employees who managed the PICO inmate's institutional career.

It is understandable that this work pattern had isolated PICO in the institution. That there was a difference between the PICO and other DVI counselors was quite evident, inasmuch as the latter, although they had the same civil service status, performed quite different duties under the pressure of heavy caseloads. PICO personnel were dealing exclusively with YAs who represented only half of DVI's population. In addition, middle management in the institution had little experience with PICO in day-to-day work because the PICO supervisor reported directly to upper administrative officials. Although the bulk of DVI's personnel acknowledged PICO's prestige in the Department of Corrections and tended to believe that it was designed according to an "ideal" treatment model, that is, psychotherapeutic, they had little opportunity to observe PICO's work or to understand its principles. As a consequence of its isolation, the DVI stereotype about PICO combined uninformed awe for psychological treatment with exasperation toward a staff group whose members made no observable contribution to the general tasks of running the institution.

As might be expected, PICO staff members had operated in a way that reinforced their differences from the rest of the institution. They knew little about the problems and duties of other personnel, and tended to devalue both the routine work of the regular DVI counselors and what they presumed to be the antitreatment stance of custody. They thought of themselves as the one group of personnel who cared about inmates and saw other employees as, at best, victims of "the system." Within PICO, all relationships were intense, among staff members as well as between counselors and inmates. Although the PICO counselors made a common front against the rest of DVI, within their own group they developed private therapeutic styles, competed in technical sophistication, and established conflicting positions in regard to professional issues that often took on strong personal overtones.

PICO counselors, whose professional education had prepared them to place high value on one-to-one relationships with clients, had learned the PICO version of treatment under conditions of strong reinforcement: high prestige, organizational isolation, and intense ingroup interaction. This group was now expected to spearhead a development that called upon counselors to share a total caseload not only with each other but also with other institutional employees; to work with custody officers as colleagues in the management of program; to assume the procedural duties of regular classification counselors; and to define treatment as problem-solving in the present. In many ways the values and skills the counselors had learned in the previous PICO model were challenged by the tasks outlined for them in the new project.

As would be true for any group, those aspects of the new role that did extend and support the activities of the old were more easily accepted by the counselors than were some of their new duties. The counselors enjoyed their increased ease of access to inmates in the living unit. They found discussions with officers and other staff members helpful in rounding out their information about inmates. And they experienced considerable satisfaction in the opportunity to manage the institutional careers of the inmates who were assigned to them for treatment.

On the other hand, the counselors found that some of the new tasks interfered with the activities to which they attached high value. Planning for individual inmates was rewarding but also confronted the counselors with those institutional limitations that blocked the implementation of ideal plans. Managing the procedural details for which they had newly assumed responsibility appeared at first to limit their time for therapeutic contacts. Task groups required problem-solving skills different from those used in group therapy, and the counselors found themselves encountering inmate hostility when they responded in customary therapeutic fashion in this new kind of group. When interest groups were first proposed, counselors were concerned that "I didn't get a professional education in order to manage recreational activities."[2]

Above all, the counselors resisted the program planning responsibility required by joint staff operation. In the later years of PICO, the counselors had been minimally involved in administrative decisions and they did not perceive staff discussion of management issues as an aid to therapeutic activities. The counselors felt that program-planning was the responsibility of the director and that she should instruct them what to do, since she had the experiential knowledge which they lacked. The psychoanalytic formulations to which the counselors were accustomed did not help them relate organization to treatment, and they perceived the researchers as responsible for the application of social science concepts to the Project's work.

Thus many of the new counselor tasks were not initially rewarding. However, because there were aspects of the new counselor role that supported the activities in which the counselor did find satisfaction, each one made an initial adjustment that continued into the second half of the first year. Essentially he came to terms with the new job by identifying in his caseload a central group of inmates to whom he offered individual and group counseling. In this little island of activity linked with his past, he gained sufficient security to live through the multitudinous new tasks whose significance he did not at first perceive.

---

[2] See Cumming, John and Elaine, *Ego and Milieu: Theory and Practice of Environmental Therapy*, Atherton Press, New York, 1962, p. 114, for the response of doctors in a mental hospital to administrative tasks necessary for recreational activities but apparently not "medically relevant."

The officers had a quite different experience in moving to the role designed for them in the Project because they were already oriented to a certain level of management as their primary function. Although they experienced other role strains, such as those in relation to their fellow officers outside the project who taunted them unmercifully about their assignment to a "ding wing" and in adapting to the changed functions of Project administration and counselors, the officers' job of supervising the living processes on the Unit continued to be basically defined as they had formerly experienced it. As program developed, almost all the new conditions served to make their accustomed roles in managing inmates on this Unit somewhat easier and more rewarding. The fact that the inmate population was both smaller and more stable than that of the ordinary living unit reduced the amount of detail for which each officer was responsible. Because all three officers (including the relief officer) were regularly assigned to C-Unit, they were able to agree on a set of working arrangements that reduced both uncertainty among themselves and the friction with inmates that appears when officers on different shifts interpret the rules differently. Discussions with counselors provided information that helped the officers deal more easily with troublesome inmates. Staff meetings were a new forum for the expression of opinions with colleagues and considerably raised the status of the officer position in their own eyes and in the minds of inmates. "They see us go off to meetings and know that we have something to say about what happens to them."

As a result of officer relaxation, relationships between officers and inmates in C-Unit gradually assumed an informality that reduced hostility and permitted an increasingly flexible, human interchange between "the man in the uniform and the man in the blues." Later, vacation and sick-leave relief officers began to report that C-Unit was a good place to work. "The inmates are easier to handle." "This is the first time since I have been in DVI that I have been asked to a meeting to discuss my work." The officers found that the new aspects of their role increased their stability, prestige, and effectiveness in job management. Accordingly, the officers in C-Unit did not experience the strain of changes in role with the same intensity as the counselors.

AD HOC INNOVATION

Because so little detailed planning had been possible before the C-Unit program began, the new jobs proposed for counselors and for custody officers had not been mapped out in advance. As could be expected, the first four months of action were characterized by considerable *ad hoc* experimentation in new activities by each staff member with little sys-

tematic coordination among the group.[3] Because each member was repeatedly faced by situations for which there were no prescriptions to
guide action, each one tended to act on his own judgment without awareness of the possible consequences for others. This somewhat random exploration of the new action possibilities produced strains for all.

The lack of coordination in role innovations was particularly observable
in the early relationships between custody officers and counselors on the
Unit. For the first time in DVI, both groups shared the same work space.
Although officers were held responsible by the institution for order in the
Unit, the counselors were perceived both by the officers and by themselves
as having a superior position in responsibility for "program." Since the
program was now, in fact, the functioning of the Unit, it was obviously a
subject for joint planning but at first the staff did not know how to use
the planning sessions. In this situation *ad hoc* innovations on the part of
either group had repercussions in the work of the other. Of the two, the
officers experienced particularly severe strain.

The divergence in status and function between counselors and officers
appeared dramatically in an early orientation session when all the counselors, researchers, and inmates were introduced to each other, while
neither of the two officers, who had made a special effort to be present,
was mentioned.[4] Officers soon found themselves confronted by inmates to
whom a room change or special arrangement in the Unit had been promised by a counselor without consulting the officer. One officer recalled
from these early days that the Project supervisor frequently appeared
during a weekend without having notified the officer that there would be
activities on the floor of the Unit, and that often officers learned about program plans from inmates before they had word from the counselors.
More than once a counselor on the Unit for an evening discovered what
he considered to be a state of tension among the inmates and called a
meeting while the officer stood by without any recognizable share in the
activities. Occasionally, serious difficulty resulted, as in one incident when
the counselors decided to hold a meeting of nonhonor inmates on the
floor of the Unit during an out-of-bounds period, and the officer, who had
helped to round up the inmates, was later "chewed out" by the watch
sergeant responsible for C-Unit along with other units. Both the supervisor
and the officers used the bulletin board for communicating with inmates,
and sometimes conflicting notices about such matters as articles permitted
in rooms or the scheduling of TV programs were posted at the same time.

---

[3] This kind of readjustment period should probably be expected even with detailed
planning.

[4] Inmates began to speak of officers as part of "staff" only during the second six
months of program.

One particularly imaginative officer explored the possibilities of his new role in ways that repeatedly got him into trouble with either the rest of the Project staff or his custodial superiors, or both. His first action was designed to make C-Unit "the best unit in the institution." He posted a special set of rules concerning cleanliness and contraband that infuriated the inmates and was not upheld by the Associate Superintendent, Custody. After the storm of protest had died down, he turned his attention to work with individual inmates. He won much appreciation from the counselors when, having observed the upset condition of a newly admitted schizophrenic inmate, he assigned him to a protected job in the Unit TV room. However, he was reprimanded by DVI officials for the same action because he had taken it on himself to change an inmate's job assignment without referring the matter to the assignment lieutenant. In another situation this officer was in trouble with both counselors and custody because he had acted beyond his assigned authority in handling an incident of sex pressure and had bypassed the counselors who were also working with the suspected inmates.

Not all the innovations of these two staff role groups were disturbing to the other, and a pattern of work that respected the contribution of each emerged. The officer mentioned above organized a card file for the Unit office in which officers and counselors recorded information that would be useful to both.[5] The counselors took turns carrying the keys for the officers when there were meetings with inmates in which the officer should participate. A tentative plan for approving room changes was formulated. The officers began to be notified ahead of time about plans for the program and so did not have to depend on information from inmates. The officers joined the counselors in planning for the first Christmas Open House, a new venture for both, and their help in outlining the procedural changes required for this activity was greatly appreciated. With these developments, the disruption of unplanned innovations was reduced.

SHARED DECISION-MAKING

The tensions inevitable when two or more role groups become responsible for decisions about issues in which all have a stake appeared most clearly in the early period in the relationships between the researchers and the counselors.

One might have expected the first collisions of disparate staff interests to occur between custody and counselors. But initially these two groups

---

[5] This device was especially useful in the early days as a symbol of joint work on a common task. It passed into disuse when informal communication between officers and counselors became customary.

maintained their separate domains of responsibility much as they had before they were put together in the one program. Everyone took it for granted that counselors were in charge of case processing and the custody officers knew little about such activities except that counselors talked with inmates. The custody officers assumed their primary responsibility for managing procedures on the Unit and, when counselors were involved in such matters, they also tended to accept the general DVI attitude that custody, at one level or another, was the ultimate authority on rules. Only in the issue of who should approve room-change requests within the Unit did counselors and officers in the initial period claim overlapping responsibilities for the same decision and discover that they had divergent interests in many cases.

There was a less clear separation of interests between the researchers and the counselors. From the beginning, both groups had been engaged in designing the broad outlines of the Project's action program. The same conceptual framework determined both the action program and the research program. The researchers were understandably concerned that the basic principles of the community model be expressed in the action program they were expected to study, while the counselors were more interested in maintaining activities in which they were already secure. The researchers were also considerably more sophisticated in using the social science concepts that supplemented the psychoanalytic formulations to which the counselors were accustomed and often took the leadership in discussing how these should be implemented in the program.

The confusion between the two groups was heightened both because the role of participant observer was new to all members of the Project, and because the PICO researcher had previously shared in the clinical work of that phase. Accordingly, the counselors initially saw the added research staff as potential service personnel. When, as we have noted, the counselors resisted the program-planning responsibilities inherent in their new role, the researchers tended to take over, thus increasing counselor apathy. As a consequence, a number of early plans were proposed by the researchers and adopted without sufficient examination by the counselors who had to implement the plans.

In spite of the fact that the researchers became aware of the problem and identified the appropriate contribution of research to action planning, they were handicapped by a stereotype within the Project that reappeared from time to time, namely, that the researchers had a monopoly on ideas and were therefore responsible for telling the action people what to do. It was some months before program-planning was actually a joint activity involving all role groups in the Project, with each contributing to ultimate solutions from the perspective of different kinds of competence.

NEW STAFF-INMATE RELATIONSHIPS

Possibly the most severe readjustment faced by all staff members involved the new types of roles permitted to inmates. Each staff member had been trained to relate to inmates under conditions that made him unilaterally responsible for decisions. The rules administered by the custody officer often reduced his interchanges with inmates to a routinized impersonality. The professional conventions of the counselor also limited the possible kinds of interaction between himself and the inmates. In the new activities inmates were expected to become participants in decision-making. Relationships between staff and inmates were to be characterized by the spontaneity and honest expression of opinion that is more frequently found in normal social interchange. In the transition from distance-producing patterns for inmate-staff relationships to the kind of management that raised the status of inmates, almost every sort of staff and inmate interchange became ambiguous and anxiety-provoking.

For instance, the counselors tended at first to open committee discussions with the implicit assumption that inmate opinion would be the final arbiter of all issues. It took time for the staff to identify those decisions for which responsibility could be delegated entirely to inmates; those areas in which joint decisions were appropriate; and those that had to be reserved by staff for decision after discussion with inmates. One officer resolved the problem he experienced by segmenting his roles with inmates. When he was supervising the Unit he was the tough authority; when he sat in meetings with inmates he asserted that no holds were barred and that no consequences would follow regardless of what was said in the meeting; while in more informal conversations with inmates he tended to discuss his personal ambitions in a way that implied an unreal mutuality. Since all staff had now become more open to unstructured communication from inmates, each staff member found himself approached about matters that properly should be taken to one of his colleagues. Staff members frequently overresponded, each acting as though every inmate request must be dealt with favorably by anyone to whom it was addressed.

As could be expected, inmates were severely affected by such uncertainty in staff operation. Some of the hostility and frustration expressed by inmates in the early days can be understood as a reaction to this kind of uneasy staff behavior.

INCONGRUENCE BETWEEN STAFF ROLES IN THE PROJECT AND IN DVI

A different kind of strain was experienced by all staff members as they interacted with personnel in the rest of the institution. DVI's staff had been prepared for the new duties assumed by Project staff members primarily by announcements, with little information about how C-Unit activities would be coordinated with the work of divisions within DVI. Most important, DVI was unprepared for a project in which management functions were distributed throughout all echelons of personnel.

The DVI assignment lieutenant was puzzled when counselors appeared in his office to confer about proposed job changes for inmates, and he often made disruptive decisions about the programs of individual inmates without thinking to involve the C-Unit counselors in the plans. The Associate Superintendent, Classification and Treatment, did not expect to deal with a counselor, grade I, about the availability of musical records for the C-Unit Holiday Committee. The watch sergeant assumed he would continue to supervise the C-Unit officers as he did in any other housing unit although they were now directly responsible to the Project supervisor. The chief of the maintenance division would accept requests from C-Unit only through the Associate Superintendent, Custody. And the Superintendent was puzzled, even alarmed, when he realized the extent to which policy issues were being openly discussed with both inmates and lower-level staff before proposals from the Project were communicated upward.

These encounters constituted "role shocks" for both Project staff and institutional personnel. Unfortunately, the problems so generated could be handled only on a case-by-case basis because there were no regularized patterns for coordination between the activities managed according to the Project's model and those of other divisions in DVI.

EMERGENCE OF THE STAFF WORK GROUP

The staff became a group out of sheer necessity two months after the first inmates had been admitted to C-Unit. The inmate committees had resigned in anger saying, "Learn to do your own job before you talk about helping us."[6] Serious upsets in program plans had been experienced because communication with DVI's upper administrative officials had not been consistent. Every staff member was determining his own activities without reference to the total coverage of a common task, with the result that everyone was over-extended and exhausted. There was evidence of duplication of effort and interference with each other's work, even in such minor details as the ducating of a single inmate by more than one counselor or group leader for the same hour.

The first staff meeting, in which each member was equally involved and willing to state problems openly, occurred on November 17, 1960. It was

---

[6] See pp. 68–69.

angry in tone because each staff member was highly critical of the others; but at last the staff were talking about "what we need." Each member knew from his own experience that he had to have the support of a co-ordinated staff plan and each was ready to give top priority to developing "better communication among ourselves." The staff therefore decided to retrench the group program temporarily and to schedule as many staff meetings as necessary for the discussion of "what we are doing and why." It was further agreed that time spent by counselors with inmates would be devoted to enlarging staff knowledge of the inmate population, with special attention to inmate leaders, regardless of their positive or hostile orientation to the C-Unit program. With this information, the staff should be able to plan action about inmate needs.

This meeting ended with general consensus that "now we are getting somewhere." However, the next two discussions were characterized by apathy and an unfriendly silence. The staff members had stated their problems but still did not know how to get started in joint problem-solving. For each, it was "those others" who had to change. At this point there was a still more serious crisis to be faced, which involved the move of the first YAs to honor status.[7]

With this added evidence that coordination of activities was essential if any program was to continue, the staff settled down to work. In two weeks they outlined a manageable group program together with a ration-ale for the use of each kind of group.[8] Because they had been collecting information about the inmate population,[9] they were able to relate the proposed group program to identified inmate needs and to agree on the use of different approaches to each of the various subgroups. Assignments of individual staff members to responsibility for groups were made by staff agreement that each approved investment of time was essential to the total program. After this task was completed, for the first time the staff were able to consider openly and without rancor a serious error made by one member (the director) in communicating with another through an in-mate. The staff were beginning to learn that the community program was the responsibility of all and that one member had to support the work of others if a major failure involving everyone was to be averted. They were also learning that it was both safe and necessary to examine mistakes in open discussion if all were to learn what was needed in order to do the job.

---

[7] See pp. 115–118.

[8] See pp. 73–76.

[9] In securing and formulating information about the total inmate population and its subgroups, officers demonstrated one aspect of their unique usefulness to the total task.

In December, 1960, immediately following this sequence, the staff had two very satisfying experiences in using inmate groups to help staff in problem-solving. In each, an *ad hoc* inmate group was convened to work with the staff concerning a serious incident in Unit life: one was a case of pressure for sex involving a YA; and the other, information that a Mexican gang had accumulated a set of knives. Because the staff had made provisional analysis of inmate social organization in the Unit, they were able to select the right participants (from both staff and inmate points of view) for each of the groups. With the advice and help of the inmate leaders, it was possible to bring the inmate who had been under sex pressures safely back to the Unit from protective custody. In the meeting with the ethnic group leaders, arrangements were made to have the accumulation of knives turned over to staff. The patterns for problem-solving that had proved successful for the staff as a group had now become available for use in problem-solving with inmates. The success of these experiences in group problem-solving eased some of the tensions and provided the staff with experiences that would be exploited repeatedly during the following months.

PROBLEM-SOLVING IN THE STAFF WORK GROUP

A number of factors contributed to the emergence of a staff work group capable of exercising responsibility for problem-solving management. In the first place, as we have noted, the staff were surrounded by an environment that was responding with anger to inefficiency and refused to grant requests presented haphazardly. However, punishment from the outside would not have been sufficient to have brought this set of individuals together as a problem-solving group.

It was more important that already all staff members had been exposed fragmentarily to the rewards potential in the new situation. Both the counselors and the officers had been permitted to continue their accustomed patterns of operation long enough to find that the new setting facilitated some activities in which they already found satisfaction. Both were repeatedly placed in situations in which more power than they were accustomed to command was available for use in controlling their own and the inmates' destinies, provided only they could learn to use that power effectively. In the initial chaotic weeks there had been momentary successes resulting from coordinated action between two or more members of staff that encouraged them to experiment further,[10] although at first

---

[10] See custody officer-counselor cooperation in planning for an actively schizophrenic inmate in Chapter IX.

most staff members were unclear why some actions were successful while others resulted in failure. Through this period the short working papers produced by the director, each addressed to the analysis of a commonly experienced problem, helped to focus staff attention on contributing factors and on alternatives.[11] In the successful experiences in dealing with serious problems in inmate behavior occurring between November 17 and December 22, 1960, each staff member had gained first-hand knowledge of group problem-solving as a useful process. When the administrative situation was stabilized by the appointment of the second supervisor, in late January, 1961, the staff were ready to implement their group program for inmates and to undertake additional problem-solving activities.

It was no accident that the staff first operated as a productive group in managing the Interest Group program. This was a new venture for everyone, so there were few preconceptions drawn from past education or experience that had to be defended in any course of action undertaken. The program was formulated under two stringent conditions: the staff had to find a way to establish less strained relationships with inmates; and, given the serious limitations on time, any action had to be justified on the basis that it could be maximally effective in getting to inmates. Status differences among staff tended to disappear in this situation because the idea that seemed workable was more important than who had the idea. The abilities and skills of all staff members were seen as potentially usable in such an endeavor. As staff decided together, "We are going to put staff energy into facilitating the Research Seminar, the Music Group, the English-Speaking Group for Mexicans, and the Painting Group, because this way we reach four quite different subgroups among the inmates"; the words justifying action had the same meanings for everyone. Throughout the life of the Project it was notable that staff became most clearly a responsible group when designing a program that was new to all for which discrete responsibilities had not already been routinely allocated. Such an experience often had beneficial effects for the management of other situations in which role strains were more severe.

The Interest Group activity contributed in other ways to staff cohesion and communication. For one thing, staff members who did not ordinarily talk with each other outside meetings were now conferring. Interest Groups met on several evenings a week and often more than one was scheduled for the same evening. It was therefore necessary that several staff members—counselors and researchers alike—should take responsibility for evening duty one night a week. Often a counselor who had planned with inmates for a group meeting needed to pass on information

[11] See, for instance, Exhibit 4, pp. 104–106.

about the plans to the person who would be responsible for general supervision of the Annex on the evening that meeting was scheduled. This meant sharing responsibility, reporting back, and the exchange of suggestions in order to ensure the continuity of program. For the first time, one staff member learned what the other was doing and found he could trust another person with "his" inmates. When the Chess Club or the Fine Arts Group disbanded, there was general understanding of the difficulties. Everyone was interested in the productions from each group, whether it was Big Mac's tape-recorded introduction to a blues record or the unexpectedly strong painting coming from the brush of an inmate who had been known up to that point only for his moodiness and disorganization. One heard less about "my group" and more about "our program."

Perhaps the most important factor in the success of the Interest Group Program was the fact that for the first time the staff as a group were dealing in a concerted fashion with needs actually experienced by inmates. They were facilitating inmate requests and suddenly found themselves welcomed among inmates. When inmates and staff were freed of the inmate perception of staff as "trying to change me" and joined in explorations of common interests, both staff members and inmates revealed themselves as much more attractive persons than either had expected. Staff members glowingly reported these experiences of mutuality with another part of the community and spoke of using the new relationships to facilitate the next steps in situations where more strain between them could be expected.

CHARACTERISTICS OF THE STAFF WORK GROUP

Several phenomena appeared spontaneously in the work of the staff as a group and continued to be characteristic of staff work in periods of high creativity. First, each staff subgroup began to be interested in the work of others. Counselors undertook to formulate a revised plan for case recording and conferred with secretaries about fitting the new procedures into the flow of their work. At the request of secretaries, counselors, and researchers two meetings were called to coordinate their procedures. Custody officers pointed out that they did not know what the counselors did. It was discovered that both officers and counselors were wasting time because officers could not answer inmates' procedural questions and therefore had to refer them for interviews with counselors when a short answer from the officer, provided he had the information, was all that was required. Accordingly, three weekly staff meetings were devoted to introducing the officers to case processing. When evening training sessions for the staff were considered, the planning committee tried to find a time convenient for all staff groups, including officers and secretaries.

At the same time, role groups called meetings for themselves whenever the problem under consideration did not involve others. The researchers met regularly so they would be under less pressure to talk about their own business in meetings of the action staff. The secretaries called *ad hoc* meetings to determine responsibilities in the pool or asked administrative staff to sit with them when new problems were identified. The counselors and the supervisor met occasionally to discuss such matters as classification procedures; and the lieutenant supervisor met on occasion with his officers. These meetings tended to be short, task-focused, and called only when there was a need. There was increasing evidence that everyone knew what a meeting was for and was able to use meeting time selectively and with expedition.

At the same time, a number of new roles emerged, or persons with one primary role took on new tasks. Secretaries became leaders of interest groups. The inmate clerk position emerged as significant for leadership in program activities. Volunteers and students were used as group leaders. A chaplain intern in the institution commented that "a community should have a chaplain" and shared in the C-Unit program during his six months of training. These persons including inmates were involved in staff work sessions whenever it was appropriate for their jobs. Later when parole officers were assigned to the Project, the work on the days they could be present was focused on pre-parole planning, and the staff meetings scheduled were used to coordinate the work of the parole agents with that of the resident staff.

Throughout this period there was increasing pressure from all groups for a systematic introduction to the conceptual framework of the Project. Staff now wanted to know, not just "why are we having an Interest Group Program," but "how does each part of the program fit within an organized perspective on managing a community." For some months the agenda of regular staff meetings had included what was called "training"; but each week there were urgent action decisions to be made and the more general topics were postponed. In addition, no one staff meeting could involve all members of each role group because of shift schedules.

Accordingly, a staff committee undertook to organize a ten-week series of evening meetings to be led by the director. These meetings, scheduled from late July to early October, 1961, were attended by all researchers, counselors, and secretaries on their own time.[12] Most of these individuals did supplementary reading as well.

---

[12] During this period there were changes in the administration of the Project, and the new supervisor found it possible to attend only the later sessions. Two custody officers had planned to attend but personal emergencies interfered.

The training program was focused on the use of community in treatment, emphasizing the staff role in managing the kind of community needed for resocialization. The sessions were organized as discussions in which the staff made formulations on the basis of their own recent experiences as to how behavior could be understood as the product of persons interacting with their social environment; how change in behavior involves change both in persons and in the patterns for relationships available to them; how helping people change their environment also helps them grow as persons and so affects behavior; and how modifying the system of social relationships in which persons live contributes to their resocialization. In each meeting, illustrations from current staff behavior (both successful and ineffective) and commonly remembered inmate behavior were used to provide concrete referents for conceptual formulations. Almost immediately, discussions in staff meetings took on a new resonance as one or another staff member made a proposal "because as we were saying last night if we do this we ought to get this kind of result." A kind of shorthand device for communication developed among the staff. One would hear the chief secretary comment when assuming a new task, "See—'flexible role system' "; or a counselor would begin a proposal by saying, "Now according to the 'treatment model.' . . ."

Problem-solving in the staff group evidenced the same characteristics we observed when studying the processes by which the inmates became creative participants in the official program. In both groups there was evidence of increasing interest in the operation and needs of subgroups. Both staff and inmate groups changed in character from collections of mutually defensive individuals to task-focused organizations. Honest criticism was welcomed while hostile griping diminished. In the staff work group as in inmate groups, new roles appeared and task groups readily formed and engaged in activities on an ad hoc basis. And at the same time both staff and inmates showed increasing interest in the larger community within which they acted.

PROBLEM-SOLVING MANAGEMENT AND INMATE CREATIVITY

It is important to note that the period during which the staff functioned as a work group rather than a collection of employees coincided with the period of creative program for inmates described in Chapter III. But more than a temporal relationship connected staff problem-solving with similar inmate behavior.

The reciprocity between the staff work group and inmate participation in official program seemed to operate as follows. Staff perception of what was possible in work with inmates was clearly limited by the experiences of staff members in their own work group. What staff did not perceive as possible for themselves they could not provide for inmates. However, when the staff did give their attention to working as a problem-solving group, they had both new experiences to use in designing their work with inmates and a new fund of information for understanding the problems they were attempting to solve. The inmates' response to the newly provided opportunities, in turn, reinforced staff's ability to be aware of their own operation. Staff were thus freed to explore still better modes of operation for themselves and to make similar patterns available to the inmates.

The Staff-Inmate Group. This reciprocal process can be observed in action by following the changing plans devised by staff for communication between staff and inmates about total Unit concerns. To understand why a year was required to design an effective mechanism for this kind of communication, we must start with the planning period preceding the action program.

From the beginning it had been agreed that some form of communication between staff and inmates about the concerns of the total Unit was essential to building a resocializing community. However, it was not easy at first to see what device could ensure such communication. Two possible means were rejected in the planning period. The "community meeting" involving all staff and inmates was not considered because of the lack of facilities for accommodating so large a group. Meetings of each inmate caseload, led by its own counselor, were rejected because of the PICO history of competition among counselors and the fear that such a procedure would establish three disparate communities, each attached to one staff member and inaccessible to the others. After much discussion in the planning period, a tentative plan was adopted, establishing a Staff-Inmate Group to meet weekly to consider "the health of the Unit." This group was composed of all available staff members plus seven inmates chosen by staff to act as representatives of inmate opinion during one week of office. This pattern for staff and inmate communication about Unit problems was used during the first three months of Unit operation.

As could have been anticipated, the first Staff-Inmate Group plan satisfied no one. No group met together long enough for the inmate members to learn to trust each other. Large issues identified at one meeting could neither be explored nor resolved by those concerned because there were no provisions made for continued discussions by the same persons. Most inmates spoke only for themselves, if they spoke at all. Inmates complained that they had no means of identifying the opinions of their fellows before a meeting or for reporting back after it. As was noted earlier, this first plan resulted in distorted communication between staff and most of the inmate population.

The first Staff-Inmate Group plan had been devised before the staff had been exposed to the realities of inmate association. The staff had naïvely assumed that the inmate "grapevine" would ensure rapid transfer of information from one inmate to another; and that any inmate, given the official designation of "representative," would be used by other inmates for communicating information to the staff. The staff also feared that the election of representatives by inmates would establish a political machine in which only "dukes" would have access to communication with staff.

The first plan for inmate-staff communication had established a staff-controlled mechanism that not only determined which inmates—"those ready for the role"—should participate, but also provided that no inmate group concerned with policy issues should develop strength through continuity of membership. In part, because the staff feared open communication among their own members and perceived power as more often destructive than not, they had created in their own image an organizational device for work with inmates in which neither free communication nor power could develop.[13]

During November and December, 1960, the staff became a group and did something about their own faulty communication system. Their first accomplishment was designing a rational plan for inmate-group activity. At first, the staff considered dispensing entirely with any community-focused group because of the obvious deficiencies of the Staff-Inmate Group plan as it had operated up to this time. However, at the insistence of the researchers that some symbol of community should remain if the program was to be more than a disjointed collection of small groups, the staff drew up a blueprint for a new kind of Staff-Inmate Group.

Inmate representation was enlarged to include ten staff-selected inmates and three Unit-elected representatives to DVI's Inmate Advisory Council. The ten inmates selected by staff would act as representatives of the C-Unit population for four weeks at a stretch, while the Inmate Advisory Council representatives would continue in office for the three-month period provided by their election to that office.

The staff hoped by this new plan to use the Staff-Inmate Group as a training ground for those inmates perceived by the staff as ready for community-focused activity, to widen the communication channels by

---

[13] It is significant that, although the official name for the Project's action program was the "Inmate-Staff Community," the need of the staff to control revealed itself in the title "Staff-Inmate Group" assigned to the body responsible for communicating about community interests.

reaching a larger number of inmate subgroups, and to maintain this "citizen" role accessible to all inmates who could be encouraged to think of the Unit as important. The staff were not yet ready to open communication channels freely to inmates and so continued to maintain considerable control. However, they now sufficiently perceived the necessity of open communication between staff and inmates to include elected inmate representatives in the Staff-Inmate Group, and to permit an inmate group with sufficient continuity in office to influence policy and to report staff operation more accurately to the inmate population.

The new plan was put into operation in January, 1961, after the appointment of the second supervisor. At first, there were no Inmate Advisory Council representatives available to meet with the Staff-Inmate Group because up to this point C-Unit inmates had not cared to run for election. However, at the next regular institutionwide election there was a lively political campaign in C-Unit and three new men, previously not noticed by staff as inmate leaders, were elected to the Inmate Advisory Council, thereby also becoming members of the Staff-Inmate Group.

At first, the new plan did not work much better than the earlier arrangement. Inmates clearly perceived the Staff-Inmate Group as a small Inmate Advisory Council designed for bargaining between C-Unit inmates and staff. Attending the weekly meetings broke the routine of work or academic assignments and so appointment to the office was not actually resented. On the other hand, the only task of the group, as understood by the inmates, was to present requests and gripes to the staff. "Since C-Unit is different, why can't we see TV for an hour longer in the evenings?" "My mattress is terrible. Holes clear through to the springs. Why can't I move into that empty room with a better mattress? Why not get new mattresses for the whole Unit?" "What are the staff going to do about the noise in the TV room?" "If staff can do all they claim to do, why didn't I get the job change I wanted?" These challenges were presented in a desultory fashion, and an answer about institutional limitations resulted in sullen withdrawal or whispered side conversations obviously insolent in tone.

Although a better organizational form had been provided for communication, the general atmosphere remained one in which inmates proved over and over again that "they aren't going to do anything for us." When one staff member tried to respond to the more general issues involved in the TV room noise problem, another would divert the focus by commenting on underlying feelings expressed by an individual. Even a momentarily lively conversation soon lost its momentum under these conditions and the ensuing glum silence finally would be interrupted by another impossible-to-grant request. The lieutenant supervisor, in disgust, labeled the meetings as "gimme sessions" and commented that this kind of thing always happened when dealing with inmates in any group that might have action consequences.

By this time, however, the staff were ready to identify problems, to schedule themselves for work, and to examine a wider range of alternative measures for improving performance. Therefore, they did not assign all the blame to the inmates for the unsatisfactory operation of the Staff-Inmate Groups. Nor did they consider dispensing with the community-focused group simply because a second device did not seem to be working well. Recognizing that the new Staff-Inmate Group plan still did not provide for the ultimate goal, adequate communication between the staff and the total population, the staff settled down to consider how the present device could be improved.

Because the staff had learned to consider their own behavior when the program proved ineffective, they first observed that staff activity in the Staff-Inmate Group had much to do with its erratic performance. They agreed that each staff member spoke as an individual in the Staff-Inmate Group meetings without referring to common staff concerns, at times even deflecting a line of discussion initiated with inmates by another staff member. Often staff members responded directly to each other's comments, actually competing for inmate attention. As one researcher said, "If you listen, you'll hear more staff voices than inmate voices." In addition, the staff noted that they had failed to orient each new collection of representatives to the task of the Staff-Inmate Group and its place in the total program. A counselor commented, "The inmate representatives act as though they had never heard about the Staff-Inmate Group in an orientation meeting." Because neither staff nor inmates understood why they were together, there was always an initial period of fumbling. If one group did begin to develop a focus, it was only toward the end of the four weeks when they were about to be disbanded.

In April, 1961, the staff modified their own pattern for work with the Staff-Inmate Group, assuming for the first time responsibility for acting with the inmate representatives as a group. They planned each four-week period as an intensive reorientation to the C-Unit program, with special attention in the first meeting to the importance of the Staff-Inmate Group for the whole community. The inmate representatives would be invited to initiate subjects for discussion but the staff would also go to each meeting with an agreed-upon problem concerning which they needed inmate opinion, thus dignifying the meeting as having a function for the staff's share in the community's work. A task-focused, rather than a therapeutic approach, was accepted as appropriate for staff participation in these meetings; and all staff members agreed to support each other in stimulating discussion among the inmates. Each group of inmate representatives would be encouraged to initiate a project on its own, with the assurance that it could continue as a working committee if its project was not completed by the end of its four weeks' tenure.

The response of the inmates was immediately rewarding. Inmate work groups appeared in response to the staff work group, as can be seen in the development of such projects as the Welfare Fund in June, 1961. Given greater freedom and responsibility, the inmates invented previously unused processes for reaching a larger proportion of the total population. Polling processes were devised for use when the issue concerned every inmate in the Unit. Individual representatives "interviewed" men casually available on the Unit about controversial questions in order to supplement the opinions of friends, returning to the next session of the Staff-Inmate Group with penciled verbatim notes to report the variety of points of view so discovered.

In June the director believed that both staff and inmates were ready to consider a still more effective organization for public communication about issues. She suggested that caseload groups, meeting under the leadership of each counselor, be used to involve every inmate in the consideration of community issues. The idea was greeted by staff with some interest. However, the new Staff-Inmate Groups were now working so well that staff were busy implementing the new projects proposed each month, and the suggestion of caseload groups was dropped at this time with little discussion.

The caseload group idea was reintroduced in the August staff meetings by the counselors after the staff training discussions about the importance of free, public, and comprehensive communication for building a resocializing community. Now that they realized why they wanted community groups, the staff expeditiously identified certain already available devices for communication with all inmates. Each counselor would meet with half of his caseload (roughly 20 men) once a week. The hour freed in the institutional schedule for group counseling would be used for such meetings, thus avoiding a mass withdrawal of C-Unit inmates from their regular assignments in the work and educational programs. Each group session would combine discussion of current issues in the C-Unit community with matters specific to the work of the counselor and his caseload; and each group would elect two inmate representatives to meet weekly as a Unit Council with the entire staff. Administrative staff and custody officers were to be involved in the Half-Caseload Groups in rotation in order to expose all inmates to all the staff and to help coordinate the staff's perspective on inmate concerns. Research observers would follow the trends in each group. The staff work group, on one hand, and the Unit Council, on the other, would provide the integrative mechanisms.

At long last, the staff could conceive of a communication system for inmates that included everyone while leaving room for subgroup differentiation, chiefly because they had created this kind of communication system for themselves and found it good. Although at an earlier period staff members had been distrustful of policy groups led by individual counselors, fearing competition and disparate loyalties, they now thought of each other as representing the whole staff in whatever they did with inmates. Consequently, they were able to take advantage of the division of labor already provided by the assignment of caseloads to counselors, and to drop the additional complicating structure they had used to establish "checks and balances." Most important, open communication among themselves had been experienced as a support in accomplishing the work they wanted to do. They were therefore able to see the usefulness of free communication for the inmates' participation in the community.

In examining reciprocal problem-solving between staff and inmates and the consequent increase in staff's ability to manage efficiently, it is important to note that the first step had to be taken by staff. At each stage, inmate behavior was responsive to the assumptions about working relationships expressed by the staff in the patterns they provided in program and in the way staff members related to each other around a task. When the staff were fearful of communication and attempted to control rather than to free participation, inmates responded anomicly. When staff opened communication channels to a degree but continued to function without self-direction, inmates assumed the stereotyped "gimme" approach customary when inmates are offered undefined access to discussion with officials. When the staff themselves became a task-focused work group, inmates responded by becoming task-focused.

To initiate this process, the staff were required to include their own behavior as a work group among the dimensions to be considered when trying to understand inmate behavior.[14] Only after they accepted this as a necessity were they able to choose between alternatives, that is, to modify a program device or to change the way they were using that device. Each successful new experience in problem-solving in the staff work group increased the staff's information about the social process for which they were responsible and extended the range of acceptable alternatives to be used in managing their work with inmates. Because these experiences were cumulative, staff could approach each succeeding problem with increased flexibility.

---

[14] A similar finding emerged in the Austin Riggs Center Community development from 1950 to 1953, as reported by Robert B. White and Joan Erikson to the Massachusetts Psychological Association, May 17, 1953, in an unpublished paper, "Some Relationships Between Individual Psychotherapy and the Social Dynamics of the Psychiatric Sanitarium."

We must not neglect the inmate contribution to the expansion of problem-solving management in C-Unit. Inmates were not just passively responsive. As soon as the inmates were freed to join with staff and with each other in task-focused activities, they developed their own patterns of problem-solving, assuming some responsibilities formerly reserved for staff and vastly widening the pool of human resources available for community activities. The end result was a process by which staff and inmates learned from each other, with both inmates and staff contributing according to their abilities and functions. Such a reciprocal process proved, in the C-Unit experience, to be essential for a community involving both officials and inmates.

THE PROBLEM-SOLVING STYLE OF ADMINISTRATION

Up to this point we have been able to tell the story of staff operation in the Project with minimal reference to the administrative activities facilitating the development of problem-solving management. Throughout the first year, administrative personnel were related to other Project staff primarily as members of the staff work group with certain leadership functions. In large part the visible roles of administrative personnel were similar to those of other staff members. They were participants in meetings, consultative resources, and part of the pool of employees who led inmate groups and counseled individual inmates. Executive activities as distinct from participation in the staff work group rarely occupied the foreground of staff attention because they facilitated staff operations as a body responsible for management rather than dictating them.[15]

This relative invisibility of administration during the creative period of the C-Unit community program was documented in a number of retrospective interviews with counselors, officers, and inmates who had been with the Project during its several phases. All of them reported minimal awareness of the executive activities of the director and the lieutenant supervisor who had shared administrative responsibility for the Project from January to August, 1961. One officer said, in remembering this period: "The director did much of the work when we were first getting organized. . . . In relation to staff she never decides, but she makes suggestions that are taken up by other members of the staff who then get it thrashed out. The supervisor usually makes the decisions that could only be made by him." Inmates reported, "We never knew just what the lieutenant supervisor actually did, but he got things done."

---

[15] See the story of changing designs for staff and inmate communication on pp. 155–160 for an example of administrative ability to wait for the staff's readiness to act.

In the C-Unit experience, this style of administration seemed essential to support the staff's responsibility for problem-solving management. It was characterized by three kinds of administrative activity:

1. Many planning and policy-making functions, usually reserved for administration, were specifically delegated to the staff work group or to some appropriate subgroup within it. When administrative personnel made the ultimate decisions that could be made only by them, the issues had been first discussed openly by the staff and the final action was reported back so that the staff could determine how they would take the next steps to implement the decisions.

2. Administrative personnel operated with the staff as members of the work group, contributing from the special perspective of leaders much as any staff member contributed from his particular position. The special responsibilities of administrative personnel as members of the staff work group were threefold: (a) to maintain the perspective of the task and of the governing ideas in the discussion of issues; (b) to enlist the active contribution of every relevant individual; and (c) to support other staff members in problem-solving by providing a model of this process in administrative behavior.

3. Administrative personnel made arrangements for the program so determined with the appropriate officials in DVI without burdening the staff work group with the details of this executive function. Information gained during these explorations was reported back in terms of issues that should be taken into account in staff deliberations rather than in the details of the process as it was experienced by the administrators.

By the end of the first year every staff member relied on this style of administrative activity to provide the conditions for maintaining the staff work group in its responsibility for problem-solving management.

THE STAFF WORK GROUP AND COMMUNITY

The preceding description of staff operation during the Project's first year provides clues to why organizing the staff as a work group, in contrast to the usual bureaucratic pattern for official relationships, enabled them to build community in their work with inmates. Several processes occurred because of the staff work group that could not otherwise have been expected. In the Project's experience these processes were necessary if the staff were to be able to operate effectively in a community with inmates.

1. Participation in the staff work group enlarged the perspective from which each staff member performed his part of the program with inmates.

As the individual staff member helped to design the way the common task was to be implemented he learned how his daily activities and those of other staff members affected the work of each in accomplishing the joint goal. He gained much information about how inmates functioned throughout their institutional life, especially in those areas outside the purview of his particular job. And each member learned a broader set of generally applicable skills than those required for his specialized function as he shared with his colleagues in developing the various problem-solving methods. Because of his membership in the staff work group each staff member saw and responded to a complex and interrelated reality as he performed his specialized function in program; and had access to a greatly increased array of informational and skill resources.

2. The staff work group provided the individual staff member with an anchoring reference group that supported his allegiance to official values as he worked with inmates. A member of the staff work group did not approach work with inmates as an isolated official executing the orders of remote superiors. Rather, he represented the strength and authority of the total staff work group whenever he acted with inmates. Each staff member was accordingly less vulnerable to the seductions of the delinquent culture surrounding him. Each found it easier to be a secure and flexible authority, since both he and the inmates recognized the broad legitimation that superseded personal idiosyncrasy and arbitrary rules in his official behavior. And each staff member relied on the approval and comradeship of his colleagues rather than on inmate response for the pride, support of values, and affective satisfactions so necessary for the person who undertakes the wearing challenges of work with offenders.

3. In participating in the staff work group, each staff member practiced under the guidance of his colleagues the problem-solving role he was expected to perform in his program activities with inmates. Thus continuity between his role as member of the staff work group and his role as official with inmates was established, helping to build the communication between official world and inmate world so necessary for a community of interests between them.

4. The sharing of goals and responsibility experienced by the individual staff member in the staff work group removed many of the bureaucratic restrictions from his exercise of initiative on the job, permitting him to see new facets of the social reality with which he was dealing and to respond flexibly within the guidelines for task performance established by himself together with his colleagues. Such new insights and potentialities, in turn, enriched the perspectives and resources of the total staff.

5. The involvement of persons with various functions in the staff work group emphasized the treatment implications of all staff activities and

made it possible to act on them. When program became "what all staff members did in work on the task," it was possible to see the custody officer's procedures for distributing bed linens, the management of a holiday program, and the secretary's share in facilitating written communications as contributions to the resocializing process of equal importance with the counselor's interview with an inmate. All staff activities were means for managing human resources to accomplish a task; and all were treatment in that the "way of managing" determined the ultimate value message about relationships among people that would be received by the inmates. Management and treatment were accordingly integrated in staff functioning and philosophy through the mechanism of the staff work group.

As we shall see in the next chapter, the work group pattern for organizing staff was drastically different from the bureaucratic pattern for establishing relationships among staff; and it had quite different consequences for the relationships that became possible among staff and inmates. At the end of the Project's first year, a number of changes in personnel and in the relationships between the Project and DVI reintroduced the bureaucratic form of organization into Project staff operation. In the next chapter we shall examine what the quite different conditions for staff work under bureaucratic patterns meant for the role of officials in the C-Unit community.

VII - RETURN TO BUREAUCRACY

IMPORTANT changes in the work patterns of the Project staff were precipitated by changes in administrative and counselor personnel beginning in August, 1961, and continuing until April, 1962. In August, a new supervisor replaced the lieutenant who had acted as interim supervisor since January, 1961.[1] In September and November, two counselor positions were vacated and replacements were not secured until January and April of 1962. A new administrative position was created and in November, 1961, a lieutenant was appointed as assistant supervisor. Two secretaries among the group of four who had participated in the staff training sessions left during the fall months. Many of these changes were due to promotional transfers within the Department of Corrections. They were clustered in one period because several new civil service lists had been announced in August, 1961, and Project employees had rated top positions on each list.

Coincidentally, this period of staff change occurred at the end of the first year of Project operation, and many of the inmates first admitted to the Unit were leaving on parole, with new inmates replacing them. Two caseloads were without counseling service except for emergencies from early in November, 1961, until the middle of January, 1962, and few newly admitted inmates could be assigned immediately to a permanent counselor.

---

[1] The new supervisor was not available for full-time duty until the middle of September.

In addition, the remaining staff were repeatedly experiencing contact with the institutional "ceiling" on program. Although the actual limitations on continued expansion were not explicitly stated until after the institutional decision against further changes in the C-Unit honor system was made in December, 1961, it was clear throughout the fall of 1961 that there was pressure on the Project to conform more closely to DVI's current patterns. In the episode of the screen removal request described in Chapter IV, both staff and inmates had experienced a letdown in expectations about the degrees of freedom remaining for the further expansion of inmate responsibilities. Many planning meetings, whether composed of staff, or staff and inmates, evidenced the hesitancy of the participants to invest energy in developing proposals that might never be implemented.

Outwardly, the basic program for work between inmates and staff continued as usual during this period, although two major projects remained on the drawing board until January, 1962: the Welfare Fund and the Half-Caseload Groups. Volunteers, a student, two secretaries, and the director helped the remaining counselor carry the fall semester Interest Group Program. Monthly C-Unit dinners involving all staff and inmates with guests from the wider institutional staff were scheduled in a separate mess hall. A second Christmas Open House was managed successfully. Most important, the long-awaited "Bridges to the Community" program was staffed, beginning in August, 1961, by parole agents from all the districts in the state; and C-Unit inmates for the first time received the help in parole-planning they had been eagerly awaiting. The frequent appearance of parole agents to some extent maintained the image of staff as adequate in resources, even though many individual services could not be provided with consistency. A cadre of inmate leaders, trained in the events of the preceding year, carried many responsibilities formerly reserved for staff and helped to maintain among the inmates a mood of expectation.[2]

However, a major change appeared in the performance of the remaining staff that cannot be explained simply in terms of unusual work pressures or limitations on the expansion of program. Because of a number of factors, by the time new staff members were secured the remaining staff were no longer operating as a problem-solving work group, but as a collection of individuals, each relying on his own resources for discharging the responsibilities assigned to him. The gradual shift toward isolated adjustments by Project staff members accompanied by an increasing sep-

---

[2] The inmates were now able to depend on their own resources in skills and knowledge to carry out certain projects that did not require constant administrative facilitation by staff. For example, the football team was organized in January, 1962. (See Chapter V.)

aration between treatment and management functions was, in part, a response to changes in the style of Project administration.

CHANGES IN PROJECT ADMINISTRATION

At the beginning of September, 1961, two changes in administrative organization and behavior were instituted within the Project.

THE EXECUTIVE COMMITTEE

DVI's Superintendent changed the executive structure of the Project at the time the third supervisor was appointed in August, 1961. In his opinion many issues confronting Project administration were too sensitive for discussion in the presence of subordinates. Accordingly, he established, beginning in September, 1961, a Project Executive Committee, consisting of the Associate Superintendent, Custody, the Supervisor, and the director. (When the second lieutenant was appointed as assistant supervisor in November, he replaced the Associate Superintendent, Custody, as the representative of custody on the Executive Committee.) This Committee departmentalized the Project by establishing three independent authorities, each responsible for a specialized function: treatment, custody, and research. These executives were instructed to resolve the issues affecting their separate groups of subordinates in discussion among themselves.[3]

The operation of the new Executive Committee essentially removed the Project's administrative personnel from membership in the staff and eliminated the management function of the staff work group. Staff meetings could no longer be in the same sense work sessions. The Project's administrators reported to the lower-level staff the limits already established by upper DVI administration before the critical problems had been formulated by the Project staff in terms of their own experiences. By the time an issue was introduced for staff consideration, the direction of action had been determined in discussions from which the relevant action staff had been excluded, leaving only details to be considered by the staff members who were responsible for implementing the program with inmates.

Although the researchers noted that this was a critical event in the Project's history, the action staff continued at first to behave in terms of the old norms for staff work group operation. In fact, the more regular participation of the Associate Superintendent, Custody, in the discussion

---

[3] The head secretary disgustedly announced, "In this Project there are too many chiefs and too few Indians."

of Project problems was welcomed by all as a direct communication line between the Project staff and DVI's administration. However, additional changes were introduced into the staff work group by the patterns of administrative activity used by the newly appointed third supervisor.

A CHANGE IN THE STYLE OF ADMINISTRATION

With the appointment of the third supervisor, a noticeable change in the style of Project administration occurred. A graduate social worker with experience in DVI, the new supervisor combined a clinical approach with a traditional bureaucratic use of authority in his activities with staff. He preferred to discuss real issues in conferences with individuals, often focusing more on feelings than on tasks. He used staff meetings for reporting both his own activities and the decisions of upper DVI administrators, involving staff primarily in the discussion of procedural details. Increasingly, this style of administration dramatized the supervisor as the one who was responsible for the program and his subordinates as persons who carried out instructions.

The fact that, as a new appointee to the Grade III position, the new supervisor was on six months' probation was partly responsible for his maintaining this behavior. Since this was his first administrative position, he was closely supervised by the Associate Superintendent, Custody, who trained him in the orientations expected of a "strong" supervisor in DVI. Although the rest of the Project staff encouraged the supervisor to adopt the patterns that had proved useful during the first year of work, they had no control over his ultimate appointment at a permanent supervisory level. Under these conditions, the staff could not counteract the administrative mistakes—as viewed from the perspective of the Project's model—that were beginning to have a cumulative effect on staff functioning. Nevertheless, the staff group did not easily give up the communication patterns that had proved so useful to them, and by the end of the first month, members from several staff groups asked for a meeting with the new supervisor to consider what was happening.

On September 29, 1961, the secretaries, counselors, and researchers convened with the supervisor and director and the issues were outlined. The chief secretary drew two pictures on the blackboard showing "how we were organized before" and how "we are now since we changed." In the old period "We were unified." Now "there is a split between research and service." "Everything is falling apart." The current problems listed by the staff included: (1) Research administration was now distinct from program administration and this caused complications in the secretarial pool and confusion for the counselors. (2) Secretaries were no longer invited to staff meetings when appropriate, "We feel like a bunch of peons." (3) Plans for the participation of parole agents in the program had been established without preliminary discussion with the staff, and the counselors were now undertaking new duties that had not been adequately provided for in the administrative plan. (4) Room changes were now authorized by the supervisor without reference to counselors or custody officers. (5) Staff assignments involving relations with DVI's administration had been inappropriately delegated downward, for example, the assignment of the Welfare Fund committee to a counselor who could not facilitate this complicated program at the upper levels of DVI's administration. (6) There was little communication from the supervisor ahead of time about changes in the schedule for staff activities. Together the group recognized that some of these difficulties were to be expected during a period of transition; and certain immediate adjustments were made to restore coordination among researchers, secretaries, and counselors. The staff left the meeting with the hope that a beginning had been made in reestablishing the staff work group as a body with management responsibilities.

However, the ability to communicate openly that had been temporarily reestablished in the meeting of September 29 was not apparent at later staff meetings. In October the second counselor left the Project, and by the middle of November the staff work group had virtually disappeared as a recognizable entity.

By the time the lieutenant joined the staff as assistant supervisor in November, 1961, staff and administration were distinct systems within the Project, rather than parts of one work group. The "staff" had become a collection of lower-level employees, each individually related to a member of the executive triumvirate. Although staff meetings continued, the Project's administration had now become the locus of decision-making, more responsible to authorities outside the Project than to the staff. Because less was now known about how decisions were reached, staff members experienced the consequences of administrative activity without sharing the responsibility; as a result, administration, as distinct from work on a task, became an important focus for staff attention. A dissident subgroup appeared among counselors and secretaries who expressed their dissatisfactions in gripe-session lunches away from the institution's grounds. The supporting tradition of the staff work group had disappeared, and staff members now adapted themselves individually to a flow of work that increasingly took on the character of procedural implementation of plans determined outside their immediate experience. It is significant that open criticism disappeared from formally convened staff discussions and by December the counselors were questioning the usefulness of all staff meetings.

CONDITIONS AFFECTING THE SECOND STAFF

The additional new staff members, a lieutenant as assistant supervisor and two counselors, were appointed November 15, 1961, January 1, 1962, and April 1, 1962, respectively. It is clear that, together with the new supervisor, they faced a situation that was drastically different from that confronting the first staff; and that their resources for dealing with it were more limited.

THE POOL OF HUMAN RESOURCES

The staff group of which these new appointees became members was more narrowly constituted than before. Researchers and secretaries had become satellite role groups no longer actively involved in action planning. The director's role had become one of "training," although she continued to act as a counselor for a few inmates; her contribution to the management of program was made primarily through private conferences with the supervisor and she could no longer initiate action. Only one counselor and two custody officers remained from the original staff work group and they had lost any hope that the management patterns of the previous year would be reinstated. Two role groups now made up the staff responsible for program: the three counselors with their supervisor, the three custody officers with their lieutenant.

BACKGROUNDS

Like the first staff, the new staff members were all prepared by their backgrounds and experience to accept a traditional bureaucratic approach to the Project's task. The lieutenant and the first new counselor had had long experience in DVI and were already highly respected for their procedural efficiency and loyalty to the bureaucratic norms. The second counselor had had experience in a county sheriff's office. Their educational backgrounds were diverse in many ways—high school, undergraduate public administration, and criminology—but were similar in that each lacked any systematic introduction to the skills of therapeutic interviewing and group leadership.

The major differences between this staff and the first were twofold: except for the new supervisor, they lacked the discipline of using ideas as guides to job functioning usually gained in professional education; and except for one of the counselors they all had achieved recognition within DVI as good workmen, a status each desired to maintain. Although the two new counselors had read casework literature, they shared with the lieutenant a somewhat idealized conception of "helping relationships" patterned after the PICO model of individual psychotherapy. Each new staff member in his own way anticipated that in the Project he would continue to manage his job as he had in his previous work experiences, while learning skills in the new and different area of "treatment." Thus all the new staff members were prepared by preconceptions developed in previous experiences to maintain the separation of treatment from management now increasingly characteristic of Project activities; and none of them expected as they entered the Project to make the revolutionary changes anticipated by the first staff.

ORIENTATION

Because the new staff members came into the Project at widely separated times, each went through his initial period of disorganization alone. The new supervisor saw each of them as requiring orientation primarily to the treatment, or counseling, functions of his new job. Accordingly, the supervisor dealt with them much as he would have with new students in casework. Each was asked to sit in on groups led by the supervisor to observe his group techniques; and each selected certain cases for "intensive" work, submitting process recordings of interviews for supervisory conferences on casework techniques. Documents from the Project's past were provided for reading; and institutional manuals were used to teach procedures. But at no time were the new members exposed to staff activities in which they could experience directly what was meant by problem-solving management.

The new staff members responded, as might be expected, in two ways. Each tended to feel inadequate when introduced to the mysteries of "helping relationships" concerned primarily with feelings and evaluated in terms of the "depth" of material produced by the client; and each restored his sense of competence by resolutely establishing procedural order in the work that had been accumulating for him, using management patterns that had been successful in previous jobs.

PROBLEMS OF SUCCESSION

The situation of the new staff did not demand the same reorganization of perspectives that had been required of the original staff group. Because many basic program issues had been resolved during the first year, the

Unit program was fairly stable and could now absorb considerable strain without threatening the breakdown in functioning that had confronted the original staff. As a result, the new staff were not required to examine their own behavior as a possible source of difficulties that could be more easily explained by lack of staff time or by reference to the unacceptable behavior of inmates.

Furthermore, the new staff were administering a program that had been formulated by a previous staff. For the original staff, program had been their own creature, a tool they designed under the duress of resolving difficult problems. They felt free to modify program as need arose because what they had made they could change if the task could be accomplished better in some other way. In contrast, for the second staff, program was something to be learned and to be administered according to the prescriptions of a still mysterious "treatment model."[4] By exchanging one staff group for another without an overlapping period of orientation, the program had ceased to be perceived as a tool for flexible response to need and had become an institutionalized pattern to be administered. The new staff members approached their work as learners who needed to establish order in a complex new experience rather than as creators.

Thus as it emerged from the period of disorganization precipitated the previous August by staff turnover, the second staff, with its ranks complete at the beginning of April, 1962, had already established its work patterns according to the patterns characteristic of the usual staff operation in DVI.

SEPARATION OF MANAGEMENT FROM TREATMENT

The drastic changes in project administration and staff composition just reported had serious consequences for staff action as measured against the prescriptions of the community model for resocialization. The progressive separation of management from treatment and the disappearance of problem-solving as a basic process in staff operation is revealed in a series of events dating from January through August, 1962.

DIVISION AMONG STAFF GROUPS

The first critical incident occurred in January, 1962, when all the new staff members except the final counselor had been appointed. It reveals

---

[4] For instance, when implementing the Half-Caseload Group plan the following January, the new staff operated mechanically without having experienced the problems the groups were expected to correct.

how difficult problem-solving had become for the staff since the Executive Committee had reintroduced structural divisions into the staff work group.

The Third-Tier Incident. In one two-week period during January, 1962, the diminishing ability of the staff to mobilize for problem-solving management resulted in an incident with serious consequences for the staff, for the inmates, and for the community in which they were all members.

On the Monday of the first week, three inmates approached the administrators individually about a group of Mexican YAs who were causing excessive noise at the end of the top-floor tier. The inmates who reported the problem were quiet, intellectually inclined A#s who had difficulty pursuing their leisure-time interests—reading, study, and hobby craft—in their rooms because of the customary noise in the Unit. Over a period of time these men had been gradually assigned to rooms in a relatively quiet location in the Unit, the window end of the top-floor tier. A group of younger Mexicans had recently formed the habit of congregating in this area on evenings and weekends, talking and singing loudly, beating the walkway railings as though they were bongo drums, and kicking their heels against the doors of the adjacent rooms.

The inmate who reported the problem to the director was one of her counselees, long a constructive leader in the C-Unit community. According to his statement, this kind of difficulty had occurred twice before, but each time the third-tier men had managed to "educate" the annoying group, persuading them to show consideration for the inmates in the surrounding rooms. The senior men living on the third tier had tried the same approach with this new group. They found that "the population is shifting so much with all this new intake that the old C-Unit magic doesn't work." He said that all the A#s from previous honor units understood there was a rule that, although inmates could visit at each other's doorways, no groups were allowed to assemble in the walkways of the upper two tiers.[5]

At this point in the Project's history, the director could offer three alternatives to her counselee. He might go to the supervisor or to the lieutenant, or both, as the persons who were now the responsible administrative officials in the Project. He might bring up the matter in the Half-Caseload Group to which he was assigned. Or he might rely on the director to introduce the subject to the Executive Committee. The inmate responded that it would look as though he were "snitching" if he alone spoke about this matter in the Half-Caseload Group. He decided to ask the director to draw

---

[5] Although no such rule was discovered, it was a strong norm among honor men that the area in front of a man's room was not to be used except by his own visitors and as a passageway for those going to other rooms.

administrative attention to the problem. Essentially he was relying on her to set in motion the longstanding C-Unit process by which staff designed the means to enable inmate subgroups to gather information, analyze issues, and handle, with staff help, a potential conflict among themselves.

The director talked with the supervisor and the lieutenant and learned that they had also been approached about the problem. They agreed to discuss the situation at the following Friday staff meeting when both counselors and custody officers would be present; and that the Unit officers would be alerted to keep an eye on the third-tier area. The director suggested some initial information-gathering steps to indicate to the inmates that the staff were responding to the problem, for instance, by asking the two third-tier inmates who had been strong leaders in the Unit program to consider with the Executive Committee the possible courses of action. The lieutenant felt strongly that the "complainers" should be seen only as individuals since otherwise they would just reinforce each other's "gripes." The director commented that seeing them together might help them mobilize their own resources for coping with the problem, but the lieutenant could not agree.

On Wednesday three of the director's counselees, each of whom lived close to the end of the third tier, reported that feeling was running high on the Unit. They felt the situation had reached a boiling point and that they had done their share by first trying to handle the problem and then by asking for staff help. Since these men had always heretofore been reliable in their evaluation of events on the Unit, the director tended to believe that something was seriously wrong.

In the regular weekly executive meeting that afternoon, the director once again proposed that group problem-solving processes be initiated. The lieutenant was still firmly opposed to discussing the matter with the "complainers" as a group and was equally unwilling to take action to identify the members of the Mexican group, since this would be asking the third-tier men to "snitch." He felt it should be left to him and his custody officers to administer the rules, and that, since the officers had observed no signs of trouble, no rules were being violated. The director proposed that the complaints could be seen as evidence that two subgroups in this situation had needs that required administrative attention. The supervisor was more interested in what he believed to be the personal pathologies of the complaining inmates and said that the counselors should deal with these individuals about their attitudes. In view of the evident lack of administrative consensus, the director agreed that action should be postponed until all the staff could consider the issue.

The problem was discussed in a staff meeting including both counselors and custody officers on Friday afternoon. The officers reported that the far end of the third tier was a difficult area to police or observe. They tended to feel that the "complainers" were just "sniveling" and that actually they were more concerned with sleeping than with study. The director called attention to the fact that the noisy inmate group were Mexicans who had little to do during free periods, and noted that no Interest Group Program had been provided for inmates with limited personal resources since the previous summer. This point interested the counselors. They went on to discuss the possibility of identifying the Mexican group and providing a program for them, although no attention was given to finding them another place to congregate during the weekend. The officers were instructed to watch the third tier carefully.[6]

On Monday of the second week the director talked with the inmate who had first reported the problem to her and found him in a state of near panic because a half-finished knife had been observed in the third-tier trash can. He reported that the Mexican group had been provocatively noisy during the weekend, so much so that seven men who lived at that end of the third tier had had to leave their rooms for the yard or other spots in the Unit in order to avoid giving physical expression to their anger. One of the seven—a Project clerk—had shouted in his frustration that he would see to it that the Mexican inmates were moved, and all the third-tier men were concerned that, because he was the inmate clerk who handled the C-Unit room transfer sheets for the Project lieutenant, he had seriously exposed himself by this thoughtless threat.[7] None of the third-tier men had seen any evidence that the Unit officers had noticed, or taken action regarding, the unusual noise on the Unit during the weekend free periods.

In her regular conference with the supervisor immediately after this interview, the director reported the appearance of the knife. The supervisor said he had been trying to identify the members of the Mexican group in order to organize them in an evening Interest Group. There was some discussion of calling the "complainers" together. The director said she was uneasy about the effect of such a step on the inmates so long as the staff members were so divided among themselves about the definition of the problem.

By the following Wednesday a generalized anxiety had spread among C-Unit inmates because a remark of the supervisor to an inmate clerk had been interpreted to mean that staff were defining the problem as a "racial issue." In the regular Executive Committee meeting, it was evident that

---

[6] Note that no one considered using the new Unit Council as an appropriate body for the discussion of these issues.

[7] See case of Jack in Chapter IX.

the Project administrators still had no plan for action. The lieutenant felt that the initial mistake had been made when the quiet inmates had been allowed to move one by one to the third tier and that they now formed a "clique." The supervisor proposed a meeting with the third-tier inmates to tell them no rules were being violated and that they should stop fussing. The director protested this definition of the situation by allocating blame. In her perspective, both groups had legitimate rights and needs that were not being met. She said it was important not to stereotype one group as "all right" and the other as a "clique of complainers," noting that the men living at the end of the third tier were a collection of quite different individuals and were, in fact, a less cohesive group than the Mexicans who were annoying them.[8] By the end of the Executive Committee meeting, the only plan was to call the third-tier men together the following Monday if matters had not been settled over the weekend, although no one was clear what would be done at the meeting.

The following day, Thursday, an inmate not directly involved—an older Mexican who had been active in developing the Welfare Fund plan—approached the director, saying there was trouble on the Unit, and "his people" were involved. He thought the difficulty was being caused by staff but that if the director knew about it, she could put a stop to it.

In the Friday afternoon staff meeting of the second week, the third-tier problem was again the chief topic for discussion. The staff defined the two groups more clearly than before. The Mexican group, having little else to do, liked to congregate on the third tier because it was out of the way of traffic and overlooked the visitors coming into the building. They treated this spot as the street corner where they hung out and acted in their accustomed ways. The third-tier men, however, had moved to this area in the Unit because they desired peace and quiet for their more studious pursuits.

Although each set of inmates appeared to have a reasonable point of view, members of the staff began taking sides with one or the other. The custody officers felt that the trouble would cease if the two loudest "complainers" were moved to rooms away from the area as a warning action to the others. Some counselors gave top priority to the needs of the Mexican group for more staff attention. And still others felt that the interests of the third-tier men should be protected while another spot was provided for the gatherings of the Mexican group. As the meeting progressed, certain issues were clarified and feelings among the staff calmed sufficiently to decide that all inmates would be asked to "cool it" over the weekend with the promise of staff action at the beginning of the next week.

---

[8] Substantiated by sociometric data obtained earlier in the month in the inmate system survey.

Unfortunately, the only action on which staff could agree was to call a meeting of all inmates from both sides of the controversy for 1:00 P.M. on the following Monday afternoon. The inmates were not prepared for the meeting, receiving word of it only when the ducats for Monday were distributed on Sunday evening. On Monday morning all the involved inmates were upset and several of the A#s threatened to ignore their ducats, even though such a refusal would be grounds for disciplinary action, because they felt the meeting was dangerous in an inflamed situation. The Mexican group members had had no previous communication from the staff about the problem and vaguely anticipated some sort of "trouble." The uninvolved Mexican who had communicated with the director had been ducated to the meeting, thus exposing him, along with the third-tier men who first brought the problem to the attention of the staff, to the suspicion of "snitching."

At noon of the third Monday the staff met to consider what they would do in the impending meeting. After a period of anxious and unfocused discussion, the director proposed that the real issue making it difficult for staff to get together was the conflict between the custody position and the treatment position; and that finding a way to reconcile these two approaches in the joint management of the community was the Project's job. The lieutenant, who had hitherto remained tense and silent, responded by pointing out that he was in charge of custody in the Project, that this was a custody matter, and that his authority had been ignored throughout the whole incident. The staff listened with understanding and asked him what he would propose. In a short time he was explaining how the staff should approach the inmates in the meeting as "talking over with them a common problem on the Unit that staff and inmates should consider together." The staff left to reassemble with the inmates in a more relaxed frame of mind, although they still had no specific plan to offer for resolving the problem.

The meeting did not accomplish what staff had hoped. The supervisor, while insisting that no inmate had "snitched,"[9] introduced the subject by placing the burden on a "group of complainers." The third-tier men responded defensively, saying that "certain people should learn consideration for others." The Mexican who had approached the director confidentially was asked directly by the supervisor what he thought should be done, but he disclaimed all responsibility. The younger Mexicans squirmed in their chairs and had little to say except one, who said that he had not realized they were making so much noise. Two third-tier men expressed appreciation of the Mexican group's desire to get away from the confusion

---

[9] *Snitch:* usually defined as an inmate who has actually betrayed another inmate.

on the floor of the Unit and proposed that another place be found for their activities. The staff contribution was primarily to state that no rule was being violated. The third-tier men went away feeling that staff had given the Mexican group permission to be as annoying as they wished and had put them in the position of snitching, despite staff insistence in the meeting that no one had snitched. The general impression left with the inmates was that they were perceived as two warring cliques who should be good boys and not annoy each other.

There were no overt incidents following the meeting, but relationships among inmates and between staff and inmates remained strained. The third-tier men now felt themselves under surveillance by custody as a "clique" and under suspicion by other men in the Unit as possible "snitches." Three inmate leaders dropped out of community activities. An Interest Group was established for the Mexican inmates, but a lasting breach had been created among subgroups within the C-Unit community.

In retrospective interviews, two inmates who left the Unit some months later, after having been with the program from the beginning, independently dated widespread inmate disillusionment with staff from this episode, stating that it was at about this time that the word "snitch" was redefined among C-Unit inmates to mean any inmate closely associated with staff and therefore in a position to betray his fellows.

Consequences for Staff Operation. In this incident it is evident that staff opinions were now being formed outside the staff work group in private communications that occurred primarily within the three segments of the administrative structure. As a result, staff meetings were no longer used for a free exploration of issues after which the staff could adopt a common position; they tended rather to be forums for the restatement of perspectives already adopted under the leadership of one or another of the authority figures in the Project.[10] Although a momentary understanding of controversial interests among the staff had been achieved, it came too late to permit the gathering of information through work with the involved inmates. Accordingly, the step-by-step process by which subgroups are progressively involved in problem-solving was bypassed, with staff acting at the last only to require a direct confrontation between two mutually threatened inmate groups who had not been prepared for this step.

The consequences for staff operation were unfortunate. Instead of having experienced successful problem-solving in a management task, the

---

[10] This identification with separate administrative groups was not uniform, and the counselors aligned themselves individually. It was at this point that the counselors suggested that fewer staff meetings be scheduled so "we can get on with our work."

new staff had learned primarily to be wary of talking with each other or with inmates about real problems. Each staff member felt justified in his own opinions and uneasy about expressing them because no resolution in action integrated their various perspectives. At a meeting a month later, scheduled by staff request to clarify the administrative roles in the Project, the Third-Tier Incident was mentioned as an example of the confusion that can arise when role conflicts are not dealt with directly in the course of action. Although the meeting had started fruitfully, the feelings of certain staff members about this event were so strong that the others refused to discuss the role problems placed on the agenda by their own request.

In the daily log for that day the researchers noted that the staff had apparently ceased trying to deal with intrastaff conflicts through open discussion. They listed a number of recent behaviors of individual staff members all designed to bypass the disagreements anticipated if matters were brought to the point of open discussion in a formally convened meeting.

MANAGEMENT WITHOUT TREATMENT

In spite of its withdrawal from the free discussion of issues, the new staff did mobilize for efficient procedural work. With the appointment of the final counselor, its ranks were complete at the beginning of April, 1962, and the backlog of work accumulated during the period of staff vacancies was beginning to disappear. However, the elimination of treatment implications from management functions, now increasingly characteristic of the new staff's operation, appeared with particular clarity when they undertook to design a new program for the classification of C-Unit inmates.

The C-Unit Classification Committee. In the regular institutional program, the Classification Committee made all the major decisions affecting each inmate's program. This Committee, composed of representatives from several divisions DVI, determined inmate security ratings, assigned individuals to work and educational programs, reviewed grades, and scheduled YAs for parole board hearings. Since the regular institutional Classification Committee handled these matters for the entire inmate population, it worked under the pressure of limited time and was necessarily restricted in its discussion of issues with individual inmates. The members of the Committee were departmental representatives of administrative divisions and seldom actually knew the inmate whose case was under consideration; therefore, their decisions were based primarily on information available in the short notes found in the record. Although the inmate usually appeared at the Classification Committee meeting, his presence did not ensure his participation in the decision process. It did, however, allow the Committee to communicate its decision directly to him. On the presumption that each such decision was crucial for the individual inmate, the Project had originally proposed to bring each C-Unit inmate together with the staff members who knew him best for the purpose of making classification decisions. A C-Unit subcommittee of the institutional Classification Committee was the device suggested for achieving this goal.

Although C-Unit had long had its own discipline court, it had never insisted on having its own classification subcommittee, partly because the Project had a weekly calendar in the regular Classification Committee's schedule and the staff found this participation with a representative group of institutional personnel a useful link with the larger DVI program. However, in March, 1962, DVI's administration proposed that it would be more efficient for the regular classification committee to turn this duty for C-Unit inmates over to the Project staff.[11] Accordingly, plans were initiated to establish a C-Unit classification subcommittee to meet once a week in the Unit TV room.

The new staff undertook this assignment to create on its own with considerable enthusiasm. The assumption of classification duties raised the status of most C-Unit personnel and made each more influential in the treatment of individual inmates. The Unit lieutenant would assume the program assignment duties for individual inmates usually reserved for the institutional assignment officer; each counselor would be able to present the cases he knew intimately; and for the first time in the history of DVI, custody officers at the Grade I level would sit as active participants in decisions affecting the programs of individual inmates. Because one of the new counselors had extensive classification experience the new procedures were outlined with great efficiency. The plans were discussed with the inmates, who expressed general approval and made suggestions about how to use the TV room for this activity. The first meeting of the C-Unit Classification Committee was scheduled in an atmosphere of anticipation and general agreement.

However, in the preparatory discussions, the possibility that this change in management could also increase inmate participation in the treatment of their fellows aroused considerable inmate interest. For a long time C-Unit staff and inmates had discussed establishing some process by which fellow inmates under the guidance of staff could consider the wel-

---

[11] The C-Unit calendar took considerably more time because more detailed and complicated plans were under consideration, and each inmate was asked to contribute to the discussion before a decision was reached. It is important to note that this plan was proposed by upper administration and did not grow out of staff planning for the desired next steps in the development of the C-Unit community.

fare of individuals in the Unit population. The goal was to include an inmate's peers within the range of social resources officially used for helping the individual. A number of devices for achieving this goal had been considered: the involvement of inmates in discipline decisions; the establishment of a "discipline group" made up of chronic violators; and an inmate committee to join with staff in approving advancement to honor status. None of these suggestions had proved feasible, but the idea continued to appear from time to time in inmate discussions with staff. Now that C-Unit was to have its own Classification Committee, the inmates suggested that they, as well as staff, might participate in the classification discussions that determined the treatment of their fellows. With tentative staff agreement a specific proposal was formulated that, as a first step, all inmates ducated for a particular classification calendar should sit as observers during the hearings. Two values were expected to accrue from this experience: (1) all inmates would get better acquainted with the way official decisions were made; (2) this first step would provide experiences to be used in designing processes for more active inmate participation in considering the welfare of individuals.

There was much discussion of the inmate observation proposal in the Half-Caseload Groups during the two weeks before the first meeting of the C-Unit Classification Committee meeting. However, the staff, in the press of handling procedural details, did not systematically consider whether this was the best means for involving an inmate's peers in discussion about his institutional career. No staff decision about inmate observation had been reached by the time of the first meeting of the Committee.

As the staff and the inmates scheduled for this calendar assembled in the Unit for the initial C-Unit Classification Committee meeting, the first inmate to be called asked the supervisor if inmate observers might be present during his hearing. As he entered the TV room to take his place at the table with staff, all the inmates ducated for this session followed him and arranged themselves on the benches, where they remained during the next two hearings. At this point, a counselor passed a note to the supervisor, saying that the next case involved a psychiatric report. The observing inmates were ushered out of the room, with no explanation to the individual whose hearing had been announced. When the following case was called, the inmate observers returned to the TV benches and remained throughout the rest of the session.

This event caused considerable concern for both inmates and staff. Inmates were curious about the one case they were not permitted to observe, and the man himself was embarrassed by the speculation of his fellows. The counselors were upset that they had not been informed ahead of time that inmates were to be permitted to observe, and reported that they were handicapped in presenting their cases because certain details had to be repressed for fear of repercussions for the individual inmate among his fellows. With little further discussion, the staff agreed to dispense with inmate observation of classification procedures, and the incident passed into Project history without clarification.

In this incident we can observe several evidences of the new staff's definitions of management and treatment and the consequent separation between these functions in their operation. First, the new staff did not notice that the process for which they were designing procedures was one of treatment decision-making. They expeditiously took care of time and place arrangements and established the relationship of the C-Unit committee within the institution's hierarchy of classification subcommittees. But they ritualistically followed DVI's customary pattern for determining who should participate and what questions should be addressed without asking what pattern might best ensure that good treatment decisions resulted from classification processes. Thus they dealt with what was essentially a design for treatment decision-making as simply a set of procedures. Second, the new staff at no time attended to the far-reaching consequences for inmate and inmate-staff relationships inherent in the inmates' proposal that they be involved in considerations of individual inmate welfare. The staff had an intuitive sympathy for the inmates' curiosity about the procedures affecting themselves, but had no apparent awareness that the whole design of the community would be advanced toward the Project's model if inmates were now to share in considering the welfare of their fellows. Third, the staff evidenced no ability at this point to see that the establishment of a C-Unit Classification Committee, even if dealt with as a procedure, was an important symbolic communication to inmates about official perceptions of inmates and about official values governing relationships between staff and inmates. Having made what they considered to be a procedural mistake, they corrected its management but did nothing to clarify the impact of this experience on inmate perceptions. Finally, "treatment" was now increasingly conceived of by this staff as "private," occurring between the individual inmate and staff about matters too sensitive to be shared with his fellows. Because the staff no longer perceived for themselves that peers could be helpful in matters of concern to the individual, they did not know how to design such a process for inmates.[12]

---

[12] We do not intend to suggest that the collection of inmates who happened to be scheduled for a particular session of the Classification Committee was necessarily the appropriate peer group for considering the welfare of an individual inmate. If the staff had consciously intended to create a device for involving an individual's

Therefore, any device that might officially involve fellow inmates in an individual's treatment was permanently eliminated from consideration in the C-Unit program.[13]

Staff Training. Just as the staff training sessions conducted the previous summer had revealed a staff work group deeply involved in its responsibility for managing a community, so the staff training program scheduled for ten weeks in March through May, 1962, displayed the second staff's inability to think about management activities as having implications for treatment. The sessions were scheduled by the supervisor as substitutes for one of the two weekly staff meetings,[14] and were led by the director for the purpose of introducing the new staff members to the basic ideas of the Project. Because the second staff had had no experience in problem-solving work in their own group, the presentation of material about how they might create a problem-solving community lacked commonly accepted referents in behavior and was academic rather than related concretely to action. A discussion of the staff work group's influence on inmate participation in the community produced tension rather than enlightenment because the staff members were too uncomfortable to discuss current examples of staff behavior.

In response to requests from the supervisor and other staff members, the director modified her training plans, and the remaining sessions were devoted to the less tension-inducing topic of elementary interviewing

---

peers along with staff in classification decisions, they would have sought some means for bringing together inmates who were already significantly related to the individual whose institutional career was under consideration. The point of the classification story is that the C-Unit staff, as they were operating at this point of time, could not perceive the resocializing potential in the inmates' interest in understanding decisions made about each other and in their readiness to open individual concerns to the examination of peers. As a result, the staff took no responsibility for designing a device that might increase the treatment power of a necessary official process by involving socializing peer relationships in making its decisions effective.

[13] It should be noted that the general institutional group counseling program in DVI, although expected to encourage inmates to help each other with "problems," tended to focus discussion on inmate problems of two kinds: personal difficulties experienced on the outside under conditions not observable by the inmate's immediate peers; and shared inmate gripes about staff and official program. As a setting for problem examination, group counseling was resolutely protected against action consequences. The Project proposal had been that inmate peers should be encouraged to help each other deal with immediate problem situations under the guidance of staff and that such discussions should influence official and inmate action in relation to individuals.

[14] It is important to note that in this case the supervisor planned training for the staff, whereas the first staff organized training for itself; and that action staff meetings were now considered dispensable because there were relatively few management decisions requiring staff discussion.

skills. Treatment had been relegated by this staff to the one-to-one relationships in which the personal problems of inmates could be discussed;
and their key concern proved to be "How can I keep a relationship with
the inmate and still exercise the necessary authority?" The answer to this
question was inherent in the earlier subject matter relating the exercise of
authority in management to treatment, but the staff had not been able to
hear because the pressures in their own situation provided too many
strains toward compartmentalizing these two functions in separate kinds
of staff activity.

STAFF VERSUS INMATES

A month later in June, 1962, the "Moving Skid Row" incident, described
in Chapter V, revealed a staff now completely unaware of the effect of
management processes on the relationships between staff and inmates.

It will be remembered from the Moving Skid Row story that the staff
had attempted to resolve their own recurring problems of inmate requests
for room changes and inadequate supervision of the nonhonor rooms by
moving skid row to the ground floor. In the process they freed a block of
rooms for honor status men in the desirable area of the third tier. As a
subsidiary provision, one room change by request was to be permitted
each honor inmate in the order of seniority after arriving in C-Unit. These
related decisions were reached in a June, 1962, staff meeting, and implemented the following week.

This time there was no planned discussion between staff and inmates,
although there is nothing more crucial to an inmate than the location of
his "house." Inmates had received incorrect information from the officers,
and some had put in their requests for specific rooms (although the request was to be for a room change, not a particular room). The lieutenant
and a counselor together assigned men to the newly vacated honor rooms
in the order of seniority, beginning at the least favored end of the third
tier. When the transfer sheet was posted, there was a great uproar among
the inmates. In an effort to postpone the moves until after discussion, the
inmates drew up a petition (the first since the early days of C-Unit)
signed by over half the men in the Unit and submitted by an inmate committee requesting a meeting with staff. No meeting was called, and the
leaders of the protest group were subjected to severe staff censure.

The staff made no effort following this episode to consider what had
caused the trouble. Most staff members, administrators, counselors, and
custody officers alike, were angry and disgusted that their liberal action
had not been appreciated. They agreed, "No matter what you do for inmates you can't please them."

Nevertheless, we should note the staff actions that ensured an unfavorable outcome. The series of decisions that had pleased staff had not been a result of problem-solving among role groups. Rather, they were reached through a bargaining process between counselors and custody in which custody received better access to supervision of troublesome inmates; counselors received some freedom to approve reasonable requests for room changes, although this freedom was strictly limited by the seniority rule; and honor inmates, without being asked what they wanted, received access to the desirable rooms on the third tier formerly occupied by skid row. Inmates were prepared for these major changes in the "zoning" of their community by announcement, but they were not asked to discuss the plan before the changes were made. When inmates requested a restoration of the rights of C-Unit—a meeting with staff—they were ignored and those who had dared to take leadership in criticism were stigmatized as "trouble-makers." The staff, now oriented to operate in a way that did not include problem-solving either in its own work or in work with inmates, were surprised and angered because inmates had questioned management and were not grateful for a benefit bestowed by an upper authority.

In this incident we see a staff lacking the crucial information about inmate interests that they needed in order to make appropriate decisions and unable to understand either inmate operations or their own. Management of procedures had taken over the relationships between staff and inmates, except in the privacy of the individual interview; and the staff had resolved its own conflicts by establishing a common front against the inmates on management issues while relegating treatment to the therapeutic interview with the individual. In the C-Unit community there were now staff on one side, and on the other, inmates without rights, who could choose to be clients.

LACK OF CORRECTIVES IN THE
NEW STAFF'S EXPERIENCE

In spite of the many obvious influences that pressed the second staff toward its final adaptation in the Project, we need to ask why its members did not see what was happening and correct their behavior before the problems became so cumulative that they were irreversible. These were not ill-intentioned people. Each member had desired to be a part of the Project and was dedicated to the accomplishment of its purposes as he understood them. Repeatedly alternative courses of action had been suggested by the director, who had led a former staff in the problem-solving activities of the first year. Why, given leadership support and the evidence of their own experience, did the second staff not challenge the traditional patterns for work that were smothering the community of which they talked?

In early attempts to explain the change in staff operation from the first to the second staff the answers to this question seemed to lie in two directions, one specific to the C-Unit experience and the other suggesting more extensive implications.

INEFFECTIVE LEADERSHIP

First, the director was never in an administrative position with the second staff to ensure their being rewarded with success when they did attempt to follow her lead in problem-solving management. Proposals for action in terms of the problem-solving framework did not work when implemented by administrative personnel with contrary orientations. In addition, the increasing separation among the three authorities in the Project seriously limited the information available to any one executive about what was going on among the various subgroups within the C-Unit community. Both analysis of problems and recommendations for action suffered accordingly; and any one person's proposal to remedy a problem situation tended to be limited in usefulness because it was based on inadequate information. In consequence, the staff never learned what the words of the Project's model meant through successful action. Like the inmates, who do not become resocialized unless they live the new values they speak about, the second staff never learned through action to be problem-solving managers.

CONTRARY ORIENTATIONS

More fundamentally, the new staff members lacked any intellectual perspective from which to question either what they were doing or the consequences of what they did. Each in his own way lived in terms of a self-consistent set of orientations about human beings and the necessary relations among them that made such matters as the separation of management and treatment and the fundamental opposition of inmate and staff interests seem inevitable. The orientations that constricted their imaginations have their roots deep in the religious and economic history of our society; and it is no accident that such assumptions about man and his social relations find their most thoroughgoing expression in our institutions for dealing with offenders.[15]

---

[15] See "Puritanism and Deviancy," in Kai T. Eikson's *Wayward Puritans*, John Wiley and Sons, New York, 1966, pp. 185–205, for an explication of the influence of puritan cosmology on the governing philosophy of prison management in the United States.

In general, all the members of the second staff acted on the following notions about human relations.

Bureaucratic Work Patterns. First, the new staff members were committed to the work relationships of the traditional correctional bureaucracy. In this model, authority to make decisions is delegated upward and tasks downward. Public communication among staff members is determined by a strict code as to what is appropriate between persons operating at different levels of authority. Tasks are allocated to persons in positions rather than to groups, thus focusing responsibility on the individual while limiting his resources for carrying responsibility to his own knowledge and skills. The efficient management of organizational procedures is equated with the attainment of the organization's goal. Accordingly, the performance of assigned tasks becomes an end in itself and rules determine the narrow limits within which discretion can be exercised in all matters touching management.

These assumptions about relations among staff in the accomplishment of duties establish an intellectual as well as organizational dichotomy between management and treatment. Since treatment, by definition, cannot be rule-bound, it is relegated to the limited area in which latitude for invention can be allowed by management, primarily to verbal interchange between a staff member and an inmate in a strictly defined "treatment situation." Thus treatment becomes what one does in those limited areas not governed by rules and in the time left over after the primary business of management is accomplished.

Individual Responsibility. Reinforcing the bureaucratic model for relations among staff, with its implied separation of management and treatment, was a more general assumption about the nature of human beings. In this perspective, the individual whether worker or client, is held solely responsible for his behavior. Whether he is perceived as exercising will or driven by intrapsychic forces beyond his conscious control, the primary dynamics producing behavior are conceived of as internal. The individual can choose to change his behavior either by learning a lesson from punishing reactions to his behavior, or by seeking professional help. In either case it is the individual who has to change.

This perspective on human behavior makes no provision for the dynamic interaction of person and environment in the production of either inmate or staff behavior. The organization of social relationships in this environment is not perceived as influencing the individual's psyche or as evoking from him one kind of behavior rather than another. The organization is a given and it is the individual's responsibility to adapt in an acceptable fashion.

Such a view of behavior screens out of awareness a crucial body of information about the behavior to be changed, that is, the influence on behavior of the way relationships are organized. The social work supervisor, the custody lieutenant, and the well-trained bureaucrat in the second staff all maintained different assumptions about the internal forces affecting the behavior of inmates, but all three were equally unable to see that the way staff were organized affected the way both they and the inmates behaved. Accordingly, they were all equally unable to observe and understand a large component of the reality they were expected to modify.

Discontinuity Between Treators and Clients. Furthermore, this perspective does not recognize any similarity between treatment relationships and work relationships. The person in treatment is to be changed. He is in a dependent position; the relationship is focused on him as an inadequate person; and there is no mutuality between him and the change agent. In contrast, work relations with colleagues are established among persons who are presumed to occupy their positions because they do not need to change. In the work situation, attention is focused away from the person and toward the position; and mutuality in discharging obligations is assumed. Given this dichotomy between "clients" and "treators," there was no reason for the members of the second staff to believe that examination of staff behavior could help in understanding inmate behavior.

Given this set of orientations, some more explicitly formulated than others but all mutually reinforcing, the members of the second staff lacked an intellectual basis for questioning their operation and its consequences for the C-Unit community.

THE ORGANIZATIONAL ENVIRONMENT

In retrospective analysis, a third even more potent factor has been identified to explain the inability of the second staff to adopt new orientations and to gain the satisfactions in building community that had been experienced by the first staff.

During the second year, much more than in the first, the Project was itself being managed by its organizational environment much as it was expected to manage the inmates in C-Unit. Without explanation from upper administration, the Project had been required to revise its administrative structure and to reintroduce functional divisions into its processes for exercising authority within the Project staff. A procedural change with important treatment implications, for example, the establishment of the C-Unit Classification Committee, had been established to serve institutional convenience, not because it made the C-Unit community more effective in treating individual inmates. At the beginning of the second year, the Associate Superintendent, Custody, proposed that C-Unit be used as a special treatment unit for identified troublemakers in order to relieve the congestion in the adjustment center. The Project's urgent report that the honor system procedures were handicapping its work fell on deaf ears; further exploration of this issue and its consequences was forbidden. Throughout the second year administrative personnel from the Project went like inmates with "gimmes" to upper authorities who held the fate of the Project in their hands and who could grant or deny requests without involving Project personnel in a problem-solving process that took into account both institutional necessities and Project requirements. Just as the organization of the staff groups within the Project determined the kinds of relationships that developed between staff members and inmates and among inmates in C-Unit, so the organization of decision-making in the larger institution as it affected the Project determined the relationships that the Project staff would use in its own work. What was not permitted in relationships between the Project and its organizational environment could not flourish within the Project itself; and ultimately the patterns of the governing institution proved more powerful than the ideas with which it took issue.[16]

It is little wonder, therefore, that the history of the second staff parallels in reverse the development of the first staff. Communication among Project staff members became "privatized" and segmented. Opposed rather

---

[16] A complete analysis of the relations between the Project and its upper authorities would include a discussion of the way the Department of Corrections dealt with DVI as a subunit within itself. DVI's upper administrators were themselves often in the position of approaching the controlling authorities in the State Department with "gimmes" that could be either granted or denied, depending on the orientations of the current office-holders rather than on an exploration of problems in the light of common goals. In a major sense, the Project itself had not grown out of DVI's formulated needs and goals for its own development. Rather, the Project was imposed on DVI's administrators by upper authorities who were more concerned with pressures in the larger system than for the immediate welfare of DVI as a part of that system, much as the honor system and the Executive Committee were imposed on the Project's organization by DVI. Thus the Project's experience with DVI was coherent with the authority relations institutionalized throughout the entire correctional system. It was as true that DVI administrators could not provide for the Project what they did not experience as acceptable in interaction with their own authorities, as that the Project's administrators could not provide for the C-Unit inmates what was not consistently supported by the immediate authorities in its institutional environment. Under these circumstances the flexibility toward change that was provided by DVI's administration during the first year of the Project's experience is important evidence of the fundamental good will of DVI's administrators as persons; and the return to status quo on which they insisted during the second year occurred at a point where subunit development explicitly threatened the organizing principles of a larger system.

than complementary subgroups appeared. Information about the social phenomena with which the staff were expected to deal was restricted both in content and in distribution, and progressively less time was devoted to the information-gathering steps required for problem-solving. Management at all levels became increasingly procedural as planning and policy decisions were made without explanation by upper administrative officials; in consequence, the staff lost ability to perceive the treatment implications of management at any level. And as the Project staff increasingly operated as though it were simply one link in DVI's hierarchy for delegating authority upward and responsibility downward, management within the Project became the business of staff as representatives of DVI's administration, not of staff and inmates together. Ultimately the interests of staff and inmates in C-Unit were explicitly structured in opposition to each other, except in the private communications possible in the treatment interview. By the end of the second year segregation among staff and between staff and inmates had supplanted community except in the outward forms.

RELATIONSHIPS BETWEEN STAFF WORK GROUP, THE OFFICIAL PROGRAM, AND INMATE EXPERIENCE

The work of two different staff groups provides impressive evidence that the way the staff are organized as a work group has important consequences for the kind of program they provide and for the nature of inmate participation in the program. In the Project's experience, when the staff group was organized for problem-solving management, task-focused activity appeared among inmates, both in their interaction with staff and in their relationships with each other. When staff managed by fiat and restricted problem-solving to treatment activities, inmates evidenced increasing conflict among themselves and with staff.

Our data suggest that a major factor determining the nature of relationships between inmates and staff in program is the organization of the staff work group. The staff of necessity use those organizational forms acceptable to themselves when designing the official program for work with inmates; and individual staff members operate with inmates according to assumptions established in their work among themselves. Throughout the history of the Project, relations among inmates appeared to be responsive to patterns existing in staff operation. Thus we propose:

The more effectively the staff operates as a problem-solving group the more effective will be the problem-solving processes used by staff members in work with inmates and the more the relationships among inmates will take on the character of socially constructive problem-solving.

If this proposition holds, the organization of the staff work group becomes an appropriate object for study when examining an attempted resocialization program. In the behavior of the staff group one will find important indices to what is occurring in the official program with inmates as well as to the nature of the less observable social relations established by the inmates among themselves. By the same token, the patterns for work established by the staff group will tend to reflect those used by its larger organizational environment. It seems clear that management by problem-solving at any level can induce problem-solving processes within the subgroups for which it is responsible but remains dependent for continuance on the support of similar decision-making processes in the larger system in which it is lodged.

In the next chapter we shall examine in more detail the notion that management by problem-solving can affect the system of relationships developed by the inmates among themselves by examining the inmate system within C-Unit and the means by which the first staff gained influence within it.

VIII - THE INMATE SYSTEM

THE PROJECT saw relationships among offenders in prison as one of the most powerful socializing forces to which the inmates are exposed. Traditionally the influence of prison inmates on each other has been characterized as almost uniformly antiofficial, so much so as to constitute an active barrier to staff efforts to communicate positively with prisoners.[1] Since the Project wished to mobilize all socializing influences available in the institution in support of resocializing goals, one of its chief management tasks involved encouraging inmates to relate to each other outside the official program in ways that supported what the staff were trying to do in the official program. Only so, it was believed, would the staff have access to understanding and dealing with the real problems of inmates, and be able to rely on inmate norms that could permit individual inmates to be guided in action by the values the staff were seeking to establish in the C-Unit community.

Influencing the inmate system in C-Unit proved to be a very different management problem from that of organizing the staff. By definition, the inmate system does not include staff members, who neither observe nor directly control the way inmates relate to each other away from staff. The

---

[1] A summary of the literature on inmate systems in traditional correctional institutions is found in Sykes, Gresham M., and Sheldon L. Messinger, "The Inmate Social System," in *Theoretical Studies in Social Organization of the Prison*, Social Science Research Council, Pamphlet 15, New York, 1960, pp. 5–19.

Project staff could control the flow of resources to the inmates, and so establish certain limits on their activities, but they could not determine what the inmates would do with such resources. Accordingly, the Project staff were forced to develop a strategy for dealing with the inmate system in C-Unit that used indirect means for influence. Something about the kind of resources staff used and the way such resources were provided would have to be relied on to influence the patterns by which C-Unit inmates would organize themselves to perform the social tasks necessary for any group of persons who live closely together.

Every institution has a strategy for dealing with its inmate system. The Project early learned that the main thrust of DVI's strategy was to minimize the ability of inmate groups to achieve cohesion and complexity in order to make it difficult for inmates to organize against staff. In the Project's perspective the resulting inmate system would necessarily be too atomized and primitive to act positively in support of resocializing values.

Accordingly, the Project's first arrangements reduced inmate mobility in C-Unit and allocated staff services to the housing unit in order to gain a strong inmate system in which the bonds developed among inmates would be intensified by the fact that both living and service activities were shared among them over a period of time. In addition, staff arranged for a four-month intake period during which inmates were selected randomly week by week. This arrangement ensured a period of flux during which the C-Unit inmate system would be in the process of forming its patterns; and so, conceivably, would make it somewhat more accessible to staff influence in forming those patterns.

Beyond these provisions to encourage a strong inmate system and to provide a period of flux before inmate patterns in C-Unit were fully established, the Project staff had no explicit notions about what their strategy for influencing the inmate system in C-Unit would be.[2]

A PROJECT STRATEGY DEVELOPS

In the early period many staff members did not even have a very clear idea of what an inmate system is. They tended to think of it, not as people who would necessarily organize their relationships because they lived to-

---

[2] The theory available at the time (early 1960) was concerned primarily with describing the inmate systems characteristic of maximum security institutions with inadequate resources. Compared with these institutions, DVI is a medium security institution relatively rich in men and material resources. It was therefore necessary to develop theory in a form appropriate to such a setting that would lead to prescriptions for action.

gether, but as the "inmate code," a rigid set of antistaff norms inevitably adopted by imprisoned persons and controlling individual inmates primarily through fear. During the proposal-writing period, state and institutional administrators as well as Project staff members talked of changing this code by "breaking the inmate system," somehow disposing entirely of the power maintained by inmates over their fellows.

CHANGING STAFF PERSPECTIVES

Only after a period of experience in the program did the staff recognize that relations among inmates always exist outside the interchanges with staff and that they influence all inmate behavior with staff. An important clarification of staff expectations occurred in a staff meeting in March, 1961, with the statement, "We are not trying to get rid of the inmate system. We are trying to influence it so that its norms will support individual inmates in resocialization efforts."

Although the inmate system was by then perceived as capable of either supporting or limiting the effectiveness of the official program, many persons on the staff still thought more of a culture shared by a collection of individuals than of a social system with its own tasks, leaders, interacting subgroups, and patterns for forming and communicating norms. Two recurrent issues reflected the staff's conceptions about the social entity with which they were attempting to deal.

First, the repeated expectation of the staff that a desirable inmate system would evidence itself in a consistent expression of positive feeling toward staff and program revealed that they still thought of the inmate system as a collection of individuals who might one by one be separated from the "code's" influence and encouraged to accept staff's orientations in entirety. The inmate enthusiasm that appeared in response to the Interest Group Program was very gratifying in contrast to the noisy hostility of earlier days. A natural human hope appeared that this glow of good will from individuals would characterize all inmate-staff interactions once every inmate had been "reached." Repeatedly staff members had to remind each other that "our goal is not to have everybody love us." Staff were sobered by noting that problem-solving always brings real differences into open expression; that many stands taken by inmates would oppose staff value positions in one respect or another and that inmates, given choices, formed subgroups to carry on outside the program the value dialogue initiated in work with staff. This perspective helped to correct staff expectations that the inmate system would ultimately become undifferentiated from staff relationships and official values.

Second, so long as staff action to influence the inmate system was conceived primarily in terms of adequate staff coverage reaching inmates as individuals, there continued to be issues among staff members about the appropriate disposition of limited staff time. Those who saw the inmate system as an interactional entity with resources to be brought into cooperation with official purposes believed it strategic to invest much staff effort in the natural inmate leaders who could influence the norms affecting all C-Unit inmates. Those staff members who thought of the inmates primarily as individuals to be influenced one by one through relations with staff saw the inmate leaders as individuals who "could take care of themselves" in using program resources. As a result they emphasized the necessity of focusing staff attention on the "less adequate individuals. . . . We are putting too large a proportion of our scarce resources into inmates who are already strong." In spite of these differences both kinds of work with inmates continued within the official program, and evidence that both approaches helped to influence the informal relations among inmates was increasingly apparent during the latter part of the first year.

It was only during the staff training sessions in August, 1961, that the service staff formulated a conception of the inmate system as a dynamic social unit, including and affecting all inmates in C-Unit, interacting within itself to select leaders, enforce norms, form subgroups, and generate the activities necessary for any group of persons who live together. This formulation, attained by the staff through engagement with a little known social reality, emerged along with a C-Unit inmate system that was capable of handling its own operation during two racial disturbances in the general institution in a fashion unique in DVI's history. At this point the service staff was ready to move toward a more sophisticated formulation of the nature of the particular inmate system with which it was dealing and to define the means by which that system's operations could be observed, predicted, and influenced.

THE ORIGINAL C-UNIT INMATE SYSTEM

If staff had been able to hear what was being said, the noisy statements by inmates in the early days about the problems created for them by transfer to C-Unit would have told them much about the norms, tasks, and means of the original C-Unit inmate system. It will be useful to review here some of the data presented earlier in order to make more explicit the orientations of the first C-Unit inmate system that needed to be modified if inmate relationships were to contribute to building a resocializing community.

1. *The norms of the inmate system proscribed close association with staff.* Relations between staff and inmates were almost uniformly formulated by the inmates as dangerous, safe only if strictly controlled by inmate

norms. One orientation group said: "What makes you think we want to know you better? How would you like it if seven of us walked into your living room uninvited?" For the inmates, moving the counselor offices into the Unit meant "more surveillance," reducing still further the freedoms available in those short periods of time when inmates mingle with relative spontaneity, and increasing the probability of disciplinary writeups during these periods. A deeper fear was linked to time. "You mean to keep us here longer so you can *help* us." "If staff knows you better, it might not be so good when you go to the Board."

A more vaguely formulated general discomfort about relations with staff was also expressed by the inmates, revealing an increased sense of inadequacy and jeopardy under the C-Unit plan for closer relations between staff and inmates. "It makes me feel like I'm being analyzed. I wonder if something's wrong with me." "Talking to staff makes me uncomfortable. It's easier to talk to inmates." "I've been taught to keep my mouth shut. It's a hard habit to get out of. I feel watched." "Staff always wants us to say yes. Here in C-Unit I don't know what you want me to say." "What do you want us to talk about? You want us to cop out?" "I feel like I'm walking on thin ice." "There's always some string attached." "Getting to know staff makes you do harder time." In general, the staff's wanting to know inmates better was expected to endanger the remaining freedoms of inmates, trap them into betraying themselves and their fellows, and keep them in prison longer "for their own good."

2. *The inmate system norms permitted close association between an inmate and a staff member only when the subject for discussion, such as the "personal problem," was unlikely to lead to revelations about other inmates.* An inmate could take a personal problem to a counselor and talk with relative freedom. To maintain this freedom, according to the inmates, officer and counselor functions must be strictly separated. "How come that officer is always asking our names? I don't want no policeman to know my name. If it comes down, you may not be in it, but the man knows you, he writes your name down. It's different with counselors." "Officers are two-faced." "Custody doesn't trust any of us." "The other day I got called down by a counselor for talking in TV and I thought he was out of line. It threw me off guard. That's the officer's job." "Did you say the officers were part of *staff*?" "What's with all these bulls asking your name and creeping around?" "Officers can't help. They aren't trained. That's the counselor's job." Although inmates recognized some advantages in having counselors more easily accessible, the counselors were supposed to restrict their activities to helping inmates against an otherwise hostile institutional world. The proposal that counselors would be interested in behavior on the Unit

and that officers would be interested in knowing individual inmates was seen as reducing the ability of all inmates to keep the operations of the inmates among themselves hidden from staff scrutiny and interference.

3. *The inmates expected to receive certain necessary resources from the official system to support their own activities. First, staff were expected to provide an externally enforced orderly routine that protected the individual inmate from the disruptive behavior of his fellows.* Suggestions that the inmates pool their resources with those of staff in controlling behavior on the Unit were met by a uniform retort, "That's your job." "A convict doesn't tell two others to stop gunseling. That's the officer's job. That's what he gets paid for, isn't it?" "Inmates can't judge another inmate." Requests for inmate help in resolving the A#-YA conflict in the TV room met with a similar response: "The final answer is not up to us anyway. Why didn't you come in with a plan all set up before you started C-Unit?" "If we had fixed rules and went by them, everything would be all right." Inmates expected staff to provide an orderly routine governed by explicit and consistently administered rules. If an individual inmate got caught violating these rules, "That's his hard luck; it doesn't affect my time." Within this framework of enforced conformity, protecting the individual inmate against his fellows, the invisible social controls of the inmate system apparently could operate comfortably to support individuals in doing their own versions of short and easy time.

4. *In addition to depending on the official organization for a consistent framework of rules and sanctions, the inmates expected the official world to provide privileges and material comforts.* The Project staff were challenged from the first: "What are you going to give us? It sounds like we have to do everything." "What am I getting to make up for the things you are taking away by putting me in C-Unit?" But inmate norms restricted official giving to material comforts or relaxation of rules. "I'm interested in goodies." "How about color TV?" "If C-Unit is different, how about an extra hour viewing TV at night?" "Why don't we get to go to the yard any time we want to?" When help in problem-solving was offered as a kind of giving, inmates routinely retorted, "You're not able to help anybody. An inmate has to do his own time and his own parole." "A con either straightens up or he doesn't. He has to do it for himself." "If you do find out what your problem is, you've still got it. It's up to the individual. People are different." "You staff have your own problems." "There isn't anything we can do about our problems in here. You have to be out on the streets."

5. *Within the framework of official control, the inmates used their own patterns to maintain order, to orient new inmates to the expectations of the*

inmate system, and to ensure a common front vis-à-vis officials. Although
the inmates were usually unwilling to describe their own mechanisms for
the control of behavior and clearly did not expect to use them in open cooperation with staff, they did acknowledge that means to control individual behavior existed and that these would be used to supplement whatever controls were exercised by staff. It will be remembered that the first
orientation group decided: "We'll get TV programming all set and then
when new inmates come in, they will just have to go along." An officer was
told, "Okay, you want a quiet Unit, leave it to the A#s and you'll have your
quiet Unit." Later, after the breakdown of the TV Committee, staff was
again told, "You make too much hassle over TV. Leave it to us and we'll
run it." The intimation was that inmates would exercise control in their
own way inasmuch as staff did not act, but that the means they would use
would not be revealed.

The inmates were more willing to describe the nonviolent means they
used for controlling the behavior of individuals, primarily the use of discussion among themselves both to educate the new recruits to the Unit
and to reach agreement about the propositions all inmates would support
when confronting staff. Inmates attending the first orientation meeting of
any new group would often report "no questions to ask" because "the other
inmates ran it down to me when I moved into the Unit last night." The
first group of 20 inmates revealed that they expected to use this educating
process with the next selectees when they decided to settle on TV procedures as a group and then "tell the new men as they come in that this is
the way we do it in C-Unit." In the first few weeks, "old" C-Unit inmates
asked to participate in the orientation sessions with staff and on occasion
joined the group to make their own statements to the new recruits. "They'll
accept it from an inmate when they wouldn't from staff." Early inmate
requests were for space on the Unit where committees could meet without
staff present to prepare for official committee meetings, and for a Communications Committee that would send reporters to sit in on all groups
and to write inmate statements about what happened. The first request for
change in the honor system involved permitting nonhonor men the freedom of the floor immediately after dinner, "so we can all get acquainted
and agree among ourselves about the plans we want to propose." These
control mechanisms evidenced a large investment of effort by the inmates
to ensure a united front in relations with staff.

6. *The norms of the inmate system assumed that each inmate would
distrust other inmates and that each would pursue his own goals—"doing
his own time"—without concern for others except when their particular
interests happened to coincide.* The meeting notes of the first four months

are full of somewhat guarded inmate comments expressing perhaps even more distrust of fellow inmates than of staff. "You can't expect inmates to take responsibility. They wouldn't be in here if they could be responsible." "If the sports fans are to have their time on TV, there has to be an official memo on the bulletin board. The Bugs Bunny crowd[3] won't pay any attention to an agreement." A YA speaking about YAs: "Give them honor keys and they'll go wild." "We don't want inmates to have a say about who gets an honor key. Inmates shouldn't judge other inmates." "I don't talk because the other inmates might laugh." "YAs don't deserve any privileges." "All it takes to wreck things is a few hostile inmates." "They're not friends—call them 'associates.'" "They're just a bunch of cons like me. I'll never want to see any of them outside."

Along with this distrust of each other went disregard for the needs or problems of other inmates. "Nonhonor inmates shouldn't have a say." "If they don't like sports, send the nonsports to another Unit. Then the honor men can view what they want." "The trouble is you guys are just thinking of yourselves." "I want to know what's in it for me." "If everyone has a say, it won't do any good." In addition, there was the recurring implication that one man's gain was probably a loss for another. "In C-Unit the YAs have too many privileges that I had to work for. I've lost status. What are you going to do for the honor men to make up for what the YAs have gained?" "You're just using us for guinea pigs so you can make it better for other inmates five years from now. I don't care about them. It's my time you're messing with."

7. *The first C-Unit inmates recognized three patterned adaptations according to which the individual inmate might do his own time.* The inmates in the Research Seminar told the staff what form individual adaptations could take within the institutional inmate system as they had experienced it. When the Seminar members were asked about subgroup formation on the Unit, the research staff proposed that up to this point inmates had identified two sets of subgroups: A#-YA; and Negro, Mexican, and white. The inmates responded firmly that this was not the way they saw the inmate population. In essence they said: "There are three kinds of inmates. There are other 'wise' inmates like us who know how to do time. Then there are the 'gunsels,' who are always getting into trouble with the officers and making trouble for other inmates. They have an idea about how to do time, but it is the wrong idea. And finally, there are the 'oakies.' They don't wash; they sit around and do nothing but maybe play the guitar, sniff, go on trips. They don't have any idea about how to do

---

[3] *The Bugs Bunny crowd:* YAs desiring cartoon programs as opposed to sports.

time. They're nothing." In the superficially controlled jungle that constituted the inmate's social world, they reported that the individual had three
choices: he could conform outwardly to official requirements while establishing his own sub-rosa way of life; he could join others in conflict with
both the official world and other inmates; or he could retreat into a half-
world where dreams wiped out consciousness of time, its use and its
obligations.

At that time the C-Unit inmates apparently did not recognize a fourth,
or problem-solving adaptation, as a viable alternative for the individual.
Much later, Big Mac, with his parole date set for six months later, decided
to drop out of program, as do all "wise" inmates, since he no longer needed
to "take it (what he did with his time) to the Board." To his surprise, "I
found I couldn't do it. Since I have been in C-Unit I learned to do time by
working at projects. Now, I just don't know how to do time any other
way." In a later section of this chapter we shall document the appearance
of a problem-solving adaptation as an acceptable mode of doing time
among the C-Unit inmates.

As we review these norms and expectations, accepted by the original
C-Unit inmates to govern their behavior, we note that they were highly
constricting, concerned more with proscriptions and protections than with
positive efforts to ensure inmate welfare. However, they do reveal that the
inmate system, like other social systems, performed the tasks required by
any group of persons who habitually associate with each other. For instance, the inmate system had established mechanisms for securing resources from the official system in the form of information, material goods,
privileges, and permissions to use time and space in given ways. It distributed these resources in various ways so that they became available to individual inmates for use in the pursuit of their particular patterns for
doing "short and easy time." It controlled relationships among inmates to
avoid the spread of overt conflict between competing subgroups. And it
inducted new inmates into the established official and inmate patterns
while providing means for inmates to cope with the tensions arising from
having to conform to these patterns. However, one peculiar feature of the
inmate system in C-Unit at the time was that, unlike many social systems,
it did not have ways of establishing collective goals involving the welfare
of the group and transcending particular individual needs, nor did it have
the mechanisms for mobilizing resources for the pursuit of such shared
goals even if they had existed. Its patterns were limited to protecting the
individual inmate from unnecessary interference from either staff or his
fellows as he acted in his own interest.

To involve inmates as resocializing partners, the staff would need to
influence the norms and processes by which the C-Unit inmates went
about organizing their own social relationships.

THE PROJECT'S STRATEGY

Although it was many months before the staff were able to make explicit their strategy for influencing the inmate system in C-Unit, the tools for a strategy were built into the program from the beginning, and the strategy emerged in action even as the staff groped for understanding.

The underlying framework for the Project's strategy was set by the original stipulations that inmates would remain in C-Unit as long as they stayed in the institution, and that the housing unit itself would be the basis for service. These conditions eliminated two props supporting the usual inmate modes of adaptation to DVI. First, escape from difficult relations with peers by moving to another housing unit was no longer possible. If trouble or conflict developed in C-Unit, it had to be dealt with by some means other than flight. Second, inmates in C-Unit could not insulate their participation in groups with staff from observation by their own immediate peers. Such insulation was frequently possible for inmates in other units, since often the members of a particular group of staff and inmates had no relation to one another except in that group. In C-Unit, however, the decision to make the housing unit the basis for community meant that when an inmate acted in a group with staff, he was acting before other inmates with whom he was directly related in the inmate system. Consequently, in contrast to the rest of DVI, interaction of inmates with staff in C-Unit was a functional part of the inmate system itself, not simply behavior somewhat remotely controlled by general inmate system norms.

Within this framework, the Project's official program combined two kinds of activities in its emerging strategy for influencing the inmate system in the direction of support for community values. It provided opportunities for inmates to work individually with staff on their own immediate problems, in an effort to reduce the demands they made on their fellows and to increase their abilities as individuals to become problem-solving resources to each other. And it deliberately designed the official group program as a means through which inmates could work openly with staff on the tasks of the inmate system.[4]

The outlines of the Project's strategy for influencing the inmate system in C-Unit can be observed in action during the noisy, unsettled four-month period of deliberately created social fluidity.

As we have seen, assignment to C-Unit was a disturbing event for most of the selectees, arousing contagious hostility and anxiety in many. This event, with its unknown consequences for individual goals, became the

---

[4] In a historical perspective, it must be emphasized that these activities were only gradually seen as elements of a coherent strategy.

first significant bond among inmates who did not yet know each other; and for each the concerns stimulated by this event tended to intensify more personal anxieties. The creation of C-Unit obviously confronted the new and as yet unformed inmate system of C-Unit with a massive version of one of its major functional problems, the management of individual tensions in a way that avoids behavior dangerous to all.

While the C-Unit inmate system was still in flux, the Project offered both its personnel and the program as official resources for dealing with tension, thus becoming a partner in forming new patterns for managing tension. All kinds of groups, some formally convened (as in the Orientation Sessions, the meetings of the Staff-Inmate Group, and the Committees), and others operating informally (as in the Bull Sessions) were provided as forums in which inmates could state their immediate problems in the presence of staff. Counselors were available to individuals to hear and respond to their particular versions of the more general problems. Procedures were established to legitimate and facilitate problem discussion among the inmates themselves, for example, a small office was provided for committee meetings, nonhonor men were given the freedom of the Unit floor after dinner for mingling with their fellows in a situation where talking was not proscribed, and a Communications Committee was established.[5] During holidays, special programs were provided to help inmates manage the tensions characteristic of holiday periods.

This use of the program to provide for discharge of tension in officially approved discussion and action served the purposes of both the staff and inmates through a single set of activities. The staff learned about real inmate problems and about the means inmates were accustomed to use in resolving problems. The inmates were helped to establish communication among themselves and were assisted in handling their uneasiness in a way that avoided the expression of this tension in behavior potentially damaging to the interests of all.

This experience in assisting the inmate system with one of its important tasks provided the model for the Project's basic strategy for influencing C-Unit's inmate system. In essence it consisted of legitimating the inmate system's tasks and using the official program, in both individual relations and groups, as the means through which inmates could perform these tasks with the help of staff.

This strategy accepted the fact that each system needed the resources of the other. What the inmate system needed from staff was official assist-

---

[5] Inmates had requested these opportunities in order to maintain control under inmate norms independent of staff. However, the staff legitimated these inmate system activities, thus opening channels for influence over inmate norms.

ance in managing the tensions of individuals, controlling disruptive behavior, establishing means for transmitting information throughout the system, and supporting inmates in helping each other. The staff, in turn, became increasingly aware that it needed an inmate system that would: (1) permit individual inmates to relate openly to staff in problem-solving ways; (2) allow the problems and tensions of daily inmate life to be shared with staff so that staff could deal effectively with issues of real concern to inmates; and (3) develop and effectively pursue community goals that transcended the immediate needs of particular individual inmates. During the first year the official program became the means through which both inmates and staff began to work at the tasks of each simultaneously, each influencing the other in the process.

A DIFFERENT C-UNIT INMATE SYSTEM

By the end of the first year it was evident to all observers that a new set of relations between staff and inmates and among inmates had been established in C-Unit. As we have seen, inmates in C-Unit were talking to all kinds of staff not only about personal problems, but about the day-to-day problems on the Unit. Even such a touchy matter as race relations had become a proper subject for formal and informal discussion between staff and inmates. C-Unit inmates could and did express concern about the welfare of their fellows and were able to mobilize their resources for "the good of the whole" as evidenced in the Welfare Fund and in the Unit response to institutional disturbances outside the Unit. Information gained from staff was moving accurately and helpfully throughout the Unit. And inmates who were known by staff as leaders among their fellows were also obviously leaders in the official program.

Moreover, there is considerable evidence that the patterns established during the first year continued to guide inmate behavior into the second year of the Project despite the loss of staff, the change in the nature of the staff work group, and the high inmate turnover that occurred in the fall of 1961.[6] In early October, an A# newly admitted to C-Unit, who was very

---

[6] In all, 59 inmates—30YAs and 29 A#s—were admitted during the four months—September through December, 1961. The average expected intake for a four-month period was 40 inmates, 20 YAs and 20 A#s. This increased intake was caused by the high number of releases occurring a year to eighteen months after admission to C-Unit. It is evident that the C-Unit inmate system lost a large proportion of inmates who had been socialized into its patterns at a time when staff were less able to assist in the induction of new inmates because of the loss of experienced personnel.

angry about his reassignment, insisted that the Project could not be selecting its population randomly. "All C-Unit inmates look alike to me. You're probably selecting so your record will look good. I've never seen a unit where so many men look as though they are going to make it on parole. So many guys always up there talking to the officer, running errands, and doing things for him." In late October the Holiday Committee asked that the C-Unit Christmas celebration include a special religious service for all C-Unit men. The C-Unit football team, with its widespread inmate support involving loyalty to the Unit as a whole, was a project of January, 1962. It is evident that C-Unit inmates could not have successfully organized so complex an undertaking unless communication pathways had been open, patterns for mobilizing their own resources had been available, and sentiments of loyalty to the Unit had been widespread. And as late as the end of January, the Third-Tier Incident began when several inmates who were having trouble with another group first used customary C-Unit processes for "educating those other guys" and then brought the problem to staff for help in resolving it.

From such observations it is reasonable to surmise that during the first year the inmate system in C-Unit changed significantly in the directions sought by staff, and that these new patterns survived in C-Unit at least until the Third-Tier Incident in January, 1962.[7] Certainly the observed interactions among inmates and between inmates and staff strongly suggest that problem-solving had become an accepted mode of inmate adaptation in C-Unit, that communication from inmates to staff about important matters in the Unit was relatively frequent and open, and that inmates could define and effectively pursue shared goals.

However, the observations provide only a sketchy picture of the inmate system in C-Unit and do not permit a systematic comparison of C-Unit with the rest of DVI. Consequently, in order to present a comparative perspective on what was happening among inmates in C-Unit, we turn to a survey of inmates conducted in C-Unit and two other housing units.

In the weeks just prior to the Third-Tier Incident, nearly all inmates in C-Unit were interviewed, and in the following months random samples of inmates in an honor unit and a nonhonor unit were interviewed with the same questionnaire.[8] It will be recalled that inmates earned honor status at DVI by accumulating seniority in terms of time without disciplinary

---

[7] Evidently, during the first several months of the second year of the Project, up until the Third-Tier Incident, "what ought to be" remained the same for many inmates, even though lack of staff postponed the expression of these expectations in a vigorous action program. Subsequently, a number of inmates reported that the Third-Tier Incident crystallized emerging inmate uneasiness about the new staff and established a permanent split between inmate interests and staff interests.

[8] The design and administration of the survey is described in detail in Appendix B,

infractions, and that as a consequence, there were larger proportions of
A#s and older inmates in an honor than in a nonhonor unit.[9] Moreover,
inmates in the honor unit tended to have lived in the unit for a longer time
than was the case for inmates in the nonhonor unit. In these respects,
C-Unit was between the other two units, and consequently if the program
of the Project had no real effect, we should expect the survey findings for
C-Unit to lie between those for the honor and the nonhonor units.[10] In
fact, this turned out not to be the case.

Using the survey data we can address directly two central questions
about the effectiveness of Project strategy in influencing C-Unit's inmate
system: Did problem-solving adaptations become fairly widespread and
accepted in C-Unit? And was there more extensive communication in
C-Unit between inmates and staff about inmate concerns than in the other
units? We shall begin by examining the nature of relationships between
inmates and staff in an effort to establish the extent of problem-solving
adaptations. Then we shall inquire into how inmates with problem-solving
adaptations participated in the inmate system. And finally, we shall look
at communication from inmates to staff concerning matters important to
the inmate system.

INMATE RELATIONSHIPS WITH STAFF

Since some contact between staff and inmates is necessary if they are to
communicate about important matters and if problem-solving relationships are to develop and be sustained, we shall look briefly at the data
concerning frequency of interaction between staff and inmates. Then we
shall turn to the main question, that of problem-solving behavior in inmate-staff interaction.

---

and the construction of various indices used in the analysis is given in Appendix C.
The complete questionnaire is included as Appendix E.

The survey was not administered earlier because the instrument was not completed and pretested until late December, 1961. Ideally, C-Unit inmates should
have been interviewed in August, at the peak of inmate solidarity around the
Emergency Plan, to reveal the maximum differences between C-Unit and the rest
of DVI. However, the evidence for significant carryover through January, 1962, is
sufficiently strong to warrant using the survey data gathered then for documenting
these differences. It might be added that the completion of interviewing in C-Unit
prior to the Third-Tier Incident was one of those fortunate accidents that sometimes happen in social research. If the incident had occurred several weeks earlier,
the findings of the survey might have been quite different.

[9] See Chapter IV, especially the section "The Honor System in DVI."

[10] See Appendix D for a comparison of the three units on these and other background
characteristics. Aside from legal status, age, time in unit, and time in DVI, the
differences between all three units are relatively small.

TABLE 3. *Inmate Reports of Contacts with Day Housing-Unit Officers, by Housing Unit*

| Frequency[a] | | Housing Unit | | |
		Nonhonor Unit	Honor Unit	C-Unit
		Per Cent		
At least once a week		56	45	68
At least once a month but less than once a week		18	17	18
Less than once a month		26	38	14
	Total	100	100	100
	Base	(57)	(60)	(120)

[a] Item 95: "On the average, about how often do you talk to [the day housing-unit officer]—either on business or just conversation?"

FREQUENCY OF INMATE CONTACT WITH STAFF

Although no necessary minimum amount of contact could be specified ahead of time, we have already seen that the C-Unit program was designed to increase frequency of interaction between staff and inmates. Despite the increased opportunities for interaction with staff in C-Unit, an inmate housed there could choose to avoid contact with counselors and officers almost as easily in C-Unit as elsewhere, since most interaction was voluntary except for the bare minimum necessary for procedural matters. However, looking across the first row in Table 3, we see that C-Unit inmates were the most likely to report talking with the day housing-unit officer at least once a week, and similarly, the top row of Table 4 indicates that C-Unit inmates saw the evening housing-unit officer more often than did other inmates. It is also clear from the first two rows of Table 5 that the increased availability of counselors in C-Unit was accompanied by greatly increased formal contact. Moreover, when we consider informal inmate contacts with counselors, which were almost completely voluntary in contrast to the formal contacts arranged through ducats, we find that 43 per cent of the C-Unit inmates reported more than one informal contact per month, compared with 3 per cent of the inmates in the other two units.[11]

[11] The informal contacts question is item 84 in the questionnaire: "On the average, about how often do you talk with [your counselor] *without* a ducat—for instance, before or after group counseling, on the Unit, or other places?"

TABLE 4. *Inmate Reports of Contacts with Evening Housing-Unit Officers, by Housing Unit*

		Housing Unit	
Frequency[a]	Nonhonor Unit	Honor Unit	C-Unit
		Per Cent	
At least once a week	33	64	82
At least once a month but less than once a week	7	18	8
Less than once a month	60	18	10
Total	100	100	100
Base	(57)	(60)	(120)

[a] Item 105: "About how often do you talk with [the evening housing-unit officer]—either on business or just conversation?"

TABLE 5. *Inmate Reports of Formal Contacts with Counselors, by Housing Unit*

		Housing Unit	
Frequency[a]	Nonhonor Unit	Honor Unit	C-Unit
		Per Cent	
At least once a week	0	0	20
At least once a month but less than once a week	33	22	47
Less than once a month	67	78	33
Total	100	100	100
Base	(57)	(60)	(120)

[a] Item 83: "About how often do you see [your counselor] on a ducat [formal pass]?"

In addition to relating with unit officers and counselors, inmates in C-Unit as well as elsewhere could seek out still other persons among the institution's employees. A work instructor from a previous assignment, an officer with whom the inmate had become acquainted when living in a different unit, the chaplain, or the coach might become for any individual inmate the person to whom he turned for occasional support or advice. Since C-Unit staff provided easy access to counseling service, we might have expected that C-Unit inmates would make less use of staff outside the Unit than would inmates with much more limited access to counselors. On the contrary, we see in Table 6 that increasing their resources in the Project did not reduce their readiness to establish relations with official persons not regularly responsible for them. In fact, C-Unit inmates behaved in this matter much as did the honor-unit inmates.

Finally, all inmates in the institution were encouraged by the administration to use some of their leisure time in group activities, although such participation was voluntary. Since each approved group had to be supervised by some staff member, such groups provided inmates with an additional role-relationship in the program involving both officials and peers. In the general DVI program, weekly group-counseling classes were available for most inmates. Other groups included clubs for bridge and chess, teams for the various sports, and such activities as the Gavel Club (for public speaking) and Dale Carnegie classes. The Inmate Advisory Council was available to elected representatives from each of the living units, attracting inmates interested in the bargaining process between the inmate population and the DVI administration. In comparison, the C-Unit group program was considerably richer in the number and variety of activities available to the population it served than was the general institutional program. Even so, most of the C-Unit groups were voluntary, and some C-Unit inmates chose not to take part in any group.

TABLE 6.   *Inmate Reports of Informal Contacts with Other Personnel, by Housing Unit*

| | | Housing Unit | | |
Frequency[a]		Nonhonor Unit	Honor Unit	C-Unit
		Per Cent		
At least once a week		12	23	23
Less than once a week		2	4	12
No "other" staff member mentioned		86	73	65
	Total	100	100	100
	Base	(57)	(60)	(120)

[a] Item 40: "How often do you see [person named as 'other']?"

TABLE 7. *Inmate Participation in Group Activities for Youths and Adults in C-Unit and DVI*

	Legal Status			
	Youths		Adults	
Participation[b]	*Comparison Sample*[a]	*C-Unit Population 9/60–6/62*	*Comparison Sample*[a]	*C-Unit Population 9/60–6/62*
	Per Cent			
No groups	28	3	11	5
Group counseling only	47	11	35	13
One to three events other than group counseling[c]	20	26	24	31
Four or more events other than group counseling	5	60	30	51
Total	100	100	100	100
Base	(143)	(133)	(123)	(133)

[a] The comparison sample was drawn from the DVI population according to the same criteria as the C-Unit population.
[b] SOURCE: Official ISCP and DVI records.
[c] The "events" counted here were defined as a group other than group counseling holding one or more meetings in any one month, regardless of the number of meetings of that particular group during the month. This definition underestimates the number of events for C-Unit inmates, since almost all C-Unit groups met weekly, while many non-C-Unit groups met only once a month.

Table 7 presents the data on group participation for YAs and A#s in C-Unit during the first eighteen months, as compared with participation by a sample of YAs and A#s living outside C-Unit over that same period.[12] It is evident that inmates in the comparison sample during this period had limited exposure to the group program, while in C-Unit most inmates had participated in some group activity. Over half of both the YAs and the A#s in C-Unit are recorded as having participated in four or more monthly group events during this time compared with less than a third in the rest of DVI.

Further, looking at the YAs, we see that C-Unit YAs participated more

---

[12] This comparison sample was drawn at random from the same pool of eligibles as the C-Unit population.

extensively in group activities than did YAs in the rest of DVI. This suggests that C-Unit staff had somewhat more access than the staff in the rest of the institution to a large part of population customarily left out of group activities.

It is apparent that inmates in C-Unit reported more contact with all kinds of staff than did other inmates. This readiness to approach staff became customary in C-Unit, and inmates were frequently seen talking informally to counselors other than their own, as well as with administrators and researchers, whenever these persons appeared in the Unit. In fact, it was almost impossible to conduct any business on the Unit without also spending time with the inmates on the floor who clustered around to report progress, ask questions, or open discussion on some matter, which might range from personal problems to more general topics such as the honor system, the pros and cons of a current project, or the problems of parole. This expanded interest in informal contacts with official personnel extended to visitors to the Unit, who often commented on the spontaneity with which C-Unit inmates approached strangers, introduced themselves, inquired about the visitors' interests, and offered information.

PROBLEM-SOLVING RELATIONSHIPS WITH STAFF

Extensive contact between inmates and staff was an essential precondition for the emergence and stability of problem-solving interaction. Problem-solving behavior, however, depended on the way staff members acted in their relations with inmates. In addition to simply talking with an inmate, a staff member had to engage him in dealing with matters considered important by the inmate, and in a way that meant that real issues were being dealt with honestly and realistically.

Relationships with Individual Staff Members. If a problem-solving relationship existed between an inmate and a staff member, the inmate should have experienced two conditions:

1. The content of interaction between the staff member and the inmate included more than just routine procedural matters, and it involved "talking serious," which in inmate argot means talking about important matters in a relatively honest and direct way.

2. The staff member's response was felt by the inmate as understanding of inmate problems, appropriate to the roles required by the tasks at hand, and not involving overt conflict.

While these two conditions do not guarantee the presence of a problem-solving relationship, they can provide a usable index since the absence of either clearly makes a problem-solving relationship improbable.

TABLE 8. *Problem-Solving Relationships Between Inmates and Various Staff Members, by Housing Unit*

	Housing Unit		
Staff Members	Nonhonor Unit	Honor Unit	C-Unit
		Per Cent[a]	
At least one unit officer	9	12	28
Counselor	10	13	41
At least one supervisor	16	17	31
Other personnel	0	5	6
Base	(57)	(60)	(120)

[a] Percentages do not add to 100 because an inmate could have a problem-solving relationship with more than one staff member.

To obtain a measure of the extent of problem-solving relationships, every inmate interviewed in the survey was asked a series of questions about each of several staff members: the day and evening housing-unit officers; his counselor; his morning and afternoon work supervisors or instructors; and any other staff member with whom the inmate felt particularly at ease. For each staff member, the inmate was asked if he talked about more than just routine business; if he "talked serious" with the staff member; if he thought the staff member understood inmates; if he felt he was treated in an appropriate role such as student or workman by the staff member rather than "just like another inmate"; and if he and the staff member got along. When an inmate responded affirmatively to all of these questions, the relationship between him and the staff member was classified as problem-solving.[13]

The results of this procedure are tabulated in Table 8. Looking across each row, we see that for every category of personnel except "other," C-Unit inmates were more likely to report problem-solving relationships. One particularly interesting finding is that C-Unit inmates more often reported problem-solving relationships with work supervisors, vocational instructors, and teachers than did inmates in other units. This supports the idea of the Project planners that problem-solving activity, once started, would tend to spread into relationships not originally affected by the pro-

---

[13] The construction of this index and the specific questions for each staff member are described in greater detail in Appendix C.

TABLE 9. *Number of Problem-Solving Relationships Between Inmates and Individual Staff Members, by Housing Unit*

Number of Problem-solving Relationships with Individual Staff Members	Housing Unit		
	Nonhonor Unit	Honor Unit	C-Unit
	Per Cent		
Two or more	5	13	35
One	25	13	29
None	70	74	36
Total	100	100	100
Base	(57)	(60)	(120)

gram.[14] Further, looking at Table 9, we see that C-Unit inmates were more likely than other inmates to have problem-solving relationships with several staff members.

C-Unit Groups. In addition to the questions about relationships with individual staff members, C-Unit inmates were asked about their participation in the C-Unit group program. However, in the questionnaire, the same questions were not asked about groups as about relationships with individual staff, and consequently, the index of a problem-solving relationship is somewhat different. Specifically, an inmate's experience in a C-Unit group was classified as problem-solving if he saw the other inmate participants as not putting on a front merely to impress staff, not "sniveling" (special pleading in a complaining, unmanly way), and not "snitching" (informing on other inmates), and if he thought the group accomplished something for C-Unit as a whole.[15] Again, these conditions do not ensure the presence of a problem-solving relationship but only make it more probable, and their absence surely renders a problem-solving relationship unlikely.[16]

---

[14] Moreover, the more problem-solving relationships an inmate had within C-Unit, the more likely he was to have problem-solving relationships outside the Project, which gives additional support to this idea.

[15] A more complete discussion of this index is contained in Appendix C.

[16] Unfortunately, a corresponding series of questions was not asked of non-C-Unit inmates about their experiences in officially sponsored groups. At the time the questionnaire was constructed, the reasoning was that the officially imposed constraints on discussion in non-C-Unit groups made the emergence of problem-solving be-

By this criterion, 43 per cent of the inmates who recalled having participated in the C-Unit group program also reported a problem-solving relationship in the C-Unit groups. It should be noted that only about half the C-Unit sample did recall in the interview that they had participated in C-Unit groups,[17] so that actually only 22 per cent of the total C-Unit population were classified as having had a problem-solving experience in the C-Unit groups. These latter figures seem quite small in view of the importance of the groups within the C-Unit program. However, it should be recalled that the program itself was considerably less extensive during the fall of 1961 because of the lack of staff; in addition, there had been a large turnover in the inmate population during this period.[18]

Nevertheless, of those inmates who had participated in the group program, two out of five reported a problem-solving experience.[19] It appears that the group program in C-Unit was at least somewhat successful in developing the problem-solving patterns of interaction between staff and inmates that were necessary as a precondition if the groups were to be a means for the staff to influence the inmate system in the desired direction.

The survey data, then, support the observational impression that C-Unit inmates were more likely than others to establish problem-solving relationships with individual staff members, and, further, that a fair number of C-Unit inmates who participated in C-Unit groups had experienced some problem-solving interaction in these groups.

PROBLEM-SOLVING ADAPTATIONS

We saw earlier that inmates reported to staff that there were three ways of adapting to institutional life: manipulative conformity, overt aggression,

---

havior virtually impossible, and that very few inmates outside C-Unit participated in groups other than group counseling, so that in any event, little information could be gained by asking about noncounseling groups outside of C-Unit. In retrospect, this omission was undoubtedly a mistake.

[17] This was ascertained by item 28: "Have you belonged to any of the groups or committees that are especially for C-Unit?"

[18] Of the inmates in C-Unit for three months or less at the time of the survey, 37 per cent recalled participating in the group program, compared with 58 per cent of the inmates in C-Unit for more than three months.

[19] This proportion is about the same for inmates in C-Unit three months or less and for those in C-Unit for more than three months. It should be remembered, however, that recent groups in C-Unit had often been conducted by staff members who were new to the Project's use of groups; and that because of the recently established institutional "ceiling" on changes in C-Unit program, many group activities, since September, had resulted in disappointment for those inmates used to accomplishing goals through C-Unit groups.

TABLE 10. *Number of Problem-Solving Relationships,[a] by Housing Unit*

		Housing Unit		
Number of Problem-solving Relationships		Nonhonor Unit	Honor Unit	C-Unit
		Per Cent		
Two or more[b]		5	13	40
One		25	13	30
None		70	74	30
	Total	100	100	100
	Base	(57)	(60)	(120)

[a] Includes relationships in C-Unit groups.
[b] These inmates are classified as having a problem-solving adaptation.

and withdrawal. Each of these adaptations makes unlikely the development of problem-solving relationships in the official system or that any individual inmate would report more than one problem-solving relationship with staff. An inmate may establish one "good relationship" with a single staff member, while at the same time relating antagonistically to "those other bastards." In contrast, a problem-solving adaptation implies a general way of relating to other people that should be expressed in similar relationships with several staff members.

In general, then, inmates with more than just one problem-solving relationship[20] were classified as having a problem-solving *adaptation*. Using this index, we can proceed in the next section to investigate how inmates with problem-solving adaptations fared in their relations with other inmates. In Table 10 we present the percentages of inmates in each housing unit having none, one, and two or more problem-solving relationships. Using this criterion, it is clear that there were considerably more inmates with problem-solving adaptations in C-Unit than in either the honor unit or nonhonor unit.[21]

[20] C-Unit groups are included. Comparing Table 10 above, with Table 9, we see that inclusions of C-Unit groups increases the percentage with two or more problem-solving relationships from 35 to 40, which does not affect the major conclusions. However, inclusion of the groups gives a more complete picture of C-Unit inmates.

[21] This finding cannot be attributed very reasonably to selection biases. First, the percentage of inmates with problem-solving adaptations increases with length of time spent in C-Unit. Second, the selection procedure itself was partially random-

SUMMARY

The findings presented in this section indicate clearly that C-Unit inmates had more contact with staff than did inmates in other units. Further, it appears that relationships between staff and inmates were more likely to be of a problem-solving nature in C-Unit than in the other two units. And if we classify inmates with two or more problem-solving relationships as having had problem-solving adaptations, then C-Unit inmates were much more likely than others to have had problem-solving adaptations. This evidence gives considerable support to the observations of staff that the C-Unit program, in addition to allowing for increased contact between inmates and staff, stimulated the emergence of problem-solving adaptations, which were evidently rare in the rest of the institution.

PARTICIPATION IN THE INMATE SYSTEM

A comparatively large proportion of the inmates in C-Unit apparently had problem-solving adaptations to the official program. However, the question remains of whether these inmates were isolated or an isolated segment in the C-Unit inmate population, or whether they participated actively in the affairs of the inmate system as a whole. To the extent that inmates with problem-solving adaptations were actually involved in inmate-system activities, the Project succeeded in transforming problem-solving into a viable adaptation to institutional life.

FREQUENCY OF INTERACTION AMONG INMATES

Our first concern is whether inmates with problem-solving adaptations were isolates. To assess this, two questions were asked in the survey:

156: "Thinking now of the past month (or time you've been in the Unit), would you say you spent more of your time on the unit by yourself or with other men?"

157: "When you're with other men during your free time on the Unit, how many men do you usually associate with?"

The responses to the first question are presented in Table 11 which gives the percentage answering "about half" or "over half," among inmates with

---

ized (see Appendix A). And third, when various background characteristics are introduced as control variables, the finding in Table 10 is unaffected (see Appendix D for further discussion).

TABLE 11. *Inmates Spending Half or More of Spare Time in Unit with Other Inmates,*[a] *by Housing Unit and Type of Adaptation*

	Housing Unit		
Type of Adaptation	Nonhonor Unit	Honor Unit	C-Unit
		Per Cent	
Problem-solving[b]	[1][c]	[5]	54[d]
	(3)	(8)	(48)
Nonproblem-solving	41	54	57
	(54)	(52)	(72)

[a] Item 156: "Thinking now of the past month (time you've been on the Unit), would you say you spent more of your free time on the Unit by yourself or with other men?"
[b] Two or more problem-solving relationships.
[c] Figures in square brackets are absolute numbers rather than percentages. Square brackets are used when the base for percentaging is less than 10.
[d] Read: "Of the 48 C-Unit inmates with problem-solving adaptations, 54 per cent spent half or more of their spare time with other inmates."

and without problem-solving adaptations, within each housing unit. Looking at the first row in the last column, we see that 54 per cent of the C-Unit inmates with problem-solving adaptations spent half or more of their spare time in the unit with other inmates. This compares with 57 per cent among the C-Unit inmates with nonproblem-solving adaptations. The responses to the second question are presented in a similar way in Table 12. It is clear that inmates with problem-solving adaptations were as likely as others to associate with their peers.[22]

From these findings we can conclude that having a problem-solving adaptation did not isolate an inmate from association with other inmates. Conceivably, however, inmates with problem-solving adaptations formed a distinct and separated segment in the inmate population, associating with each other but not with outsiders. This question can be addressed because in C-Unit we were able to gather sociometric data, and thus an

---

[22] It is worth noting that in both Tables 11 and 12, honor unit and C-Unit inmates had about the same amount of contact with peers, but the nonhonor unit inmates had less. This reflects the fact that inmates in the nonhonor unit had less freedom to associate with one another, because of the greater restrictions existing in nonhonor units generally, than did inmates in the honor unit and C-Unit. If we did not have this finding, we would have some reason to suspect the validity of the data.

TABLE 12. *Inmates with Three or More Associates in the Same Unit,[a] by Housing Unit and Type of Adaptation*

Type of Adaptation	Housing Unit		
	Nonhonor Unit	Honor Unit	C-Unit
	Per Cent		
Problem-solving	[1]	[7]	58
	(3)	(8)	(48)
Nonproblem-solving	48	62	58
	(54)	(52)	(72)

[a] Item 157: "When you're with other men during your free time on the Unit, how many men do you usually associate with?"

inmate's own adaptation could be compared with those of the inmates with whom he associated.

Each inmate was classified into one of three categories in terms of the proportion of his associates with problem-solving adaptations. An inmate was placed in the first category if over half of his associates had problem-solving adaptations; in the second if half or fewer, but at least some, had problem-solving adaptations; and in the third if none of his associates had problem-solving adaptations.[23] Further, each inmate was classified by his own type of adaptation. The results are presented in Table 13, which gives the percentage of C-Unit inmates falling into each of the three categories, by the inmate's own adaptation. Looking across the top row, we see that 21 per cent of the inmates with problem-solving adaptations associated mainly with others having problem-solving adaptations, compared with 29 per cent of those with nonproblem-solving adaptations. This is directly contrary to what would be expected if problem-solving inmates associated primarily among themselves, for in that case, a majority of the inmates with problem-solving adaptations should fall into the over-half category. Moreover, looking at the bottom row, we see that only 17 per cent of the nonproblem-solving inmates had no associates among problem-solving inmates, which again is contrary to the idea that the inmate system in C-Unit was divided into relatively isolated subgroups.

[23] These categories were chosen because they speak most directly to the hypothesis to be investigated below. However, the conclusions are unchanged if different categories are used.

TABLE 13. *Adaptations of Inmate's Associates, by Inmate's Own Adaptation (C-Unit Only)*

		Inmate's Own Adaptation	
Adaptations of Associates (proportion problem-solving)[a]		*Problem-solving*	*Nonproblem-solving*
		Per Cent	
Over half		21	29
Half or less, but at least some		59	54
None		20	17
	Total	100	100
	Base	(44)	(72)
	No answer	4	0
	Total cases	48	72

[a] See the main text for a description of these categories.

There is substantial evidence, then, that the inmate system in C-Unit was not split into two segments, one composed of inmates with problem-solving adaptations and the other not. Instead, it appears that inmates participated in the network of interaction without regard to type of adaptation.

FRIENDSHIPS AMONG INMATES

Thus far we have considered the quantitative characteristics of participation in the inmate system. In this section we turn to the nature of interaction among inmates and consider expressions of friendship among inmates.

It will be recalled that when the first C-Unit population was being assembled, the inmates in effect told the staff that their relations with each other were characterized by distrust. Inmates were not wanted as friends on the streets. Other inmates were seen as "just a bunch of cons like me." "I'll never want to see any of them outside." "They're not friends—call them associates." "I associate with them while I'm here because I have to." Subsequent observations throughout the first year, however, suggested that this attitude might have changed in C-Unit.

TABLE 14. *Inmates Wanting Half or More of Associates as Friends After Release, by Housing Unit and Type of Adaptation*

	Housing Unit		
Type of Adaptation	Nonhonor Unit	Honor Unit	C-Unit
		Per Cent	
Problem-solving	[2]	[6]	75
	(3)	(8)	(48)
Nonproblem-solving	59	48	67
	(54)	(52)	(72)

In order to investigate this matter in the survey, we asked each inmate to name the other inmates with whom he associated frequently.[24] Then we asked the following question about each of his associates: "On the streets would you want him as a close friend, a friend but not really close, just an associate, or wouldn't you want to associate with him?" Inmates were then classified into two categories: those who wanted half or more of their associates as friends, and those who wanted less than half of their inmate associates as friends after release.[25] Our main concern is with how inmates having problem-solving and nonproblem-solving adaptations participated in friendship relations. Consequently, in Table 14 we compare inmates with and without problem-solving adaptations in terms of friendship. We see that, here again, having a problem-solving adaptation did not cut an inmate off from his fellows.[26]

Another, somewhat more subtle, point can be made from the data in Table 14. Looking at the second row of the table, we see that among in-

---

[24] In the honor and nonhonor units, fictitious names were asked for. See items 158–170 in Appendix E.

[25] For each associate, the response was counted as "yes" if the respondent answered either "close friend" or "friend but not really close." There were in all six refusals to answer in the honor unit and eight in C-Unit, over the whole set of items. These were classified as "no" on the assumption that negative attitudes were being concealed.

[26] Although the differences between inmates with and without problem-solving adaptations are too small to be reliable in their own right, they are consistent with the idea of a "spread of effect." Further, when length of time in unit is taken into account, the differences increase slightly. We believe that there is in fact a tendency for inmates with problem-solving adaptations to have more friendships than other inmates.

mates with nonproblem-solving adaptations, those in the honor unit tended to want fewer of their associates as friends than did inmates in either the nonhonor unit or C-Unit. To understand this, we recall that part of the basic philosophy of control in DVI was to separate the individual psychologically from his peers so as to prevent organized opposition to the administration. It appears that this effort was successful for certain inmates, who conformed consistently to the rules and thereby gained honor status, but who were less likely to form friendships with other inmates. In the nonhonor unit, however, we find a large proportion of those inmates for whom this strategy failed, and there we see a higher rate of friendships among inmates. The crucial point here in terms of the Project strategy for dealing with the inmate system is that in the nonhonor unit, friendships among inmates were fairly frequent but were formed in an atmosphere of antagonism toward officials, while in C-Unit, many friendships arose, but these occurred in an atmosphere of fairly open communication with staff. Thus, the friendships in the nonhonor unit can be interpreted as evidence of inmate cohesiveness against officials, but the opposite appears to have been true in C-Unit. The DVI strategy for dealing with the inmate system resulted in one set of inmates who conformed but tended to be psychologically isolated from one another, and another set who conformed less but tended to be closer to each other. In C-Unit, it appears that inmates were able to form friendships and at the same time interact cooperatively with officials.

SUMMARY

It seems evident that not only did many C-Unit inmates have problem-solving relationships with officials, but also that such inmates were not isolated from their peers. Rather, they tended to be well integrated into the network of informal associations and were as likely as others to form friendships.[27] It was essential that this opportunity to participate in relationships with his fellows be available to the problem-solving inmate in C-Unit if this adaptation was to become a realistic possibility for more than the occasional individual who was already psychologically separated from the other offenders with whom he was forced to live.

---

[27] Additional data presented in Appendix C further support this conclusion by showing that inmates with problem-solving adaptations were at least as likely as others to be involved with other inmates in such practical matters as expressing inmate concern with rules and procedures needing change, listening to the personal problems of other inmates, and doing something about the disruptive behavior of other inmates.

COOPERATION BETWEEN THE INMATE AND
OFFICIAL SYSTEMS

But the Project's goals for a resocializing community required more from its inmate system than a general tolerance permitting its members to cooperate with staff without suffering social isolation. It sought nothing less than active cooperation between inmates and staff in identifying the real problems of inmate daily life and in designing patterns for their resolution. Such a goal required inducing an inmate system sufficiently congruent with other subsystems in the community—official program and the staff system—to permit its members to practice problem-solving openly wherever they moved in social relations and to encourage the pooling of community resources in problem resolution regardless of the location of such resources within the different subsystems.

Such a community could not be assumed to exist if the problem-solving inmates in C-Unit segregated their participation in the inmate system from their relationships with staff, even if as individuals they were exposed to beneficial staff influence. Accordingly, the final question to be addressed with the survey data is whether or not inmates in C-Unit actually brought matters of concern within the inmate system into their relationships with staff as individuals and in official program. To the extent that the staff effort to build an integrated community was successful, we should find a tendency for C-Unit inmates who were involved in functionally important inmate-system activities also to communicate with staff concerning those same activities.

Earlier we outlined in general terms some of the functional problems that must be met in order that stable relations among inmates might persist,[28] and we have seen a number of instances of C-Unit inmates communicating extensively with staff about critical events and problems within the inmate system. To reinforce these observations with data from the survey we will consider social control as one of the activities contributing to the stability of inmate relations.[29] Not only is social control a critical matter in any social system, but as we have seen, inmates clearly attached a great deal of importance to the problem of enforcing norms among themselves.[30]

The following questions in the survey dealt with social control processes within the inmate system:

---

[28] See p. 200.

[29] Data on two other topics are presented in Appendix C. The findings are essentially the same as those presented here concerning social control.

[30] See pp. 197–198.

126: "There'll be some inmates who do things that bother the other men in the Unit—like too much noise, fires; maybe some racial tension. When things of this sort get really bad, do you talk with other inmates about it?"

127: "How about with staff?"

128: "Would you talk about it to the inmates causing the trouble if they weren't friends of yours?"

Positive responses[31] to both the first and third questions suggest that an inmate both participated with others in evaluating the disturbing behavior as violating inmate norms and was willing to act as an agent in enforcing these norms. Such inmates, it seems reasonable to suppose, were more likely than others to be concerned with social control in the inmate system.[32]

The question now is, of these inmates concerned with social control, how many were likely also to discuss the disruptive behavior of other inmates with staff? Such communication to staff is, of course, an extremely delicate matter in view of the widespread inmate proscription of "snitching" and "ratting." Nevertheless, observations by staff suggested that, while this inmate norm was retained in general, the inmate definition of what constituted illegitimate informing in C-Unit apparently shifted to permit a much wider range of inmate communication about problems caused by other inmates to staff. The data from the survey support this impression: 42 per cent of the C-Unit inmates who were concerned with social control reported they would talk to staff about disruptive inmate behavior, compared with 25 per cent and 21 per cent in the honor and nonhonor units.

Further, inmates with problem-solving adaptations should have played an especially prominent part in communication to staff about activities in the inmate system, since problem-solving adaptations, as conceived by the Project, entailed joint consideration by inmates and staff of matters important to both. As can be seen from Table 15, this is indeed the case: C-Unit inmates with problem-solving adaptations who were concerned with social control were especially likely to talk with staff about disturbing inmate behavior.

These findings are reinforced by similar results concerning other topics of communication between inmates and staff.[33] Clearly the survey data

---

[31] For the first question a positive response was defined as a "yes" answer to both the question itself and the probe, "Would these be inmates in the unit?" For the second and third questions, positive responses were defined as "yes," as opposed to "undecided" or "no."

[32] About one-fourth of the nonhonor-unit inmates and one-third of the honor-unit and C-Unit inmates responded positively to both questions 126 and 128, and were thus classified as concerned with social control among inmates.

[33] See Appendix C.

TABLE 15. *Inmates Talking to Staff About Disrupting Inmate Behavior, by Housing Unit and Type of Adaptation (Inmates Concerned with Social Control Only)*

	Housing Unit		
Type of Adaptation	Nonhonor Unit	Honor Unit	C-Unit
		Per Cent	
Problem-solving	[0]	[2]	50
	(0)	(5)	(18)
Nonproblem-solving	21	20	36
	(14)	(15)	(25)
All types combined	21	25	42
	(14)	(20)	(43)

support the observational impression that inmates in C-Unit had come to rely on the official program in dealing with the problems of daily life among inmates. It appears, then, that the Project's strategy altered the inmate system in C-Unit in a fundamental way. Not only were "good" relationships established on an individual basis with particular inmates, but in addition, by making the official system more permeable to legitimate inmate influence, the inmate system became more accessible to influence by the staff. In working with inmates to deal with problems important within the inmate system, the staff gained the opportunity to affect the ways inmates handled these problems among themselves; and to the extent that these opportunities were used effectively, the development of a community with common patterns for action became possible.

COLLECTIVE GOALS IN THE C-UNIT INMATE SYSTEM

From the perspective of a staff trying to induce an inmate system that would be an active resource for resocialization, an important fact about the C-Unit inmate system is not captured by the survey data: the emergence of goals within the inmate system that transcended the needs of particular individuals. The presence of such goals in a resocializing community is essential for several reasons. For one thing, only when such goals exist can the structure of roles in the peer group be complex enough to offer the range of alternative opportunities and demands necessary to support a wide and various exposure of individuals to resocializing experiences. Further, there is the simple fact that any stable community outside the artificial environment of the institution does have collective goals, and part of the task of resocialization involves teaching inmates how to participate in the determination and attainment of goals broader than their own personal needs. Finally, collective goals furnish a source of identity and pride that are probably essential props to the self-esteem and security of individuals who are experiencing extensive modification of their social functioning in a situation otherwise characterized by degradation and deprivation.

Most of the evidence for the emergence of collective inmate goals in C-Unit has already been presented. One of the first signs that C-Unit inmates were beginning to share a collective identity capable of supporting shared goals came in April of 1961 just after the Unit's first experience with a racial disturbance in the institution. In group after group, as well as in individual encounters with staff, inmates spoke to staff about how "safe" it had felt to be able to go back to C-Unit from the yard. The inmates said, "You don't shoot at a C-Unit man. You've been in groups with him and you know he's all right." "In C-Unit everyone knows everyone's a regular." "The Unit was relaxed. Most people went about their business. That's the kind of contagion that swept our Unit." "Everyone was kind of helpful. They were worried about the guys who hadn't gotten in yet." Out of this experience came the first suggestions that C-Unit might be handled differently during institutional emergencies, suggestions that developed into a concrete inmate goal later formally approved in the Emergency Plan after the second such episode.

In May a group of inmates proposed that a Gunseling Counseling Group be established to "help gunsels." This suggestion was met with such inmate comments as, "Give them an office. Then with some responsibility they'll straighten out." And at about the same time, the Seminar Working Group decided not to recommend that YA intake be screened to eliminate bad actors from C-Unit because you "don't deny a guy help if you think you can give it to him." Here we see inmates proposing that C-Unit, inmates as well as staff, had a collective responsibility toward certain inmates who in fact tended to disturb others by their behavior.

In the development of the Welfare Fund we see a similar pattern. The idea arose first with a collective concern about inmates without funds to buy cigarettes and other commodities and was quickly transformed as a means for mobilizing inmate resources for other goals as well, such as providing Unit-owned swimming suits and building a C-Unit library.

The creation of the Football Team was an inmate goal that, perhaps more clearly than any other, symbolized a collective C-Unit identity and pride in the Unit.

As a final example, the Goodbye Party for the researchers in August of 1962 was accomplished by the mobilization of inmate resources with a minimum of facilitation by staff. The Goodbye Party was organized by a "Special Projects Interest Group," established to plan special events for the "Unit as a whole." The inmate who organized the group, in an interview shortly after the January survey, said:

> I guess I was trying to be a psychologist when I picked that group. I didn't go after men I liked, but rather men I thought would have something to offer and would work on each other to bring out the best in each. For instance, there's Gary. Now he's an introvert, usually doesn't have much to say, but you should see him in there pitching in our group. And Al. Now on the Unit everybody—inmates and staff—thinks he's a real bad gunsel, and he acts that way on the Unit. But in our group he is just as serious and mature as the rest of us. An entirely different guy. And take Bob, he's sort of artistic and when you talk with him as an individual he's pretty inflexible in his ideas. But somehow our group makes him able to see other people's points of view and be ready to change his mind about some things. I didn't plan it that way but when I got the six picked, I had representatives of all three races, of young and older inmates, and of all three stages in the Unit: about ready to go out, newcomers, and those who have been in for a while.

In this manner inmates in C-Unit came to be seen by their fellows not simply as persons who were liked or disliked, but also as potential human resources to be organized to achieve certain goals for the Unit as a whole.

It is within this context that the differences between C-Unit and the honor and nonhonor units must be understood for their relevance to the goals of the staff. The evidence is, we think, strong that the Project staff had found a way to influence the inmate system so that it could in time become an important resource in the resocialization effort. However, in emphasizing these positive facts about C-Unit, we must not forget that the achievement was only a partial one. Many areas of inmate life remained taboo as topics for frank discussion between most inmates and staff. Significant numbers of inmates were not reached either directly by staff or indirectly through the more positive functioning of the inmate system. Conflict and distrust among inmates and between inmates and staff were undeniable facts even when the community was at its best. Nevertheless, the signs of actual change and the potential for further change were unmistakable.

A MODEL FOR INTERACTION BETWEEN THE INMATE AND OFFICIAL SYSTEMS

Although C-Unit and its staff never became in actuality the resocializing community that was implicit in the original plans, the changing inmate system in C-Unit enabled the staff to formulate a model for the relations between the inmate system and its official system that should characterize a more fully developed resocializing community.

In most institutions, three systems of activities and relationships can be identified: the staff system, composed of relations within the staff itself; the official program, consisting of relationships among inmates and staff that are established and administered by the staff system;[34] and the inmate system. Each of these systems has a structure of roles and tends to develop a complex of symbols and values in terms of which situations are perceived and evaluated. However, as correctional institutions are usually organized, these subcultures are segregated from one another so that the same situation is defined and evaluated differently in the inmate system, the official program, and the staff group.[35] In effect, when staff and inmates meet in the official program, the staff person wears his official and professional mask, and the inmate puts up a "front," each protecting his activities in the staff or inmate system from observation by the other. Inmates feel staff won't "level" with them, and staff members feel inmates are "putting on a shuck." Consequently, the official program operates as a barrier between the inmate and staff systems, so that although the two often are concerned with the same problems and have compatible interests, they tend to operate unilaterally, with limited recognition of how much each depends in fact on resources provided by the other.

In contrast, in a resocializing community, interaction between inmates and staff in the official program should lead to the development of a culture that is common to both the inmate and staff systems, so that situations are defined and evaluated in much the same way within the inmate system, the official program, and the staff system. In such a community, each side legitimates the concerns of the other, and the shared framework of symbols and values allows the two systems to develop common goals, identify tasks of importance to both, and share their resources in accomplishing these tasks. In both the inmate system and the official program, there are fewer constraints to deter persons from entering into problem-solving relationships with others, whether those others be inmates or officials.

According to this model, the individual inmate is provided with a rela-

---

[34] What we have been calling the "official system" consists of the staff system together with the roles provided for inmates in the official program.

[35] The phenomenon of a single set of individuals (e.g., staff) participating in two social systems with incompatible cultures is common. See, for example, Warriner, C. K., "The Nature and Functions of Official Morality," *American Journal of Sociology*, vol. 64, September, 1958, pp. 165–168. Generally, in such cases overt conflict is avoided by segregating role performance in one system from visibility in the other. For a more general statement, see Coser, Rose L., "Insulation from Observability and Types of Social Conformity," *American Sociological Review*, vol. 26, February, 1961, pp. 28–39.

tively open-ended range of opportunities for relating to both peers and staff, and he should find sufficient congruity between his experiences with peers and with staff to maintain a sense of personal continuity as he moves from role to role. Within the broader range of social opportunities, each inmate will locate that segment within which he can move freely at a given time. There will always be some inmates who drastically. limit their participation in that portion of the range that involves relations with staff. But the opportunity for expansion in both directions will be present for each individual, instead of the range being artificially limited by inmate or staff norms. And even those individuals who remain most distant from staff will be affected to some extent through a network of peer relationships that permits, and in fact depends on, open interchange with staff.

In thinking about this model, which is an extrapolation from, rather than a description of, the C-Unit experience, it is important to recognize that the inmate system created under these conditions will be powerful and organizationally sophisticated. Inmates will have a great deal more influence over each other's behavior under this model than in a modern, bureaucratically organized prison that seeks to control through segregation and policing. In this one respect, the inmate system under the model is similar to those found in many of the older prisons described in the literature, which also have extremely powerful inmate systems. In these latter institutions, the basis of inmate power is, of course, quite different, since it rests on covert collusion between staff and members of an inmate elite, who receive from staff the means of power over other inmates and in return exercise this power partly to maintain the appearance of order and overt staff control.[36] In a resocializing community, staff control is also exercised in large measure at second hand and through an inmate elite. However, staff influence is maintained through a process of joint problem-solving between inmates and staff, and the inmate elite does not have anything like a monopoly since nearly all inmates are involved in one way or another in problem-solving activities with staff.[37] In this situation, the social relations of the inmate system become available as a resource for resocialization.

---

[36] See Cloward, Richard A., "Social Control in the Prison," and McCleery, Richard, "Communication Patterns as Bases of Systems of Authority and Power," in *Theoretical Studies in Social Organization of the Prison, op. cit.*, pp. 20–48 and 49–77, for descriptions of these mechanisms of control. For an analysis of the differences between such institutions and DVI, see Wilson, Thomas P., "Some Effects of Different Patterns of Management on Inmate Behavior in a Correctional Institution," *op. cit.*, chaps. 1 and 2.

[37] From this it follows that if effective problem-solving were blocked for a substantial period of time in a resocializing community, a dangerous situation could develop in the inmate system. Either the inmate system would be deprived of sufficient

SUMMARY AND CONCLUSION

Our purpose in this chapter has been to examine the changes brought about in the inmate system by the C-Unit program. The Project's strategy for influencing the inmate system in C-Unit was based on two fundamental provisions: inmates and staff were assigned permanently to C-Unit, and the housing unit was made the basis for service. The strategy itself consisted of giving legitimacy to the functional tasks that needed to be performed by the inmate system and using the official program as a means through which inmates could perform these tasks with the aid of staff-provided resources. In carrying out this strategy, the staff relied on problem-solving interaction with inmates as the mechanism for defining jointly with inmates the nature of specific problems to be dealt with and the appropriate courses of action. Through this strategy, the staff hoped to create a strong inmate system that was capable of defining and effectively pursuing collective goals and controlling the behavior of its members, but which at the same time permitted the emergence of problem-solving as a common mode of adaptation and allowed widespread communication from inmates to staff concerning problems important within the inmate system.

The evidence we have been able to accumulate, both from observations and from the survey, appears to support the impression that this strategy was in fact beginning to work in C-Unit.

However, the purpose of all this was not to create change for its own sake; rather, it was to provide one of the essential elements in a resocializing community. Only when events in the inmate system are open to joint examination and influence by staff and inmates is it possible to design and carry out treatment strategies that include the whole range of significant experiences of an individual inmate and to draw upon relations with peers as a resource in the resocialization effort. In the next chapter we turn to the problem of how the combined resources of the inmate-staff community might be organized to contribute to the resocialization of individual inmates.

---

power to control its members, or, if it remained powerful, it could move in a direction hostile to staff.

It is perhaps worth noting that social control in C-Unit was apparently quite effective once the program had become established. Although the disciplinary data available are subject to a number of difficulties, so that a thorough analysis is not warranted, the basic fact is that the C-Unit rates were noticeably lower than those in the rest of DVI after the first six months.

IX - INDIVIDUAL CAREERS IN C-UNIT

IN THIS CHAPTER we turn our attention to the individual inmate, and how the combined resources of the community could be channeled to meet his unique needs and capacities. We wish to make two points: (1) An additional action group, not yet described, was needed to engage the individual in the experiences appropriate for his resocialization. (2) The community itself contributed to the treatment of the individual offender by providing the conditions for resocializing action by the individual.

THE RESOCIALIZING TEAM

The action group held responsible by the Project for individualizing treatment was potentially composed of all those persons—officials, peers, family members, or others—who were personally significant to the individual inmate during his life in C-Unit. Because each of these persons exercised a direct influence on the inmate, they were considered by the Project to be the active socializers in his life. The task of the Project was to enable these persons to make an impact on the individual in the desired direction.

In ordinary life, persons who are connected only because each is directly involved with one individual often do not become related to each other. In consequence, the influence of each tends to affect only one aspect of the individual's situation and may even conflict with that of others. Sensitizing an individual to moral issues calls for constantly exposing him to situations that would provide salient experiences. Accordingly, the Project encouraged those persons directly related to a particular inmate to become aware of themselves as a "team" with responsibility for intensifying the resocializing impact of that inmate's experiences while he was a member of C-Unit community.

The inmate's counselor was expected to identify these otherwise unconnected persons and involve them in action. In C-Unit he would be greatly aided by the fact that the organization of the Unit made informal and formal communication between the counselor and certain of his team partners a regular occurrence: the three custody officers, the leaders of groups, the parole agent, administrative personnel, and inmates. More initiative would be required to involve other persons such as the teacher and the work supervisor who were responsible for the inmate's institutional program outside the Project. But it was the counselor's task to be aware of those persons who should be included in the resocializing team and to maintain communication among them about the individual with whom they were all concerned.

The operation of the team was expected to accomplish more than a sharing of information. Each team was charged with developing a strategy for work with the individual at the focus of their attention. The strategy would guide the team members in planning the style of the treatment approach, in timing and grading the tasks to which the individual would be exposed, and in selecting the value emphases to be maintained during treatment.

The use of the strategy did not imply that each of the influential persons in an inmate's life would become a therapist. On the contrary, the Project emphasized the usefulness of exposing the inmate to a number of persons with distinct functions in preparing him for the variety of roles he would be expected to perform in the free community. The strategy was expected to coordinate the influence of the various team members by making explicit the nature of the problem with which all were dealing, the general pattern of work, and the contribution of each to the common goal.

The Project had planned to devote its first year to building the kind of relationships between staff and inmates that would support the development of resocializing teams. The work of the second year was to be focused on refining the skills in problem analysis and strategy planning needed for effective team operation. As we have seen, the loss of trained staff and the reorganization of the Project at the end of the first year refocused the Project on issues other than the treatment of individual inmates. Accordingly, there was less study than had been hoped of the ways in which the resocializing community becomes effective in the lives of individuals.

However, in the Project's two years, enough experience accumulated to support the idea that resocializing teams appear spontaneously in an inmate-staff community and that they can be used to adapt the pooled resources of the community to the needs of individual inmates.

The cases reported in this chapter have been selected from a limited pool of records. The use of teams was not consistently characteristic of staff work in C-Unit. Often, when team activity was, in fact occurring, the counselor recorded only procedural decisions and his own interaction with the inmate. However, from the beginning, the director kept a record of those team processes in which she was either directly or tangentially involved. In the second year she shared with one counselor a study of 17 cases from one of his Half-Caseload Groups.[1] Also in the second year a series of case conferences were used to train the Project staff in the use of the resocializing team.

From among these limited sources for data, we have selected those case stories that (1) best illustrate the resocializing team in various kinds of action, and (2) suggest, through their differences, the range of possible strategies needed when working with a population of institutionalized offenders.

RESOCIALIZING TEAMS IN ACTION

During the first year of the program, resocializing teams emerged in an *ad hoc* fashion, primarily because in C-Unit several staff members who were concerned with a single inmate were accessible to each other for communication about a common problem.

---

[1] Walter China, the counselor who participated with the director in this study, was a Project staff member from early in its first year through the period of reorganization. His patterns for work with inmates were developed during the period of maximum resources and, so far as the organizational environment made it possible, he continued to work in the same fashion. His caseload was composed of inmates from the northern part of the state in order to limit the number of parole agents with whom he would need to confer. One of his two Half-Caseload Groups was selected for study because he had kept inmate friendship groups intact in assigning inmates to each group.

The study was conducted as follows: The director interviewed each of the inmates, in a sequence determined primarily by the accidents of availability, without having consulted the counselor or the official record about the individual whom she was to interview. During the interview she used the diagnostic guide to be presented in a later section of this chapter. After recording the interview, the director formulated the apparent problem and proposed a resocializing strategy which was then compared with what the counselor was actually doing. Meanwhile the counselor recorded his own work with each of these inmates, including his own problem analysis and strategy, as well as the involvement of other team members in the resocializing work.

DENNY

The first treatment team to go into action appeared in response to an emergency during the second week of intake. Among the new YAs was a revoked parolee, eighteen-year-old Denny, whose appearance reminded one of a sick and hunted animal, hair awry and clothes disarranged on his bony frame. He talked to anyone who would listen about the two radios in his head that sent him contradictory orders; what he needed was a third radio to tell him which order to obey. On the first morning the Unit officer discovered Denny's serious enuresis and, observing his "readiness to blow," moved him to a room next to the custody office where he could be closely observed and given help with his bedding. In the orientation meeting, Denny began to talk incoherently. When a counselor redirected the discussion in an effort to focus the startled inmates away from his bizarre behavior, Denny wandered off talking to himself. After the meeting, Denny went as required to his temporary work assignment as an orderly in another unit and "blew his top" when given instructions about his duties. By the end of the first day the counselor and the C-Unit officer had together arranged for Denny to be assigned to C-Unit as a full-time orderly. The officer gave Denny responsibility for the TV room where he could be alone most of the time endlessly dusting the same areas over and over again between periods of watching TV.[2]

From the record it was learned that Denny was a diagnosed schizophrenic who at an earlier period had received shock treatment in a mental hospital. During his stay in the reception center just prior to his selection for C-Unit, he had been placed in the adjustment center in order to protect him from physical mishandling by other inmates. The Project staff members said among themselves: "If we keep that guy out of protective custody for one week we will be doing well."

After four months it was possible to write about Denny:[3]

---

[2] If Denny had not been in C-Unit, it is probable that neither the counselor nor the Unit officer would have been able to influence what happened to Denny after he "blew up" on his work assignment. If he had lived in any other unit, Denny could have been disciplined, sent to the hospital, or confined to protective segregation, depending on the perceptions of the watch sergeant or lieutenant who handled the matter.

The freedom to use Unit jobs supervised by Project staff, such as orderly or inmate clerk, as work placements for inmates who evidenced either special needs or special potentialities was an important asset in programming for individuals in C-Unit.

[3] The quoted reports have been edited for clarity in this context. It is evident in this case that Denny's illness had entered a period of remission quite possibly because of the support he received in C-Unit.

A few weeks later he was well organized enough to be made head orderly of C-Unit and allowed to answer the telephone (although at first he tended to sing over the phone). [Denny] began to sit in on groups as they met on the floor of the Unit and to make occasional rational contributions to the discussions. Later he asked for a school assignment and is now in half-day remedial reading. At this point he has earned his honor key; presents a totally different appearance as to hair and grooming; was recently baptized and has entered seriously upon Protestant religious activities; talks about goals for himself in the institution and for the future. The team for this inmate has been the morning custody officer, the counselor, the remedial teacher, and the chaplain. This team has been able to work effectively because Denny was in a system that could be at first almost totally protective and could flexibly widen opportunities as he became less disorganized and more responsible.

During his ten months in C-Unit Denny's social world gradually widened. He related in some way to each member of the Project staff. Fellow inmates picked up the staff's protective attitude, and more than one of the older men occasionally tutored Denny during the evening hours when he pored over the school books he carried with him everywhere. Denny gradually became more capable of meeting normal expectations in his work, although he still occasionally had fits of defiant rage in response to job instructions. After one such outburst later in his stay, Denny's counselor and the lieutenant supervisor (who acted together as C-Unit's discipline court) agreed that he was now able to accept the appropriate disciplinary action. As a result he lost his honor key as would any other inmate under similar circumstances. Denny accepted this decision with a certain kind of pride and earnestly set to work to earn back his key. Additional milestones were noted when Denny could be moved to a location in the Unit away from the officer's close supervision and when he was appointed to the Staff-Inmate Group for four weeks, an assignment in which he performed acceptably. When he was considered for parole release, Denny was torn between two desires. He dropped in to the director's office, saying, "I've grown up so much I hope they look at my good record and say I'm ready to go home. But, don't tell anyone, I think it would be good for me to stay a while longer."

The final team member, Denny's parole agent, was appointed to the Project just before Denny was to be released to his family. Fortunately, his parole agent was in the institution on the day Denny received word that his stepfather had refused to have him in the home and that no other placement was immediately available. At first Denny was in a storm, refusing to leave his room for dinner call or to talk with any staff member. The supervisor[4] and the parole agent remained on the Unit into the early

---

[4] Denny's counselor had recently left the institution and there had been no replacement.

evening. They finally engaged Denny in a discussion of the situation, persuading him that the parole agent would be able, on his return home, to communicate to Denny's family the facts about his progress since they last saw him. Subsequently, Denny left to live with his family on his scheduled release date. The staff hoped that the parole agent with this introduction to the problem and to the treatment methods found useful in the institution could continue the support that both Denny and his family would need in the months ahead.

By the end of his stay in C-Unit, Denny's resocializing team included all the Project staff, several officials outside the Unit such as the chaplain, the remedial teacher and the parole agent, and a number of inmates. One of the counselor's principal functions was to help the other team members, especially the custody officer who was Denny's first work supervisor, understand what could and could not be expected of Denny at any particular stage of personality integration. With little formal conferencing, a common strategy of protection combined with the gradual introduction of normal expectations and responsibilities was adopted by everyone. The more mature inmates joined the team operation without explicit invitation from staff, participating in roles that emerged because of the team activity. Surrounded by this relatively cohesive social world and confronted with the limited challenges that his disorganized self could master, Denny's overt symptoms passed into remission. For at least this brief period his self-image changed from that of a victim of internal disorder to a perception of himself as able to accomplish goals in a benign environment.

CARLOS

Carlos presented a quite different order of problem. He was the twenty-year-old YA leader of a self-identified Mexican clique whose members were lodged both in C-Unit and in other housing units in the institution. Carlos had been committed to DVI for leading a gang fight in which several persons were injured. His record revealed a long history of drunkenness, pitched battles with Negroes, and general hoodlum behavior. Early in his life Carlos had been placed with respectable Mexican foster parents who still cared about him although they were now nearly ready to cease trying to keep him as a member of the family.

As the staff observed Carlos swaggering among his followers, they realized they had the core of an organized ethnic conflict group within the Unit population. Carlos was built to be a fighter, stocky and broad shouldered. He was also very likable, particularly when his customary defensive scowl gave way to an engaging grin. Although he was intelligent, he was shy in conversation, and when he could be drawn into discussion he used a simple but picturesque argot that came out explosively. Verbally as well as muscularly, he expressed feelings simply and directly. Abstractions were not for him. He responded to early explanations of the Unit program by saying, "I don't dig all that. Man, you sure lost me."

After three months in C-Unit, the record shows:

Work with [Carlos] began when his counselor started conferences with him together with his foster family who want him to come back to them when he is released from the institution but who cannot accept his delinquencies. While conferences with him and his family were proceeding, the boy talked with his counselor about his desire to be a leader and his feeling of inadequacy because of his lack of education. He was appointed as a TV orderly and elected chairman of the TV committee, representing it at several staff-inmate conferences. When he earned his honor key, he was thrust into a real conflict because his former gang companions outside C-Unit felt he should have refused this evidence of cooperation with staff. The episode of the knives, the crucial decision point for Carlos, followed an evening ruckus in which he first led a rat-packing group against the Negro clique and then cooled it off.

The "episode of the knives" illustrates the staff's *ad hoc* use of inmate groups to solve problems that were critical for staff and for the Unit, and at the same time to confront the individual with value issues of importance for him. For Carlos the problem was explicitly one of identity and conflicting allegiances. Would he give his loyalty to the squares represented by his respectable foster family and the staff, or to his hoodlum peers who acknowledged his fighting ability and leadership? The report reads:

The week began with a Mexican clique leader,[5] who is in an identity crisis (deciding whether to remain a gunsel or to turn square) coming to his counselor and asking what would happen if he turned in several knives. Recently, his clique had become obvious on the Unit, collecting at the end of the Unit hall each evening and involved over the weekend in what was close to a racial fight with a similar Negro clique. The counselor asked Carlos to give him his knife and brought him to a meeting with the director and the supervisor. As a result of this discussion, two of Carlos' friends turned in their knives to their counselors; the rest of the weapons were thrown away and Carlos reported, "The Unit is clean." A meeting between the Mexican leader and the leader of the Negro clique with staff laid the base for continuing meetings designed to deal with tensions which, as the boys said, "are ready to be triggered off by just any little thing." At the end of this process the staff learned that it had been planned to "come down" (a battle between Mexicans and Negroes) on the morning of the Saturday Christmas party; and that "it has been called off" because of this series of conferences. In connection with the earlier ruckus between Mexicans and Negroes, led by Carlos but then terminated by him, Carlos said: "Man, I thought something must have happened to my mind. The way I've been brought up you

---

[5] Carlos.

fight for your pride. But there I was, the first time in my life I couldn't hit him."
And later, "I've learned you don't have to have a knife to be a man."

Carlos continued as leader of his clique but now his friends on C-Unit
were all trying to earn their honor keys to be with Carlos. They asked for
a special interest group for themselves "where we can do something with
our time besides teach the youngest how to do an armed robbery." Carlos
was beginning to discover an acceptable way out of his value conflict: he
could lead his friends in socially approved action.[6]

Throughout his stay in C-Unit Carlos had his ups and downs, at one
moment devoting his energies to the Interest Group Program and entering
into projects for the total Unit, and at another organizing his friends
against the Negroes "who are getting too salty." The counselor continued
to work with Carlos, with his foster family, and with his peers in the
English-Speaking Interest Group. After nearly a year Carlos was released
to live with his foster parents under the supervision of a parole agent who
had recently been assigned to the Unit.

Eighteen months later the parole agent reported that Carlos was still on
parole and still struggling with his conflicting identities, although he was
approaching a more stable resolution. He had married "a respectable girl
with considerable intelligence and patience." The first few months of mar-
riage had been rocky, with Carlos alternating between short periods of
work and long periods of roistering and fighting with his gang friends. The
parole agent reported: "Now he has a baby, Carlos is taking things more
seriously. He has settled down to a job and is working hard for the first
time. He told me he has decided he can still be friends with his old crowd
and not have to join in their fights. He says, 'That's too young for me
now.'"

In this case the core team included the counselor, the evening officer,[7]
the foster parents, administrative personnel, other inmates, and the parole
agent. What Carlos had needed from C-Unit was an opportunity to exercise leadership in legitimate activities that he could enjoy; training in the
social skills necessary for leading a group in contrast to leading a fighting
gang; endless patience while he learned how to "cool down," or manage,
his impulses; and a parole plan that could hold him in the open community while he "grew up."

---

[6] In the staff's perspective it was equally important that Carlos was becoming a part
of the resocializing teams concerned with his friends.

[7] The evening officer was responsible for appointing TV orderlies and organizing
their work.

ALLEN

Allen was a member of the first group of 20 C-Unit men. A clean, well-built, blond, twenty-three-year-old A# who "carried himself like a man," he was restrained but intense in his anger at the way his life had been disrupted by assignment to C-Unit. It was he who pointed out firmly that the "code" made staff and inmate association impossible. Allen was working full time for his federal certificate in air engines and wanted to complete his work before his parole date, which he hoped would be set for soon after his next Board appearance. He welcomed no interference with his single-minded drive toward his objective.

Later the counselor learned that Allen was the child of his middle-class parents' old age, the only boy in the family. He early broke away from his mother's querulous complaints, "How *can* you when you know my heart is weak?" and his father's distant disapproval, to become a playboy. Allen was already smoking marijuana in the ninth grade and his adolescence was one long series of parties, wild automobile chases, accidents, and progressive use of drugs until he became a mainliner. As he said, "I was *bad*. I stole from those who cared for me." On the few occasions when he was caught his parents paid fines, restitution, and legal fees. There had been one point in his late teens when Allen became interested in a girl and decided to straighten up. But her father, a policeman, refused to let her have anything to do with Allen, and he threw himself back into the wild life in a way that seemed to ask society to stop him. At age twenty-one he was sent to his first institution as an adult felon on a burglary charge connected with his addiction.

Before Allen came to C-Unit, the institution had already done much for him. He had graduated from high school and had received training in servicing air frames and air engines under the instruction of a strong, warm teacher who acted as a substitute father figure for Allen. Although he studied much in the evenings, Allen had also developed his interest in art. In his spare time he painted gaunt figures in various attitudes of imprisoned despair. In spite of his seriousness, Allen was respected among the "wise inmates." He could do time "without sniveling"; and he could "hold his mud."

C-Unit provided three additional experiences for Allen: counseling addressed to "why did I get into trouble"; opportunity to assume a responsible role in a community; and help with parole planning. When he began to see the possibilities in the C-Unit program, Allen was quite explicit about what he needed and serious in making use of his opportunities.

Allen's use of counseling followed the traditional pattern of casework with a client who has both motivation and capacity for insight. He examined his confused and bitter relationships with his parents and began to free himself from the guilt and need to punish, so obviously acted out in his delinquencies. An important clarification occurred after he had written his parents the good news that his parole date had been set far earlier than he had expected. His mother's answering letter expressed no gladness; it merely stated that they did not want him to come home. Shortly after, when his parents visited for the first time in months, they did not ask about his parole plans and spoke only of their own arrangements for retirement. Allen told his counselor: "At first I was angry and bitter. Then I thought to myself, I hurt them a lot; they are old and absorbed in their own problems. I suddenly realized that what I always wanted them to give me was never there for me to have anyway. I know now this is what it is and it won't be anything else. I sat down and wrote them how disappointed I was that they didn't care about my parole, but that I could understand how it felt to them. They haven't answered me but they showed my sister the letter and told her how glad they were to get it."

The C-Unit program engaged Allen's interest as a community in action. He participated vigorously in the Research Seminar; helped to untangle the communication problems that developed between the Music Interest Group and the institution's Inmate Advisory Council over the programs taped for use in the institution's radio program; and was a strong member of both the Seminar Working Group and the Orientation Committee that it sponsored. In these groups he related well with various staff sponsors, using the group process directly for social learning without special help from his counselor.

The parole plan required special permission to accept an out-of-state airplane servicing job and was difficult to implement. There were many conferences with Allen, his sister, and the parole agent, and a six weeks' delay in Allen's release because of uncertainties in the employing organization. During this period Allen used the counselor for support in dealing with the anxiety arising from his decision to wait in the institution for this job rather than to accept immediate release to a make-work job with no future.

Two years later Allen was back in the state with money in the bank and plans to enter college. He spent a short time with his parents getting their house and yard in order before moving to the college town. He told this story about using his C-Unit experience in relations with his co-workers during the air servicing job.

I was supervising the crew pretty much the way we ran the Music Group—everybody with his job to do, but everybody pitching in wherever an extra hand was needed. I signed for the work we did as a team. Then this new superintendent was appointed. He went by the book and everybody had to stick to his own job. The men were unhappy and so was I. So I went to the superintendent and told him how we wanted to run it. He suggested I had too little experience for the job; so I said if he was uneasy about my ability after six months of successful supervision I would go back to being a mechanic. I tried this for a while, partly because I liked to get my hand back on tools. Then I realized I wasn't going to be happy working for him. So I resigned from the company. I did it in a way so there would be no hard feelings and I'll be able to get a good work reference.

Comparing this vignette of mature behavior in an anger-provoking situation with the cold hostility that Allen had expressed in his early C-Unit relationships, the counselor to whom Allen made this report was glad he had had an opportunity to experiment in a more protected setting before he tried himself in the complexities of outside employment.

In Allen's case almost everyone he dealt with in C-Unit became a member of his resocializing team because Allen was independently using his widening experiences to practice the insights he gained in counseling. With both staff and inmates he was engaged in learning the meaning of human bonds and of responsibility beyond his immediate goals for himself. The counselor was active with other members of Allen's team chiefly to secure opportunities for him. He talked with Allen's work instructor and arranged for a typewriter to facilitate weekend study. He secured a research clerk appointment for Allen after his technical training was completed. And he involved the parole agent, Allen's sister, and the work instructor in the complicated planning necessary to arrange for the job to which Allen was released. But because Allen sought out ways to act in terms of acceptable values, the counselor did not need to engage the resocializing team in formulating an explicit strategy for treatment. In this respect, Allen represents a small segment of the total correctional caseload found in the institution.

CASES WITHOUT TEAM SUPPORT

There was, however, one kind of case for which the team never developed spontaneously. Until there was a device for convening the resocializing team, the counselor often struggled with difficult or "nuisance" cases without the support of the relevant personnel. Some inmates were so firmly identified in the minds of DVI officials as "troublemakers" that decisions about discipline or work assignments were made without consulting the counselor. Thus the counselor's work could be seriously handicapped by the unwillingness of other staff members to support his efforts. Eric's case is a good example of lack of responsiveness from the potential team.

ERIC

In Eric's case six months passed before the counselor could mobilize a team, and then it was Eric's peers whom he first used as co-resocializers. At first, all the relevant staff members, custody officers, and work instructors alike saw Eric only as an "agitator," a "nuisance," a dealer in contraband, and a dangerous leader in fomenting racial strife. Eric reciprocated the feeling. "I think I know how to let staff know only what I want them to know about me." "I like to needle that officer, hang around, make comments about what he doesn't do right, agitate him."

When Eric came into C-Unit he was a twenty-year-old A# who had been in at least three previous institutional placements since he was ten years old. Just before his present commitment to DVI, he was known in the community as one of the leaders of a dangerous neo-Nazi gang. In the institution he associated with other self-proclaimed racists. His criminal career had started at age ten with a widely publicized homosexual experience involving an older man, and since then he had been involved in a notorious teenage gang, organized theft and burglary, firesetting, and various sexual exploits. As Eric said, "I like being chased by cops, the excitement of pulling a job. I've tried all kinds—checks, burglary, robbery, theft—and having the cops shoot my car off the road. I've always been like that. There wasn't anything I wouldn't do, even as a little kid, to stir up a crisis." "I don't know anything I want to do that would be square enough. If I took up photography I would probably go in for pornography." There had been two stretches of peace in his life—six months in the wilds of Mexico on the ranch of a friend's father, and eight months in a military service where he was selected for special training in handling explosives. Both of these experiences had been terminated by Eric himself, who simply walked out to return to his home community where he was always in trouble.

At first, it seemed that the counselor was important to Eric only for two reasons: (1) Here was one more official to manipulate, needle, and bully into arranging special favors; and (2) interviews with the counselor provided an opportunity, irresistible to Eric, to brag about the criminals he had known, the jobs he had "pulled," his power in the inmate system, and his ability to annoy and outwit institutional officials. "I can tell you these things without getting them jammed back down my throat like with other counselors."[8] The counselor listened, facilitated requests when they were appropriate, refused to get angry when "baited," but did not intervene to

---

[8] Eric's stories included descriptions of how he had previously frustrated psychiatrists and caseworkers by refusing to talk.

protect Eric from disciplinary action when he was caught stealing, sniff-ing,[9] or hiding contraband. Along the way, he quietly challenged Eric's more obvious distortions of facts by lending him books such as William L. Shirer's *Rise and Fall of the Third Reich: A History of Nazi Germany*, and by commenting. For instance, when Eric talked enthusiastically about a young woman he had met at the Christmas Open House, the counselor pointed out, much to Eric's consternation, that he had evidently been able to like a Jew.

Since Eric expected a counselor to try to reform him, such a stance on the part of an official was incomprehensible, requiring further investiga-tion. The formal and informal contacts between Eric and the counselor grew more frequent, from seven in the second month of Eric's stay in C-Unit to as many as fifteen a month half a year later. The counselor be-gan to hear about Eric's "hero" father whom he had never known; his mother, her boy friends, and the hated stepfather; his sister with whom he had been sexually involved; and later about Eric's fear of losing his masculinity in the long period of institutionalization.

When the counselor had identified Eric's buddies, who were also neo-Nazi, he arranged for occasional joint interviews, especially with one friend who had just been denied parole for another year. The counselor recorded: "Since these two seemed to be pretty close friends, it seemed that it would be possible to assist each one in helping the other." From Eric and his friend, as well as from other inmates who associated with them, the counselor received confidences about the life they planned to live after getting out of the institution, "somewhere in the wilderness away from society where nobody can tell us what to do."

The model for this future was Hitler and his band of intimates. The lead-ing inmates in the group had some German heritage. They were intensely racist. As Eric said: "I think there is such a thing as a superior race and superior men." "As far as I am concerned niggers are all dirty, foul, and loud." As part of their cult they had collected and hidden in their rooms a swastika flag, newspaper clippings about the plight of modern Germany and the tortures of concentration camps, and drawings of "survival equip-ment" planned for their wilderness camp.

After he was convinced that Eric had dropped his connection with the institutional neo-Nazi group, the counselor had these mementoes brought to him, reviewed them with the Unit officer, disposed of the items that were clearly forbidden, and gave written permission for the innocuous

---

[9] *Sniffing:* inhaling fumes from some volatile liquid like ditto fluid or glue to induce a feeling of intoxication.

material to kept in Eric's room.[10] In spite of this care, Eric's room was cleaned out by officers searching the institution after a self-proclaimed Nazi leader in another unit was discovered, and Eric was sentenced to isolation with an additional postponement of his Board hearing. The counselor was particularly distressed at this new setback because several of the more mature inmates in C-Unit had observed his work with Eric and were going out of their way to be friends with him. As one inmate said, "It's the counselor I feel sorry for. All that good work going down the drain." The counselor was concerned that after this additional punishment Eric would withdraw completely from his new, more positive contacts.[11]

However, in his discussions with Eric and his friends, the counselor had learned about the interests they had in common. They talked of a group for learning Spanish and Portuguese and a photography group, but finally settled on an Interest Group to study the history of World War II. This group did not last long because of the intensity of feeling aroused between pro-German and anti-Nazi inmates. Finally, Eric's group of friends coalesced in an Explorers' Club devoted to the study of survival techniques. At each session the counselor presented a problem, for example, the individual was lost in a swamp, or he had clues to a buried treasure. The conditions of each problem were specified, and after each man had decided what he would do under such circumstances the various proposed solutions were discussed. In the process each individual's ability to assess reality and deal with actual conditions was revealed, and the members who proposed improbable solutions were challenged by their fellows. Value issues arose, such as the relations between whites and Negroes in the South and the responsibilities to the government of a citizen who comes into money unexpectedly, for example, by finding a treasure. The opposing positions were argued by the inmates themselves. Even more significant, the group members began to criticize each other when the irresponsible behavior of one or another interfered with the work at hand. At one point Eric, who up until then had perceived himself as in absolute command over his friends, was nearly expelled from the Club because of his domineering behavior.[12]

---

[10] A memorandum signed by a staff member was provided to inmates who kept articles such as books or craft supplies in their rooms to prevent their removal as contraband during the periodic room searches.

[11] In DVI, as it was then constituted, Eric might well have been sent from isolation to administrative segregation had he not been assigned to C-Unit.

[12] This group illustrated the kind of problem-solving activity that remained possible even after the change in staff functioning reported in Chapter VII.

The counselor explicitly formulated his strategy in using this group for dealing with Eric as "getting inside his fantasy and using it to confront him with actual problems in his social reality."

When Eric was being disciplined by his peers he began to reach out to both staff and fellow inmates. He took to dropping in on other staff members in their offices and agreed to have an interview with the director: "Mr. C. told me I could be honest with you."[13] The clique became less tightly knit and Eric began to associate more frequently with other men, some of whom were positive leaders in the C-Unit program. Although he had never played football before, Eric was one of the active organizers of the C-Unit Football Team.[14] After many efforts to get Eric placed in some job more challenging than the garbage detail, the counselor found a custody officer, the field house lieutenant, who would take him on as his full-time clerk. Under this tough boss who liked men and sports, Eric began for the first time to do well in an institutional assignment. By this time Eric's devotion to his counselor, his less frequent discipline infractions, and his consistent effort to be civil with staff had become obvious to everyone. As a consequence, the counselor met more responsiveness when he approached other personnel about their contribution to work with Eric.

No one, including the counselor, believed that what was happening in C-Unit for Eric could be sufficient to ensure a good prognosis, given his evident and deep-seated pathology.[15] But when one compares Eric's habitual expression of ugly contempt at the time he was first admitted to C-Unit with the picture taken of him at his second Christmas Open House while he was explaining the Explorers' Club display to visitors, it is evident that during his fifteen months in the Unit Eric had accumulated some experiences different from many others in his life. He had learned something about how to satisfy his taste for the dramatic in legitimate ways. A few of his criminal values had been challenged. He had experimented with new roles. Perhaps most important, he was no longer sure he wanted the loneliness revealed in his interview with the director when he said flatly: "If you really want to know how I see the world, I don't like people."

Eric was only one of several members of the Explorers' Club who were approached best through a strategy that used the interaction of peers under the leadership of an adult. However, the relevant staff members could have helped the counselor much earlier if there had been a way to convene the resocializing team for discussion of problems and strategy. For

---

[13] For a detailed report of the director's interview with Eric, see Studt, Elliot, *A Conceptual Approach to Teaching Materials: Illustrations from the Field of Corrections,* Council on Social Work Education, New York, 1965, pp. 81–89.

[14] At one point the team manager (Big Mac, who was a Negro) had to protect Eric from a beating administered during scrimmage. He told the team, "You don't go after one of your own."

[15] In late 1964, Eric's counselor, who was then a parole officer, reported that Eric had successfully completed eighteen months on parole. Shortly after, he was reported missing.

too long the counselor worked under the handicaps of custody's readiness to see Eric and anyone he associated with as "troublemakers," and the refusal of various work instructors to give Eric another opportunity to learn a trade. As a result, more than once it was impossible to reward Eric with added responsibility at a point when he was ready to align himself more actively with the values represented by the C-Unit program. Lacking means for activating the resocializing team, the rest of the staff behaved as though Eric's resocialization was solely the counselor's responsibility. Obviously the staff needed a device that would bring the relevant personnel together to consider this kind of difficult inmate.

CONVENING THE RESOCIALIZING TEAM

After the second counseling staff had been recruited, it was possible to work slowly toward the formation of organized resocializing teams. The case conference, attended by all the Project staff and by those personnel in the institution who were also working with the inmate whose case was to be considered, was the device used to establish the concept of the resocializing team in action. In the conference one counselor presented a case with which he was having particular difficulty. As might have been expected, each counselor chose for his conference the case of an inmate who was characterized as a "nuisance," that is, an inmate who was chronically in trouble and who was limited in personal and social resources. Shortly before each conference the director assumed a temporary role in the team by scheduling an interview with the inmate whose case was to be discussed.

WILBUR

Wilbur is a good example of the institutionally perceived nuisance. He was a recently admitted nineteen-year-old Negro YA who had already managed to get himself thrown out of the DVI school and dismissed from a culinary assignment. In desperation he had finally been assigned to the least demanding of all jobs, that of corridor orderly. His talk was a mumble, difficult to understand. Staff members tended to believe that he deliberately distorted his speech as a way of expressing hostility. Because his offense was burglary with aggravated assault he was perceived as potentially dangerous.

The team reporting at Wilbur's conference included the counselor, the two Unit officers, his former schoolteacher, the corridor officer currently supervising Wilbur's work assignment, the parole agent to whom Wilbur would ultimately be released, and the institution's supervisor of group counseling who had talked occasionally with Wilbur. The counselor reported that Wilbur frequently demanded adjustments in his schedule and was apparently unwilling to accept institutional regulations. In his opinion Wilbur put on an act, pretending to be duller than he actually was in order to get out of work. The two Unit officers had noted that Wilbur seldom understood an order and that when it was repeated he became surly. The evening officer had also observed that Wilbur was frequently the butt of jokes arranged by other inmates. The teacher had been unable to get consistent work from Wilbur and had dismissed him from school because he distracted the other students by acting the buffoon in response to their needling. The officer in charge of corridor orderlies said Wilbur repeatedly wandered away from his post when not closely supervised and was insolent when reprimanded. In the pre-parole groups, the parole agent observed that Wilbur was easily triggered by provocative comments from other inmates into long mumbling tirades, during which the other group members covertly snickered. The group counseling supervisor felt that some potentialities were hidden beneath Wilbur's surly manner but had no suggestions for reaching him. Each member of the team was frustrated in attempting to deal with this resistant individual who consistently caused minor trouble. Up to this point each official had been coping as best he could in isolation from his co-workers.

In this review of common experiences the team identified certain perceptions shared by all the members. Wilbur was obviously and disagreeably hostile but seldom showed overt rebellion. He was demanding and at the same time seemed unable to understand or accept the minimum expectations of the inmate role. He acted in any group of inmates in such a way as to bring ridicule on himself while expressing the covert hostilities of all. Each staff member who had dealt with him felt vaguely that Wilbur could do better if he only would.

The director's report of the interview with Wilbur added information suggesting a possible explanation for his irritating behavior. Wilbur had described his impoverished childhood in the deep South. He had little memory of his parents and reported that an older sister had taken care of the brood of younger children. Wilbur had left school at age ten to help finance the household. As he talked, the director noticed how clearly he was expressing himself and commented that she had not heard him speak so well before. Wilbur responded that his sister was the only adult with whom he had ever really talked and that he had always found it easier to talk with women than with men.

He went on to tell how he had left home at age eighteen, going West to look for work. He got a job as a dishwasher in a bar where a white waitress befriended him and finally invited him to come to her room after work. Late one evening Wilbur went to the store at the address she had mentioned just as it was about to close. When the storekeeper insisted that the waitress had moved and refused to say where she had gone, Wilbur thought the man was lying to him because he was a Negro. He picked up a heavy piece of wood lying nearby, intending to frighten the man into revealing her whereabouts. The storekeeper pulled a gun from under the counter and pointed it at Wilbur who hit out in fear. Graphically he described over and over his horror at seeing the man fall; his realization that he must run; and grabbing the loose money on the counter with some confused thought that this action would influence people to look for a burglar. Wilbur left town, found himself in another state, and obtained an agricultural job where he was working steadily two months later when he was arrested. It was then that he learned the storekeeper had been seriously injured as a result of the blow.

Now in the institution, Wilbur found himself repeatedly losing all awareness of his surroundings while he relived for endless moments the horror of the assault. "I keep asking myself how could I have done that? Did I really do it? I've never hit a man before." Whenever Wilbur was absorbed in this inner dialogue, he responded angrily and incoherently to an interruption from anyone, often realizing afterward that once again he had been "insolent" to an officer. He spoke of his continuous feeling of irritability as people around him, inmates or officials, forced themselves on him, interrupting his compulsive inner search for what had happened and why.

When Wilbur's own perception of what was happening was taken into account, his behavior took on new meanings. The conference group noted that he did not seem committed to a delinquent orientation and that he had probably done well not to get into trouble at an earlier age. As a Negro from a deprived southern background, suddenly located in a western metropolitan area where his social position was much less strictly defined, he must have had difficulty identifying what behavior was and was not acceptable. Actually he seemed to have shown ingenuity and steadiness in locating and keeping work. Much of his apparent stupidity about institutional requirements might be attributed to the fact that never before had he been exposed to institutional living and he was learning to adjust to this experience in a fairly sophisticated inmate population. Added to all these disorienting factors was the psychological shock associated with his offense. The staff team agreed that Wilbur's report of what he experienced inwardly was sufficiently congruent with the behavior they had observed to explain much that had previously been interpreted as deliberate efforts to annoy staff.

Out of this discussion with its fresh perspectives on a problem that was about to become fixed in expectations and behavior, a strategy emerged with a place of importance for each staff member. The counselor would not attempt to use scheduled interviews at this time but, through frequent, more informal contacts with Wilbur, would offer a warm, supportive relationship as a framework for handling the expected procedural difficulties with minimal excitement and threat. The work supervisor would explain duties patiently and would respond to the occasional hostile outbreaks with encouragement rather than disciplinary writeups. Meanwhile the counselor would search the institutional program for a job assignment in which Wilbur could learn, "where at first not too much would be demanded of him," and with a supervisor who could both understand his limitations and be relaxed in response to his occasional hostilities. The possibility of getting Wilbur into a remedial reading class with a woman teacher would also be explored. And finally, recognizing that peer relationships were very important in the life of this isolated individual who was rapidly being trained by his fellows as their clown, the officers and all other Project staff would communicate in various ways to C-Unit inmates that this was an individual to be protected rather than pilloried. At this point Wilbur would not be encouraged to take part in discussion groups. First group experiences should be like those provided by the Music Interest Group where Wilbur could participate on the fringe of activities if he chose, and other group experiences would be offered as he showed ability to undertake them. The team, once convened, had created for itself a treatment strategy much like the plan that had emerged spontaneously in action in the case of Denny, whose need for protection and gradation of stress had been more immediately evident to the entire staff.

By the end of the conference the staff shared a sense of closure, accomplishment, and hope. This good feeling increased the following week when reports began to come in from various persons in the institution that Wilbur's behavior had "improved." When they considered what had happened, they agreed that surrounding a confused inmate with officials who understood what they were doing and why might well result in changed attitudes in both inmate and staff.[16]

One of the most important consequences of the case conferences was the hope and enthusiasm that emerged among staff members—both those new to the Project and outside personnel—who, after having become used to working in isolation, experienced the benefits of sharing their perceptions and together designing a way to deal with frustrations. Some of the most useful insights were attained during the informal luncheon meetings preceding each conference when the director and the inmate's counselor went

---

[16] A year later Wilbur was pointed out to a Department of Corrections official who was visiting C-Unit as a strong inmate leader positively related to staff.

over the case with each of the staff members who would be reporting their experiences in the discussion. Although the case conferences were infrequent because of scheduling difficulties,[17] the Project staff learned by preparing for them that informal discussions could be managed much more frequently than they had realized and could therefore be used in establishing active resocializing teams for more cases. They also found that a conference on one case often had value for work with other similar cases.

It was no accident that the cases selected for conference presentation were all "nuisance" cases. No other inmates are so wearing on staff and in few cases does the individual staff member so much need the reassurance of his fellow workers' support. At the same time it is this kind of inmate who most needs the cohesive social world that only the activization of the team can provide for him. Many nuisance inmates present a quite different behavioral picture (as did Wilbur) as soon as their life space is saturated by official relations that are consistent and informed by understanding. The change of inmate behavior in response to changed staff behavior does not constitute resocialization. But substituting mutual responsiveness for mutual irritation is essential for starting the resocializing process. In the atmosphere of hope and openness to potentiality created by the resocializing team, it often proved possible to assess the actual problems more realistically and to establish a strategy that could be modified as developments warranted.

The case conference should not be perceived as an end in itself, nor is such a formal convening of the team essential to get teamwork started in all cases. The primary function of the conference is to pull the team members out of the pressured routine of their normal duties for the purpose of taking a new look at a problem that is becoming stereotyped in their minds. In the group setting each member experiences both the comfort of knowing that others also find the inmate difficult and an unexpected widening of perception as others describe the same behavior in somewhat different terms. In the free space provided by the scheduled conference each team member is able to experiment hypothetically with proposals for action that would not occur to him when he is under immediate pressure. In this kind of atmosphere old patterns can be disrupted and new constellations can emerge in creative problem-solving. The team members take expanded selves back to their daily work, using perceptions and energies previously uninvested in the case. As the inmate responds, a new and self-reinforcing dynamic is initiated in the interaction between the inmate

---

[17] For instance, the heads of the various DVI divisions were reluctant to release their employees to attend even when they were actively involved in work with the inmate whose case was to be discussed.

and his environment. This change in the direction of human interaction is a necessary first step in the resocializing process.

GUIDELINES FOR PROBLEM ANALYSIS AND STRATEGY DESIGN

It was not necessary for every member of a resocializing team to conceptualize what he was doing in order to be a useful participant. It was important for some member of the team, preferably the counselor, to have a systematic framework for thinking about the dimensions of the problems to be treated and the elements of resocializing strategies. These conceptions provided guidelines for helping the team examine case situations and design plans for treatment.

An outline of guiding questions was used for identifying among the many facets of the person's social functioning those especially pertinent for understanding his problem in behaving as a moral person.[18]

THE PERSON

—What is his perception of the nature of relations among people in the social world as he knows it?

—What is his image of himself, as he is and expects to be, in this social world?

—What moral orientations guide his participation in social relations?

THE PERSON IN HIS BASIC SOCIAL ROLES

—How have his family experiences affected, and how do they now affect, his readiness for morally responsible behavior?

—What experiences with peers, in the past and present, influence his moral behavior?

—How do his past and present experiences with persons in official positions of authority affect his ability to perform in an acceptable fashion?

—How have his experiences in the community's opportunity systems prepared him for competence in normal social roles or diminished his ability to use opportunities for learning and doing?

---

[18] This outline for differentiating among the problems of offenders was first formulated by the director during a fourteen-month study (in 1957–1958) of inmates in a young man's reformatory financed by a grant from Russell Sage Foundation. One version of this diagnostic guide, together with studies of 17 C-Unit inmates, has been published in Studt, Elliot, *op. cit.* In that volume the cases of Eric and Wilbur have been presented in somewhat different form.

INDICATORS FOR STYLE OF TREATMENT

—What produces stress for the person and how does he react to stress?

—What does the person perceive as help and how does he respond to offered help?

These guiding questions directed the staff's attention to the problem for which resocializing treatment was responsible and had competence, the individual's moral adaptation. The diagnostic focus was on those aspects of the interaction between an individual and his social environment that determined how values were currently being expressed in his behavior. The purpose was neither an explication of his intrapsychic dynamics per se nor a description of his socialization over time. Rather the diagnostic goal was an ordering of the information available to staff about an individual's moral functioning that led directly to a hypothesis for resocializing action in the present.

Although not all the relevant data have been presented in the case stories of Denny, Carlos, Allen, and Eric, sufficient information has been given to show in each case how the individual's perception of social relations, his self-image, and his moral orientations combined in interaction with his role experiences to establish a problematic pattern for relating values to behavior. We can use these stories, therefore, to illustrate how the diagnostic guide, presented above, helped the staff assess the presenting problem in social functioning, sketch the main outlines of an appropriate strategy for resocializing intervention, and differentiate the style of case management to be used with each inmate.

The four cases illustrate quite different problematic patterns for relating values to behavior, each of which appears with some frequency in correctional populations.[19] In Denny's situation we see a person sufficiently disorganized in his ability to perceive or deal with social reality that his behavior tended to be determined by any persons in his environment who provided the external direction on which he depended. His apparent lack of guiding values reflected his inability to use any dimension of order in his external reality for managing his inner chaos. In contrast, Carlos, as we first saw him in C-Unit, was deeply engaged by the oversimplified code of a conflict gang whose war with society's code was largely incidental to the fact that its members sought impulse satisfactions in socially dangerous

---

[19] It is important to note that each case is an especially clear example of a broader, more comprehensive category; and that these four types are not presumed to be exhaustive of the possible kinds of problematical value patterns to be found in correctional populations.

activities. His own values of pride, manliness, and loyalty were not in themselves bad; they needed to be supplemented and attached to activities through which he could mature as a member of a complex community. On the other hand, Allen gave explicit allegiance to many of the conventional values of the usual American business man, such as independence, ambitious striving, and efficiency in the use of resources. His problem can be understood as that of a person whose neurotic guilt toward his parents both made him vulnerable to committing behavior that actually violated his value code, and restricted his capacity to establish the bonds with other persons required for acceptable participation in the group endeavors of the normal community. Finally, in Eric we see a person who had adopted an explicitly antisocial set of values; his tastes and behavior were consciously chosen to defy socially accepted values and to attack those persons who tried to live according to such values.

It is equally clear that each of these four types of value maladaptations required a different treatment strategy. Denny needed a world in which morally responsible persons provided nurturance while gradually introducing him to the simple social tasks he must master in order to survive. In such a world he could be expected to develop behavior patterns congruent with the values of his protectors. Carlos, in contrast, needed an opportunity to engage in a wide variety of action roles in a social structure that could reward his own values when they were expressed in acceptable activities, encourage the development of other values, and teach him the social skills essential for managing his impulses in a complex society. Allen needed psychotherapy to reduce his need for punishment together with opportunities to learn the satisfactions of the effective bonds that Carlos already valued so highly. And Eric needed a comprehensive resocializing experience designed to change the nature of his core value system.

It is important to note that each strategy used all the available socializing means: individual counseling, work, education, peer interaction, and relationships with responsible authorities. The strategy did not specify the use of a single method. Rather, it encouraged each member of the resocializing team to adapt his own method for exercising influence to the identified problem, the stage of resocializing work, and the individual inmate's ability to handle stress and use help. Thus counseling could mean for Denny a semi-paternal, pervasively available, supporting relationship; active social planning for Carlos; and structured interviews directed to insight development for Allen. The use of peer relationships for resocializing purposes could vary from the provision of additional nurturing persons, such as Denny's inmate tutors; to the organization of a socially demanding task group such as that Allen found in the Seminar Working Group; to the use of peers for challenging orientations and behavior as in the Explorers' Club interaction with Eric.

Furthermore the resocializing strategy was never static. At one stage in an individual's development one treatment method could assume salience only to become background support at a later stage. With Eric, the use of a tightly knit peer group seemed necessary before he could relate positively with official authorities other than his counselor. Denny could use participation in peer groups only after many officials—the counselor, the teacher, the chaplain, and the custody officer—had helped reorient him to the real world. And Allen spent some months in counseling before he began to use task groups for active social learning. The strategy established a style of management for the resocializing team's work with an individual, encouraging a flexible and cohesive response from the social environment to that person's needs, stage of development, and emerging capacities.

The Project's use of treatment strategies depended on the fact that each inmate was a member of a resocializing community in which all kinds of problems at all levels of social development were being dealt with at the same time. We saw that when Denny was ready to participate in groups he could take his place in activities already established by better-organized inmates like Allen. Carlos was helped to move from gang leadership to group leadership because he could represent his friends in groups whose other members did not assume a gang orientation. Allen took one step in learning compassion for those less capable than he when he tutored Denny. And the counselor's work with Eric was supported when quite different kinds of inmates noticed the counselor's "good work" and stepped in to help. In each case, as the individual grew and could undertake additional tasks, new treatment approaches could be used and new experiences in helping and being helped became available in the informal associations of the Unit. In an important way, each of the strategies was possible only because it was implemented in a community that could accommodate them all at the same time; whose array of treatment resources was correspondingly broad; and whose daily life offered a wide variety of experiences in which values could be tested in action.

Thus the role of member in a resocializing community was one component of each of the possible treatment strategies developed for individual inmates. The strategy was intended to set in motion a dynamic process in an individual's life that would extend far beyond his participation in formal treatment roles and could keep pace with his growth by exposing him to various kinds of social tasks. The Project hoped that when an individual had mastered the variety of challenges available to him in the C-Unit community, he would be ready to undertake the still more complex tasks of the diverse community waiting for him outside the walls.

RESOCIALIZING CAREERS

A resocializing career is more than a collection of treatment roles. It is lived by a person who fashions, from the experiences available to him, a unique statement in action of who he is and expects to become. Such a career is possible only when the individual is able to test in the complexity of daily action the insights, values, and social skills gained from his exposure to segments of the treatment program. The resocializing community is designed to provide the organizational conditions necessary for the integration of desirable modes of adaptation that occurs in a resocializing career.

Jack's case illustrates what we mean by a resocializing career. After telling his story we shall examine the evidence that community, as a certain kind of arena for action, was an essential condition for the emergence of his resocializing career.

JACK

Jack was the tough, independent product of an Irish slum in the East. When he was admitted to C-Unit in its second month of operation, he was twenty-two years old, a slight, wiry A# committed for armed robbery, and was within three months of his annual Parole Board hearing. Everyone expected that his parole date would be set at this hearing because Jack had done very well in the institution. He had no discipline writeups. He had achieved a special status in the refrigeration shop where he was assigned during the day as a helper and an advanced student. His duties included responsibilities in the electrical shop, where he had a similar status, and he was used by both instructors to coordinate the work of the two shops. Accordingly, Jack had much more freedom of movement in the work area than other inmates. He used keys usually reserved for the instructors, and was responsible for issuing tools and supplies. The instructors had already referred Jack as a potential employee to business owners in their home community.

In C-Unit Jack was explicit in his criticism of the initial program, making his points with a direct honesty that differed from the sullen or merely provocative comments offered by many inmates. He did not seem to have close ties with any of his fellow inmates. At one moment he seemed gregarious and friendly; at another, brusque to the point of rudeness. In group discussions he was as independent toward inmates as toward staff, challenging any idea with which he disagreed regardless of who proposed it. He attended Bull Sessions frequently, but often walked out with a ges-

ture of impatience when other inmates seemingly lost the point of the discussion and used the session to complain or tell long-winded stories of
their personal experiences. He wrote and signed lucid articles for the first
newspaper, stating his code for inmate behavior and criticizing both the
nonhonor inmates and the program that subjected those who had already
earned honor status to the added tension created by the presence of nonhonor men. Because Jack seemed tenacious in grappling with subjects that
interested or bothered him and, in spite of his impatience, had evident
capacity for ordering ideas, he was invited to join the Research Seminar
scheduled for January, 1961. He accepted, expressing interest in finding
out "what the Project is really all about."

At this point Jack was participating actively in the new experiences
offered by the C-Unit program. Unfortunately, the program, as yet un-
developed, was not able to fulfill its implicit commitments to Jack in a
crisis that entailed serious consequences for his institutional career.

The critical incident occurred the day before the first Christmas Open
House in 1960, two and a half months after Jack had been admitted to
C-Unit. It was initiated by two homosexually inclined YAs who reported
to one of the C-Unit officers that Jack and another C-Unit A# had subjected them to sex pressure in the refrigeration shop. When the supervisor
learned of this incident, he secured permission from the Associate Superintendent, Custody, to investigate the facts in *ad hoc* conferences involving
both the inmates and the relevant staff. Jack was the only one of the four
inmates who responded with interest to this new way of handling a potential disciplinary infraction. He talked openly about his own fringe involvement, reporting that he had known something was going on in connection
with the two YAs and that he had participated in the joking byplay. He
refused sturdily to give information about any other inmate, stating only
that the wrong A#s had been fingered. By the end of the day (a Friday),
the Project staff, who had also consulted with the two work instructors,
were convinced that no overt act had occurred and that Jack was not involved in the pressure operation, although the other three inmates had
probably been working up to something. During the conferences, commitments were made by all the inmates to cool off the sex activity on the Unit
over the weekend. With the permission of the Associate Superintendent,
Custody, all four were released to the Unit with no discipline report in
their records.

However, one of the YA inmates was disappointed by the lack of dramatic response to his story and late that afternoon told his tale to an officer outside the Unit. This officer reported to the captain who was in charge
of the institution in the absence of other administrative personnel. He
promptly transferred the two A#s to isolation and the two YAs to protec-

tive segregation, where they remained over the Christmas weekend. By the following Wednesday, Jack and the other A# inmate had each been sentenced to twenty-nine days' isolation and their parole hearing dates had been postponed for three months.[20] In addition, they had been recommended for transfer to another prison. Two weeks later the Project staff had accumulated enough information about the incident to have Jack's transfer rescinded, but they had not been able to clear his record or reinstate his parole hearing date. After nineteen days in isolation, Jack was returned to C-Unit, his isolation sentence having been commuted to time served.

At this point, Jack was a bitter, hostile isolate on nonhonor status who talked with no one. He attended the Research Seminar meetings but did not contribute to the discussions. Jack's counselor had left the institution soon after the first supervisor resigned and the director was temporarily responsible for the uncovered caseload. Observing Jack's obvious distress, she offered him weekly interviews "for a month or so." Without any expression of interest Jack agreed to this proposal.

Jack came warily in answer to his ducats. He asserted that no person could help another. To seek help was "weak" and "dependent." He not only had to do his own "straightening up," he also wanted to be completely independent: "Getting involved in obligations only causes trouble." The counselor said it was not necessary to decide what they might do together until after they had had a chance to get acquainted. "It takes time to know whether you can trust another person and both you and I have to test what is possible. Furthermore, you have had good reason not to be sure you can trust me." She suggested that he help her prepare for writing his Board Report, by telling her about what led up to his commitment to DVI.

Jack came alive in spite of himself in telling about his adventures. He had been a slum street kid during his early life, "always fighting and doing crazy things." "There's nothing I haven't seen or tried. I like all kinds of people. It doesn't matter to me how they get their sex or how they make their living if I like them." In his early teens Jack had been sent to a boys' correctional school. "I guess the police wanted to get me off the streets. Anyway they were mad at me because I wouldn't tell them who did it."

Since his stay in the first institution Jack had been much on the road. "Suddenly I want to take off, just see a new place." He hitchhiked and stole cars for transportation. He would stop in a new town for a while, work and make friends, and then leave for another destination. Once he simply took a room in a strange town and stayed in it for a week. "I didn't

---

[20] A disciplinary report involving postponement of the date for a Board hearing would almost automatically ensure a denial of parole for another year.

go out except for food. I just wanted to be alone." In this way he explored the South, the Middle West, and the far West, although each time he returned home again. On his most recent trip he had left home for California "because I was on parole and I heard the police were looking for me." He insisted he never wanted to see his family again, and that they were not interested in him.

In each of his exploratory travels Jack had made temporary friends. There was a man who let him ride with him for three days. "He let me sleep in the car, even though he didn't know anything about me. At the end of the trip he offered me a job. I still have his name and address." One time Jack had found a young couple stranded at 2:00 A.M. after a car accident and had rounded up help for them. With concern Jack described the girl's hysterical distress as she had walked up the roadway toward his car. There was a Mexican family who had befriended Jack and with whom he later shared his earnings when the man was out of work. A schoolteacher was now Jack's only correspondent.

The commitment offense involved two men whom Jack had met in a bar and who wanted help with the holdup of a taxi driver. "It was a silly thing. I was working and didn't need the money. But they were so dumb they would have botched it up. I took the bullets out of the gun ahead of time or somebody would have got hurt. I gave them most of the take and told them to get out of town. But they were too stupid. I got caught because I went back to town to make sure they got away." When the counselor agreed that it did seem silly to get himself locked up for a deal like this, "almost as though you wanted to be stopped," Jack expostulated grimly that nothing in the world was so painful as being "cooped up, not able to take off when I want to." "I can't see settling down to one place, nothing but family and work. I get tired of a place and the same people, want to see something new. I want to see the whole world before I'm ready to settle."

In the last interview before Jack's delayed Board hearing he dropped his wary reserve for a short moment, asking seriously, "Why do you think I get into trouble?" The counselor responded that she knew only the little about him that he himself had told her. He seemed to have been saying that he had never learned which people to trust and perhaps that he did not believe people ever could trust each other. When he started to get close to someone, he moved away or did some crazy thing that made him have to go away. She thought he must be very lonely. Later, after the Board hearing, the counselor asked what had happened. "They asked me why I kept getting into trouble. I told them what you said—I don't trust people. It made sense." Jack got the denial he had expected and settled down in March, 1961, to do another year.

Up to this point the work with Jack had been psychological first aid

extended to a deeply distressed person who had been unwillingly introduced into a system that had first engaged him and then failed him in
action. Because Jack seemed so forlornly isolated from his fellows, as well
as from staff, the director invited him to join the Newspaper Group where
he could associate with other inmates in a task-focused, emotionally neutral setting. Because she was staff sponsor for this group, she was able to
see Jack occasionally without seeming to force a counseling relationship on
him. She therefore continued Jack on her caseload. In April the newspaper
editor resigned, and Jack, irate at the careless way the reporting work had
been managed, took over the editor's job in a frenzy of plans for "getting
this thing properly organized." Suddenly, at the end of one newspaper
planning conference Jack said, "Will you take me on for regular counseling? I've decided I need help."

Jack did not know what he meant by help; it was just something that
happened in a weekly counseling session. Perhaps his request was simply
a plea for human attention in a desperately bleak life. But the counselor
needed a sense of direction to start her work with him. She used the previously outlined guide for case analysis in assessing Jack's problem as it
had been revealed in his behavior up to this point.

The Person. Jack sees the *social world* as composed of independent human
units, each enduring alone the consequences of his own and others' acts. Each
person in this world is self-determining and makes his choices in terms of what
he "wants." There are many evidences that Jack is uneasy about close relations
among these isolated human units. This uneasiness has probably been intensified
by his recent disciplinary experience.

In this social world Jack reportedly sees himself as a free agent, exploring
wherever his curiosities lead him with no formulated goal except experiencing
the "new." Not quite so clearly verbalized is an underlying perception of *himself*
as a maker, doer, and organizer.

Jack has a clear *code of values* for himself to which he is passionately loyal;
and he ruthlessly applies this code to the behavior of other people. These values
include: strict honesty about one's own opinions, not "ratting" on other persons,
individual freedom from middle-class moral prescriptions concerning sex and the
stability of family life, orderliness and good workmanship in the performance of
tasks.

The Person with Peers and Officials. With peers Jack operates erratically. His
curiosity, love of adventure, and sheer drive to organize lead him into peer relationships, legitimate and illegitimate, in which he appears to offer leadership.
This kind of involvement, however, is rarely stable, partly because in Jack's
world the individual is guided only by what *he* wants, partly because of Jack's
ambivalence about human closeness. When a relationship starts, something
"foolish" is done and trouble results, or Jack gets one of his "moods" and turns
brusque. "If I don't want to talk to a guy, I tell him to go away. Or I shine him
on[21] and go to my house." Because Jack is so critical of others and tends to su-

---

[21] *Shine him on:* inmate term meaning to ignore by refusing normal responses to communication.

perimpose his drive for order on everyone associated with him in a task, he may be resented by his peers in group activities.

With *officials* Jack accepts the rules of the game, provided the management of affairs is efficient, the rules are clear, and he is treated "like a man." Although he is capable of loyalty and learning when authority offers him responsibility (as with the two shop instructors), he is deeply distrustful of officialdom in general and basically hostile to it. When Jack likes someone in authority he probably perceives him as "different," not really part of the official system.

Indicators for Style of Treatment. The greatest source of *stress* for Jack is restraint on freedom to move about and to follow his curiosities by engaging in new experiences. In part, personal relationships are distrusted because they imply this kind of restraint. Jack also experiences stress when, in the performance of a task, he is not free to make, organize, and experiment. He has two reactions to stress, both of which disrupt already tenuous associations with other people: (1) quick anger, and (2) "black moods," both followed by withdrawal.

For some reason not yet known, Jack perceives *help* as dangerous. It seems associated in his mind with weakness, loss of self, dependency, and intolerable obligations. Perhaps also with hurt? Although he reportedly often acts to help others, he is particularly uneasy about receiving "credit" for such actions. When he gives help it is because he "wants" to, not because he is a person of good will or others are in need, and giving help must not lead to entangling obligations.

The Problem. Jack's early delinquencies seem best explained (without further information) by the fact that he lived in an area where it was easier to be delinquent than not and in a family without resources to prevent such behavior. His current problem is much more complex, involving his inability to maintain the stable human relationships that are necessary to implement his drive for accomplishment. He has therefore established as a life pattern a restless search for experience of any kind that is almost guaranteed to get him into periodic trouble.

The Initial Strategy. The first task is to get Jack related once again to the C-Unit community. Over time the components of work with Jack should include:

A central person who can live with Jack through the painful process of learning that it is safe to relate closely with another human being.

Other officials with whom he can practice relationships of varying degrees of closeness.

An environment rich in opportunities for learning, assuming responsibility and organizing.

Task-focused group activities with peers so that in a relatively neutral setting he can get feedback about how his behavior affects others and interferes with the attainment of his personal goals, and can at the same time learn to give loyalty to goals that supersede his own immediate interests.

It took an additional five months to get Jack as ready to experiment within the C-Unit community as he had been just before the disciplinary incident. At the beginning of this period there was no resocializing team because Jack remained aloof from all Project staff.[22] He did throw himself

---

[22] The counselor did confer with Jack's work instructors and both were supportive team members throughout Jack's stay in the institution.

into the work of reorganizing the newspaper with a kind of furious energy. He changed the paper's makeup; bullied reporters who were late with copy; retyped all submitted stories, editing out the excess of big words which he called "Webster's Disease"; conducted interviews with administrative personnel about program changes; and ran the ditto machine himself to be sure that each issue was published on schedule. As a first step in relating Jack more widely with the Project staff, the counselor transferred the Newspaper Group (for which she had been responsible) to a woman secretary who had had newspaper experience and who could help Jack with the technical skills required by the editing job.

Clearly the director's first task as counselor was to establish some basis for communication between herself and Jack. This was not easy to do. Jack was wary. He wanted to be told what he should talk about and argued heatedly that any topic the counselor proposed had "nothing to do with being helped." He refused to talk about his daily life in the institution because "I don't talk about other inmates." His work in the shops was "going all right." His feelings were "none of your business. Anyway I feel fine." From time to time, however, Jack did relate stories of his wanderings, and occasionally there were conversations that were plain fun for both the counselor and him as he described his various escapades with humor and vivid details. Such interviews tended to end with some deeply thoughtful comment, as when he spoke of his feeling for the Catholic chaplain at the first correctional school who had baptized him. In these comments one glimpsed a carefully protected tenderness in Jack's perceptions of others.

The counselor quickly learned that she could not use these momentary revelations as stepping stones to further communication because Jack immediately closed up against what he called her "prying." It was four months before he offered his first indication of trust. Shyly at the end of one session he told about his plans for his work future. He wanted to have a business of his own that combined the two trades he had learned in the institution, and he wanted to organize the business so that customer needs could be met more efficiently than is possible in the usual commercial pattern. This would involve employing different kinds of skilled workmen under one management. Jack had worked out this plan in considerable detail. Jack said, "I was afraid you would laugh." Then he went on to tell how he was devoting many of his free hours to reading about the business methods he would need to use in order to accomplish this goal.

The crucial turning point in the counseling process occurred a month later. Jack's stories had by now revealed that almost always he had left his current home base because "there was a woman I wanted to get away from." When the counselor asked what had happened with the woman he had just mentioned, Jack reacted with fury. "What business is it of yours? What happens between me and a woman is our affair and nobody else's." The counselor responded: "Jack, you asked for help. When you tell me about experiences that had something to do with your getting into trouble, I can't understand what they mean unless you tell me about them. Lots of times, just when we get to talking about something that is obviously important to you, you slam the door on me and then get very angry when I push a little. You know, you don't have to come for counseling and if you would rather we will quit. But if you want help, then you will have to be prepared for me to push a bit on closed doors when it seems important, even though I know this will be painful to you." Jack said: "I know, I always slam doors on people."

The counselor recorded later: "This was a crucial conference in which Jack's basic defenses against trusting another human being were acknowledged between us and he committed himself to wanting to learn how 'not to slam the door on people' as he had always been accustomed to do." From then on, a question, "So you would like to slam the door again? May I push a little?" was usually enough to bring a rueful grin to Jack's face and get him talking once more.

At this point Jack was once more ready to explore the possibilities of the C-Unit program, and during the second five-month period the process proceeded much as it might have if no disciplinary incident had supervened. As he became active in the C-Unit community Jack experienced both the satisfactions and anxieties that human engagement inevitably engendered in him.

The new period was initiated by Jack's decision to leave his job in the shops and return to high school for a half-day assignment. He had decided that he needed a full high school education to equip himself for the work he wanted to do; he had already accumulated more hours of technical training than was usually permitted to a single inmate. A newly vacated inmate clerk position was available in the Project, so Jack was appointed clerk to the C-Unit staff for the half-day period when he was not in school.[23]

In his work as clerk in the Annex offices, Jack was quickly involved with each of the C-Unit staff members. He reorganized the clerk's job and took on additional tasks for keeping the population statistics in order. With great pleasure he reported to the counselor an experience with the lieutenant. On discovering that Jack needed a new kind of form, the lieutenant took him to the printing shop where he was consulted as the responsible

---

[23] Because of limited teacher time, few inmates could attend school more than one half of each workday.

person about the makeup of the forms, the number needed, and when needed. The counselors found Jack helpful in keeping ducat lists in order. Later, when Jack learned that the courses he needed for graduation from high school were not available in the school's curriculum at this time, the research staff offered him a research clerk's position as a substitute assignment for the second half-day of his schedule.

The glow of being liked and approved inevitably stimulated worries for Jack. When the lieutenant was absent for a day Jack impulsively made certain decisions that could have been left for the lieutenant's return and waited anxiously for his reaction, expressing great relief when he received approval. There was a day when Jack's figures did not match those in the DVI control center. His tension pervaded the Annex atmosphere until he had ferreted out the mistakes that had been made on both sides. At the second Christmas Open House several staff members introduced him to visitors as one who should have credit for certain aspects of the C-Unit program. Jack spent the next weekend writing a long statement (never submitted to staff) explaining why he was going to resign from the clerk's position. Later, when talking with the counselor, he associated his heightened sensitivity with his new relations with staff, saying: "Whenever I get tied up with a lot of people who like and trust me, I hurt someone. I need to get away before that happens. It bothers me when people start giving me credit. Something bad always happens next." Jack did not resign. Instead, he took on the research clerk job. But the next week he was in despair because, having sensed that his counselor was angry (in a business transaction involving several people), he wrongly attributed her feeling to some arrangements he had made independently in connection with his program change. "When I get close to someone I always hurt them. I was afraid I had hurt you."

It was possible to allay Jack's rising panic in his new experiences with human relations primarily because, ever since he had decided not to "slam the door" in counseling, he had been using the counseling sessions to disentangle the threads in his earlier relationships with an abusive father ("I'm just like him"), a weary but kind mother, and exploiting older women friends, all of whom had contributed to his current emotional vulnerability. Essentially one theme had been explored over and over again, "When I get close to people they hurt me, and then I hurt them."[24]

The path of counseling had not been smooth. Once Jack had decided abruptly to quit counseling because "All it does is make me feel bad. I feel good all the time except when I talk to you. I don't see how feeling bad

---

[24] During this period Jack initiated correspondence with his parents to which they responded.

can help me. It's better to forget such things. I can't change them now."
But the next day he was waiting at the counselor's door asking urgently
for a five-minute talk that turned into an hour's conference. As the outlines
of Jack's earlier relationships were established and distinguished from
current realities, Jack's use of counseling increasingly focused on his experiences in the here and now of the C-Unit community.

During this same period Jack had become actively involved with his
fellow inmates. In these relations he experienced directly the irritation of
his peers evoked by his domineering manner. He accepted an appointment
to the Staff-Inmate Group and undertook a one-man, unsuccessful campaign to get large community meetings "where everything can be hassled
out with everybody present" established in the C-Unit program. From
books on newswriting lent to him by the sponsor of the Newspaper Group,
he wrote a four-page style guide for his reporters and turned group meetings into work sessions in which every submitted article was scrutinized
for style. The sponsor reported: "Jack started out by being quite dictatorial
toward the other reporters. He was startled when they took one of his
articles apart and showed him that he was making the same mistakes.
After the first shock, he took the criticism in good part and has written two
much better articles since." Jack was one of the active organizers of the
football team, and although he had never played football before, he volunteered for the quarterback job, because "no one else wants to take that
job on. We all know that Big Mac will play quarterback in the real games."
However, when Jack, who belonged to a Half-Caseload Group led by another counselor, ran for the office of representative to the C-Unit Council,
he did not win the election, because as the group said, "You dominate
every discussion." Jack was so chagrined by this experience that he did
not even tell his counselor about it.

It was just at this point that the staff let Jack down once again. A serious
disagreement among the staff that was never properly resolved led to conflicting actions toward a group of inmates of whom Jack was one.[25] Because Jack was a Project clerk, he was particularly vulnerable with his
fellows and was temporarily under suspicion from some of them. At the
next counseling session Jack stamped out of the office, saying bitterly:
"Twice I trusted the staff. All it got me each time was a hassle and I was
the one who got hurt. I won't use people. I won't use you. I won't be dependent on people. I'm through with counseling." In spite of the fact that
this episode should have been avoided and could have had serious consequences, the many strong links between Jack and his new social world
were maintained in most essentials. The counselor continued to see Jack

---

[25] See The Third-Tier Incident, pp. 173–178.

in connection with appropriate business. In two weeks Jack had weathered this emotional crisis and was back in counseling, ready to work on the preparation of his next Board Report. He was especially concerned for fear he would lose his temper at the parole hearing when under questioning from the Board.

Jack's third phase, terminated by his release on parole four months later, was full of good experiences for him. The counselor obtained from the Associate Superintendent, Custody, a complete exoneration for the homosexual incident (based on the official record), and attached it to the Board Report after Jack had read it. Jack had joined an Art Appreciation Interest Group led by a teacher from a nearby city. One counseling session was devoted to his glowing discussion of "Those guys like Frank Lloyd Wright, Beethoven, and Van Gogh; they had everything against them and look what they did with their lives." He organized a Painting Interest Group and arranged for an inmate artist from outside C-Unit to be the teacher so that he could begin to do some of the things he was learning about. He told the counselor, "Things like organizing the art group and the football team—they're helping me learn how to work with men the way I want to do when I have my own business. Painting, I've never done that before. I don't know how to say it. It's just satisfying.[26] I don't know what is happening to me. It's just that I am having so much fun."

The new and more mellow Jack began to receive the respect and affection of those about him with a shy humility very different from his earlier alarm reaction at the mention of "credit." A letter written for Jack's record by the volunteer leader of the Art Appreciation Interest Group (and seen by Jack) said in part:

Jack has displayed genuine academic interest in the arts. . . . He has always been sincere and moved by the art forms and his questions illustrate true esthetic feelings and growth. However, Jack has even more than these qualities. Without a doubt he is a group leader and the other members in our group respect him. He shows a deep sense of integrity and is not held back by difficult problems. He seems to search beneath outward appearances. . . .

Jack gained respect from many C-Unit inmates for his performance in the thankless position of understudy for Big Mac's position on the football team. He began to speak to the counselor more understandingly of both his peers and the staff. "I can understand a lot of those guys you would call gunsels. They gripe about the program a lot. They just don't realize that administration and custody and counselors all have to work together

---

[26] Jack's parting gift to the counselor was a pastel drawing of a woman's head based on one figure in the Sistine Chapel murals.

to make a project like this go, and that it takes more time to get all these different people together on a plan. Those guys put on a front and the biggest front of all is saying they don't want any part in the program."

When Jack went to his Board hearing in May, 1962, he came back grinning. "You know, I actually enjoyed talking with them. When I came out of the room laughing, the other inmates who were waiting their turns looked at me as though they thought I must be sick in the head or something." A week later Jack learned that his time had been set for immediate release on approval of parole plans. His former instructors utilized their business connections in a nearby town to get Jack a job in the kind of work he had been trained to do. The day before his release the inmates in the Art Appreciation Interest Group pooled their own goodies to give Jack the first parolee goodbye party in the history of C-Unit.

Because at the end we see a very likable Jack with an integrity and ability worthy of respect, we should not forget his potentialities for being dangerous to himself and to society. Jack's insatiable curiosity got him into everything that was going on in the Unit, legitimate and illegitimate, and it was hard for him to learn to be realistically protective of himself when his "honesty" was challenged. Two weeks prior to his last Board hearing it took the combined efforts of his own and Eric's counselors to persuade him to give up the overt evidences of his association with Eric until after DVI's administration had become more relaxed about neo-Nazis in the institution. Jack's interest had been challenged by Shirer's *Rise and Fall of the Third Reich,* and he wanted to finish the book, which he had borrowed from Eric's counselor. Furthermore, he was contemptuous of the institution's official policy. "They think they are trying to stamp out fascism. I never saw anything more fascist than the methods they are using." It was only when he realized that he might be in real danger of another false accusation just before a Board hearing that he reluctantly turned the materials he was reading over to Eric's counselor. In addition, when Jack was given freedom to act he had difficulty locating the limits of his responsibility except by trial and error. It was easy for him to overstep these limits without intending to. He loved the freedom to design his own way of working granted him in the inmate clerk job, saying, "Up here I do lots of things I don't really have to do because no one tells me just what I have to do and how." Although he was quick to learn from his mistakes, he was seldom careful to analyze what needed to be done before acting. Any mistake he made tended to stimulate excessive anxiety that could lead to impulsive withdrawal from work on the current problem.

During the retrospective research interview for which he volunteered the day before his release, Jack summarized his C-Unit experience: "My counselor helped me by teaching me not to hold anything back; to trust people and not to look at it one-sided. And also she taught me to make choices. This was important for the clerk's job. Up here (in the Annex) lots of decisions were left up to me and I was working with free people who let me decide how I was going to do the job. I learned a lot from working with them."

The Project's last report about Jack was that he was working steadily, attending Junior College at night taking technical courses related to his work, and was about to be married. But the continuance of a new mode of adaptation depends both on the person and on the social system in which he is functioning. One wonders to what extent the free community, with its greater complexity and limited concern for the individual, has been able to provide Jack with opportunities to continue the kind of life that he found "satisfying" and "lots of fun" in C-Unit.

Jack's whole story reveals the action of a community that supported the development of a new orientation to social relations. But in following the story of a person it is easy to ignore the organization's contribution to this process unless it is examined directly. What difference did it make to Jack and to the people working with him that they were operating in a community rather than in a segmented organization patterned according to the more traditional correctional bureaucracy?

ORGANIZATIONAL CONDITIONS FOR RESOCIALIZING CAREERS

The C-Unit community provided at least three organizational conditions for the emergence of Jack's resocializing career:

1. The organization placed high value on the individual. Its norms prescribed both flexible responsiveness to individuals in different situations and continued investment in the individual as his needs and capacities changed.

2. The organization was sufficiently coherent to allow the individual to move from one role to another with minimal conflict among roles and maximum reinforcement of new learning.

3. The organization provided a transitional role for the inmate focused on the relevance of present experiences for a desired future.

We can summarize the evidence in Jack's story that these conditions contributed to his resocializing career.

VALUING THE INDIVIDUAL

Jack's own highest value was his insistence on being himself no matter who liked it. Only a system that also valued the individual could have helped Jack change in the ways he expressed his individuality. We can observe the conditions that made it possible to respond flexibly to Jack as a person of worth in at least three activity areas.

Problem Identification and Resolution. The C-Unit community approved the open statement of experienced problems, including the expression of criticism and differences of opinion. An important correlate of this norm committed the organization to change itself in response to useful criticism and to delegate responsibility for helping to accomplish change to the person making the criticism. Only a system with these norms could have tolerated Jack's attacks and encouraged him to adopt the values of the community by involving him in its creation.

Control of Behavior. The C-Unit community valued discriminating action in cases of misbehavior more highly than routinized consistency. The staff's original attempt to deal with the homosexual incident followed this norm. The psychological damage that resulted when a rule-bound decision from upper administration interrupted this process was more profound because Jack had responded with trust to the Project's individualizing approach. It was important, however, that the organization undertook to undo the damage it had helped to cause and to rectify the injustice through securing Jack's exoneration. It was also important that staff could differentiate between Jack's curiosity about the history of Germany and dangerous neo-Nazi involvement and so could help him avoid a second serious interruption in his resocializing career.

Use of resources. The Project staff as community leaders assumed continuing responsibility for finding and using resources as needed by the individual's changing capacity. This commitment required special inventiveness with a person like Jack who continuously opened up new opportunities for action once an initial investment had been made. Thus his appointment to the inmate clerk job led to a reorganization of population accounting and the need for new forms. Securing the volunteer teacher for the Art Appreciation Interest Group was followed by plans for the Painting Class, requiring complex arrangements within the institution to approve the use of an inmate instructor from outside C-Unit. In Jack's case, staff had to be ready to expand resources as each new investment opened up possibilities for still other experiences. In the cases of other inmates quite different kinds of continuing investment might be needed, such as finding ways to reward the limited efforts of a more passive inmate, or holding the line against manipulation while keeping open the opportunity for legitimate problem-solving. But whatever the nature of the individual's need and capacity, the initial commitment involved the staff in continued investment, within the limits of the possible, in that individual's career.

COHERENCE

When the individual is being asked to integrate new modes of adaptation, he should not at the same time be vulnerable to conflicting demands from the people who are important to him. One of the most important contributions of the resocializing community to the individual is the opportunity to maintain a value consistent self as he moves from one role to another.

In Jack's story there were two incidents in which the C-Unit community failed Jack in this important respect: the homosexual incident; and the Third-Tier Incident when as Project clerk he was subjected to conflicting staff actions and resulting suspicion from his fellows. On both occasions Jack was exposed by an ineffective organization to conflicting pressures from inmates, counselors, custody, and administration. This kind of failure on the part of a resocializing community has much more serious consequences for the individual than a comparable failure in the free community where no obligation to support a drastic change in an individual's social functioning has been accepted.

In spite of these episodes, Jack's experience with different segments of the C-Unit community was sufficiently coherent to reveal the importance of this organizational condition for the development of a resocializing career.

Staff Work Group. Jack's image of the social world as a collection of unrelated, mutually dangerous human units was first challenged by his experiences in the role of clerk to the staff work group. Here was a group of persons with various functions who, so far as Jack could observe, behaved well in terms of a shared task. As clerk he was able to work with each staff member on part of that task while differentiating among them in terms of personal attraction and kinds of communication. In this experience he found, as he said, that "administration, custody, and counselors all have to work together to make a program like this go, and it takes more time to get all these people together on a plan." For Jack, the staff work group offered a new action model for task-oriented relations and a chance to experiment with a role for himself in such a system.

Inmate System. Having achieved this conception of desirable social relations, Jack was able to experiment with this new model in his association with peers. For instance, it was important that the C-Unit inmate system was sufficiently complex to undertake the kind of tasks, such as the newspaper and the football team, in which Jack could both offer leadership and experience the teamwork required to achieve group goals. The norms of the C-Unit inmates were sufficiently congruent with those of staff to make it acceptable for inmates to work with counselors in supporting the resocialization of their fellows, as Jack did with Eric's counselor. And when Jack performed his role of fellow inmate in the same way he behaved with staff he received the same rewards of appreciation and affection from his peers.

Treatment. It was especially important that Jack's role in counseling was an integral part of the community in which he was trying out new ideas. Jack could probably not have learned to trust and work with a variety of people if he and the counselor had examined the problems of his past in an artificial setting, remote from the world in which he was living out the same problems day by day. Jack was both too suspicious and too disciplined by the "code" to have shared verbally with the counselor the details of what he was up against in his everyday life as an inmate. Because the counselor and Jack were both observing and participating in the same social reality, she could help him relate his understanding of the past to his current experiences and could design new and increasingly challenging social tasks in which he could test his developing insight.

The coherence potential in the C-Unit community is nowhere better observed than in the spread of effect from Jack's work with his counselor to his experiences with the staff work group to his new relations with his peers. Each of these experiences was salient during a different period in Jack's resocializing career as he moved from trust in one relationship to task-focused work with several persons to a still wider arena for give and take. Each succeeding phase was made possible because Jack was able to maintain personal continuity as he moved among his diverse roles in treatment, job, and peer group in the C-Unit community.

TRANSITION

A third organizational condition for a resocializing career is the transitional nature of the individual's membership in the institutional community. There are two elements in the term "transitional" as it is used here: (1) The organization is conceived of as a temporary rather than a permanent base for the individual; and (2) the experiences it offers are expected to be relevant in preparing the individual for the desired future. The resocializing career of the individual within the organization is thus inherently goal-oriented rather than an end in itself.

There are many evidences in Jack's story that he perceived a direct relevance between his experiences in C-Unit and the goal he had set for his future life. The plan for the business he hoped to build in the future was modeled after the Project scheme for bringing together a variety of "experts" in one organization; and his own role in that business was to be the organizer who would facilitate these experts in getting the best possible service to customers. He thought of the football team experience and the painting class as "helping me learn how to work with men the way I want to do when I have my own business." But the resocializing community does not have to have this kind of exact relevance for the future to be effective. Jack may never own his own business. But if, as seemed to be true of him, he achieved some competence in differentiating among human relationships, in trusting when and to what extent it is appropriate to trust, and in engaging in acceptable task-focused activities without imposing his own patterns on everyone else, his resocializing career in C-Unit had general relevance for any kind of acceptable future in the free community.

In the C-Unit approach, community was an essential condition for resocializing careers. Within this larger matrix formal treatment methods of many different kinds could be introduced and used. But they were always considered tools for transforming the rich complexity of daily life into resocializing experience, not program units with independent goals. C-Unit was dedicated to preparing offenders to become socially competent members of a community rather than the subjects of different kinds of treatments. For this goal the various treatments had to be subordinated to and gain their meaning within a program in which all aspects of life had a potential for resocializing experience.

Thus the Project proposes that *resocializing treatment is the way you manage the social relations within which the offender spends his institutional time and that each treatment method is one kind of management process.* This proposition rejects the artificial dichotomy between treatment and management that has plagued the correctional agencies since the introduction of treatment programs. It further suggests that reform of correctional institutions be refocused away from the proliferation of special units demonstrating one or another treatment method, and addressed to the fundamental reorganization of the relations among the human beings who live and work within the walls.

THE UNREACHED

The cases we have presented up to this point all show some movement in the direction of the goals formulated by the Project for the individual's resocializing experience. It has been necessary to use such cases in order to make explicit the dynamics of the resocializing process.

However, it was always clear to staff that many of the C-Unit inmates failed to use the resources of the community for work toward resocialization. Many factors contributed to these failures. In certain cases lack of staff time or skill was obviously responsible. In others, even when much staff effort was invested, the inmate himself seemed to lack the essential qualities needed for work toward the desired goals.

The staff learned by experience, though never by systematic study, to recognize certain kinds of cases that responded poorly even when much effort was invested.

There was the occasional passive, blunted individual who watched life go by without apparent curiosity, interest, or concern. His bland lack of communication, even in action, made it almost impossible to identify anything that he experienced as a problem. Joint work between such an inmate and staff seldom occurred because of his sheer lack of engagement with any aspect of the life available in the institution.

Quite a different sort of person was seen in the seventeen-year-old illiterate Mexican alcoholic, who was hyperactive, irascible, and daily in trouble somewhere in the institution. He experienced problems vociferously, but even after months of patient living with him through his crises he had learned little more than not to swing from the third-floor tier railings in C-Unit. He became something of a pet with the staff because so much effort was expended on him, but no one was surprised when five months after he was paroled, he was seen again in the institutional corridors waving gaily to his former counselor.[27] Lack of capacity for social learning in any relatively normal situation seemed the major problem in this sort of case.

An entirely different kind of problem was presented by the inmate who had ability to engage himself and considerable inherent capacity for learning but who still remained unreached. The case of a sophisticated and complex drug addict with literary talent and clerical skill comes to mind. When he came to C-Unit he had already been four and a half years in the institution and during this period he had exhausted the patience of all officialdom by his ability to engage staff interest in his behalf only to use each new opportunity maliciously. His only pleasure seemed to derive from denigrating manipulation of staff. For nearly two years the Project staff held the line with him, offering him opportunities while refusing to

---

[27] If the original Project proposal had been put into action, this individual would have been readmitted to C-Unit in order to build current treatment on the foundation of his previous ten months' experience in C-Unit.

be manipulated. There were periods when everyone was observing with hope and pleasure the apparent emergence of a new adaptation. At the end, however, he managed to create a situation in the institution concerning his job placement over which the Project had no control. He told his counselor: "For the first time I realize that I am responsible for the messes I get into." But by this time no further opportunities for helping him test this new understanding in action could be mobilized in the institution chiefly because no appropriate work supervisor would have him. Accordingly, the Project's commitment to continued investment in the individual could not be honored. He ended his days in the institution in a routine culinary position, sullen and vindictive to the last. Three months after his parole the Project learned he was back in prison somewhere.

And finally, there was the rare individual who had to be eliminated from the Unit population because he was aggressively criminal toward other inmates, constituting a serious danger to others unless supervised more restrictively than was possible in C-Unit. One such inmate was the duke of the pressure gang that dominated the skid-row subsystem of C-Unit's early days. He coldly sent his lieutenants to do his dirty work and efficiently recruited and trained the weaker YAs to accept his domination. The Project staff were never sure that they might not have found some way of dealing with him if he had entered the Unit after its organization was more stable. But at that point in its history, the Project had no adequate resources to challenge this explicitly predatory person and his damaging operation toward other inmates.

There is sometimes more to be learned from the study of failures than from the examination of apparent successes. But the first step in such a study requires explicating the process to be evaluated. Careful examination of failures requires a situation with more control over variables than was commanded by the C-Unit Project. The presence of the unreached inmate in C-Unit is a continuing challenge in the search for knowledge about how to resocialize society's outcasts, raising many important questions about policy, organization, and treatment methods. But the answers to these questions await other projects in the years ahead designed to test the propositions formulated here and elsewhere in the literature.

C-UNIT AND LIFE ON THE STREETS

Life in C-Unit was never an end in itself. The entire Project was a voyage of discovery, seeking to identify those aspects of institutional life that could be used to make the life inside a more adequate preparation for life on the streets. The ever-present question was: What is going on now

among the human beings in the institution that has relevance for free life
and therefore can be used as learning experiences designed to move inmates toward socially acceptable futures?

Paradoxical as it may seem, the most important sign that an inmate was
engaging himself in the resocializing process appeared when time in the
institution became important to him *not* in terms of its ending date but in
terms of experiences in the here and now. When the inmate could say
in his own way, in action, or in words as did one inmate, "I've learned that
who I am today here matters for who I can be on the streets," then continuity between the imprisoned self and the free self had been established
and current experience could affect the nature of that future self.

People grow only when present life is real to them. Making present time
a matter of real life was the Project's primary means for contributing to
the futures of the inmates who lived in C-Unit. The findings are not in
about their failures or successes on parole. But recidivism statistics will
never properly reveal what happened for C-Unit inmates during their
lives in the Unit. Many variables enter into the parole experience that cannot be controlled by the institution nor anticipated as the inmate leaves its
doors and becomes the man on the streets. What the institution can do is
to offer the inmate an opportunity to be a man today. If he accepts this
opportunity, then he receives the priceless gift of time that is significant
for his personal continuity in life. When this has happened for the inmate,
the responsibility for offering him continued opportunity to be a person of
worth rests with the free community.

X - RETROSPECT

IN THIS CHAPTER we ask the reader to consider with us what was learned in the C-Unit experience about the resocialization process and about the kind of organization needed to accomplish resocializing goals.

RESOCIALIZATION

An important outcome of the C-Unit experience was the transformation of intuitive perceptions about what offenders need into a provisional model for the resocializing process. Although we could not evaluate what happened in the lives of C-Unit men in terms of behavior on parole, we did see inmate behavior in the institution change in the desired direction under certain conditions and regress under contrary conditions. From the perspective of model-building the disintegrating phase of the C-Unit program provided data that were as important for understanding blocks to the growth of community as were the data of the developmental period for studying how inmate creativity could be released.

With the help of the "men of C-Unit" certain vague beliefs about what might happen in persons' lives under resocializing conditions have become tentative propositions about the dynamics of individual resocialization. Certain of these are paramount.

1. The stress, degradation of previous selves, and separation from the distractions of the normal community involved in imprisonment constitute

useful, if not necessary, conditions for initiating a resocializing process. Not all offenders now sent to prison need such drastic pressures to change in order to ally themselves with official helpers; and many would do better if the pressure to change, potential in imprisonment, were used over a shorter period of time. Even under present conditions the disruption and need to reintegrate initiated in the individual by imprisonment (and maintained to some extent by the anticipation of release) sets in motion a dynamic that can be used with many inmates to influence the direction of change.

2. Because resocialization is concerned with correcting moral discontinuities and with reinforcing or, in some cases, helping to establish internalized value systems congruent with viable community participation, four conditions seem essential if the personal crisis introduced by imprisonment is to be used for resocialization.

a. *A valued role as member of a community* for the person who is to be resocialized. This role restores the individual's dignity as a person, gives immediate and realistic content to hope, and establishes the matrix of obligations and rights that is essential to moral functioning.

b. *Opportunity for each member to participate in the definition and enforcement of the norms required for acceptable social interaction in a community.*

c. *Opportunity for each member to learn values through action in his own behalf,* by making choices, experimenting with alternatives, and experiencing consequences.

d. *Support for value learning through coherence among the various relationships in which the inmate participates,* such as those he experiences in treatment activities, in various segments of official program, and in the inmate system.

3. Adequate diagnosis and treatment of the moral difficulties of individual inmates are greatly facilitated by a community setting that provides opportunities for positive moral behavior. Such a setting makes it possible to differentiate between moral pathology and responses to pathological situations. It also provides the range of resources necessary for flexible responses to the various forms of social maladaptation evidenced by imprisoned offenders.

4. It can be inferred that resocialization is occurring in some degree in the life of the individual inmate when present experience in prison becomes: (1) significant for its own sake, and (2) relevant for his future life in the free community. At such moments personal continuity is established between the imprisoned self and the free self, hopefully permitting the individual's active use of the lessons he has learned in prison under the stress of the problems he encounters after release.

5. Regardless of what has been accomplished in influencing an individual's orientations and behavior during his stay in the resocializing community, the ultimate effectiveness of these new learnings for his behavior in the free community will depend on continuing support during the parole period. Ideally his release to parole should occur when he is ready for greater responsibilities than those possible in prison; should constitute advancement to a higher status "member of the community" role than that available to him in the prison community; should provide free access to opportunities for performing the normal social roles required of any community member; and should specifically support a continuing moral adaptation through means similar to those used in the resocializing community.[1]

The model for the resocialization of individual offenders directs attention to the offender and his community as the crucial actors in the correctional process. In this perspective prison and parole are not conceived of as accepting sole responsibility for the community in doing something to the offender that will make him once more a faceless unit in an anonymous mass. Rather, correctional activity is seen as a mediating process for healing a broken social relation between a community and a person, with both having had to become aware of and responsive to the other. In this total process the institution's proper mission would seem to be that of establishing conditions that enable the offender to prepare himself for the responsibilities of life in the free community; and that of parole establishing the conditions that enable the offender and his community to work together toward his ultimate reintegration into normal social functioning.

ORGANIZING FOR RESOCIALIZATION

Resocializing agencies have a double interest in social relationships. They aim to encourage clients to change the ways in which they relate to others. And in this effort their proper tools—if not their only tools—are relationships among persons: among staff members and among clients, and between the clients and their communities. The way such relationships are organized is thus crucially important to th ̣ resocializing agency; they must provide a proper matrix for personal hange, both encouraging such

---

[1] In following a number of C-Unit leaders during the years since their C-Unit experiences, it has become evident that the newly released parolee often experiences a demotion in status from that he achieved in the resocializing community, together with a marked reduction in support and severe limitations on opportunities to participate in appropriate roles. Further study of what happens on parole to those who have been treated in prison is essential both for understanding the total process required to restore offenders to normal social functioning and for designing effective corrective treatments.

change and furnishing opportunities for its realization. Much of the Project's effort was invested in the attempt to discover that organization of human resources best fitted to achieve the aim of inducing and supporting a capacity to change social relationships.

It seems clear on the basis of the C-Unit experience that the current organization of correctional agencies is poorly designed if the test be the encouragement of capacity to change. C-Unit was never permitted to develop in full the alternative model of organization toward which it was striving. However, we can summarize the Project expectations that were supported by experience, its discoveries about the nature of the resocializing community, the reasons for the disintegration of the emergent inmate-staff community on C-Unit, and certain organizational issues that await explication.

SUPPORTED EXPECTATIONS

Of first importance is the finding that inmates are not inherently and massively antisocial in their orientations. When an environment existed in which the dignity of inmates as persons was respected, most C-Unit men acted in support of the values essential to community. Given legitimate means in the official program to work on their own problems with the help of staff, most inmates used the approved mechanisms in preference to sub-rosa activities. In this process they evidenced a degree of creativity and concern for the welfare of others that surpassed the expectations of many persons who were accustomed to think of inmates as hostile children. It is clear from the C-Unit experience that inmates constitute a tremendous pool of ordinarily untapped human resources for accomplishing the official goals of the correctional institution.

Equally important is the finding that many institutional staff members have more to give to resocializing work than is usually permitted within the limitations of traditional job descriptions. When professional and technical personnel were offered expanded opportunities to contribute as members of a staff work group, they evidenced capacities not previously apparent in their work. Growth, inventiveness, and sharing characterized the performance of staff in each of the Project role groups during the period when problem-solving norms were primary in the relations among staff. Thus the Project expectation that potential but unused resources for resocializing work existed among the persons already employed by the institution was confirmed.

Also in line with Project expectations was the fact that an important means for releasing the creative energies of both inmates and staff proved to be changing the way persons were related to each other in the accomplishment of tasks. Providing inmates and staff with roles that made them responsible for their own behavior in solving problems of significance to them increased their investment and made them accessible to training. When either inmates or staff experienced demotion to less responsible roles at the hands of upper authorities, they responded with outward conformance and the public use of approved words, *but* they did not learn. Management, in its primary function of establishing the roles through which people work at tasks, thus proved itself to be one of the most powerful tools in the resocializing treatment.

EMERGENT FORMULATIONS

The Project's most important discoveries concerned the nature of the resocializing community. Several propositions about the critical dimensions of the resocializing community model emerge from the C-Unit experience.

1. The resocializing community is essentially political, dealing with the value issues involved in the governing of men. The issues with which both the offender and his community must come to grips, if he is to become a viable participant in the free community, are those of justice under rules and the rights of the individual, the control of deviance and the encouragement of diversity, the individual's obligation to community welfare and the preservation of self-interest. Problems in these areas, for which both the offender and his community are responsible, brought the individual to correctional attention in the first place; they must be dealt with directly in the process of restoring him to free status in the community. Any part of the corrective process, whether instituted in prison or on parole, must accordingly be prepared to focus attention on the basic relationships between a person and his organized community; and to use, among other means of influence, the political activities necessary for maintaining the democratic values of our society in the relationships between the individual offender and his social groups.

2. At the heart of these issues, and of the means for dealing with them, are the processes used for maintaining social control. Neither psychological intervention to modify the orientations of the offender nor procedures for securing his welfare are sufficient, alone or in combination, to accomplish the goal of his restoration to viable participation in the free community. Unless the institutions for control used in dealing with the offender are congruent in values with those expressed by the institutions for psychological treatment and welfare to which he is also exposed, the central issue is avoided and the effectiveness of every corrective effort is seriously vitiated. Thus the resocializing community must be concerned from the

outset with the means used for social control and the way these are integrated with the other processes used in managing the offender's return to
free status.

3. Segregation as a primary means for social control is opposed in principle to control by community. Control by community relies in large part
on social relationships to support acceptable behavior, using manipulation
or the exercise of force by an outside authority sparingly and only as otherwise uncontrollable situations require such intervention into the normal
control processes. Thus the resocializing community will be characterized
by a more complex system of social control than can be provided by a
system that depends primarily on segregative means; and will use social
control for different ends, that is, the encouragement of individual initiative and responsibility rather than the maintenance of conformity per se.

4. The traditional bureaucratic form of management currently adopted
by correctional agencies is severely limited as a means for facilitating the
processes of social and personal change established by the resocializing
community. The bureaucratic organization necessarily focuses on the orderly performance of established routines that often become ends in themselves because goals are assumed. When modification of goals and of the
social processes affecting cultural values is more important for the agency's
product than are the means by which goals and values are implemented,
then bureaucracy is an inappropriate form of organization.[2] The outlines
of the organizational model that can facilitate human creativity and
growth have not been fully established, although many tentative efforts
to create one are evident throughout our society. The resocializing community is one of the enterprises that express this more general groping toward an appropriate form of organization for accomplishing social and
personal change.

5. The relationships between the resocializing community and its organizational environment are critical for the emergence and maintenance
of a resocializing culture within the community. When there are ultimate
decision-makers outside the resocializing community, the system pressures
on them, their goals and orientations, and the processes for communication
between them and the smaller unit are critical for what happens within the
community itself. Any successful resocializing community must give high
priority to designing its relationships with the higher authorities who determine its fate.

6. Given a supporting environment, the kinds of relationships that will
obtain within the resocializing community are primarily determined by

---

[2] Crozier, Michel, *The Bureaucratic Phenomenon*. University of Chicago Press, Chicago, 1964, pp. 6–9.

the way the official staff organizes its own relationships. Problem-solving norms and processes must characterize the relationships among staff members if these are to appear in the activities through which staff and inmates work together and in the relationships established among inmates.

7. The inmate system within the prison community is an essential participant in the work of the resocializing community and can be influenced to support official goals. Although the strategies for inducing a cooperative inmate system are still embryonic in formulation, the C-Unit experience strongly suggests that the inmate system is not the inevitable barrier to resocializing work traditionally assumed, but that it reflects quite directly the official organization to which it responds. It is clear, however, that the resocializing community cannot be bifurcated into staff and inmate systems; that it must achieve an arena of activity within which staff and inmates talk a common language and act in terms of commonly accepted norms; and that establishing this domain for joint work between these primary segments of the community tends to induce a supportive system of relationships among the inmates themselves.

8. The resocializing community is never a problem-free community. Instead, it may seem especially problem-prone since it values rapid identification and direct confrontation of problems, together with problem-causing responsive change, above the smooth operation that often obscures problems by ignoring them and their consequences. The maturity of the resocializing community is measured by its lack of anxiety in accepting that problems are inherent in social relationships; its willingness to examine and deal with the fundamental sources of problems in either the structural or psychological aspects of social functioning; and the effectiveness of the processes it establishes for making necessary changes.[3]

9. It is clear that the Project never proposed to establish a "people-changing" therapeutic community. In the usual formulation of that treatment model the ideal role for staff and inmates is that of therapist, and all situations are to be used for intervention into intra-psychic difficulties. In contrast, the basic role of all persons in the C-Unit community was that of "citizen," and performance in situations was evaluated by the achievement of individual and group welfare through effective work at present tasks. In the course of the C-Unit experience and in later analysis, this critical difference between the "resocializing community" model and the more usual image of the "therapeutic community" became increasingly clear. It was

---

[3] Jacques, Elliot, *The Changing Culture of a Factory*. The Dryden Press, Inc., New York, 1952, p. 300. "Our definition of social health in an industrial community would picture a factory not so much free from problems, as one capable of tackling in a realistic way whatever technical, economic, and social problems it may encounter."

a basic Project assumption that people change as they act in their own behalf in response to real adaptive tasks; and that the life task facing the
offender in prison is to use the situation forced upon him by his change of
status to become a different kind of community member in the present as
well as upon release. This task might or might not require personality
change. It would require some change in the offender's social relations and
in his ability to maintain the values of community in his day to day behavior. Accordingly, although the C-Unit community included resources for
providing therapy where such intervention was needed by individuals, its
basic design was geared *not to "doing things to people to change personalities" but to creating the conditions under which people could change
themselves through changing the way they worked together on common
tasks.*

CONDITIONS FOR DISINTEGRATION IN C-UNIT

Three particular failures to achieve the desirable organizational conditions for a resocializing community seem to account in large part for
C-Unit's inability to stabilize the potentialities for community that
emerged toward the end of the first program year.

Of primary importance was the fact that the community was never permitted to design its institutions for control in congruence with the values
espoused in its welfare institutions. Sentencing, the honor system, and the
DVI discipline process all remained static throughout the Project's life,
reflecting a quite different model for relating staff and inmates from that
proposed by the Project. Under these circumstances C-Unit inmates
gained tangible and visible rewards from the larger system only for conformity as individuals, not for active participation in building community.
The sanctioning system imposed from outside the Project was a powerful
force maintaining the "do your own time" orientation among the C-Unit
inmates. The fact that nothing could be done to change the means for
dealing with deviant behavior created strong pressures against open community discussion of this critical area. The community's inability to act
except in procuring amenities ultimately led to a sub-rosa acknowledg-
ment between staff and inmates that the C-Unit community was an arti-
fact, not a dynamic and effective social entity. "Shuck" and "front" superseded commitment and respect, and "community" and "problem-solving"
became the false verbal coinage of a realm in which one did not "talk
serious" in public.

The lack of problem-solving connections between the Project and upper-
level administration in DVI was in large part responsible for turning the
C-Unit community into an ineffective satellite. For a period of time prob-

lem-solving appeared in C-Unit as the dominant process in many social relationships. But the dynamics of change so released were quickly blocked when the Project's controlling environment continued to make decisions that reflected a different philosophy of action. The administration of the larger institution could not be drawn into the problem-solving process within the Project, nor was it able to support such a process between itself and the Project administration. In consequence, the administration of the larger institution could neither understand nor respond positively to the Project's requests for increased responsibility.

The cooptation of the C-Unit community was completed when a Project supervisor was appointed to reinstate within the Project the style of administration characteristic of the larger institution. The critical importance of administrative style for the problem-solving process is revealed in the difference between C-Unit's programs in the first and the second years. In almost any staff position other than that of the administrator, an experimental program can rely on role design to encourage appropriate performance on the part of either professional or technical staff. But the responsible administrator's role cannot be designed and enforced by his subordinates. If he is not able to perform as a leader in problem-solving because of his own commitment to that mode of operation and with positive support from the larger institution, the problem-solving process cannot be instituted or maintained in the activities of the staff.

ISSUES RAISED BUT NOT RESOLVED

Several issues were highlighted in the C-Unit experience for which the available data offer no guide to resolution.

Population Selection. During the course of the action program two selection processes were proposed as alternatives to the random process used to collect the study population. One proposal was to screen inmates for C-Unit for motivation and capacity to use the resocializing process. The second was to use C-Unit as a special treatment program for the more inadequate and disturbed inmates in DVI.

The Project was opposed on principle to both of these selection processes:

1. The Project was not proposing a single treatment method appropriate for an identifiable kind of inmate. Rather, it conceived of the role of member in a problem-solving community as a basic requirement for treating the social maladaptations of every imprisoned offender. The Project recognized the variety of treatment strategies that would be necessary to specify the community experience for inmates with different kinds of

problems. But it had no criteria that would differentiate inmates who needed to experience acceptable problem-solving within a community from those who had no such need.

2. The Project was opposed to any segregation of inmates in groups that carried the negative label of "especially sick" or "especially bad." The role "member of the worst community" was not conceived of as a treatment tool but rather as a means for inducing secondary deviance.

3. The Project was concerned with preparing inmates for life in the free community where the individual must be able to take value positions, select appropriate reference groups, and give aid as well as receive support. The heterogeneous population of the resocializing community provided the variety of exposures in action required to teach both the weak and the strong these fundamental social skills.

Nothing in C-Unit's experience led the Project leaders to question these principles for selecting the inmate-staff community population. But certain questions about the meaning of a randomly selected population for the more capable inmates within it did recur from time to time in the course of the action program. Would more have been accomplished if staff energies had been devoted less to those who were minimally capable of learning and more to those who were ready to undertake basic changes in their lives? Did the high status achieved by the more capable inmates in C-Unit actually disadvantage them for the free world where they would once again find themselves at the bottom of the social ladder? If the inmates who should never have been in prison because of their actual social competence had been removed from the C-Unit population, would it have been possible to use the complex process of the problem-solving community in treating the less adequate remaining population? And if not, did the whole community approach depend for success on the exploitation of strong inmates in the treatment of the weak?

The Project was keenly aware that perhaps a third of its population would have been better treated through adequate services in the free community. Since these individuals were held in prison by forces that could not be influenced by the Project staff, it was deemed particularly important to keep them acting in their own behalf in preparation for release. But the presence of the more capable inmates in C-Unit was not a necessary condition for the problem-solving community. The Project continued to distinguish between the community problem-solving process and the program that develops because certain individuals rather than others compose the community. If inmates like Big Mac and Jack had not been present in C-Unit, the program would have been quite different. Less complex activities than the Welfare Fund could have been expected. The program as a whole would have been less like the normal activities of the open community. Probably it would have been necessary to work with a smaller population and to provide a richer proportion of staff to inmates. But the process would have been the same. Those individuals in such a population who actually used the process for their own growth would have achieved high status in that particular community. And transition to the free community would have faced them on parole, as it did many men who had become C-Unit leaders, with a renewed degradation unless special provisions were made by the community that received them.

Maintaining the Problem-Solving Culture. C-Unit's experience does not help us answer the question, How can the problem-solving culture of the resocializing community be institutionalized once it has been established? The data do suggest that the staff work group is the primary culture carrier in work with a transitional inmate population. The question of maintaining the problem-solving culture therefore focuses attention on stability of the staff.

Several practical problems contribute to the difficulty any project such as C-Unit might expect to experience in maintaining a stable staff culture. The small multifunctional staff unit required for the resocializing community can never provide sufficient opportunities for promotion within its own system to hold all the lower-level staff whom it trains. Because civil service examinations are administered periodically, promotional opportunities for all staff tend to cluster in time, with the possibility that all or most of the members of one or more of the role groups might need to be replaced within a short period. Because of the intensive training and personal development gained by a member of a problem-solving staff work group, its incumbents can be expected to rate promotions more quickly than do persons in more traditionally designed positions. Thus a program like C-Unit can expect a more serious problem in frequency of staff turnover than do more routinized divisions within the State Department. Yet it was evident in the C-Unit experience that it was far more difficult to train new staff in the problem-solving process once the basic structure of the program had been established than it was during the period when all staff members were required to deal with the critical issues involved in creating a new community.

Given C-Unit's experience, we can only guess at the measures that might have helped to maintain the staff culture in spite of rapid staff turnover. Certainly it would have been important to ensure continuity of administrative style during the period while new staff members were selected and trained. It might have been possible to arrange for staggered terms of office in the Project, permitting the work group to orient one new member at a time, and to commit each to a term of participation that allowed for the development of necessary skills. Such a plan would have required state level attention to the careers of employees who moved into the Project and then out. Perhaps more attention could have been given to selecting new recruits for the Project who were particularly well equipped to adopt the problem-solving approach in order to reduce the length of time required for their orientation.

Ultimately any plan for stabilizing the problem-solving process as it was developed in C-Unit during its first year was the responsibility of upper-level decision-makers in the institution and in the Department of Corrections. The Project could make clear the conditions for stability; it could not control the flow of personnel into and out of its staff work group. Structural supports from the larger organizational environment, such as long-range personnel planning, are evidently required if organizational change is to be nurtured and allowed to develop to the point where it can actually institutionalize the problem-solving culture. And maintaining that culture will always depend in large measure on the way the leadership role of administration is defined and executed.

Bridges to the Community. C-Unit: Search for Community in Prison has presented no systematic findings on the Project's attempt to integrate the parole process with the resocialization program in the institution. There are several reasons for ignoring in this document one of the Project's major proposals of the early planning period.

Parole agents were not assigned to the Project until early in the second year of program. The parole agents from the larger districts were rarely the persons who supervised C-Unit men after release. And the frequent changes in agents assigned to C-Unit limited their ability to contribute to the program.

In the few instances where a parole agent learned to know inmates whom he later supervised in the community, major advantages in the plan were apparent. An occasional problem inmate went out to an ingenious parole plan that proved successful largely because he and the parole agent had known each other over a period of time and the parole agent had had the benefit of the Project's experience with the inmate. The frequent presence of parole agents did enrich the Unit program and helped to focus the work of both staff and inmates on present tasks as they related to the future. But ultimately it proved impossible to coordinate from the vantage point of a single institution the complex and separately administered state divisions of institutions and parole for YA and A# inmates drawn from many distant geographical areas. The Project staff saw enough value achieved in individual cases to be sure that continuity between the institutional and parole experiences is a critical factor in successful resocialization as tested by performance in the community. But they were also convinced that basic changes in the relationships between institutional services and parole services are required to provide continuity of experience for all offenders who are released to parole.

THE COSTS OF ORGANIZATIONAL CHANGE

Evaluation of the Project's findings and limitations leads directly to questions about the ability of the larger systems in C-Unit's environment to support the process they had authorized. It seems clear in retrospect that the major flaw in the original plan was to leave unspecified the implicit commitments of DVI and the Department of Corrections when they established a small subsystem charged with initiating organizational change. Before the action program started, no one was clear about the nature of the costs expected of the larger systems responsible for the ultimate outcome. Today it is possible to be somewhat more specific about the implications of an administrative decision to initiate planned change in one of its subsystems.

At least three commitments from top administration seem to be necessary if the stated goals of a project like C-Unit are to be achieved. These commitments involve adopting principles to govern administrative action during the life of the Project.

1. *Commitment to Reciprocal Change.* Throughout the life of the C-Unit program, upper administration appeared to assume that the Project, once authorized, could maintain the change process within the confines of its relatively tiny inmate-staff community without calling on its organizational environment for reciprocal change. DVI and the Department of Corrections were prepared to make necessary procedural adjustments such as those required to assign parole agents to C-Unit or to establish a C-Unit Classification Committee. But they were apparently totally unprepared for the fact that changing the role of the inmate in the C-Unit community would call for corresponding changes in the role performance of all employees in any system, including both the institution and the Department of Corrections, that directly affected the development of the C-Unit program.[4]

---

[4] We came to call this the "one thing leads to another" principle. It is worth emphasizing that *neither Project personnel* nor correctional administrators realized at the outset the extent of matters that would be called into question by Project operations. Some of these matters would have required reconsideration of policy, and perhaps law, beyond the established purview of Department of corrections administrators.

Essentially the effectiveness of planned change in C-Unit depended on the ability of upper administrators to provide problem-solving roles wherever C-Unit activities intersected with other parts of its organizational environment. This stipulation should not be read to mean that C-Unit needs were expected to supersede other interests whenever there was an encounter with other divisions and authorities in its environment. It does mean that, when C-Unit acted through its personnel as part of a larger whole, it should have been able to use the problem-solving process that had been established as the critical norm for relations among its own subsystems. Only the authorizing administrations could establish conditions that permitted C-Unit to relate through problem-solving, rather than hierarchal, processes with its relevant environment; and to establish such conditions upper administrative personnel would themselves have had to act in terms of the orientations, goals, and values inherent in the role changes established for C-Unit operation. Without such changes in role performance by officials, outside C-Unit but related to it, C-Unit personnel could not maintain the problem-solving roles established for work within its own boundaries; nor could they contribute to the spread of change throughout the larger institution.

Change in one subsystem becomes viable only as reciprocal change in role definition occurs at the relevant points of connection with the total system. The commitment to responsive change is one of the costs of planned change to be assessed whenever a large organization assigns responsibility for initiating change to a subsystem within itself.

2. *Commitment to the Discipline of Ends.* A special instance of commitment to reciprocal change directs attention to the way responsible administrators in the larger organization make decisions about the unit that is responsible for initiating change.

Throughout the action program Project leadership found it difficult to engage its critical decision-makers in the discussion of issues formulated

---

The most important example is sentencing. It was quickly apparent that for maximum effectiveness sentencing decisions should have been congruent in philosophy and fact with other reward and penalty decisions in C-Unit. This implied a degree of influence over such decisions by inmates and prison staff members not contemplated—indeed, opposed—by the philosophy and practice of those who set sentences and parole dates during the C-Unit Project. (It will be recalled that adult sentences were set by a board, the Adult Authority, independent of prison administrators, and that the institutional counsellors who knew the inmates were not permitted to make recommendations. The sentences of Youth Authority wards were also set by a board also independent of the prison administration, although certain minimal recommendations from institutional staff were expected to guide the Youth Authority Board in making decisions.)

in terms of ends to be achieved. The system to which upper administrative personnel were geared focused the attention of high-level decision-makers on the means to be used rather than on the analysis of alternatives, the prediction of consequences, and the implications of these for progress toward a goal. As a result, many decisions about the Project were procedural in nature and frankly designed to avert an imminent crisis. Often by the time decisions were made few alternatives remained; and the means selected more often served the purposes of smooth administration than the Project's mission of establishing change through problem-solving.

The success of planned change efforts depends in large measure on the ability of organization leaders to examine all relevant information, to predict the consequences of action, to authorize an array of appropriate means, and to delegate the choice of means to those who are responsible for action to achieve goals. The administration of a large organization that uses a subsystem to initiate change makes an implicit commitment to accept the discipline of ends over means in making character-determining decisions about that subsystem. The cost of an administrative shift from a focus on means to a focus on issues, goals, and process should be openly faced before change action is authorized.

3. *Commitment to Clients.* A final commitment assumed when initiating change by the administration of an organization responsible for a subject population is to the clients affected in the course of experimentation.

Those who authorize planned change in a prison must assume responsibility for opening up the wells of creativity and growth in the lives of persons who are dependent on the organization. Unless the administration is committed to fulfilling over time the promises implicit in the changed inmate role, it would do better to leave the inmates alone to make their own adaptations to difficult realities, protected by their limited expectations of the official world. First to engage the vulnerable discarded persons of our society in creating a community based on the dignity of the individual and then to degrade them once more to the status of things to be manipulated is to repeat the societal rejection that brought them to the prison. The consequences of such an abrogation of trust (even if not intended as such) are more severe because of the painful effort invested in the attempt to establish relationships of trust. Once the inmates have been given back their voices, administration must be ready to maintain its commitment to open communication among men so long as it is related to the involved individuals.

Thus an important cost to be assessed when initiating planned change is the commitment to continue the new relationships with the inmates who are subjected to change. If these organizational costs are not recognized and provided for, the human cost in the lives of those for whom the organization is responsible, is indefensible.

* * *

The logic of the C-Unit experience leads us to reject the current intramural controversies between custody and treatment, between one form of correctional treatment and another. The question at issue is, What is the task and what is the proper use of the available resources for accomplishing this task? Since the only effective resocializing resources are relations among people, it is obvious that the critical question confronting correctional administration is, How do you organize people so that the outcome of their work is more adequate social beings?

The answers to "How do you organize for resocialization?" will not be found in administrative manuals or in treatment textbooks. Its principles can be discovered only as free people and offenders together are set the task of creating communities where moral values take precedence over all others in the daily socializing processes of life. Such communities will not be tidy in the bureaucratic sense. Problematic, self-critical, continuously in flux; creating, demolishing, and re-creating as problems and resources change; they will frighten the bureaucrat and stretch the administrator's capacity for leadership. But they will be dealing with the stuff of real life insofar as they engage each individual in the intimately personal discovery of what it means to be a responsible social being.

APPENDICES

SELECTION FOR C-UNIT

SELECTION of inmates for C-Unit was governed by a variety of factors, some of which were discussed in Chapter II. The purpose of this Appendix is to outline systematically the criteria employed in the selection of the C-Unit population.

In the absence of other considerations, the Project would have liked to have had a population representative of the population of DVI as a whole. On the one hand, such a population in C-Unit would have provided the Project with inmates presenting a wide range of behavior and correctional problems, which would have facilitated identification of different kinds of offenders and the development of appropriate means for treating each. On the other hand, a population representative of the institution as a whole would have made the findings of the Project indisputably relevant to the rest of the institution, a consideration of some importance in view of the understandable skepticism of correctional administrators toward special projects using highly selected populations. In fact, however, complete representativeness was not possible for reasons given below. Instead, it was necessary to create two "eligible pools," one for youths and one for adults, and then to select randomly from the eligible inmates.

CRITERIA

The need for two eligible pools, one for youths and one for adults, arose from the legislative requirement that equal numbers of youths and adults be chosen for C-Unit.[1] Although the criteria determining eligibility for the two pools were roughly the same, there were also some important differences.

Time. To be eligible for C-Unit, an inmate had to have a minimum of six months and a maximum of eighteen months left to serve in the institution before probable release on parole. This criterion was established because C-Unit was conceived as a pre-release unit from which inmates would be paroled directly. It was believed that too short a stay in C-Unit before parole would not lead to significant effects, and too long a stay was believed likely to result in inmates becoming stale or satiated with the program. Somewhat arbitrarily, the time limits were set at six and eighteen months.

For *youths* this criterion was initially interpreted to mean that only YAs coming directly from the reception center were eligible for C-Unit, since the average length of stay of YAs in DVI was only about twelve months. After a year and two months of operation, however, it was discovered that some youths transferred to DVI from other institutions should also be included in the eligible pool, and selection was changed accordingly.

For *adults,* application of the time criterion usually required estimating the probable action of the Adult Authority board at the inmate's next hearing, since when an A# was granted parole, his release date often was less than six months after the hearing date. Not infrequently these estimates were overly optimistic, and a number of A#s stayed in C-Unit longer than eighteen months.

Geographical Limits Related to Parole. To be eligible for C-Unit, an inmate's probable parole plans had to be for release to a district in or near one of the three major metropolitan areas in California: Los Angeles, San Francisco Bay, or Sacramento-Stockton. The reason for this limitation was the special parole program planned for C-Unit, which could be implemented only in these areas. Consequently, inmates likely to be paroled out-of-state or to remote areas were excluded from the eligible pools.

This criterion affected youths and adults almost identically.

Ex-PICO Cases. Inmates who had participated in the PICO project were ineligible for C-Unit. A few youths and adults otherwise eligible had served previous sentences in DVI as YAs and had been part of the PICO

---

[1] The original PICO project dealt only with youths. In extending the project to PICO—Phase II, the legislature stipulated that at least half the inmates be youths. See Chapter II which describes the planning phase of the C-Unit Project.

project, in which they had received intensive counseling from counselors who were now part of the C-Unit Project. In order to avoid the complex clinical problems that conceivably could arise, the few such inmates were excluded from C-Unit.

This criterion applied identically to youths and adults.

Adjustment Center. Inmates currently in the adjustment center were not eligible for C-Unit. C-Unit was designed as a medium-security unit and did not have the facilities thought necessary by the institutions for handling inmates designated as adjustment center cases. Consequently, inmates in the adjustment center were excluded from the eligible pools.

For *youths,* this criterion meant that YAs designated in the reception center as requiring adjustment-center housing immediately upon entering DVI were ineligible for C-Unit. Because of their short stay in DVI, these youths did not become eligible even if they were subsequently released from the adjustment center to the DVI general population.

For *adults,* current adjustment-center status meant ineligibility, but after release from the adjustment center, an adult might become eligible.

Administrative Requirements. Various exclusions from the eligible pools were required for administrative reasons.

For *youths,* the main administrative exclusion consisted of all cases committed to the Youth Authority by juvenile courts. These cases were subjects in a study being conducted by the Youth Authority itself, and they were excluded from C-Unit to avoid introducing an extra variable in that study.

In addition, youths likely to be paroled to Alameda County (Berkeley and Oakland) were excluded to avoid conflict with another research project.

For *adults,* there were two overlapping exclusions for reasons of institutional convenience. First, adult commitments specifically assigned to DVI because of certain job skills essential to maintaining the physical plant, or who were assigned to such status after arriving at DVI, were ineligible for C-Unit. These inmates, known as the adult work crew, often had irregular or special hours of work and carried responsibilities the administration thought would be interfered with by the C-Unit program.

Second, adults living in a special minimum-supervision unit, L-3, were excluded from the eligible pool. These inmates, largely members of the adult work crew, had earned special privileges and had been formally rewarded by assignment to L-3.

THE PROBLEM OF BIAS

The complexity of the criteria defining the eligible pools precludes any simple judgment of the representativeness of the C-Unit population. To the extent that the best-behaved adults were assigned to L-3, and the worst-behaved youths to the adjustment center, the C-Unit population was like the population of the other general population units in DVI. But the variety of other factors operating makes even this a hazardous guess. Ideally, extensive background data could have been gathered on a random sample of DVI inmates, as well as on the C-Unit population, and a statistical analysis used to explore the extent of selection bias. Unfortunately, the project research staff did not have the resources to carry out this task.

However, there is some indication that the C-Unit population did not differ too greatly from that part of the DVI population living in the general-population honor and nonhonor units. After the Project had been in operation for little over a year, a survey was conducted of inmates in C-Unit and two other housing units in the institution,[2] and some background data were gathered for both C-Unit and non-C-Unit inmates. These data, presented in Appendix D, suggest that, at least at the time of the survey, the differences between C-Unit and the other units were not great.

---

[2] See Appendix B.

SURVEY DESIGN AND ADMINISTRATION

A LARGE part of the discussion of the inmate system in Chapter VIII is based on a survey conducted among inmates in C-Unit and two other housing units in the winter of 1961–1962. In this Appendix we give a brief description of the technical details of the design and administration of the survey.

THE QUESTIONNAIRE

The survey was designed to gather systematic evidence to check the observational impressions of the Project staff concerning the differences between the inmate systems in C-Unit and the rest of DVI. For this purpose, it was necessary to gather rather specific information concerning inmate behavior and relations, and it was decided to use interviews rather than self-administered questionnaires in order to reduce the problems of inmates having to cope with a complex and detailed questionnaire.

In framing questions about specific inmate behavior and relations within DVI inmate argot was used whenever it proved to be the most economical and transparent wording. Inmate informants were consulted frequently on matters of wording, intelligibility, and inmate willingness to answer, in order to avoid gross mistakes. In addition, the questionnaire was pretested four times to assess the effects of major modifications.[1] The final version is presented in Appendix E.

---

[1] The pretest samples, except for the last, were not included in the final survey samples. The last pretest was conducted using C-Unit inmates, and the version used was so close to the final one that these inmates could be reinterviewed briefly to complete their schedules.

SAMPLES

The C-Unit sample consisted of all inmates who had been in C-Unit for at least two weeks as of December 31, 1961. The two-week criterion was imposed because it was felt that this was the minimum time needed by an inmate to adjust to the disruption in his routines and expectations occasioned by being moved into C-Unit. Originally, the C-Unit sample consisted of 122 inmates, two of whom refused to be interviewed, leaving a final sample of 120.

The non-C-Unit samples were obtained in two stages. First, an honor unit and a nonhonor unit were selected randomly from the housing units in DVI. And second, within each unit, inmates were sampled randomly with a sampling ratio of one in three. The samples for honor and nonhonor units consisted of 60 and 57 inmates, respectively, none of whom refused to be interviewed.

The nature of the non-C-Unit sample was determined by the overall concern with inmate systems in housing units and by the limited interviewing staff, consisting of just the three Project research associates. The first of these considerations required comparisons between housing units, which meant either a random sample large enough to guarantee substantial numbers from each housing unit or a cluster sample by housing unit. In view of the shortage of interviewers, the latter course was taken, and even then it was necessary to sample within only two housing units rather than interview all inmates in both of them.[2]

The total sample of 237 inmates, then, consists of nearly the universe of C-Unit inmates at the end of 1961, together with a two-stage cluster sample by housing unit drawn from the rest of the institution.

ADMINISTRATION OF THE SURVEY

The questionnaire was administered in individual interviews lasting from about thirty-five minutes to an hour and a quarter, depending on the respondent's verbal skills and the number of sections of the questionnaire applying to him. The C-Unit inmates were interviewed over a period of

---

[2] The small number of interviewers was a more severe restriction than may appear. Because of the institutional schedule and other obligations of the research associates, it was feasible for an interviewer to schedule an average of only two interviews a day. Thus a large sample would have taken a long time to interview, which would have led to the danger of serious distortion of the results because of events within the institution.

one month, from the middle of December to the middle of January, and the nonhonor and honor unit inmates over a like period, from the middle of February to the middle of March.

Each inmate in the sample was sent a formal pass, which he had to honor. Once in the interviewer's office, he was told about the survey and its confidential nature, and he was then asked if he would be willing to participate. As noted earlier, all but two C-Unit inmates stayed for the interview. In general, the impression of the interviewers was that rapport had been good, despite the likelihood that many inmates chose to be interviewed either because of fear of reprisal or in order to escape for an hour from the daily routine. It had been anticipated that many inmates would participate out of fear despite assurances, and consequently great care had been taken in designing the questionnaire to avoid questions that might arouse unnecessary anxieties. Subsequent analysis has shown no evidence challenging the general impression of inmate cooperativeness and relative frankness.

STATISTICAL TESTS

It will be noted that no tests of statistical significance have been reported in the analysis of the survey data. The decision not to use such tests was based on two considerations. First, the sampling design for the survey does not approximate the statistical models underlying currently available tests of significance. Consequently, it is not clear how ordinary nonparametric statistical tests should be interpreted for this study, and preparation of tests more appropriate to the sampling design was impractical. Second, even if appropriate statistical tests were available, it is not clear that their use would have made much difference in the interpretations and conclusions. The main point is that on the basis of observations, a *particular* pattern of findings was anticipated, that is, consistent differences in specified directions. In such a situation, if all of the observed differences are in the right direction, even if some are not highly significant statistically, the line of interpretation is supported, but if any one finding runs in the wrong direction, then the interpretation is not supported no matter how statistically significant the rest of the findings may be.[3]

---

[3] A similar argument is presented by Seymour M. Lipset, Martin Trow, and James Coleman in *Union Democracy*, The Free Press, Glencoe, Ill., 1956. We would argue that the predictions in the present study were more highly specified by prior observations than were their hypotheses, so that a single negative finding would have had more serious consequences for interpreting the C-Unit data than Lipset and his associates felt would have been true for their material.

PROBLEM-SOLVING ADAPTATIONS:
Index Construction and Additional Findings

THIS APPENDIX presents some material concerning problem-solving adaptations that could not be included in Chapter VIII. The first section describes in detail how inmates were classified in terms of types of adaptation and gives the specific questionnaire items used in constructing the index. The second section reports some additional findings concerning problem-solving adaptations and communication among inmates and staff that were mentioned in Chapter VIII but could not be presented in the main text.

TYPES OF ADAPTATION

It will be recalled from Chapter VIII that inmates spontaneously identified three kinds of adaptation: "wise" inmates, who do their own time; "oakies," who sit around and do nothing except perhaps sniff glue or tell stories; and "gunsels," who make trouble for themselves and other inmates. In addition to these, the Project sought to generate a fourth type, which we have called the "problem-solving" adaptation. We attempted initially to locate all four types of adaptation using the survey data, and it proved possible to identify both problem-solving and wise adaptations. However, among the remaining inmates, it was difficult to distinguish between oakie and gunsel adaptations in a way that seemed reliable, and consequently these were treated as a single "alienated" category.

The index of type of adaptation was constructed in four steps: (1) Each inmate was asked a series of questions concerning his relation with each of six staff members: his counselor, the day and evening officers in his housing unit, his morning and afternoon work or school supervisors, and any one "other" staff member designated by the inmate as one with whom he got along well. In addition, C-Unit inmates were questioned about their participation in C-Unit groups. Using these questions, each relation of each inmate was classified in terms of whether it reflected a problem-solving, wise, or alienated adaptation. (2) Each inmate was given a problem-solving score, a wise score, and an alienated score, each obtained by simply counting the number of relations of a particular type in which the inmate participated. (3) The scores for a given inmate were combined to form an estimate of his overall type of adaptation. (4) Finally, the main concern in the present study is with problem-solving adaptations, so that once inmates had been classified as "problem-solvers," "wise," or "alienated," the latter two types were combined to form a single "nonproblem-solving" category.[1]

RELATIONS WITH INDIVIDUAL STAFF MEMBERS

The procedure for classifying the relation between an inmate and a particular staff member will be illustrated for the case of the counselor. The same method was used for the other staff members, the specific questions differing only so as to make them pertinent to different staff roles.[2]

Problem-solving relations between an inmate and a staff member can be characterized by two attributes: the presence of shared goals,[3] and the existence of common understandings and expectations that permit orderly

---

[1] It might seem that distinguishing between wise and alienated adaptations among the nonproblem-solving types merely adds an unnecessary complexity. However, there are two reasons for making the distinction here. First, the rationale for developing the index is more easily presented in terms of the set of three types than with just the distinction between problem-solvers and all others. Second, problem-solvers, wise inmates, and alienated inmates should behave in distinctively different ways that can be predicted theoretically. The fact that these predictions are born out strengthens the validity of the typology as a whole in a way not possible using just the distinction between problem-solving and nonproblem-solving adaptations. On this second point, see the useful discussion of "construct validity" in Selltiz, Claire, Marie Jahoda, Morton Deutsch, and Stuart W. Cook, *Research Methods in Social Relations*, rev. ed., Holt, Rinehart and Winston, New York, 1959. The further analysis referred to is reported in Wilson, Thomas P., "Some Effects of Different Patterns of Management on Inmate Behavior in a Correctional Institution," unpublished Ph.D. dissertation, Columbia University, 1965.

[2] The C-Unit groups will be discussed in the next section.

[3] Shared goals have been called "promotively interdependent" by Morton Deutsch, in "The Effects of Cooperation and Competition upon Group Process," in Cartwright, Dorwin, and Alvin Zander, editors, *Group Dynamics, Research and Theory,* 2d ed., Harper and Row, New York, 1960, pp. 414–448.

pursuit of goals. In contrast, wise relations are characterized by the absence of shared goals but the presence of common expectations and understandings, that is, what might be called "working relations." Finally, alienated relations are characterized by the absence of both shared goals and working relations.[4] To assess the presence or absence of these attributes in an inmate's relation with his counselor, indexes of "shared goals with counselor" and "working relation with counselor" were constructed. The two indexes were then combined to describe the inmate's relation with his counselor as problem-solving, wise, or alienated.

The index of shared goals with counselor was based on two criteria. First, every inmate had to have some contact with his counselor concerning routine procedural matters, if only in preparation for reports to the parole board. It was supposed, however, that the presence of shared goals would result in communication about things over and above the minimal procedural matters that were absolutely required. Second, it was assumed that sharing goals would be associated with a certain amount of trust and honesty on the part of the inmate in talking with his counselor. The questions used as indicators of these two criteria were the following.

89. When you see [your counselor], there are a number of things you could talk about. One kind of thing is about procedures, requests, classification, assignments, board reports, and so on.

How much of your contact with him is about things like this—would you say over half or less than half?
   Almost all
   *Over half
   *About half
   *Less than half
   *Very little

92. Do you ever "talk serious" with [your counselor]?
   (IF YES:) How much do you "talk serious" with him:
   *A lot
   *Some
   Or not very much?
   No [does not "talk serious" at all]

---

[4] Shared goals should rarely occur in the absence of a working relation, since the mutual frustration resulting from the lack of a working relation should lead either to a shift of goals or to efforts to develop a working relation. Note that the goals referred to here are the specific ends sought by the individuals in the concrete situation at hand.

Positive responses to both questions were necessary for an inmate to be classified as positive on the shared-goals index.[5]

The working-relation index was based on three criteria. First, it was supposed that in a working relation the inmate would perceive the staff member as having some awareness of the inmate's point of view. Second, in such a relation, it was assumed that the inmate would see the staff member as dealing with him in ways appropriate to the particular role-relationship between them rather than in terms of the general stereotype of "just an inmate." Third, it was supposed that in a working relation the staff and inmate would get along with a minimum of overt and directly expressed hostility or anger. The questions used were the following for the case of the counselor:

85. How well do you think he understands you and your problems:
    *Very well
    *Fairly well
    Or not very well?

86. When you really need something done, can you count on him to help you out?

    (IF YES:) Would you say you can count on him:
    *Almost always
    *Most of the time
    *Or only some of the time?
    No [cannot count on him]

88. On the whole, do you get along with him:
    *Very well
    *Fairly well
    Or not very well?

Positive responses to all three questions were necessary for an inmate to be classified as positive on the working-relation index.[6]

---

[5] The positive-response categories are indicated by asterisks. The number to the left of each question is the item number in the survey questionnaire in Appendix E.

The item numbers of the corresponding questions for other staff are as follows: first supervisor: 59, 62; second supervisor: 73, 76; day officer: 96, 99; evening officer: 106, 109; "other": 42, 45. (On item 42, "Very little" was scored as negative; all other cutting points are as in the text.)

The term "talk serious" in the second question is used by inmates to describe situations in which they talk about matters important to them with relative honesty. The contrasting argot term is "shuck," meaning the inmate talks about what he thinks the other wants discussed in ways designed to please or manipulate the other.

[6] The item numbers of the corresponding questions for other staff are as follows: first supervisor: 56, 57, 58; second supervisor: 70, 71, 72; day officer: 101, 102, 103;

Using the shared-goals and working-relation indexes, the relation of an inmate with his counselor was classified in one of four categories.

PROBLEM-SOLVING: positive on both the shared-goals and working-relation indexes.

WISE: positive on the working-relation index only.

NONSCALE: positive on the shared-goals index only.

ALIENATED: positive on neither the shared-goals nor working relation indexes.

The third category, "nonscale," represents a theoretically unstable type that should occur infrequently. And, in fact, nonscale responses were rare (see Table C–1).

Using similar procedures, the relations between an inmate and each of the remaining staff members to whom he was related were classified in terms of the types of adaptation they reflected.

RELATIONS IN C-UNIT GROUPS

Participation in the C-Unit groups was an important role-relationship within the Project, and inmates were asked a series of questions about their involvement in these groups. In retrospect, it is clear that similar questions should have been asked of non-C-Unit inmates about their group experiences, but this was not done.[7] As a result, the data on group participation are limited to C-Unit groups. Nevertheless, because the groups were so central a part of the Project, it is necessary to take them into account in any consideration of the adaptations of C-Unit inmates, even in the absence of comparable information about non-C-Unit inmates.

The basic concepts of shared goals and working relations apply to groups as well as to role-relationships involving pairs of individuals. However, the questions used to measure these dimensions differ from the ques-

---

evening officer: 111, 112, 113; "other": 47, 48. (No question corresponding to item 88 was asked concerning "other" since this staff member was located by means of the question, "With whom on the staff you see now do you feel *least* like an inmate?" [item 38].) For items 57, 71, 102, 112, and 48 the response "less than half the time" was scored negative.

[7] The decision, made at the time of constructing the questionnaire, was based on two considerations. First, relatively few inmates outside of C-Unit participated extensively in groups other than group counseling (see Table 7 in Chapter VIII), so that participation in groups did not appear to be as central a role-relationship for these inmates as for C-Unit inmates. Second, from observation and interviews with staff, it seemed evident that official expectations concerning inmate behavior in non-C-Unit groups precluded problem-solving behavior as defined here. Thus the non-C-Unit groups appeared to be irrelevant to the overall concern with the emergence of problem-solving adaptations.

tions about relations with individual staff members, largely because the parallels between pair-wise and multi-person relations were not fully appreciated at the time the questionnaire was constructed.

Three criteria were used to identify shared goals in the C-Unit groups. As with relations with individual staff members, it was required that the inmate not view the groups as a "shuck" (inmates putting on a front to please staff). Further, it was supposed that if an inmate saw others as "sniveling" (special pleading in a complaining, unmanly way) or "snitching" (informing on other inmates) in the groups, then it was unlikely that shared goals existed. The questions used were the following:

34. In your opinion, how many of the inmates in these groups try mainly to make themselves look good to the staff—would you say:

   Over half
   *About half
   *Or less than half?

35. How much sniveling goes on in these groups do you think:

   A great deal
   *Some
   *Not very much
   *Or none?

36. How much snitching do you think goes on in these groups:

   A great deal
   *Some
   *Not very much
   *Or none?

A positive response to all three questions by inmates participating in the C-Unit groups was taken as indicating the presence of shared goals.[8]

Only one question was included in the questionnaire that can be viewed as reflecting working relations in the C-Unit groups. Although an inmate may not have perceived his own goals as coinciding with the goals of the groups, he might nevertheless have seen the groups as useful in producing results benefiting the inmates in C-Unit. That is, the groups may have been viewed as an effective vehicle for pursuing inmate interests irrespective of whether or not these interests were seen as congruent with official goals. The following question was used to ascertain if an inmate saw the C-Unit groups as instrumentally effective in terms of his conception of inmate interests.

---

[8] Participation was ascertained by item 28: "Have you belonged to any of the groups or committees that are especially for C-Unit?"

32. Do you think these groups and committees do any good for the *Unit* as a *whole?*

    (IF YES:) Would you say they do:

    *A great deal of good
    *Some good
    Or not very much good?
    No [nothing accomplished for unit]

Participation in the C-Unit groups and a positive response to this question were taken as indicating that the inmate was involved in a working relation in the group program.

As with relations with individual staff members, relations in the groups were categorized in terms of the kinds of adaptation they reflected.

PROBLEM-SOLVING: presence of shared goals and working relation
WISE: presence of working relation only
NONSCALE: presence of shared goals only
ALIENATED: neither shared goals nor working relation.

Again, the "nonscale" type appeared very infrequently (see Table C–1).

NO ANSWERS

In the above it has been assumed that an inmate answered all of the questions pertaining to relations with staff, which, of course, did not always happen. A "no answer" to a given question could arise in two ways. First, an inmate may have reported "insufficient contact" with the staff member to make the questions meaningful, in which case the questions pertaining to that staff member were not asked. Second, an inmate may have been asked a question about his relation with a particular staff member but refused to answer. These two kinds of nonresponse were coded separately.

Reported insufficient contact could have two meanings. In most cases, the inmate actually turned out to be unrelated to a given staff member. For example, an inmate assigned to the same job all day could not have a second work supervisor, and such cases were classified as "no relation." In the case of the housing-unit officers, however, a report of "insufficient contact" was interpreted as avoidance of the officer by the inmate, since every inmate had to contact the officers to get supplies and information. Consequently, such a response by an inmate was taken to mean the presence of a social relation, but one in which shared goals and a working relation were absent. Thus, for housing-unit officers, insufficient contact was treated as a negative response to the questions.

When an inmate was asked a question about his relation with a given staff member but did not answer, his refusal was interpreted to mean that he felt uncomfortable about revealing a negative or disapproved attitude. Consequently, such a nonresponse was treated as if it were a negative reply to the question. In all, nonresponses, including "insufficient contact" in the case of housing-unit officers, accounted for 9 per cent of the total number of negative responses.

SCORES

The foregoing sections describe the procedures for constructing shared-goals and working-relations indexes for an inmate's relations with staff and indicate how the indexes were used to classify these relations. The results of this step are summarized in Table C-1, which gives the distribution of type of relation, by staff role. It will be noted that the "nonscale" category accounts for a small proportion of the cases, as anticipated. Consequently, in the subsequent analysis these cases were reclassified as wise on the grounds that the responses did not evidence alienation, but they fell short of indicating a problem-solving relation.

TABLE C-1. *Relations of Inmates to Staff, by Staff Role*

	Staff Member						
Type of Relation	*Counselor*	*First Supervisor*	*Second Supervisor*	*Day Officer*	*Evening Officer*	*"Other"*	*C-Unit Groups*
Problem-solving	63	39	19	23	30	10	26
Wise	49	146	71	53	55	50	28
Nonscale	18	2	0	6	5	1	2
Alienated	170	47	32	155[a]	147[b]	5	5
No relation	37	3	115	0	0	171	176[c]
Total	237	237	237	237	237	237	237

[a] Of these, 37 claimed "insufficient contact."
[b] Of these, 48 claimed "insufficient contact."
[c] Includes 117 non-C-Unit inmates who were automatically classified as "no relation."

The second step in constructing the overall index of type of adaptation was to assign each inmate a set of scores, obtained by counting the number of relations of each type in which the inmate was involved. Thus every inmate was given a "problem-solving," "wise," and "alienated" score, and in addition, a "no relation" score. The distribution of scores, excluding the C-Unit groups, is given in Table C–2.[9]

TABLE C–2. *Problem-Solving, Wise, and Alienated Scores* (EXCLUD-ING C-UNIT GROUPS)

	Problem-solving Score	Wise Score	Alienated Score	No Relation Score
Six	0	1	1	0
Five	0	2	3	0
Four	6	20	24	1
Three	9	51	53	14
Two	38	71	64	93
One	57	65	52	94
None	127	27	40	35
Total	237	237	237	237

ESTIMATING OVERALL TYPES OF ADAPTATION

The third step was to use the scores of inmates to estimate their overall types of adaptation. It will be recalled from Chapter VIII that it might be fairly easy for an inmate to establish a "good relationship" with a single staff member but to be alienated in his relations with other staff. Thus it would be desirable to require that an inmate have many problem-solving relations before classifying him as problem-solving in his overall adaptation. Unfortunately, however, it is apparent from Table C–2 that just 15 inmates had more than two problem-solving relations and only 53 had more than one (not counting C-Unit groups). Thus, imposing too strict a criterion would have made further analysis impossible because of the small number of cases. For this reason, all inmates with more than one problem-solving relation were classified as having a problem-solving adaptation, even though there were good reasons for wanting to set the criterion somewhat higher.[10]

[9] The C-Unit groups are excluded at this point to facilitate comparison of the three units on as nearly an equal basis as possible.

[10] Twelve inmates classified as problem-solvers by this criterion had more wise relations than problem-solving relations. The rationale for treating them as problem-solvers was that the presence of the wise relations did not negate the ones that were problem-solving.

In an analogous way, inmates with nonproblem-solving adaptations were classified as having wise adaptations if they had two or more "wise" relations or if they had one wise and one problem-solving relation.[11] And, lastly, the remaining inmates were classified as having alienated adaptations.

The results of this step are presented in Table C–3, which gives type of adaptation by housing unit, with C-Unit groups still excluded. It will be noticed that as one would expect, the honor unit has a large concentration of inmates with wise adaptations, and the nonhonor unit has a large proportion of alienated inmates.

TABLE C–3.   *Type of Adaptation, by Housing Unit* (EXCLUDING C-UNIT GROUPS)[a]

		Housing Unit	
Type of Adaptation	*Nonhonor Unit*	*Honor Unit*	*C-Unit*
		Per Cent	
Problem-solving	5	13	35
Wise	53	62	52
Alienated	42	25	13
Total	100	100	100
Base	(57)	(60)	(120)

[a] This version of the index of type of adaptation was constructed without taking account of participation in the group program in C-Unit. Cf. Table C–4.

INCLUDING THE C-UNIT GROUPS

From Table C–3 it is evident that even when the groups are excluded, the main fact reported in Table 10 of Chapter VIII emerges: C-Unit inmates were by far the most likely to have problem-solving adaptations. However, in discussing the adaptations of C-Unit inmates in detail, we cannot omit participation in the C-Unit groups because of the central place of these groups in the program. Consequently, the scores for C-Unit inmates were modified by including their relations in the group program,

---

[11] It should be noted that inmates with two wise relations were similar to those with one wise and one problem-solving relation in that all had scored positively on the working relation indexes with two staff members. In addition, the latter inmates had also scored positively on the shared goals index in one of these relations, but this did not seem to be a reason for not classifying these inmates as having wise adaptations.

and the types of adaptation were changed accordingly. The results, presented in Table C–4, indicate that, in fact, only a minor shift in the overall distribution is created by including the groups: 5 per cent more of the C-Unit inmates are classified as problem-solvers than before, and there is a comparable drop in the number of inmates classified as alienated. For purposes of comparing units these differences are minor, but for purposes of comparing problem-solvers with other inmates, the more accurate classification is preferable.[12]

TABLE C–4. *Type of Adaptation, by Housing Unit* (C-UNIT GROUPS INCLUDED)

		Housing Unit		
Type of Adaptation		Nonhonor Unit	Honor Unit	C-Unit
		Per Cent		
Problem-solving		5	13	40
Wise		53	62	52
Alienated		42	25	8
	Total	100	100	100
Tau = 0.394[a]	Base	(57)	(60)	(120)

[a] Value of Kendall's tau-b. This correlation coefficient will be used in Appendix D in assessing the effects of background characteristics in the relation between housing unit and type of adaptation.

Finally, introducing the C-Unit groups raises another general question that can be settled. It is possible that the larger proportion of C-Unit inmates with two or more problem-solving relations results from C-Unit inmates having a larger number of relations overall.[13] The data in Table C–5, however, show that when C-Unit groups are excluded, C-Unit in-

---

[12] A final remark on validity can be included here. After the final form of the index was computed, a number of C-Unit inmates known to the research staff were singled out. In nearly every case the index proved to agree with the memories of the staff concerning these inmates. However, it was not possible to do this on a systematic basis, so that it is not reasonable to report a coefficient of agreement. Nevertheless, insofar as we have been able to check the index, it appears to be valid.

[13] The point here is that the criterion for a problem solving adaptation was a fixed number of problem-solving relations. Thus by chance, inmates with a large absolute number of relations should be the most likely to have two or more problem-solving relations.

TABLE C–5. *Number of Relations, by Housing Unit*

		Housing Unit		
			C-Unit	
Number of Relations[a]	Nonhonor Unit	Honor Unit	Groups Excluded	Groups Included
		Per Cent		
Two	2	0	0	0
Three	9	5	5	4
Four	53	23	41	25
Five	26	57	37	30
Six	10	15	17	31
Seven	0	0	0	10
Total	100	100	100	100
Base	(57)	(60)	(120)	(120)

[a] This score is the "no relation" score subtracted from seven, the total number of possible relations.

mates do not have substantially more relations with staff. Moreover, when number of relations is held constant, C-Unit consistently had a much larger proportion of inmates with two or more problem-solving relations than the other two units (see Table C–6).[14]

PROBLEM-SOLVING ADAPTATIONS AND COMMUNICATION

This section reports data on types of adaptation and communication among inmates and with staff that were referred to but not presented in Chapter VIII.

COMMUNICATION AMONG INMATES

One of the central points in Chapter VIII was that in C-Unit inmates with problem-solving adaptations were at least as likely as other inmates to participate in the activities of the inmate system. Although not fully documented there, it was mentioned that this conclusion was supported

---

[14] One other point is worth noting in this connection. When type of relationship with counselor is tabulated by housing unit, C-Unit inmates were the most likely to have problem-solving relationships with their counselors. This finding remains when a control for frequency of contact with counselor is introduced.

TABLE C–6.   *Inmates with Two or More Problem-Solving Relations,
by Housing Unit and Total Number of Relations*
(C-UNIT GROUPS INCLUDED)

	Housing Unit		
Number of Relations	*Nonhonor Unit*	*Honor Unit*	*C-Unit*
	Per Cent		
Two	[0]	[0]	[0]
	(1)	(0)	(0)
Three	[0]	[0]	[0]
	(5)	(3)	(5)
Four	3	0	30
	(30)	(14)	(30)
Five	7	18	36
	(15)	(34)	(36)
Six	[1]	[2]	43
	(6)	(9)	(37)
Seven	[0]	[0]	75
	(0)	(0)	(12)

by data from the survey concerning involvement in issues important in the
daily lives of inmates. Three such topics were investigated in the survey:
procedures inmates felt needed changing, personal problems, and disruptive behavior of other inmates. The question pertaining to procedures was
the following:

124. In any institution there are bound to be procedures a man won't like
—for instance, unlock procedures that make men wait too long, petty
rules, too many shakedowns, TV rules that make for a lot of hassel.
When something like this gets really bad in the unit, do you talk with
other inmates about it?

(IF YES:) Are those:

*Inmates who live in the unit
Other inmates at school, shop or work
Other inmates in the yard or field house
No [don't talk about it]

The proportion of inmates responding positively[15] is given in Table C–7,
by housing and type of adaptation. In this case, it is apparent that C-Unit

---

[15] As before, positive response categories are indicated by asterisks.

inmates with problem-solving adaptations were the most likely of all to talk with other inmates.

TABLE C–7. *Inmates Talking to Other Inmates about Procedures, by Housing Unit and Type of Adaptation*

	Housing Unit		
Type of Adaptation	*Nonhonor Unit*	*Honor Unit*	*C-Unit*
	Per Cent		
Problem-solving	[1]	[8]	54
	(3)	(8)	(48)
Nonproblem-solving	24	19	24
	(54)	(52)	(72)
All types combined	25	22	36
	(57)	(60)	(120)

Three questions were asked concerning talking to other inmates about their personal problems.

121. Do other inmates come to you with things on their minds they want to talk about?

   (IF YES:) Would you say this happens:

   *A lot
   *Some
   Or not very much?
   No [other inmates do not come]

122. What sorts of things do they want to talk about?
   *Personal problems, parole, the parole board, rules
   Mutual interests, gossip

123. What do you do?
   *Listen or give advice
   Try to avoid

Positive responses to all three questions were required for an inmate to be classified as listening to personal problems. The data are presented in Table C–8, from which it is apparent that inmates with problem-solving adaptations were as likely as other C-Unit inmates to be involved. An interesting additional feature of this table is the finding that honor-unit inmates have the highest rate of listening to personal problems, which suggests that perhaps the high level of conformity to rules exhibited by these inmates exacted a toll in high levels of personal tension.

TABLE C–8. *Inmates Listening to Personal Problems of Other Inmates, by Housing Unit and Type of Adaptation*

	Housing Unit		
Type of Adaptation	*Nonhonor Unit*	*Honor Unit*	*C-Unit*
		Per Cent	
Problem-solving	[1]	[6]	50
	(3)	(8)	(48)
Nonproblem-solving	39	60	42
	(54)	(52)	(72)
All types combined	39	62	45
	(57)	(60)	(120)

The questions dealing with disruptive inmate behavior, items 126 and 128, were presented in Chapter VIII, although the proportion of inmates responding positively to both questions was not reported there by housing unit and type of adaptation. These data are presented here in Table C–9, from which it appears that inmates with problem-solving adaptations were as likely as other inmates in C-Unit to be concerned about social control.

TABLE C–9. *Inmates Discussing Disruptive Behavior with Other Inmates, by Housing Unit and Type of Adaptation*

	Housing Unit		
Type of Adaptation	*Nonhonor Unit*	*Honor Unit*	*C-Unit*
		Per Cent	
Problem-solving	[0]	[5]	38
	(3)	(8)	(48)
Nonproblem-solving	26	29	35
	(54)	(52)	(72)
All types combined	25	33	37
	(57)	(60)	(120)

These findings support the conclusion that having a problem-solving adaptation did not tend to limit an inmate's involvement in the normal round of activities of the inmate system in C-Unit.

COMMUNICATION WITH STAFF

A second major point in Chapter VIII was that inmates involved in inmate-system activities were more likely to communicate with staff about those activities in C-Unit than in the other units, and that C-Unit inmates with problem-solving adaptations were particularly likely to do so. The findings for social control have already been presented in Table 15 in Chapter VIII; consequently, we report here only the results for procedures and personal problems.

The indicator of communication to staff about procedures was the following question.

125. Do you talk about [bothersome procedures] with any staff?

(IF YES:) Who?

*Unit officer
*Teacher, instructor, or supervisor
*Counselor
*Other
No [do not talk about it with staff]

The proportion of inmates responding positively to this question, among those talking to other inmates about procedures, is given by type of adaptation and housing unit in Table C–10. It is clear that among inmates talking to others about procedures, C-Unit inmates were more likely than others to talk to staff, and that inmates with problem-solving adaptations were the most likely of all to do so.

The indicator of talking to staff in connection with personal problems is somewhat different from those used for the other two topics of inmate concern. Inmates seldom talked to staff about the personal worries of other inmates, although on occasion they did so. However, they did involve staff in the processes of relieving tension among inmates when they brought their own troubles and problems to staff, affecting both the level of tension with which inmates had to deal and the range of responses that could be made by inmates to others with similar troubles. Consequently in this instance the question used was

120. Have you talked with any staff member in the past several weeks about something that was really on your mind?

(IF YES:) Who?

＊Unit officer
＊Teacher, instructor, or supervisor
＊Counselor
＊Other
No [has not talked to staff]

The findings, presented in Table C–11, follow the same pattern as for the other two topics.

The consistency of these results provides additional support for the conclusion that there was more communication to staff about matters important to inmates in C-Unit than in the other two units.

TABLE C–10. *Inmates Talking to Staff About Procedures, by Housing Unit and Type of Adaptation* (INMATES TALKING TO OTHER INMATES ABOUT PROCEDURES ONLY)

	Housing Unit		
Type of Adaptation	*Nonhonor Unit*	*Honor Unit*	*C-Unit*
		Per Cent	
Problem-solving	[1]	[3]	67
	(2)	(4)	(39)
Nonproblem-solving	39	30	49
	(33)	(33)	(35)
All types combined	40	35	58
	(35)	(37)	(74)

TABLE C–11. *Inmates Talking to Staff About Their Own Personal Problems, by Housing Unit and Type of Adaptation* (INMATES LISTENING TO PERSONAL PROBLEMS OF OTHER INMATES ONLY)

	Housing Unit		
Type of Adaptation	*Nonhonor Unit*	*Honor Unit*	*C-Unit*
		Per Cent	
Problem-solving	[1]	[5]	71
	(1)	(6)	(24)
Nonproblem-solving	29	29	43
	(21)	(31)	(30)
All types combined	32	38	56
	(22)	(37)	(54)

BACKGROUND CHARACTERISTICS
AND TYPES OF ADAPTATION

As INDICATED in Appendix A, the selection procedures may have resulted in a population in C-Unit that was not representative of the whole institution. The possibility exists, then, that the survey findings reported in Chapter VIII and Appendix C reflect differences in selection rather than differences in program between C-Unit and the rest of DVI. In this Appendix we examine the background data gathered in connection with the survey in terms of how background characteristics might affect the relation between housing unit and type of adaptation.

The data on background characteristics, presented in Table D–1, were gathered mainly from institutional records, but some were obtained directly in the survey. It is readily apparent from Table D–1 that the differences between the housing units are not great. Except for legal status (youth versus adult), age, time in DVI, and time in housing unit, no difference is larger than 20 per cent and most differences are less than 10 per cent. Moreover, the large differences in these four exceptional cases result from comparisons between the nonhonor and honor units rather than between C-Unit and the honor or nonhonor units. If, in fact, a selection bias had populated C-Unit with inmates much more likely to have problem-solving adaptations irrespective of the kind of program, it is surprising that no corresponding pattern of differences in background characteristics appears.

Further, the right-hand column of Table D–1 gives the value of Kendall's tau-b for the relation between housing unit and type of adaptation within the categories of each of the background characteristics. Thus, for example, when type of adaptation is tabulated against housing unit for YAs only, the value of tau is 0.378, which is virtually the same as the value for the sample as a whole, 0.394, reported in Table C–4. It is clear that background factors, taken one at a time, have no consistent effect on the relation between housing unit and type of adaptation.[1]

---

[1] The small sample size precludes holding more than one background factor constant at a time. The use of product-moment partial correlation analysis does not seem justifiable with these data in view of the violations of assumptions concerning measurement, linearity, and interaction effects that would be involved.

TABLE D–1. *Background Characteristics, by Housing Unit* (SURVEY
SAMPLES ONLY)[a]

| | Housing Unit | | | |
Characteristic	Nonhonor Unit	Honor Unit	C-Unit	Value of tau for Unit vs. type of adaptation
	Per Cent			
Youth offender	60	23	48	0.378[b]
Adult offender	40	77	52	0.416
Negro	26	10	18	0.422
Mexican-American	21	18	18	0.439
Euro-American, Other	53	72	64	0.373
Father is "white collar"	10	23	14	0.500
Skilled	30	20	39	0.423
Semi-skilled	28	23	23	0.218
Unskilled	32	34	24	0.484
Under 20 years old	54	10	25	0.324
20–24 years old	35	70	56	0.377
25 and over	11	20	19	0.501
Below average I.Q.	14	22	21	0.382
Average I.Q.	64	59	50	0.444
Above average I.Q.	22	19	29	0.382
Psychiatric condition[c]	18	10	6	0.301
None	82	90	94	0.374
Alcohol problem	40	42	32	0.368
None	60	58	68	0.403
Opiate user	22	16	18	0.373
Nonuser	78	84	82	0.408
Other drugs user	29	24	38	0.376
Nonuser	71	76	62	0.402
Homosexual experience	7	0	13	0.442
No homosexual experience	93	100	87	0.375
Parents and siblings arrested	7	0	7	0.508
Parents only	11	12	14	0.490
Siblings only	32	37	28	0.241
None	50	51	51	0.453

TABLE D-1 (cont'd).   *Background Characteristics, by Housing Unit*
(SURVEY SAMPLES ONLY)

Characteristic	Nonhonor Unit	Honor Unit	C-Unit	Value of tau for Unit vs. type of adaptation
		Per Cent		
High quartile, previous arrests	18	19	26	0.497
Md. high quartile	31	31	33	0.374
Md. low quartile	26	22	13	0.371
Low quartile	25	28	28	0.448
Prior prison terms	61	47	47	0.343
None	39	53	53	0.460
Prior jail terms: 2+	16	15	13	0.504
1	21	31	33	0.471
0	63	54	54	0.332
Narcotics as present offense	16	22	22	0.369
Person	37	32	42	0.462
Property	44	40	32	0.333
Sex	3	6	4	0.395
Parole date set	9	12	28	0.418
No	91	88	72	0.373
Months in DVI: 0–3	54	8	18	0.277
4–6	21	25	18	0.534
7–12	19	20	14	0.448
13+	6	47	50	0.453
Months in housing unit: 0–3	67	25	34	0.321
4–6	23	25	30	0.474
7–12	7	27	17	0.426
13+	3	23	19	0.510

ᵃ Within each subtable, percentages add to 100 vertically. Minimum percentage bases are: Nonhonor Unit 54, Honor Unit 57, and C-Unit 118, except for father's occupation, in which case the bases are 40, 35, and 91.

ᵇ Read: "Among youth offenders, the value of tau for the relation between housing unit and type of adaptation is 0.378." For the sample as a whole, the value is 0.394 (see Table C-4).

ᶜ Other than drugs, alcohol, or homosexual experience.

INMATE SYSTEM SURVEY QUESTIONNAIRE

(Interviewer complete items 1–4)

1. Identification Code

   _____

2. Housing Unit
   _____ Honor unit
   _____ Mainline unit
   _____ C-Unit

3. Race
   _____ Mexican
   _____ Negro
   _____ Anglo
   _____ (Other (specify:))

4. Housing Status
   _____ Honor status
   _____ Nonhonor status

NAME _____
NUMBER _____
DATE _____
START _____
FINISH _____
INTERVIEWER _____

5. How long have you been at DVI—not counting the Guidance Center?
   _____ Less than two weeks
   _____ Two weeks to one month
   _____ One to two months
   _____ Two to three months
   _____ Three to six months
   _____ Six months to one year
   _____ One year to a year and a half
   _____ A year and a half to two years
   _____ Two to three years
   _____ Three to four years
   _____ Four years or more
   _____ NA

6. Where were you before you came to DVI itself?
   _____ DVI Guidance Center (*Skip* to 8)
   _____ Other Department of Corrections Guidance Center (*Skip* to 8)
   _____ Youth Authority Institution
   _____ Department of Corrections Institution
   _____ DK
   _____ NA

7. How much time did you do on this commitment before you came to DVI?
   _____ Less than two weeks
   _____ Two weeks to one month

_____ One to two months
_____ Two to three months
_____ Three to six months
_____ Six months to one year
_____ One year to a year and a half
_____ A year and a half to two years
_____ Two to three years
_____ Three to four years
_____ Four years or more
_____ NA

8. Do you have a parole date?

_____ No

(IF YES:) About how far off is it?

_____ Less than two weeks
_____ Two weeks to one month
_____ One to two months
_____ Two to three months
_____ Three to four months
_____ Four to five months
_____ Five to six months
_____ Six to nine months
_____ Nine months or longer

9. Do you feel you're getting short to going out (even though you may not have a parole date)?

_____ Yes
_____ No

10. Have you done time in a state institution before this bit—either in California or another state?

_____ No (*Skip* to 13)

(IF YES:) What institution? (Record last commitment only.)

_____ DVI
_____ Other CDC
_____ CYA
_____ Out of state adult
_____ Out of state youth
_____ Federal
_____ Other (specify:)

11. What was that commitment for?

_____ Narcotics
_____ Sex offense
_____ Property (no violence)
_____ Person
_____ Other (specify:)

12. Have you ever been on parole?

_____ Yes
_____ No

13. What offense are you in for now?

_____ Narcotics
_____ Sex offense
_____ Property (no violence)
_____ Person
_____ Other (specify:)

14. How old were you on your last birthday?
_____ Less than seventeen
_____ Seventeen
_____ Eighteen
_____ Nineteen
_____ Twenty
_____ Twenty-one
_____ Twenty-two
_____ Twenty-three
_____ Twenty-four to twenty-nine
_____ Thirty to thirty-nine
_____ Forty or over
_____ NA

15. Which of the following things do you do in your spare time?
(Check *all* mentioned by respondent)
_____ TV
_____ Radio
_____ Study for courses or trade
_____ Look at magazines or newspapers
_____ Read books
_____ Pinochle
_____ Dominoes
_____ Chess or checkers
_____ Hobby or special interests
_____ Sports
_____ Weights
_____ Other (specify:)

16. Which *one* of these do you like the most?
_____ TV
_____ Radio
_____ Study for courses or trade
_____ Look at magazines or newspapers
_____ Read books
_____ Pinochle
_____ Dominoes
_____ Chess or checkers
_____ Hobby or special interests
_____ Sports
_____ Weights
_____ Other (specify:)

17. Do you go to Church here in the institution?
_____ No
(IF YES:) Which faith?
_____ Protestant
_____ Catholic
_____ Jewish
_____ Other (specify:)
_____ NA

18. What church were you brought up in?
_____ None
_____ Protestant (probe for denomination:) _____
_____ Catholic
_____ Jewish

_____ Other (specify:)
_____ NA

19. Have you ever been in Group Counseling here at DVI?

_____ No
(IF YES:) Are you now?
_____ Yes
_____ No
_____ NA

20. In your opinion, how many inmates in Group Counseling are there *mainly* so they can take it to the Board? Would you say:

_____ Over half
_____ About half
_____ Or less than half?
_____ NA

21. How long have you been in _____ Unit?

_____ Less than two weeks
_____ Two weeks to one month
_____ One to two months
_____ Two to three months
_____ Three to four months
_____ Four to five months
_____ Five to six months
_____ Six to nine months
_____ Nine months to a year
_____ One year or longer

22. (C-UNIT ONLY:) How did you feel when you *first heard* you were coming to C-Unit? Did you

_____ Like the idea
_____ Not like the idea
_____ Or didn't it matter one way or the other?
_____ NA

23. Would you want to move to another unit if you could (or would you, if you had a lot more time to do)?

_____ No
(IF YES:) Where would you *most* like to move to?
_____ C-Unit (*Skip* to 25)
_____ Honor unit
_____ Mainline unit
_____ L-3
_____ Any unit besides present unit
_____ NA

24. (NON-C-UNIT ONLY) Would you want to move to C-Unit?

_____ Yes
_____ No
_____ Don't know
_____ NA

25. (So far as you know) what makes C-Unit different from other units?

26. What is the thing you like *most* about living in _____ (present) Unit?

27. What do you like *least* about living in _____ (present) Unit?

(Non-C-Unit *Skip* to 37)

28. Have you belonged to any of the groups or committees that are especially for C-Unit?

_____ No (*Skip* to 32)
(IF YES:) In this (these) group(s) have you ever taken charge of doing something for the group (like heading a committee)?
_____ Yes
_____ No (*Skip* to 30)
_____ NA

29. If you had the chance, would you do this kind of thing again?

_____ Yes (*Skip* to 31)
_____ No (*Skip* to 31)
_____ NA

30. If you had the chance would you do this sort of thing?

_____ Yes
_____ No
_____ NA

31. Do you think your being in this (these) group(s) has benefited you personally at all?

_____ No
(IF YES:) Would you say it has benefited you
_____ A great deal
_____ Some
_____ Or not very much?
_____ NA

32. Do you think these groups and committees do any good for the *Unit* as a *whole*?

_____ No
(IF YES:) Would you say they do
_____ A great deal of good
_____ Some good
_____ Or not very much good?
_____ NA

33. (If "A great deal of good":) In what ways?
(Otherwise:) Why don't they do any (more) good?

34. In your opinion, how many of the inmates in these groups try mainly to make themselves look good to the staff—would you say:

_____ Over half
_____ About half
_____ Or less than half?
_____ DK
_____ NA

35. How much sniveling goes on in these groups do you think:

_____ A great deal
_____ Some
_____ Not very much
_____ Or none?
_____ DK
_____ NA

36. How much snitching do you think goes on in these groups:

_____ A great deal

_____ Some

_____ Not very much

_____ None?

_____ DK

_____ NA

37. Thinking now about the institution as a whole, when do you feel least like an inmate?

38. Is there anyone on the staff here in the institution with whom at times you forget you're an inmate?

_____ No

(IF YES:) With whom? (Probe for names.)

_____ Regular unit officers _____

_____ Present teacher, instructor, or supervisor _____

_____ Most recent active counselor _____

_____ Other (probe for one most important) _____

_____ NA

39. With whom, among the staff you see now, do you feel *least* like an inmate?

_____ No one

_____ Regular unit officers

_____ Present teacher, instructor, or supervisor

_____ Most recent active counselor

_____ Other

_____ NA

(*Skip* to 49 if no "other" is named in 38 or 39.)

40. How often do you see _____ (Person named in 38 or 39 "Other")?

_____ Every day

_____ Several times a week

_____ Once a week

_____ Several times a month

_____ Once a month or less

_____ NA

41. Where do you see him?

42. Do you see him about getting things you need—such as help with mail or visiting problems, assignment changes, special requests, a job on parole, or help with some work or project?

_____ No

(IF YES:) Would you say over half or less than half of your contact with him is about this sort of thing?

_____ Almost all

_____ Over half

_____ About half

_____ Less than half

_____ Very little

_____ NA

43. Do you joke or kid around with him?

_____ No

(IF YES:) Do you and he joke or kid around:

_____ A lot

_____ Some

_____ Or not very much?
_____ NA

44. Do you ever just trip with _____ when you see him?
_____ No
(IF YES:) How much do you do this:
_____ A lot
_____ Some
_____ Or not very much?
_____ NA

45. Do you ever "talk serious" with him?
_____ No (*Skip* to 47)
(IF YES:) How much do you "talk serious" with him:
_____ A lot
_____ Some
_____ Or not very much?
_____ NA

46. What do you "talk serious" with him about?

47. How well do you think he understands inmates and their problems? Would
you say:
_____ Very well
_____ Fairly well
_____ Or not very well?
_____ NA

48. Does he ever *deal* with you as a man instead of as an inmate?
_____ No
(IF YES:) Would you say:
_____ More often than not
_____ About half the time
_____ Or less than half the time?
_____ NA

49. What are your assignments right now?
a. FIRST ASSIGNMENT _____
b. SECOND ASSIGNMENT _____

50. Let's talk about _____ (first assignment). How long have you
been in it?
_____ Less than five days
_____ Five days to two weeks
_____ Two weeks to one month
_____ One to two months
_____ Two to three months
_____ Three to six months
_____ Six to nine months
_____ Nine months to one year
_____ One year or more
_____ NA

51. Can you tell me a little about what you actually do (on this assignment)?

52. On this job (in school) do you have any responsibility besides just follow-
ing orders or rules?
_____ No
(IF YES:) Would you say you have:
_____ A great deal of responsibility

———— Some responsibility
———— Or not very much responsibility?
———— NA

53. Do you have to do any thinking for yourself on this assignment?
———— No
(IF YES:) Would you say:
———— A great deal
———— Some
———— Or not very much?
———— NA

54. On the whole, how do you like ———————— (first assignment)—are you:
———— Very satisfied
———— Fairly satisfied
———— Somewhat dissatisfied
———— Or very dissatisfied?
———— NA

55. Who's your (teacher, instructor, supervisor) on this assignment? (If more than one, probe for one like most.)
Mr.
Miss ————————————————————————————————
Mrs.

56. How well would you say he (she) understands inmates and their problems:
———— Very well
———— Fairly well
———— Or not very well?
———— NA

57a. (ONLY if assignment is vocational shop or work:)
Does ———————— (instructor or supervisor) ever treat you like a man doing a job instead of as an inmate?
———— No
(IF YES:) Would you say:
———— More often than not
———— About half the time
———— Or less than half the time?
———— NA

57b. (ONLY if assignment is school:)
Does ———————— (teacher) ever treat you just as a student instead of as an inmate?
———— No
(IF YES:) Would you say:
———— More often than not
———— About half the time
———— Or less than half the time?
———— NA

58. How do you get along with him (her):
———— Very well
———— Fairly well
———— Or not very well?
———— NA

59. In your contacts with _____ (T,I,S), there are a number of things you could talk about. For instance, one thing would be your (school) work. How much of your contact is about this—would you say over half or less than half?

_____ Almost all
_____ Over half
_____ About half
_____ Less than half
_____ Very little
_____ NA

60. Do you joke or kid around with him (her)?

_____ No
(IF YES:) Do you do this:
_____ A lot
_____ Some
_____ Or not very much?
_____ NA

61. Do you ever just "trip" with _____ (T,I,S)?

_____ No
(IF YES:) How much do you "trip" with him (her):
_____ A lot
_____ Some
_____ Or not very much?
_____ NA

62. Do you ever "talk serious" with him (her)?

_____ No (Skip to 64)
(IF YES:) How much do you "talk serious" with him (her)?
_____ A lot
_____ Some
_____ Or not very much?
_____ NA

63. What do you "talk serious" with him (her) about?

64. (Skip to 78 if second assignment is the same as the first.) Now how about _____ (second assignment). How long have you been in it?

_____ Less than five days
_____ Five days to two weeks
_____ Two weeks to one month
_____ One to two months
_____ Two to three months
_____ Three to six months
_____ Six to nine months
_____ Nine months to one year
_____ One year or more
_____ NA

65. Can you tell me a little about what you actually do on this assignment?

66. On this job (in school) do you have any responsibility besides just following orders or rules?

_____ No
(IF YES:) Would you say you have:
_____ A great deal of responsibility

_____ Some responsibility
_____ Or not very much responsibility?
_____ NA

67. Do you have to do any thinking for yourself on this assignment?
_____ No
(IF YES:) Would you say:
_____ A great deal
_____ Some
_____ Or not very much?
_____ NA

68. On the whole, how do you like _____ (second assignment)
—are you:
_____ Very satisfied
_____ Fairly satisfied
_____ Somewhat dissatisfied
_____ Or very dissatisfied?
_____ NA

69. Who's your (teacher, instructor, supervisor) on this assignment? (If more than one, probe for one liked most.)
Mr.
Miss _____
Mrs.

70. How well would you say he (she) understands inmates and their problems?
_____ Very well
_____ Fairly well
_____ Or not very well?
_____ NA

71a. (ONLY if assignment is vocational shop or work:)
Does _____ (Instructor or supervisor) ever treat you like a man doing a job instead of as an inmate?
_____ No
(IF YES:) Would you say:
_____ More often than not
_____ About half the time
_____ Or less than half the time?
_____ NA

71b. (ONLY if assignment is school)
Does _____ (teacher) ever treat you just as a student instead of an inmate?
_____ No
(IF YES:) Would you say:
_____ More often than not
_____ About half the time
_____ Less than half the time?
_____ NA

72. How do you get along with him (her):
_____ Very well
_____ Fairly well
_____ Or not very well?
_____ NA

73. In your contacts with _____ (T,I,S), there are a number of things you could talk about. For instance, one thing would be your (school)

work. How much of your contact with him is about this—would you say over half or less than half?

_____ Almost all
_____ Over half
_____ About half
_____ Less than half
_____ Very little
_____ NA

74. Do you joke or kid around with him (her)?

_____ No
(IF YES:) Do you do this:
_____ A lot
_____ Some
_____ Or not very much?
_____ NA

75. Do you ever just "trip" with _____ (T,I,S)?

_____ No
(IF YES:) How much do you "trip" with him (her):
_____ A lot
_____ Some
_____ Or not very much?
_____ NA

76. Do you ever "talk serious" with him (her)?

_____ No (Skip to 78)
(IF YES:) How much do you "talk serious" with him (her):
_____ A lot
_____ Some
_____ Or not very much?
_____ NA

77. What do you "talk serious" with him (her) about?

78. Who is your counselor now?

Mr(s). _____
_____ Unassigned (Skip to 81)
_____ Don't know his name

79. How long has he been your counselor?

_____ Less than two weeks
_____ Two weeks to one month
_____ One to two months
_____ Two to three months
_____ Three to four months
_____ Four to five months
_____ Five to six months
_____ Six to nine months
_____ Nine months to one year
_____ One year or more
_____ DK
_____ NA

80. Have you ever talked with him?

_____ Yes (Skip to 83)
_____ No
_____ NA

81. Did you have a counselor before (a C-Unit counselor, I mean)?
_____ No (*Skip* to 94)
(IF YES:) Who was it?
Mr(s). _____

82. Did you talk with your old counselor at all?
_____ Yes
_____ No (*Skip* to 94)
_____ NA

83. About how often do (did) you see him on a ducat?
_____ Every day
_____ Several times a week
_____ Once a week
_____ Several times a month
_____ Once a month
_____ Less than once a month
_____ Never
_____ DK
_____ NA

84. On the average, about how often do (did) you talk with him *without* a ducat—for instance, before or after group counseling, on the Unit, or other places?
_____ Every day
_____ Several times a week
_____ Once a week
_____ Several times a month
_____ Once a month
_____ Less than once a month
_____ Never
_____ DK
_____ NA

85. How well do you think he understands you and your problems:
_____ Very well
_____ Fairly well
_____ Or not very well?
_____ NA

86. When you really need (ed) something done, can (could) you count on him (her) to help you out?
_____ No
(IF YES:) Would you say you can (could) count on him:
_____ Almost always (*Skip* to 88)
_____ Most of the time
_____ Or only some of the time?
_____ NA

87. Why can't you count on him (more)?
_____ Doesn't really try, not interested
_____ Counselor lacks influence
_____ No time
_____ Other (specify:)

88. On the whole, do (did) you get along with him:
_____ Very well
_____ Fairly well

———— Or not very well?

———— NA

89. When you see (saw) _____ (counselor), there are a number of things you could talk about. One kind of thing is about procedures, requests, classification, assignments, board reports, and so on.

How much of your contact with him is (was) about things like this—would you say over half or less than half?

———— Almost all

———— Over half

———— About half

———— Less than half

———— Very little

———— NA

90. Do you joke or kid around with him (her)?

———— No

(IF YES:) Do you do this:

———— A lot

———— Some

———— Or not very much?

———— NA

91. Do you ever just "trip" with him (her)?

———— No

(IF YES:) How much do you do this:

———— A lot

———— Some

———— Or, not very much?

———— NA

92. Do you ever talk serious with _____ (counselor)?

———— No (Skip to 94)

(IF YES:) How much do you "talk serious" with him (her):

———— A lot

———— Some

———— Or not very much?

———— NA

93. What do you "talk serious" with him (her) about?

94. Can you give me the name of the officer who usually runs _____ (present) Unit during the day shift—the one who's there most days of the week?

Mr. _____

———— Don't know

———— NA

95. On the average, about how often do you talk to him (either on business or just conversation)?

———— Every day

———— Several times a week

———— Once a week

———— Several times a month

———— Once a month

———— Less than once a month

———— Never (Skip to 104)

———— NA

96. When you see him, there are a number of things you could talk with him about. For instance, one thing would be about rules, procedures, and requests for supplies. How much of your contact with him is about things of this sort? Would you say over half or less than half?

_____ Almost all
_____ Over half
_____ About half
_____ Less than half
_____ Very little
_____ NA

97. Do you joke or kid around with him?

_____ No
(IF YES:) Do you do this:
_____ A lot
_____ Some
_____ Or not very much?
_____ NA

98. Do you ever just "trip" with him?

_____ No
(IF YES:) How much do you do this:
_____ A lot
_____ Some
_____ Or not very much?
_____ NA

99. Do you ever "talk serious" with him?

_____ No (*Skip* to 101)
(IF YES:) How much do you "talk serious" with him:
_____ A lot
_____ Some
_____ Or not very much?
_____ NA

100. What do you "talk serious" with him about?

101. How well do you think he understands inmates and their problems:

_____ Very well
_____ Fairly well
_____ Or not very well?
_____ NA

102. Does he ever talk with you man-to-man instead of as an inmate?

_____ No
(IF YES:) How much does he do this:
_____ More often than not
_____ About half the time
_____ Or less than half the time?
_____ NA

103. On the whole, how do you get along with him:

_____ Very well
_____ Fairly well
_____ Or not very well?
_____ NA

104. Now can you give me the name of the officer who usually runs _____ (present) Unit during the evening shift—the one who's there most evenings during the week?

Mr. _____

_____ Don't know

_____ NA

105. About how often do you talk with *him* (either about business or just conversation)?

_____ Every day

_____ Several times a week

_____ Once a week

_____ Several times a month

_____ Once a month

_____ Less than once a month

_____ Never (*Skip* to 112)

_____ NA

106. How much of your contact with him is about things like rules, procedures, requests for supplies, and so on? Would you say over half or less than half?

_____ Almost all

_____ Over half

_____ About half

_____ Less than half

_____ Very little

_____ NA

107. Do you joke or kid around with him?

_____ No

(IF YES:) Do you do this:

_____ A lot

_____ Some

_____ Or not very much?

_____ NA

108. Do you ever just "trip" with him?

_____ No

(IF YES:) How much do you do this:

_____ A lot

_____ Some

_____ Or not very much?

_____ NA

109. Do you ever "talk serious" with him?

_____ No (*Skip* to 111)

(IF YES:) How much do you "talk serious" with him:

_____ A lot

_____ Some

_____ Or not very much?

_____ NA

110. What do you "talk serious" with him about?

111. How well do you think he understands inmates and their problems—do you think:

_____ Very well

_____ Fairly well

_____ Or not very well?

_____ NA

112. Does he ever talk with you man-to-man instead of as an inmate?
_____ No
(IF YES:) How much does he do this:
_____ More often than not
_____ About half the time
_____ Or less than half the time?
_____ NA

113. On the whole, how do you get along with him:
_____ Very well
_____ Fairly well
_____ Or not very well?
_____ NA

114. Thinking now about the official staff in general at DVI—the officers and free people, some inmates say that most of the staff can be trusted. Others say you can't be too careful when you deal with staff. Do you think:
_____ Most staff can be trusted
_____ Or that you can't be too careful when you deal with them?
_____ Undecided
_____ NA

115. Would you say that most staff in the institution are:
_____ More inclined to help inmates
_____ Or more inclined to look out for themselves?
_____ Undecided
_____ NA

116. According to some inmates, most staff aren't going to care what happens to you, when you get right down to it. What's your opinion?
_____ Agree
_____ Undecided
_____ Disagree
_____ NA

117. Are there inmates whom you can talk to about the things that really concern you?
_____ No
(IF YES:) Are these:
_____ Inmates who live in the Unit
_____ Other inmates at school, shop, or work
_____ Other inmates in the yard or field house?
_____ Other (specify:)
_____ NA

118. Is there anyone on the staff you can talk to about the things that really concern you?
_____ No
(IF YES:) Who?
_____ Unit officer
_____ Teacher, instructor, or supervisor
_____ Counselor
_____ Other (specify:)
_____ NA

119. Thinking over the past several weeks, have you talked with any inmates about something that was really on your mind?
_____ No

(IF YES:) Were these:
_____ Inmates who live in the Unit
_____ Other inmates at school, shop, or work
_____ Other inmates in the yard or field house?
_____ Other (specify:)
_____ NA

120. Have you talked with any staff member in the past several weeks about something that was really on your mind?
_____ No
(IF YES:) Who?
_____ Unit officer
_____ Teacher, instructor, or supervisor
_____ Counselor
_____ Other (specify:)
_____ NA

121. Do other inmates come to you with things on their minds they want to talk about?
_____ No (*Skip* to 124)
(IF YES:) Would you say this happens:
_____ A lot
_____ Some
_____ Or not very much?
_____ NA

122. What sorts of things do they want to talk about?

123. What do you do?

124. In any institution there are bound to be procedures a man won't like—for instance, unlock procedures that make men wait too long, petty rules, too many shakedowns, TV rules that make for a lot of hassle. When something like this gets really bad in the Unit, do you talk with other inmates about it?
_____ No
(IF YES:) Are these:
_____ Inmates who live in the Unit
_____ Other inmates at school, shop, or work
_____ Other inmates in the yard or field house
_____ Other (specify:)
_____ NA

125. Do you talk about it with any staff?
_____ No
(IF YES:) Who?
_____ Unit officer
_____ Teacher, instructor, or supervisor
_____ Counselor
_____ Other (specify:)
_____ NA

126. There'll be some inmates who do things that bother the other men in the Unit—like too much noise, fires, maybe some racial tension. When things of this sort get really bad, do you talk with other inmates about it?
_____ No
(IF YES:) Would these be:
_____ Inmates who live in the Unit

_____ Other inmates at school, shop, or work
_____ Other inmates in the yard or field house?
_____ Other (specify:)
_____ NA

127. How about with staff?
_____ No
(IF YES:) Which staff member?
_____ Unit officer
_____ Teacher, instructor, or supervisor
_____ Counselor
_____ Other (specify:)
_____ NA

128. Would you talk about it to the inmates causing the trouble if they weren't friends of yours?
_____ Yes
_____ Undecided
_____ No
_____ NA

129. Suppose there were some kind of friction between you and another inmate in the Unit, and it looked like you and he might be headed for a real hassle. What would you do about it? (Probe for most likely first attempt to cope.)
_____ Try to talk to the other inmate about it
_____ Avoid him
_____ Fight him alone
_____ Get friends and jump him (Rat pack him)
_____ Other (specify:)
_____ NA

130. If it did develop into something serious, would you talk with other inmates about it?
_____ No
(IF YES:) Are these:
_____ Inmates who live in the Unit
_____ Other inmates at school, shop, or work
_____ Other inmates in the yard or field house? ·
_____ Other (specify:)
_____ NA

131. Would you talk about it to any staff?
_____ No
(IF YES:) Who would that be?
_____ Unit officer
_____ Teacher, instructor, or supervisor
_____ Counselor
_____ Other (specify:)
_____ NA

132. Do you think that if one other inmate picked a fight with you, you could count on your friends in the Unit to back you up if you started to lose?
(IF YES:) Even if it's just one against one?
_____ Yes
(IF NO:) Suppose it was two against one, against you?

_____ Yes
_____ No
_____ NA

133. Suppose you had just gone to classification and had been given a choice between two jobs. One was a pretty soft job and the other was a little harder but the kind of thing you liked to do. Suppose you chose the harder one.

Back on the Unit, another inmate starts giving you a hard time about it, calling you a "sucker," a "lame," and a "duck" for turning down a soft job. You can tell he really thinks this way, and he's trying to give you a bad reputation.

Do you think any of your friends in the Unit would speak up on your side, or would they keep out of it?

_____ Not speak up
(IF SOME WOULD SPEAK UP:) About how many—would you say:
_____ Almost all your friends
_____ Over half
_____ About half of them
_____ Less than half
_____ Or very few?
_____ NA

134. An inmate is assigned to a work crew. Some other inmates criticize him because he does more work than anybody else on the crew, but he still works as hard as he can.

a. What do you think of a man working as hard as he can even though other inmates criticize him—do you:
_____ Approve
_____ Or disapprove?
_____ Indifferent
_____ NA

b. How many men in the Unit do you think would approve:
_____ Almost all
_____ Over half
_____ About half
_____ Less than half
_____ Or very few?
_____ DK
_____ NA

135. An inmate, without thinking, commits a minor rule infraction. He's given a writeup by a correctional officer who saw the violation. Later three other inmates are talking to each other about it. Two of them criticize the officer. The third inmate defends the officer, saying the officer was only doing his duty.

a. What do you personally think about the inmate defending the officer:
_____ Approve
_____ Or disapprove?
_____ Indifferent
_____ NA

b. How many men in the Unit do you think would approve:
_____ Almost all
_____ Over half

_____ About half
_____ Less than half
_____ Or very few?
_____ DK
_____ NA

136. Two inmates are very close friends. One has a five-dollar bill that was smuggled into the institution by a visitor. He tells his friend he thinks the officers are suspicious and asks him to hide the money for a few days. The friend takes the money and carefully hides it.

a. What do you think about the friend hiding the money—do you:

_____ Approve
_____ Or disapprove?
_____ Indifferent
_____ NA

b. How many men in the Unit do you think would approve of hiding the money:

_____ Almost all
_____ Over half
_____ About half
_____ Less than half
_____ Or very few?
_____ DK
_____ NA

137. Suppose one man sees an inmate go into another man's room and steal some cigarettes.

a. What would you think about the inmate who saw the stealing letting the officer know there's cell robbing going on, without giving names— would you:

_____ Approve
_____ Or disapprove?
_____ Indifferent
_____ NA

b. How many men in the Unit do you think would approve:

_____ Almost all
_____ Over half
_____ About half
_____ Less than half
_____ Or very few?
_____ DK
_____ NA

138. A couple of inmates in the Unit threaten to give a third man a beating unless he brings some sniff into the Unit from the shop where he works. What would you think if he told the officer he was being pressured to break the rules, but didn't say who was doing it?

a. Would you:

_____ Approve
_____ Or disapprove?
_____ Indifferent
_____ NA

b. How many men in the Unit do you think would approve of this?

_____ Almost all

_____ Over half
_____ About half
_____ Less than half
_____ Or very few?
_____ DK
_____ NA

139. Suppose one man sees another inmate with some sniff in the Unit, and lets the officer know there's sniff in the Unit, but doesn't give any names.

a. What do you think about letting the officer know there's sniff in the Unit without giving any names? Do you:

_____ Approve
_____ Or disapprove? Why?
_____ Indifferent
_____ NA

b. How many men in the Unit do you think would approve:

_____ Almost all
_____ Over half
_____ About half
_____ Less than half
_____ Or very few?
_____ DK
_____ NA

140. Some men say most inmates can be trusted. Others say you can't be too careful in your dealings with other inmates. How do you feel about it? Do you think:

_____ Most inmates can be trusted
_____ Or you can't be too careful when you deal with them?
_____ Undecided
_____ NA

141. Would you say that most inmates are:

_____ More inclined to help others
_____ Or more inclined to look out for themselves?
_____ Undecided
_____ NA

142. According to some men, no inmate is going to care what happens to you, when you get right down to it. Do you agree with this?

_____ Agree
_____ Undecided
_____ Disagree
_____ NA

143. When there's a problem of some kind in the Unit, or something the men want, would you rather:

_____ Be in on the work with staff to find out what can be done
_____ Or is it up to staff to give the answers, with the reasons?
_____ NA

144. Do you think when inmates work with staff that:

_____ Anything important gets done
_____ Only a few little things get done
_____ Or it's just talk?
_____ DK
_____ NA

145. Some men feel that when there's a problem in the Unit, or the men want something, it's up to the staff to find the answer, and inmates shouldn't have to be involved in all the work and hassle. Do you:

_____ Agree

_____ Or disagree?

_____ NA

146. Here, do you feel treated:

_____ More like a man

_____ Or more like a child?

_____ NA

147. Do you have the feeling you know the ropes here in the institution, or are you sometimes uncertain about what the staff expect of you?

_____ Know the ropes

_____ Sometimes uncertain what staff expect

_____ NA

148. What makes you the angriest here in the institution?

149. What are the things officers do that make you angry?

150. What do free people do that makes you angry?

151. What are the things inmates do that make you angry?

152. Most inmates want to stay out of trouble when they get back on the streets. Aside from this, are there:

_____ Many things about yourself you want to change

_____ A few things about yourself you want to change

_____ Or do you like yourself pretty much the way you are?

_____ NA

153. Many people say the institution talks rehabilitation but doesn't really do much to help a man. Do you:

_____ Agree

_____ Or disagree?

_____ NA

154. (C-UNIT ONLY:) Do you think C-Unit has been helpful to you?

_____ No

(IF YES:) In what ways?

155. Apart from this, do you think the institution has been helpful to you?

_____ No

(IF YES:) In what ways?

156. Thinking now of the past month (time you've been in the Unit), would you say you spent more of your free time on the Unit by yourself or with other men?

_____ By self

_____ Half and half

_____ With other men

_____ DK

_____ NA

157. When you're with other men during your free time on the Unit, how many men do you usually associate with?

_____ (Code more than nine as "X")

_____ Refused to answer

158. Who are they? (For C-Unit record, names of first six; for Non-C-Unit, record race and legal status)

_____

_____

_____

_____

_____

_____

159. Would you say _____ (first) is:

    _____ A close friend

    _____ A friend but not really close

    _____ Just an associate

    _____ Or someone you don't really like?

    _____ NA

160. On the streets would you want him as:

    _____ A close friend

    _____ A friend but not really close

    _____ Just an associate

    _____ Or wouldn't you want to associate with him?

    _____ NA

161. Would you say _____ (second) is:

    _____ A close friend

    _____ A friend but not really close

    _____ Just an associate

    _____ Or someone you don't really like?

    _____ NA

162. On the streets would you want him as:

    _____ A close friend

    _____ A friend but not really close

    _____ Just an associate

    _____ Or wouldn't you want to associate with him?

    _____ NA

163. Would you say _____ (third) is:

    _____ A close friend

    _____ A friend but not really close

    _____ Just an associate

    _____ Or someone you don't really like?

    _____ NA

164. On the streets would you want him as:

    _____ A close friend

    _____ A friend but not really close

    _____ Just an associate

    _____ Or wouldn't you want to associate with him?

    _____ NA

165. Would you say _____ (fourth) is:

    _____ A close friend

    _____ A friend but not really close

    _____ Just an associate

    _____ Or someone you don't really like?

    _____ NA

166. On the streets would you want him as:
_____ A close friend
_____ A friend but not really close
_____ Just an associate
_____ Or wouldn't you want to associate with him?
_____ NA

167. Would you say _____ (fifth) is:
_____ A close friend
_____ A friend but not really close
_____ Just an associate
_____ Or someone you don't really like?
_____ NA

168. On the streets would you want him as:
_____ A close friend
_____ A friend but not really close
_____ Just an associate
_____ Or wouldn't you want to associate with him?
_____ NA

169. Would you say _____ (sixth) is:
_____ A close friend
_____ A friend but not really close
_____ Just an associate
_____ Or someone you don't really like?
_____ NA

170. On the streets would you want him as:
_____ A close friend
_____ A friend but not really close
_____ Just an associate
_____ Or wouldn't you want to associate with him?
_____ NA

171. How many friends (close and not so close) do you have in other units?
_____ (Record more than nine as "X")

172. What line of work do you want to get into when you get out?

173. Has your time here in the institution prepared you for a good job on the outside?
_____ Yes
_____ No
_____ NA

174. Do you think you'll have any trouble getting a good job?
_____ Yes
_____ No (*Skip* to 176)
_____ NA

175. Is it because you don't have enough training, skill, or education?
_____ Yes
_____ No
_____ NA

176. Are jobs scarce in the lines of work you want to get on the outside?
_____ Yes

_____ No
_____ NA

177. Do you think you'll have any trouble getting a good job because you'll have a record?

_____ No
(IF YES:) Would you say:
_____ A lot of trouble because of this
_____ Some trouble
_____ Or not very much trouble?
_____ DK
_____ NA

178. Do you think people in general look down on a man with a record?

_____ No
(IF YES:) Would you say:
_____ Most people do
_____ Some do
_____ Or not very many, look down on ex-inmates?
_____ DK
_____ NA

179. Some men say that most people on the streets can be trusted; others say you can't be too careful in your dealings with people. How do you feel about it? Do you think:

_____ Most people on the streets can be trusted
_____ Or that you can't be too careful when you deal with people?
_____ Undecided
_____ NA

180. Would you say that most people on the streets are:

_____ More inclined to help others
_____ Or more inclined to look out for themselves?
_____ Undecided
_____ NA

181. According to some men, people on the streets aren't going to care much what happens to you, when you get right down to it. Do you agree or disagree?

_____ Agree
_____ Undecided
_____ Disagree
_____ NA

182. Some people say that nowadays a person on the streets has to live pretty much for today and let tomorrow take care of itself. Do you agree or disagree?

_____ Agree
_____ Undecided
_____ Disagree
_____ NA

183. Would you say that these days a person on the streets doesn't really know whom he can count on?

_____ Agree
_____ Undecided

_____ Disagree
_____ NA

184. Would you agree that in spite of what some people say, the life of the average man on the streets is getting worse?

_____ Agree
_____ Undecided
_____ Disagree
_____ NA

Index

INDEX